International Business Economics

A European Perspective

Edited by
Judith Piggott
and Mark Cook

palgrave
macmillan

First published 2006 by
PALGRAVE MACMILLAN
Houndmills, Basingstoke, Hampshire RG21 6XS and
175 Fifth Avenue, New York, N.Y. 10010
Companies and representatives throughout the world

PALGRAVE MACMILLAN is the global academic imprint of the Palgrave Macmillan division of St. Martin's Press, LLC and of Palgrave Macmillan Ltd. Macmillan® is a registered trademark in the United States, United Kingdom and other countries. Palgrave is a registered trademark in the European Union and other countries.

ISBN-13: 978–1–4039–4219–7
ISBN-10: 1–4039–4219–6

This book is printed on paper suitable for recycling and made from fully managed and sustained forest sources.

A catalogue record for this book is available from the British Library.

A catalog record for this book is available from the Library of Congress.

10 9 8 7 6 5 4 3 2 1
15 14 13 12 11 10 09 08 07 06

Printed and bound in China

Dedicated to the memory of
Simon Williams
Dean of the Business School,
Oxford Brookes University.
A good friend and colleague.

Brief contents

Contents

Figures

Tables

Case studies

Abbreviations

ACP	Asian, Caribbean and Pacific countries	CU	customs union
AFTA	Asian Free Trade Area	DC	developed countries
APEC	Asian-Pacific Economic Co-operation	DDA	Doha Development Agenda
ASEAN	Association of South East Asian Nations	DG	Directorate General
		Disc	Domestic International Sales Corporation
BIS	Bank for International Settlements	DIY	do-it-yourself
		DK	Danish krona
CA	comparative advantage	DSB	Disputes Settlement Board
CAFÉ	Clean Air for Europe	DTI	Department of Trade and Industry (UK)
CAP	Common Agricultural Policy	EAGGF	European Agriculture Guidance and Guarantee Fund
CBI	Confederation of British Industry		
CD	comparative disadvantage	EAP	Environmental Action Programme
CEDEFOP	European Centre for the Development of Vocational Training	EBA	Everything But Arms
		EBS	electronic broking system
CEECs	central and eastern European countries	EC	European Community or European Commission
CESR	Committee of European Securities Regulators	ECB	European Central Bank
		ECJ	European Court of Justice
CET	common external tariff	ECSC	European Coal and Steel Community
CEPR	Centre for Policy Research		
CITES	Convention on International Trade in Endangered Species	ECU	European Currency Unit
		EEA	European Economic Area
CM	common market	EEC	European Economic Community
CIP	covered interest parity		
Comecon	Council for Mutual Economic Assistance	EER	effective exchange rate
		EFTA	European Free Trade Area
CP	competition policy	EIB	European Investment Bank
CSR	corporate social responsibility	EMS	European Monetary System
CPV	common procurement vocabulary	EMSs	environmental management systems
CTP	common transport policy	EMU	European monetary union

ECSC	European Coal and Steel Community	LAFTA	Latin American Free Trade Area
ERM	Exchange Rate Mechanism	LDCs	less-developed countries
ERDF	European Research and Development Fund	LIFE	Financial Instrument for the Environment
ESC	European Securities Committee	LIFFE	London International Financial Futures Exchange
ESF	European Social Fund	LSA	location specific advantage
EU	European Union	LSE	London Stock Exchange
Euratom	European Atomic Energy Community	M&A	mergers and acquisitions
		MBI	management buyin
FATS	foreign affiliates trade statistics	MBO	management buyout
		Mercosur	Mercado Comun del Sur
FDI	foreign direct investment	MDCs	medium developed countries
FSAP	financial services action plan	MFA	Multi-Fibre Agreement
FSC	foreign sales corporation	MFN	most-favoured nation
FSPG	(EU) Financial Services Policy Group	MMPA	(US) Marine Mammal Protection Act
FTA	free trade area	MNC	multinational company
FTAA	Free Trade Area of the Americas	MNE	multinational enterprise
		MPC	marginal pollution costs
GATT	General Agreement on Tariffs and Trade	MTS	Mercato Telematico dei titoli di Stato
GDP	gross domestic product	NAFTA	North American Free Trade Area
GFCF	gross fixed capital formation		
GMT	Greenwich Mean Time	NCP	national contact points
GNP	gross national product	NICs	newly industrialised countries
GPA	Government Procurement Agreement	NGO	non-government organisation
		NTB	non tariff barrier
HO	Heckscher-Ohlin theorem	OCA	optimal currency area
IATA	International Air Transport Association	ODCs	other developed countries
		OECD	Organization for Economic Cooperation and Development
ICA	International Coffee Agreement		
ICOR	incremental capital output ratio	OEEC	Organization of European Economic Co-operation
ICT	information and communication technologies	OLI	ownership location and internalisation
IGC	inter-governmental conferences	OMA	orderly marketing agreement
		OSA	ownership-specific advantage
ILO	International Labour Organization	PEST	political, economic, social and technological tool of analysis
IMF	International Monetary Fund		
IP	industrial policy	PPP	purchasing power parity
ISA	internalisation specific advantage	PU	political union
		R&D	research and development
IT	information technology	RER	real exchange rates
JIT	just-in-time	RIP	real interest parity

RTA	regional trade agreement	TUC	Trade Union Congress
SEA	Single European Act	UES	uniform emission standards
SEM	Single European Market	UIP	uncovered interest parity
SME	small and medium-sized	UK	United Kingdom
	enterprises	US	United States of America
SOX	Sarbanes–Oxley Act (USA)	UN	United Nations
SPS	sanitary and phytosanitary	UNCTAD	United Nations Committee
	measures		for Trade and Development
TC	trade creation	UNFCCC	United Nations Framework
TD	trade diversion		Convention on Climate
TEA	total entrepreneurial		Change
	activity	VAT	value added tax
TEN	Trans-European Network	VERs	voluntary export restraints
TGV	trains à grande vitesse	WDM	World Development
	(French high-speed rail		Movement
	network)	WEF	World Economic Forum
TNC	transnational corporation	WFOE	wholly foreign owned
TNI	transnationality index		enterprises
TRIPs	Trade Related aspects of	WHO	World Health Organisation
	Intellectual Property Rights	WTO	World Trade Organization

Contributors

Mark Cook BA MSc is a principal lecturer in the School of Business at the University of Wolverhampton. He is the author of a wide range of articles, books and commercial research reports on small business, disability in the workforce and the motor sport industry. He is a contributor to *The Business Environment*, 3rd edition (Prentice Hall, 2004) and co-author of *Business Economics: Applications and Strategy* (with C. Farquharson, Pitman 1998).

Alan Jarman BA LLB MA CertEd is a principal lecturer in economics at Oxford Brookes University. He has worked for the Canadian government in its Competition Office and has previously taught at Bristol University, Teesside Polytechnic and done part-time work for the Open University, WEA and Durham and Oxford Universities.

Andrew Kilmister BSc MPhil is a senior lecturer in economics at Oxford Brookes University. He is an author of various articles on models of economic development, Eastern Europe and on the motor industry.

Judith Piggott MA (Cantab) MPhil is a principal lecturer and head of the Economics Department at Oxford Brookes University. She previously taught at University College, Northampton and spent some years working in industry and local government. Her research interests are international economics (especially the World Trade Organization), and she is interested in the economics of the entertainment industry.

Haluk Sezer BSc DipEconDev MA is a senior lecturer in economics at Oxford Brookes University and was previously an economics lecturer at the Department of Economics, Leicester Polytechnic. His research interests are social welfare weights in Turkey, and he has published several articles in this area.

Acknowledgements

We are indebted to many individuals for their help in the preparation of this text. In particular a major debt is owed to those who have contributed to chapters and without whom the text could not have been produced. Also thanks to those in the Business School at Oxford Brookes University and Wolverhampton University Business School.

We would also like to thank our families for their unfailing support and encouragement.

Judith Piggott
Mark Cook
December 2005

The authors and publishers would like to acknowledge the following for permission to reproduce copyright material: The Federal Reserve Bank of St. Louis, WTO Publications, the European Commission, Edward Elgar Publishing Ltd, HMSO for material from the Office of National Statistics, *The Financial Times*, *The Guardian*, and the UN for the World Economics and Social Survey material.

Every effort has been made to trace all the copyright holders but if any have been inadvertently overlooked, the publishers will be pleased to make the necessary arrangements at the first opportunity.

Introduction

Judith Piggott and Mark Cook

Europe has been going through a period of massive change: the collapse of communism, the construction of the Single European Market, the introduction of the euro and the recent enlargement of the European Union. On top of this, of course, Europe exists within an international setting which has also undergone significant change: the technological revolution, globalisation, deregulation, the emergence of China and India as economic growth drivers, and increasing security issues. From all this change, what kind of business environment has emerged for European businesses and what has been their response to these changes? Similarly, have the European institutions helped or hindered the performance of European business? Have they eased the change or just added to it? And what changes are likely in the future?

This book aims, first to analyse the European and international environment in which European businesses work, and second to describe and explain the growth and impact of such businesses. Although these are the overarching themes of the book, the structure of the book is such that the reader can dip into the text and select those sections that are most appropriate to current needs within the context of the book as a whole. This is possible because the themes manifest themselves in differing ways. For example there are some areas where EU and international policy dominates, such as the area of trade. In other areas, such as foreign direct investment (FDI), the emphasis is much more on national policy and the strategy of firms rather than the European Union. The financial sector is probably a hybrid of the two however, with EU policies having significant impact but still national policy and the strategic policy of firms having a large say.

The structure of this particular edition has also changed from the previous two editions. Some chapters (such as Chapter 5) have been moved to earlier in the book, and we have changed some of the areas of policy that are looked at. For example we have added environmental policy and taken out fisheries and the Common Agricultural Policy because the latter only apply to certain areas of business rather than to all businesses. Furthermore given that central and eastern Europe is very much a part of the European Union nowadays, we felt it inappropriate to keep a separate chapter on the topic, and therefore it is covered in all chapters. Finally we have added new chapters on labour markets and on small and medium-sized businesses.

The book does contain a certain amount of theoretical discussion but its main emphasis is on applied analysis. It is hoped the book will encourage students from the outset of their business and economics courses to gain a wider perspective of the European and international economy than they might derive from the more narrow, home-nation view characteristic of traditional texts. *International Business Economics* has been developed for first and second-year undergraduate students taking business studies, business economics courses and European business degrees. It could also be useful for some background work on Master's courses.

Structure of the book

Chapter 1 provides a starting point, with an overview of the growth of international business as a preparation for subsequent chapters. It analyses the factors affecting growth, including the impact of deregulation and technology, and the types of growth that have occurred. The changes in merger and acquisition activities within Europe are then outlined, giving an overview of what has been happening in the various member states. The EU business environment and how it has changed is then considered, looking at the changing boundaries and the sectors in which Europe has a comparative advantage (CA). The question of how we judge which are the biggest firms, both in Europe and internationally, is then considered, as too are the major markets in which European multinationals are to be found. A number of examples are used to indicate the extent to which large firms in Europe are truly international. The chapter analyses the areas where 'big business' dominates and the reasons for the growth of merger activity within Europe.

With business becoming increasingly international, trade between countries has expanded enormously. Chapter 2 reviews the various trade theories, from Adam Smith to the newer theories of Krugman, Linder, Posner, Vernon and Porter. The usefulness of trade theory in practice is then considered in a discussion of world and European trade patterns. Finally the whole concept of fair trade and its implications are considered.

Trade in theory tells us many things, but trade in practice is another matter. The benefits arising from the trade theories mentioned above rely on the assumption of free trade. Chapter 3 investigates the reasons for trade protectionism. If free trade is so good, why do countries find such complex ways to prevent it? The main forms of this protection are then considered. The classic import tariff and its effects are outlined, and the effects of quotas, export subsidies, government procurement and other less direct non-tariff barriers (NTBs) such as bureaucracy are discussed in detail. A study of the World Trade Organization (WTO) is then undertaken, looking at what it has or has not achieved in the past ten years and what challenges face it in the future.

Chapter 4 considers a further development in international trading relations since the Second World War, that of increasing economic integration. The chapter begins by examining the various types and extent of the levels of integration. The theory behind customs unions and free trade areas is then discussed, from both a static and a dynamic point of view. The chapter continues by looking at economic integration in practice, giving an outline of the institutional development of the European Union and the newer trading blocks of NAFTA, Mercosur and ASEAN.

Chapter 5 explores the foreign exchange market. The differing types and systems of exchange rates are outlined, after which the chapter moves on to consider various models of exchange rate determination, beginning with models based on trade in goods and services such as the purchasing power parity approach, and then moving on to monetary models. The final section of the chapter deals with the process of European monetary union, and in particular the role of the euro in international markets and the prospects for the euro becoming an international currency that could rival the dollar.

Chapter 6 considers the questions of what a multinational company (MNC) is and why multinationals are important. It looks at the largest multinational companies, their country of origin and the issue of transnationality; in other words to what extent these companies are truly global organisations or nationally based with significant international operations. Differing views of the effects of MNCs are considered in the context of the debate about globalisation: what is globalisation and how may its effects be interpreted? Questions relating to both the desirability and possibility of MNC regulation are then discussed.

Many multinationals are the main purveyors of FDI, and the question of why firms undertake FDI is addressed in Chapter 7. The historical patterns and changes are first examined, then the theoretical approaches are outlined, with an attempt to explain the magnitude and direction of such investment. The ownership, location and internalisation paradigm is first outlined, followed by the various theories categorised as traditional, modern and radical. The chapter then examines FDI flows, first between major country groupings, then between Europe and the rest of the world, and finally within Europe itself. The chapter ends with a critical evaluation of the impact of FDI flows on the capital and labour markets, technology transfer, balance of payments and managerial practices of the recipient country.

Chapter 8 opens with a brief history of international capital flows, and discusses the way in which markets and institutions aid the movement of capital between countries and regions. The chapter then proceeds to look at the regulation of the international financial system, and analyses the way in which the approach taken within the European Union to the creation of a single European financial market fits into broader international financial developments. The remaining sections of the chapter look at the development of the main capital markets within the European Union, covering the money market, bond market, equity market and credit market, and concentrating particularly on the extent to which the EU countries now represent an integrated capital market.

Chapter 9 considers labour markets in both Europe and the wider global economy. It discusses the performance of the European Union in providing job opportunities during the last decade, and the need to make Europe more competitive via the Lisbon Agenda. The chapter then considers the social aspects of employment via the Social Chapter before moving on to develop the concept of labour market flexibility. Included here is a discussion of occupational mobility and the impact of skills on this mobility. A growing concern within Europe is the ageing population, and the impact of this on the labour market is developed. The mismatch between workers and skills is then considered, and the skills element is further developed within the area of labour productivity. Finally labour costs are considered at both the executive level and other levels of the organisation, through the focus on minimum wages.

Chapter 10 begins with a discussion of industry policy, in both the European Union and the United Kingdom. Industry policy and competitiveness are seen to be very closely linked concepts. The Lisbon Agenda, which seeks to establish the European Union as the most competitive economy in the world by 2010, is then considered. Two particular aspects of industry policy are looked at in some detail: state aid and its regulation, and public procurement. It is felt that in both areas more transparency is needed to improve competitiveness. The second section concerns competition policy. After a brief historical introduction, the chapter examines Articles 81 and 82 of the Treaty of Rome, dealing with restrictive and collusive practices and the abuse of monopoly power. These are considered in detail and compared with UK legislation. The recent changes to the merger regulations are also discussed. The chapter concludes that progress has been made, but there is much still left to do to achieve the Lisbon objectives.

Chapter 11 looks at some key policy areas – regional, environmental and transport – of the European Union. Regional policy is the first area of discussion, and to open the chapter the definition and need for a regional policy are considered. The chapter then compares the different EU countries' approaches to regional policy before looking at the development of EU-level regional policy. In this context an analysis of cohesion countries is undertaken and the policies used to address their particular problems are discussed. The emphasis of this part of the chapter is on a critical appraisal of regional policy, addressing such questions as whether regional policy has worked and if it is cost-effective. The next section deals with environmental policy, and begins by looking at the pressure within the European Union to develop such a policy and the ways in which it has developed. Three important areas of environmental policy are considered, water, waste and climate change. Finally this part of the chapter considers environmental standards and the difficulty there has been in getting countries to sign up to the Kyoto Agreement. A consideration of EU transport policy concludes the chapter. It indicates the slow progress in this area, particularly up to 1985. From this date, activity towards developing a common transport policy has quickened. The areas of road haulage and air transport are discussed in detail, and the chapter indicates that the European Union still has a long way to go before a number of its transport sectors become fully competitive.

Chapter 12 considers small business policy within the European Union. The chapter opens with a discussion of the size and structure of small and medium-sized enterprises (SMEs) in both the EU15 and the enlarged European Union. Comparisons are made with the level of SME activity in the United States and G7 countries. The chapter then compares the performance of SMEs with their larger contemporaries in Europe before moving on to consider SME internationalisation behaviour. In the context of small-firm internationalisation, the theories behind this type of activity, the drivers of internationalisation and the ways in which this activity takes place, for example in the development of alliances and networks, are discussed. The barriers to exporting are also considered. The chapter then considers in detail EU policy towards SMEs and finally discusses SMEs in the enlarged European economy, and the need for policy changes to accommodate these organisations.

Chapter 13 draws together the themes of the earlier chapters and highlights some of the challenges for Europe in the future.

1 The changing nature of international business

Judith Piggott and Mark Cook

Objectives

This chapter will:

- consider the growth of large firms and the reasons behind, and ways of, firms' growth
- develop the case for merger and acquisition behaviour in Europe
- consider the changing nature of the business environment in Europe
- discuss what represents Europe's 'best' firms.

Introduction

The 1980s, 1990s and early 2000s have seen unprecedented growth in international business activities, which has been prompted by a number of factors. One such factor has been the changes in the market in which organisations operate, from such things as the development of the Single European Market (SEM) and the expansion of the European Union (EU) (see Chapter 4). Reductions in trade barriers (see Chapter 3) and the development of trading blocs (see Chapter 4) also have provided further explanations of the internationalisation process. It is also important for organisations to operate globally within the global triad of Europe, the Americas and south-east Asia, and to improve their competitive position through growing internationalisation. This has been established through the growth of multinational behaviour, the development of **joint ventures** and the move towards **strategic alliances. Mergers** and takeovers have also allowed firms to reap the advantages of **economies of scale**, as has the development of technology. At the same time not all growth into international markets has been successful, and the last 15 years have witnessed a number of organisations **demerging**, selling off unwanted parts through management **buyouts**, or divesting themselves of non-core businesses. This chapter therefore considers the changing boundaries of international business, and those sectors in which Europe may have a competitive advantage.

Growth of large firms

On a macro level there are many factors that can be put forward to explain the growth of international business. The **World Trade Organization (WTO)** and its predecessor, the General Agreement on Tariffs and Trade (GATT) have reduced **tariffs** markedly on manufactured goods and markets, so that once highly protected markets have been opened up to trade. In particular reductions in barriers to trade in services have opened up an even wider variety of markets to trade. At the same time regional trade agreements have increased. The European Union is one of the oldest and best-known trading blocs, but more recently trading blocks on the American (the North American Free Trade Agreement (NAFTA) and Mercado Comun del Sur (Mercosur)) and Asian (the Association of South East Asian Nations (ASEAN) and Asian-Pacific Economic Co-operation (APEC)) continents have become established. (Chapter 4 looks at these in more detail.) In fact the European Union, NAFTA and Japan plus the newly industrialised countries (NICs) of south-east Asia (covered mainly by ASEAN), known as the **global triad**, have come to dominate world trade.

From an organisational point of view, barriers to trade within the blocs have been reduced, as is shown with the example of the SEM within the European bloc. At the same time external barriers have not been reduced so easily. One response by international organisations to the relative strength of these external barriers is to have operations in all three regions. This strategy has a number of advantages for the international organisation:

● Organisations can avoid surprises from competitors by forming alliances with foreign companies.
● By being inside the triad the organisation can ascertain the basic needs of triad consumers and then tailor its products to fit local requirements.
● With a presence in the three blocs the organisation can get its products to the richest markets very quickly.
● If a competitor develops a new product with great potential in one of the blocs, the international organisation can copy it very quickly and deprive the developer of the opportunity for sales in the other two markets.

Therefore being in each of the triad areas is important for international companies, and such areas account for over 90 per cent of **foreign direct investment (FDI)** (see Chapter 7). The extent to which the triad blocs will continue to influence the internationalisation of business behaviour depends on the relationship between the members of the triad, and the degree to which they may attempt to bar non-triad companies and countries.

Deregulation and the internationalisation process

Privatisation has played an important part in the questions of ownership, efficiency and performance of a number of industrial sectors, not only in western Europe, but also in south-east Asia, Oceania and central and eastern Europe during both the 1980s and 1990s. However, selling off state enterprises to the private sector is only one way by which state enterprises can feel the full effect of private sector forces.

Privatisation has also played an important role in the new eastern European members of the European Union. It has helped to improve state budgets, provided a means to break up state monopolies, and helped bring more efficient management and western capital into their economies. However only in a few new member countries (Hungary and Estonia, for example) have governments concentrated on the outright sale of state assets to strategic (western) investors. Others have concentrated on 'give-away' voucher type programmes or the sale of state assets to insider organisations. While such methods have helped with the speedy process of privatisation, they have not necessarily led to the creation of organisations that can benefit best from the globalisation process.

An alternative approach is **deregulation**. Deregulation allows private sector companies to compete in previously protected markets, sometimes with the public sector organisation, and at other times with the newly privatised company. Deregulation also has the effect of reducing differences between national regulatory systems, and so previously regulated national markets become more international, deregulated ones. This process of deregulation is likely to lead to the growth and internationalisation of business. For example, in the United Kingdom, the deregulation of the telecoms market took place in 1981. The result of this has been the establishment of a number of small new entrants, some of which were domestic firms while others were parts of large foreign telecommunications companies. The outcome has been that some of these companies have established a growing share of the UK telecoms market, and in so doing they have threatened British Telecom's (BT's) dominant position.

In the early 1990s a number of other European countries such as Germany followed the United Kingdom's lead in privatising their telecoms sectors. They were, to all intents and purposes, following a trend that had been established in the United States some ten years earlier, although the Europeans went further and created a **common market** for telecoms in Europe. The impact has been that the consumers have benefited with lower charges, the industry from high levels of growth and profits, and new jobs have been created.

Liberalisation in continental Europe has been slower, but the SEM has deregulated and opened up markets in, for example, banking, telecoms and air transport. Moreover, the move to a more market-based approach with regard to EU industrial policy has also been helped by the privatisation and deregulation process. Nonetheless, there still exists a large degree of protection for declining or strategic industries.

One outcome, however, from the result of the deregulation process has been the unshackling of companies that could then establish **joint ventures** and **strategic alliances**. It also led to increased merger activity as a means for companies to enhance their market position, or to act as a protective measure. For example Navistar International, a US truck maker, and MAN Nutzfahrzeuge, Europe's third largest truck maker, formed a strategic alliance in December 2004, to develop and manufacture truck components and diesel engines. Although deregulation is one of the drivers of strategic alliances in the trucking industry, another factor is that in an increasingly competitive market, truck makers have been forced to pool resources. As will be seen later in this chapter, a strategic alliance is only one form of company development but in the case of MAN, it is the preferred choice over other possible behaviour such as mergers and acquisitions or cooperative agreements, since it is viewed as a less risky market entry and product development strategy. Aside from deregulation as a driver of corporate development, the growth of technology has played an increasingly important part in company development.

The impact of technology

Technology can have an impact on the growth of business in a number of ways. It allows countries to obtain cost advantages and so a **comparative advantage** in the production of a commodity. On the back of this, it enables previously unprofitable markets to become worth considering. Thereafter organisations may export to new markets or expand into these markets via indigenous growth, or through mergers, takeovers or joint ventures. It is also possible that technology may provide organisations with products that are completely new and so allow them to expand into new external markets. Finally technology allows markets that were once believed to be separate to be joined, and thereby provides a way to overcome trade barriers, and thus competition.

The activity of **multinational enterprises (MNEs)** (see Chapter 6) can also lead to the transfer of technology, making it possible for host-economy firms to become more heavily involved in international markets. For example, the establishment of Japanese car manufacturers in the United Kingdom has resulted in car component suppliers providing products of much higher quality. The result has been to create a strong positive externality, improving the international competitiveness of the UK car-supply industry.

In terms of technological change, breakthroughs in basic science or the discovery of new innovations open large new markets. These new markets attract new investments and the entry of established and new companies. For example in the semiconductor industry the breakthrough in logic and memory devices caused the rapid development of new applications in computer, telecoms and other markets. These breakthroughs acted as structural breaks in the market, and led to the development of new companies and the decline of others.

Escalating research and development (R&D) costs can provide strong incentives for boundary change, particularly in rapidly moving technological sectors. Industries such as pharmaceuticals and aerospace often require expansion to finance investment. This encourages them to look for exports and growth overseas. High R&D costs also encourage firms to collaborate, reducing investment costs and risk. This often leads to the establishment of joint ventures, although where collaboration is not possible acquisition may be pursued in an attempt to reach a critical mass.

Technological developments have also played their part in linking and integrating markets, while leading to increased heterogeneity and market fragmentation. The technological advances in communications have revolutionised business operations, allowing them to manage on a wider geographical range. Global information systems have expanded rapidly and improved the coordination of global production and distribution logistics. Dicken (2003) also suggests that technology is one of the most important contributory factors underlying the internationalisation of economic activity. He identifies advances in communications and transport as fundamental 'space-shrinking' technologies that have facilitated the development of the global organisation. Similarly advances in telecoms have enabled organisations to monitor changes in consumer demand and competitors' behaviour, allowing a more rapid adaptation and response.

As stated above, MNEs have played their part in technological change, but they also have played a great part in the growth of international business generally (see Chapter 6). As a result, Dicken (2003) suggests that not only has the world become more internationalised but it has also become increasingly globalised. He acknowledges that global corporations still have the objectives of increasing market share or being a market leader, but he also considers that the desire for global profit is the dominant motive. The extent to which these global companies can expand, imposing their strategies and crossing boundaries, thereby improving their profits, depends on the way governments behave. Governments can be supportive of their actions or can make conditions that are not so conducive to the globalisation and enhancement of profits.

The route towards growth by organisations, for a wide range of objectives and often achieved through technology, can take many forms, such as mergers and takeovers, strategic alliances and joint ventures.

Types of growth

There are a number of ways in which firms can grow, but the means of growth is usually classified in one of four ways: horizontal, vertical, lateral and conglomerate growth. It is achieved through either organic (internal) or merger/takeover (external) growth. With horizontal growth firms expand within the same stage of production. Examples of horizontal growth include Glaxo's merger with SmithKline and Beecham in 1998, the merger of Royal Insurance and Sun Alliance to form Royal and Sun Alliance in 1996, the formal creation of HSH Nordbank at the end of June 2003, thereby marrying two of Germany's biggest Landesbanks in the northern territories of Hamburg and Schleswig-Holstein, and Imperial Tobacco's acquisition of the German tobacco firm Reemtsma Cigarettenfabriken in 2002. External horizontal integration often leads to the biggest threat to competition and increasing market power, and so it is not surprising that the majority of mergers that are investigated under home country or EU **competition policy** are of this type. Such mergers often have the potential to provide scale economies at both the plant and the firm level.

Vertical growth involves the linking of successive stages of production within the same industry. It may be forwards or backwards. Backwards is towards the earlier stages in the production chain, for example the purchase by Powergen in the United Kingdom and its US partner of an East German coalfield, and the move by a number of cement producers, such as Holcim and Cemex in 2004/5 to purchase aggregate producers such as Aggregate Industries and RMC. Forwards is towards later stages in the production process: for example the French oil company Elf found the only feasible way to develop retail outlets in the United Kingdom was to take over the independent VIP petrol retailing chain. Similarly Pearson, the UK publishing group, purchased National Computer Systems (NCS) in 2000, so enabling it to use its publishing experience to integrate with customers (students and schools) to design appropriate learning materials. Tesco provides another example by its move into retail clothing and home entertainment.

Lateral growth or integration involves the expansion of a firm into another industry. This action is seldom random, as there are usually threads connecting the products or markets. They may employ similar raw materials, technology or both. The purchase of the French company Sidel in 2001 by the Swiss company TetraLaval, although appearing to be a conglomerate takeover because the former designed and sold packaging for liquid food products while the latter designed and sold machines for the manufacture of plastic bottles and packing, brought lateral benefits since both companies had experience in the packaging and container sector.

Finally, conglomerate growth or integration involves expansion into a totally unrelated area. The takeover of Inntrepreneur, a joint venture of Grand Metropolitan and Fosters involving over 4,000 British pubs, by Nomura Securities (a Japanese securities conglomerate) is an example of this kind of expansion. General Electric's conglomerate growth in global industries such as transportation, media, healthcare and advanced materials illustrates this further.

This classification in terms of growth is inevitably oversimplified since growth can involve elements of both horizontal and vertical integration. For example Thomson-CSF, the French state-controlled defence electronics group, merged horizontally with other companies to achieve scale economies, but this also gave Thomson-CSF access to the companies' markets and outlets, and hence a rationale for vertical growth. Similarly some would term the Grand Metropolitan and Guinness merger as more of a vertical merger, since Grand Metropolitan possessed market outlets for the Guinness product range, and the Nomura/Inntrepreneur takeover could be seen as lateral, as Nomura has many property interests which fit with Inntrepreneur's ownership of public houses in the United Kingdom. Nevertheless it is useful to see how the different directions of growth contribute to achieving different objectives:

- Horizontal integration contributes to economies of scale and market power.
- Vertical integration contributes to the security of supply and outlets.
- Lateral and conglomerate integration provide diversification which can spread risks and enable companies to escape from the constraints of a sluggish or a declining market.

Transaction cost theory also provides an explanation of organisational growth, particularly through vertical integration. The substitution of internal organisations for market exchange permits the internalisation of transaction costs and a subsequent reduction in contracting and monitoring. As Williamson (1985) notes, an advantage of the organisation is that intra-organisation activities are enforced more easily and sensitively than inter-organisation activities. An organisation is more able to evaluate its own performance than a buyer, and an organisation's reward and penalty instruments may be more refined than those that exist in the marketplace.

For conglomerate growth or diversification, **economies of scope** provide one of the drivers for this process. For example, an organisation may find that in the production of one product it has spare capacity that could be used in the production of another. Here the minimum cost of producing a combined unit of both products is less than if the two products were produced separately.

But given all the advantages that could arise through mergers and takeovers this is not to say that all mergers have successful results. It is possible for **diseconomies of scale** to set in, particularly as management struggles to keep control over a larger empire, and perhaps profit figures could be much worse than expected after merger. Such problems have led to some famous **demergers**. For example, the Asda supermarket group in the United Kingdom acquired the MFI furniture chain but later sold its interest to a management **buyout**. Hanson Trust similarly sold off parts of the Imperial Group, which did not fit the wider activities of the Hanson industries. In addition problems with different organisational cultures, accounting practices and the like can contribute to disappointing performance from the newly merged organisation.

But why grow through the process of merger? What other methods are there of achieving a greater international presence?

Joint ventures

A joint venture is an arrangement under which organisations remain independent but set up a newly created organisation jointly owned by the parents. The reasons put forward to explain the development of a joint venture rather than other forms of expansion are:

- to provide economies of scale
- to overcome barriers to entry, as with Remy Cointreau's entry into the Chinese market
- to pool complementary pieces of knowledge
- to gain diversity
- to strengthen an organisation's market position
- to reduce the costs that may arise through R&D, production and marketing
- to develop complementary products (see the Chinese wine case study below).

In addition a joint venture may be preferred when the transaction costs are lower than those faced when establishing a wholly owned subsidiary.

Joint ventures have become a popular form of growth in the last decade, often used as a method to serve rapid expansion while at the same time reducing the financial risk of the partners. They are currently the prime method of moving into the Chinese economy, where the Chinese government is keen to attract investment but wants to maintain some element of state control. Similarly, joint ventures can be pursued as a means of attaining a critical mass without the risks of acquisition. This was the case in the car industry with the joint venture between Renault and Matra, which produced the Espace minivan. Renault benefited from Matra's knowledge of product concepts, design capability and manufacturing competence, while Matra gained access to Renault's marketing, distribution and service resources. A further example of this type of activity arose in early 2005 when Mazda Motor, Japan's fourth-largest car maker, agreed to set up a joint venture with China's First Automotive Works Car (FAW) (ownership 25:75 respectively). The new company is to have sole distribution rights to all Mazda-branded cars produced and launched in China.

It must be noted however that not all joint ventures are successful as a means of organisational growth. There may be disagreements between partners about the objectives of the joint venture. Problems may occur with contrasting organisational cultures, and technical know-how can be provided to potential future competitors.

The growth of Dynasty Wines in China indicates that entry into the Chinese market for western companies such as Remy Cointreau is often 'encouraged' through a joint venture route. This provides access to the market for non-Chinese companies while at the same time allowing Chinese companies to learn about the marketing, branding and technology factors that give western companies competitive advantages.

Strategic alliances

Whereas joint ventures may provide formalised arrangements between partners, networks are at the other end of the scale, providing for collaboration without formal relations through the process of mutual advantage and trust. In between these lie more intermediate relationships. One of these is franchising. Here the developer of a business idea (the franchiser) enters into a relationship with the franchisee, who is responsible for delivering the good or service. Examples of this type of relationship can be seen with Coca-Cola, McDonald's and Telepizza of Spain. The reason for the franchiser not delivering the product or service itself may be that no **economies of scope** exist, or that the delivery of the product or service to the market requires skills that the franchiser does not possess.

In addition to franchising, both licensing and subcontracting provide other forms of intermediate arrangements for organisations that allow them to expand into or control more markets. In the former the right to manufacture a product is granted to a few producers, while in the later a company chooses to subcontract particular services or part of a process.

The above provides the theoretical motives for growth and the ways in which organisations have sought to pursue the growth motive, but what has been the aggregate result of this behaviour in Europe?

Mergers and acquisitions in Europe

Various explanations can be found for **merger and acquisition** (M&A) activity within the European Union. Some M&A activity can be explained through firms trying to take advantage of free cash flows. Alternatively M&A activity can be explained through MNE strategy to enter new markets and extend their competitive advantage abroad. MNEs may also use M&A to gain strategic assets such as technology, management capabilities and know-how, or to realise economies of scale and scope through the restructuring of their businesses on a global scale, and to eliminate competitors. M&A activity can further be used to assess business dynamism and confidence, and this may go some way to explain economic performance.

CHINESE TASTE FOR WINE?

When Dynasty Fine Wines Group began producing what it claimed to be the first bottles of western-style wine in China 25 years ago, customers thought the drinks were rotten. 'Chinese grape wines had always been sweet but our wine tasted a bit sour,' admits Gao Xiaode, general manager at Dynasty, a joint venture between state-owned Tianjin Development Holdings and France's Remy Cointreau. 'In China, people think food and drinks that have a sour taste have gone bad.'

Thanks to several marketing campaigns and encouragement from the Chinese government, many consumers have since embraced wine as a fashionable beverage and healthier alternative to traditional rice spirits. The change in Chinese palates not only helped Dynasty to become the country's second largest wine producer, it also paved the way for a HK$550 million (US$70 million) listing on the Hong Kong stock exchange.

Benefiting from China's runaway economy and the increasingly chic lifestyles of its urban population, the wine retail market nearly doubled from Rmb1.9 billion in 1997 to Rmb3.4 billion (US$411 million) in 2003, according to Access Asia, a Shanghai-based research house.

The World Wine Industry Association expects wine sales in China to increase by 35 per cent in the period of 2003–08, compared with the global average of 5.4 per cent. While white wines account for more than 60 per cent of the Chinese market, red wines have seen stronger sales growth in recent months. Analysts point to the widespread belief that red wines are healthier than white wines. It also helps that red is seen as a lucky colour in China. 'Expensive bottles of red wine have become the latest "trophy drink" of the Chinese nouveaux riches, who like to drink such wines when eating out,' writes Access Asia in a recent report.

Despite the occasional Bordeaux blanc or Jacob's Creek, domestic winemakers such as Changyu Group, the country's biggest wine producer, accounted for 90 per cent of domestic sales in 2003, helped by lower prices and extensive distribution networks. Foreign brands are required to pay import duties, which dropped from a peak of 44.6 per cent in 2001 to 14 per cent last year. As a result, the average price of a bottle of imported wine is about US$10, compared with US$2–4 for Chinese wine.

Some analysts believe Chinese wineries will lose their competitive advantage, pointing to a further reduction in import taxes and a growing popularity of foreign brands among wealthy consumers. 'Our customers prefer foreign brands because Chinese wineries have a much shorter history and their production is considered less sophisticated,' says Mark Ruan, assistant food and beverages director at the Portman Ritz-Carlton hotel in Shanghai.

Yet Dynasty remains sanguine. The company's turnover for the first nine months of 2004 rose 25.4 per cent to Rmb620.9 million, while net profits jumped 40.4 per cent to Rmb96.5 million, according to the company's listing prospectus. 'Ten years ago, customers might have thought that a bottle with a foreign brand was better,' says Mr Gao of Dynasty. 'But now they realise that for the same amount of money they can buy much better Chinese wine.'

Source: Lau (2005).

Questions

1 Does the growth in demand for western-style wines indicate a growing globalisation of tastes?

2 Why might Chinese wines still possess competitive advantages against western wines?

Having grown during the 1990s, M&A activity reached its global peak in 2000 and decreased for the subsequent two years before rising slightly in 2003. In that year US company M&A activity grew due to the increase in domestic M&A activity, while that in Europe still showed a slight fall – partly explained through the delay in EU recovery (European Commission 2004).

A major impact on M&A activity during the 1980s was that the SEM led to a major restructuring of European industry, but has monetary union had the same effect? *European Economy* (European Commission 2001a) suggests that economic and monetary union (EMU) has had an ambiguous effect on M&A behaviour. In the banking and insurance sectors three of the four sub-sectors of the financial services category show that there was more growth in M&A outside the euro-zone than within it during the period 1997–2000. For the distribution, wholesale and retail sectors there were conflicting outcomes following EMU. For both distribution and wholesale sectors the growth in mergers and acquisitions was almost identical for those countries within the euro-zone compared with those countries outside EMU. In the retail sector the result of M&A in the euro-zone countries between 1997–2000 was threefold that of the countries outside the euro-zone. This could suggest that reduced transaction costs (through price transparency and the removal of exchange rate risks) have led to increased cross-border activities. However, the data suggest that M&A activity in the retail sector was driven mainly by domestic operations, for which the transaction cost effect of the euro plays only a small role.

The intensity of M&A activity in European countries can be defined as the country's share of the EU25 M&A total as target and bidder. As Table 1.1 indicates, 70 per cent of M&A activity was accounted for by the four largest economies of Germany, France, the United Kingdom and Italy. This is a result of these countries having the largest economies in the European Union and many of the largest and most powerful organisations, which have sought to retain their competitive advantage and enhance their profits through M&A activity. The share of M&A activity is higher than might be expected in the Netherlands, the United Kingdom, Sweden and Finland. All the new member states have a low share of M&A activity, with the Czech Republic, Poland, the Slovak Republic and Hungary accounting for the greatest amount from the new member states. Table 1.1 also shows that even though the level of M&A is low in the new member states, it doubled between 1990–3 and 2000–03. Most of the M&A activity in these countries came through the privatisation process.

The global pattern of M&A activity between 1995 and 2003 mirrored that of the activity occurring in both the European Union and the United States. M&A activity in manufacturing, distribution and finance sectors declined as a proportion of the total, and network and service industries were on an upward trajectory.

Table 1.2 shows the breakdown of total EU M&A. Domestic operations relative to cross-border operations have always been high in the EU25. Within the category of cross-border operations, M&A with the rest of the world is larger than that between the EU member states, and international M&A activity with the EU25 has been generally in decline since 1998. This may reflect consolidation by foreign organisations in the EU25, but it may also reflect a financial burden that is being paid by foreign firms that had to pay excessive prices for organisations within the EU during the last EU M&A boom.

Table 1.1 The distribution of M&A activity between EU member states

	1990–3		2000–03	
	Share of M&A (%)	Share of GDP (%)	Share of M&A (%)	Share of GDP (%)
UK	34.53	13.8	33.39	17.1
France	18.63	17.2	15.04	15.9
Germany	11.13	24.7	14.60	22.2
Italy	8.62	15.3	9.22	13.2
Netherlands	6.58	4.3	6.61	4.6
Sweden	6.30	3.2	6.00	7.2
Spain	5.56	7.3	3.35	2.7
Belgium	2.26	2.9	2.22	2.7
Finland	1.16	1.5	2.05	1.5
Ireland	1.02	0.7	1.59	1.9
Portugal	0.93	1.1	1.17	1.3
Denmark	0.82	1.9	1.02	1.3
Austria	0.75	2.4	0.90	0.2
Luxemburg	0.71	0.2	0.69	2.3
Hungary	0.45	0.4	0.59	1.5
Poland	0.29	0.8	0.51	0.8
Greece	0.27	1.3	0.49	2.1
Czech Republic	0.02	0.4	0.22	0.3
Slovak Republic	0.01	0.2	0.17	0.7
Cyprus	0.00	0.1	0.07	0.2
Estonia	0.00	0.0	0.03	0.1
Malta	0.00	0.0	0.03	0.1
Lithuania	0.00	0.0	0.02	0.1
Latvia	0.00	0.0	0.02	0.1
Slovenia	0.00	0.2	0.01	0.0
Old member states	99.24	97.85	98.32	96.15
New member states	0.76	2.15	1.68	3.85

Source: Securities Data Corporation Mergers and Acquisitions, Ameco.

Taking the EU15 member states separately, the share of domestic M&A activity was relatively high during 2000–01 in Greece, Spain, Italy, Portugal, Finland and the UK. For Belgium, Ireland, Luxemburg and the Netherlands, Community M&A activity accounted for the largest part of the total level of activity during 2000–01. On the whole international operations accounted for between 20–30 per cent of total M&A activity, with Ireland and the Netherlands being at the top of the range and Portugal operating at a level below the range (13 per cent).

Main targeted regions

From the early 1990s through to the end of the decade there was an increasing amount of M&A activity, and in particular cross-border M&A activity increased

Table 1.2 Breakdown of total EU M&A (percentages)

Year	Domestic	Community	International	Bidder unknown	Total
1995	58	14	20	8	100
1996	56	14	23	7	100
1997	56	15	24	4	100
1998	54	15	26	4	100
1999	56	16	23	4	100
2000	55	17	22	6	100
2001	56	17	21	7	100
2002	59	16	20	6	100
2003	58	15	21	6	100

Source: European Commission (2004).

threefold throughout that period. Cross-border M&A activity gradually replaced **greenfield investment** as the major force behind FDI flows, reaching a figure of 85 per cent (of total FDI flows) in 2000. During the next decade cross-border activity as an entry mode into new markets slowed, and greenfield development grew. Although it is the developed countries that dominate M&A activity, the same pattern of M&A activity was exhibited in developing countries, where M&A activity as part of FDI rose from almost zero in the late 1980s to half of total FDI in the late 1990s.

Table 1.3 Geographical breakdown of M&A activity in the EU15, 2000–01 (percentages)

Country	Domestic	Community	International	Bidder unknown	Total
Belgium	30.8	47.3	19.8	2.1	100
Denmark	37.5	35.7	24.7	2.1	100
Germany	48.5	26.1	21.8	3.6	100
Greece	67.9	11.5	18.0	2.6	100
Spain	53.1	25.1	18.4	3.4	100
France	48.4	29.5	20.3	1.8	100
Ireland	21.1	41.7	29.2	8.0	100
Italy	50.4	28.2	17.3	4.0	100
Luxemburg	11.7	62.2	25.0	1.1	100
Netherlands	29.6	41.2	26.4	2.8	100
Austria	35.5	32.7	24.6	7.1	100
Portugal	52.9	25.7	13.2	8.2	100
Finland	51.9	28.3	18.6	1.2	100
Spain	42.2	31.5	24.6	1.7	100
UK	52.7	15.6	22.2	9.5	100
EU	54.4	15.1	24.8	5.7	100

Source: Securities Data Corporation Mergers and Acquisitions, Ameco.

As noted earlier, the developed countries have dominated M&A activity as both bidders and recipients of FDI. During the period 1990–2003 the developed countries represented 61 per cent of M&A targets, with the EU15 accounting for two-thirds of that total. Since the early part of the current decade interest in the United States and European Union as targets for M&A activity has waned, with Asia, the rest of Europe, South America and Africa all receiving an increased proportion of global M&A activity. Part of the explanation for this trend is the deterioration in economic conditions in the European Union and the declining stock prices of bidder companies. However, a more important factor is the increased desire for a competitive cost advantage, which has caused firms to seek geographical locations to reduce their cost base in a global market. In addition this move to alternative markets through M&A activity was a means for some organisations to improve their competitive advantage abroad and gain further economies of scope and scale by restructuring their businesses on a global scale. Shifting the pattern of M&A activity to Asia and the rest of Europe allowed existing organisations to reduce their cost base and enter new and growing markets. M&A activity into Asia was helped by the aftermath of the Asian economic crisis, which brought a relaxation of the restrictions on equity participation and also a decline in the price of potential acquisitions as a result of their exchange rate depreciations and troubled economies (European Commission 2004).

In addition, since M&A activity is closely linked to FDI activity, the more 'FDI-friendly' economies have become, the greater the amount of M&A activity that has occurred. During the 1990s countries began to recognise the positive role M&A activity could have on promoting reform and the modernisation of their economies.

The new member states have benefited from increased M&A activity, but starting from a low base. From the early 1990s MNEs began to prepare for enlargement. This could be seen in the success of Poland, Hungary and the Czech Republic in attracting FDI (and hence M&A activity) as they integrated their economies with the EU15. More recently during the 2000–03 period, M&A activity has begun to increase more rapidly in the Slovak Republic, Estonia and Lithuania. However, in the future the new member states can expect to come under pressure in attracting M&A activity in labour-intensive/low-cost sectors from Bulgaria, Russia, China and India. The new member states may therefore need to move up to higher value-added M&A activity.

M&A behaviour can affect industry concentration ratios (the proportion of an industry that is controlled by the biggest firms in that industry). This appears to be the case for the smaller industrial sectors of the European Union. The general picture over the ten-year period from 1987 to 1997 is that concentrations have remained relatively static. This is contrary to expectations, given that there has been substantial M&A activity during this period and because of the SEM effect. For example market concentrations fell in basic chemicals (27 per cent in 1987 to 19 per cent in 1997) and in motor vehicles (see Table 1.4). A similar pattern occurred in the telecom and electronic equipment sector, with its C5 ratio falling from 42 per cent in 1987 to 32 per cent in 1997. Interestingly those sectors that are more sensitive to the SEM programme exhibited a higher degree of concentration in 1997 than they did in 1987, and this growth in concentration continued in both the sub-periods 1987–93 and 1993–7. However other factors influence concentration ratios too. These include

Table 1.4 Changes in the concentration ratios for various industries (C5 ratios) between 1987 and 1997

Sector	1987	1993	1997
First processing of steel	0.36	0.38	0.39
Cement, lime and plaster	0.27	0.33	0.39
Pharmaceuticals	0.22	0.22	0.22
Insulated wires and cables	0.36	0.39	0.71
Telecom and electrical equipment	0.42	0.45	0.32
Domestic electrical equipment	0.38	0.35	0.37
Motor vehicles	0.55	0.52	0.49
Railway locomotives and stocks	0.39	0.55	0.54
Clocks and watches	0.22	0.36	0.35
Dairy products	0.14	0.17	0.18
Pasta	0.37	0.35	0.38
Beer	0.27	0.26	0.32
Knitwear	0.09	0.11	0.14
Musical instruments	0.21	0.30	0.48

Source: European Integration and the Functioning of product markets, EU Commission, (2001).

turbulence at the top of the industry as a result of technological change, falling profits or management under-performance. Where the top five firms have remained the same there is some evidence that concentration ratios remained at best static and may have decreased over the 1987–97 period, but with the greater change in the 1993–7 period. Where turbulence is high because of the entry of a new firm in the top five, concentration ratios appear to grow, suggesting that a new entrant is able to obtain a higher share of the market than the firm it is replacing (Veugelers and Rommens 2002). Even though concentration rates have increased in many sectors, this still leaves concentration ratios behind those to be found in the United States.

The service sector concentration has been influenced by the nature of each service. Sectors such as distribution and road freight transport have been affected by high levels of restructuring, resulting in concentration levels increasing at both the domestic and EU levels. This is not surprising as this sector was expected to benefit greatly from the SEM and lighter regulation. Other areas of the service sector, such as retail banking, have exhibited smaller rises in concentration. This can be explained partly by institutional constraints and low adoption of the SEM regulations, and here more alliances have been seen rather than mergers and acquisitions.

The shrinking boundaries of the firm

As noted earlier some joint ventures do turn out to be failures, and when this occurs the organisation diminishes in size. It is equally possible, however, for an organisation to follow a strategic path to reduce its international activities, through a process of **divestment, buyouts** and **demergers**.

During the 1990s there were moves by a number of large organisations to divest themselves of their non-core areas, for both defensive and offensive reasons. The offensive reasons include:

- to refocus the total business and sell areas no longer required, even though they may be profitable
- to raise extra money: examples of this are British Aerospace's sale of the Rover Group to BMW and the sale of Falconbridge by Trellborg, the Swedish mining company, to raise money for its core operations
- to improve the return on investment
- to sell a family company, where there is no obvious succession.

Defensive reasons for divestment include:

- Because it is recognised that a part of the organisation does not, and is unable to, meet profitability requirements. Siemens and Vattenfall, for example, agreed in early 2005 to sell their interests in a Chinese power station to a group of investors after falling profitability.
- To avoid acquisition. BAT divested itself of a number of businesses to avoid the unwanted attention of a predator, for example.
- To prevent the organisation from collapsing because of the need for money. For example Lanxess, a German spin-out from Beyer, which is considered by some to be a collection of Beyer's least well-performing products, is likely to see divestments of the least profitable of these products in the future in order to improve the capital flow of the new spin-out. Similarly, the case study on Karstadt below suggests that financial factors have played a part in the company's divestment strategy.
- To avoid risk if the organisation is risk averse.
- To cope with the difficulty of managing a wide range of diverse activities.
- To restructure the company.
- To keep control of a major source of earnings that could be lost in the future.

Divestment may also be forced on an organisation by regulators. For example, Terra Firma Capital Partners acquired the Odeon and UCI cinema chains in August 2004, and although the UK Office of Fair Trading allowed this, it had concerns over the level of competition. Terra Firma is now considering divesting to a competitor a number of the cinemas it has acquired.

Management **buyouts** (MBOs) and **buyins** (MBIs) are also ways of restructuring and altering the boundaries of the organisation. The former occurs when the ownership of an organisation is transferred to a new range of shareholders, of which the current management team make up a significant element. (They are often the ones who initiated the move.) Examples of this were seen when Letts, the diary group, was involved in a management buyout in August 2000, and the following year purchased Filofax, and when Raleigh, the cycle company, was purchased through a management buyout in 2001. The above examples are of primary MBOs, but there also has been a growth in secondary buyouts. Venture capitalists were reluctant to get involved in this type of venture before, but they have begun to realise that if the first equity funder is prepared to invest and

KARSTADT UNDERTAKES INVESTMENT FOR SURVIVAL

In May 2005 Thomas Middelhoff, the former head of international media group Bertelsmann, became chief executive of KarstadtQuelle and pledged to accelerate restructuring at the troubled German retailer. The appointment quickly filled the gap left by the resignation five weeks earlier of Christoph Achenbach after only 10 months at the helm. Mr Middelhoff, once hailed as star of the 'new economy', had little experience of retailing, but this move brought him back into the top tier of German management circles after he had been ousted from Bertelsmann in 2002.

The department store and mail order group was in the throes of a restructuring and disposals programme after years of falling sales and injudicious diversification. Mr Middelhoff, who was brought in to head KarstadtQuelle's supervisory board in July 2005, said that hiring a new chief executive from outside would have delayed Karstadt's restructuring. He outlined plans to streamline the group's complex management structure. A '100-day programme' included plans to speed up the refurbishment of the 89 core Karstadt department stores and intensified efforts to boost sales at the mail order division, which generated more than half the group's sales.

However, Mr Middelhoff sought to dispel speculation that the ultimate goal was to break up the group. 'My job here is about a turnround and repositioning of KarstadtQuelle. It is not about the break-up of the group,' he said. Sales at some of the divisions had slumped badly as public uncertainty surrounding the troubled group's prospects over the previous few months prompted its customers to avoid large purchases. KarstadtQuelle said at the time of Middelhoff's appointment that the restructuring and divestment programmes it had announced the previous September were progressing 'as planned', with disposals proceeds to date totalling €400 million (US$512 million).

First-quarter earnings before interest, tax, depreciation and amortisation (ebitda) fell from €90 million to €73 million, excluding restructuring charges, although this was €14 million better than expected, the company said. Sales, at €2.97 billion, were 8.4 per cent lower than a year earlier.

Source: Wassener (2005).

Questions

1 What had led Karstadt to divest itself of some of its parts?

2 What is the danger behind such a divestment strategy?

support the management team, it is probably safe for them to support another management buyout. In fact secondary management buyouts have come to dominate the buyout market.

An MBI, on the other hand, is where an external management team executes a transfer of ownership, sometimes with the help of existing internal managers. The secondary management buyout described above often sees the new funders involving external management as a way of adding value to the management team. In the United Kingdom MBIs reached a peak in 2000, but dropped thereafter as the new external management failed to obviously add value to the company; they were just seen as buying themselves a job. As a result many MBIs failed and the market lost confidence in the process. Lessons have been learned from this, and it is expected that such a procedure will again be on the increase in 2005.

Part of the reason for the growth in both of these activities has been the privatisation process in the United Kingdom. In mainland Europe, however, the level of buyout and buyin activity has been much less. This can partly be explained by the greater proportion of family-owned firms and different legal and tax frameworks. Nonetheless, activity in France, the Netherlands and Sweden has been growing. It is interesting to note that most of the buyouts in continental Europe to date were the result of divestments by foreign investors.

A further driver in altering the size of international firms has been the process of demergers. Demerger activity often follows unsuccessful merger activity, and can also occur where an organisation seeks to reduce its attractiveness as a victim in any takeover activity. In 1996, Hanson chose to break itself up into more discrete parts to prevent a takeover bid and as a way of sealing off under-performing assets. Premier Foods acquired Hillsdown Holdings in 1999, when the latter was seen to be an under-performing group. Through a process of acquisitions and demergers Premier Foods has transformed itself, separating into three divisions which are highly profitable. Kraft is looking to streamline its business and could possibly demerge by selling off some famous UK brands such as Bird's Custard, Angel Delight and Dream Topping. GUS (General Universal Stores) has used the process of demerger to concentrate on its core business; it demerged Burberry in 2002 and sold its South African retailing business in 2005. Kingfisher plc demerged its high-street retailer Woolworth in 2001 to concentrate on its core business of DIY. As Kingfisher refocused its business on its core operations, the City viewed this as a positive step and this led to a rise in its share price.

The problem with any of the three approaches, and one that Thorn-EMI faced during 1997, is that demerging leads to smaller core business units, which makes the new companies vulnerable to predators.

Such has been the popularity of demergers that the activity has affected all segments of production/services during the last decade, including investment banks, telecoms firms, chemical companies, clothing companies (such as the break up of Coats Viyella), insurance companies (such as the demerger of Ina, Italy's third largest insurer) and car businesses.

Thus the last decade has witnessed major changes in both international and European business. Some companies have divested and demerged to concentrate on their core business activities as a means of improving their organisation's performance, while at the same time other companies have preferred to merge and take over other organisations as a means of strengthening their market position. It is against these two backgrounds that this chapter now considers Europe's service and production sectors, and assesses their current strengths and weaknesses.

The business environment in Europe

The European Union is made up of 25 very differing economies; all with varying levels of income, employment, sectoral importance, and foreign presence within their industries. Most statistics on this type of information refer to the EU15, because the ten new accession countries have only just joined the

European Union and therefore are not included in 2002 or 2003 statistics. However where possible information about the accession countries is generally included.

Business students often use a **PEST** (political, economic, social and technological) analysis to consider the environment or potential market of an area. Given the nature of this book, the analysis below covers the 'E' in PEST, the economic side of the EU business environment. Obviously it is not exhaustive, but it does give a flavour of the situation at present. (All data below comes from European Commission 2004 unless otherwise stated.)

The *level of income* of an economy, measured by gross domestic product (GDP), is vital for a business to judge its market. To overcome the problem of dealing with differing exchange rates, if we take the average of the EU15 as 100, an index can be calculated to show the relative GDP per head for the EU countries, and give an indication of the relative size of their markets (see Table 1.5).

The table shows that by far the richest country in the European Union is Luxemburg (twice the EU average), well ahead of the second country, Denmark (18.8 per cent above the EU average). At the other end of the scale is Greece which has only 68 per cent of the EU average GDP. As a means of comparison, the figures for the United States and Japan have been included in the table, which shows that Japan has a GDP per head 4.8 per cent higher than EU average, and the United States is 39.8 per cent higher. Information on the new accession countries shows that all have a GDP per head lower than the EU15. The nearest is Cyprus which has 76 per cent of the EU average, but Latvia only has 33 per cent.

If GDP is broken into the differing *sectors*, agriculture (including hunting, forestry and fishing) represents 2.1 per cent of EU GDP. Mining, quarrying, manufacturing, electricity, gas and water supply cover 22.1 per cent of GDP, while construction accounts for 5.4 per cent. The distributive trades, hotels and restaurants, transport, storage and communication take over a fifth of GDP (21.6 per cent to be exact), but financial intermediation, real estate, renting and business activities take more (27.2 per cent). Finally public administration, community, social and personal services account for 21.7 per cent. This shows a progressive movement towards services in the EU economy. The value added by financial intermediation and business services grew at an average of 3.1 per cent a year from 1991 to 2001. Some of this growth

Table 1.5 GDP per head (EU15=100)

EU 15	100	Italy	104.7	Japan	104.8
Luxemburg	197.4	Germany	104.1	USA	139.8
Denmark	118.8	France	101.9	Cyprus	76.6
Ireland	118.5	UK	99.9	Czech Rep.	59.5
Austria	113.5	Sweden	99.8	Hungary	51.1
Netherlands	112.3	Spain	82.4	Estonia	42.3
Belgium	106.5	Portugal	73.0	Poland	39.7
Finland	104.7	Greece	68.1	Latvia	33.3

Source: Panorama (2004).

could be the result of manufacturers and other services changing from in-house provision to external companies providing accounting, IT, advertising, training, consultancy, catering, cleaning and security.

The European Union has suggested why this change has been occurring: manufacturing organisations have tended to 'relocate their production, with relatively high wages, free trade and developments in communications driving output away from the EU towards low labour cost regions, particularly for more standardized products' (European Commission 2004: 2). If manufacturing is being relocated to lower-cost areas, the question is, is the European Union likely to become a service-based economy? How can the European Union maintain its comparative advantage in services, and is there no hope of a return to manufacturing in the more expensive European markets? The case study on Europe's international trading future later in this chapter addresses a number of these questions.

In some of the EU accession countries the figures give a different story. Agriculture generally is more important as a percentage of the economy, especially in Estonia (5.8 per cent) and Lithuania (7.1 per cent). Manufacturing also tends to take a higher percentage: 32.9 per cent in the Czech Republic and 27.1 per cent in Hungary. Further the distributive trades tend to represent a high percentage; 32.5 per cent in Cyprus, 32.1 per cent in Estonia, 35.4 per cent in Latvia and 30 per cent in Poland. However the financial intermediation and business activities account for far less: 10.6 per cent in Latvia, 15.7 per cent in the Czech Republic and 16.1 per cent in Poland. Finally public administration tends to be very similar to the EU average, the exception being Malta with 28.8 per cent at one end of the scale and the Czech Republic on 15.0 per cent at the other.

In terms of *employment statistics*, 310 million people aged 15 years and above lived in the European Union in 2001, and 174 million of these were employed or seeking work, an activity rate of 69 per cent. Across the European Union however this rate varied from 60.3 per cent in Italy to 79.2 per cent in Denmark. The activity rate in the accession countries was around 50 per cent.

The *manufacturing sector* employed 23.7 million people in the European Union in 2001 (a decline from 26.3 million in 1990). The fastest areas of growth in manufacturing were in chemicals, chemical products and artificial fibres, rubber and plastic products, and transport equipment. All tend to be research-driven, with a 'high degree of technological innovation … or alternatively marketing-driven, with brand image playing an important role in differentiating products' (European Commission 2004: 9). In the accession countries, agriculture accounted for a higher share of employment than the EU average, the highest being in Poland where it was close to 20 per cent. Similarly industrial employment tends to be higher: for example in the Czech Republic more than 40 per cent work in the industrial sector.[1]

Specialisation in manufacturing tended to show 'natural endowments of resources, reinforced by long-standing traditions, that can be an important contributing factor to the composition of a country's manufacturing sector' (European Commission 2004: 8) (see Chapter 2). An example of this is the importance of 'sawmilling and planing of wood in Finland and Sweden, stone in Spain, other wood products (namely, cork) in Portugal, and ceramic tiles and flags in Italy' (European Commission 2004: 10). There was also evidence of high-technology sectors being important in certain countries: France and the United Kingdom's specialisation in aircraft and spacecraft, Ireland's in office machinery and computers, and the Netherlands' concentration on audiovisual household goods.

The *service sector* accounted for most jobs (also reflected in the GDP figures). Over two-thirds (67.2 per cent) were employed in this sector, and in six countries this was over 70 per cent. Only in Portugal was the figure less than 60 per cent. In the new EU countries the service sector included over half the employed, but the only one coming close to the EU average was Cyprus, with 71.1 per cent.

Other factors that determine economic performance increasingly have been things like R&D expenditure, exploitation of property rights, know-how, skills, capital investment and supply networks. Taking these into account, in the Lisbon Council in March 2000 the European Union set itself the goal of becoming 'the most competitive and dynamic knowledge-drive economy in the world' by 2010. To judge this, it set up a database of structural indicators. Three of these are R&D expenditure relative to GDP, the number of patent applications per million inhabitants, and venture capital investment. To see how the European Union stands in this regard, we can compare it with Japan and the United States (see Table 1.6).

It can be seen therefore that the EU average lags significantly behind both Japan and the United States in research expenditure, but fares better in the other two categories. However it must be said that the EU average hides significant differences across the European Union, with Finland and Sweden's R&D proportion being 2.68 and 2.84 per cent respectively, and Portugal's and Greece's being 0.19 and 0.17 per cent. Similarly patents in Finland and Sweden are 320.3 and 346.4 respectively compared with Portugal and Greece at 3.9 and 5.2 respectively.

Small and medium-sized enterprises (SMEs) are seen as important in areas such as hotels and restaurants, and construction. In fact SMEs employed 87 per cent of workers in the construction industry, and 80 per cent in the hotel and restaurant industry.

Foreign affiliates trade statistics (FATS) measure the commercial presence of enterprises in other territories, so they give us another way of looking at the extent of globalisation within the European Union. This can be seen for some EU countries in Table 1.7.

Table 1.6 Selected structural indicators

Country	R&D expenditure relative to GDP, 2001 (%)	Patent applications per million inhabitants, units, 2000	Venture capital investment relative to GDP, 2001 (%)
EU15	1.28	152.7	0.05
Japan	2.11	148.5	N/A
United States	2.04	158.2	0.14

Source: Panorama (2004).

Table 1.7 Value added at factor cost (€ million)

Country	Nationally owned	Foreign owned
Denmark	66,734	8,518
Netherlands	143,931	26,865
Finland	49,421	6,788
Sweden	98,272	18,889
UK	540,963	100,858

Source: Panorama (2004).

Case study 1.3

EUROPE'S INTERNATIONAL TRADING FUTURE?

In July 2004, the European Union held a conference in Brussels centred around a report on 'European industry's place in the international division of labour: situation and prospects'. This report highlighted that the concept of the north/south division of labour was now becoming redundant due to the fall in costs of transport, communication and transactions, the opening up to trade of large economies with cheap labour (for example China and India), and the ability of MNEs to take advantage of this abundant labour through the use of advanced technologies. Given, for example China's comparative advantage in many manufacturing activities and India's comparative advantage in many services, the paper questions the future of manufacturing in Europe in the face of this low-wage competition. Will Europe have to abandon its manufacturing base and 'become instead a major market for imported products and producer of services' (Fontagné et al. 2004: 2)? It also asks, 'Are services themselves not in danger of widespread delocalization to countries which combine lower labour costs with strong skills in certain areas (the "Bangalore syndrome")?' (Fontagné et al. 2004: 2). A further question was also asked – does Europe actually need industry?

This latter question is answered by pointing out that industry does continue to play a key role in the European economy because:

● Manufacturing is maintaining its share of the volume of GDP.
● The relative fall in value added and jobs comes from price changes, and reflects productivity gains and more exposure to competition than in services.
● Services owe their existence to manufacturing in many cases.
● Often service sector workers who are unskilled or low-skilled earn less than similar workers in manufacturing.
● Manufacturing still brings technological change, innovation and higher productivity and 'plays a strategic role in terms of Europe's independence (space industry, arms, information technologies and so on) (Fontagné et al. 2004: 3).

The report puts it succinctly 'There is no longer any smoke coming out of the factory chimneys. But factories are still needed' (Fontagné et al. 2004: 3). However there is also 'an urgent need for European countries to realize that the world is changing and that this very rapid change seems unlikely to grind to a halt' (Fontagné et al. 2004: 5).

Big countries such as Brazil, Russia, India and China are experiencing rapid growth and becoming key players in world trade. They also have a comparative advantage in many goods. Similarly some smaller countries are using the increased integration globally to grow.

Two key issues were identified: technology and institutions. In terms of technology, the report states that 'Europe has missed the technological boat of the 21st century' (Fontagné *et al.* 2004: 7) and that policy is needed to reverse this trend. It assumes the United States will remain dominant technologically, and that Japan will benefit from its research over the last ten years to recover its previous place, but the European Union, it is argued, needs to catch up and put in place the Lisbon Agenda which sets objectives for a knowledge-based society.

The second issue concerns the fact that the poor quality of the new competitors' institutions is holding back their growth, but that it also means they can maintain low living standards and low labour costs, which keep them competitive. Should these improve, living standards should rise

and intra-industry trade would flourish – so bringing gains to EU industry. Should this not happen, the result would be the 'co-existence of a rich North with an ageing population and substantial social safety nets, alongside a South which is pressing home its cost advantage' (Fontagné *et al.* 2004: 9). To counter this, the report suggests the European Union should play a full role internationally to improve the situation for the sake of its industry.

Source: summary of Fontagné and colleagues (2004).

Questions

1 Do you agree with the report that Europe still needs manufacturing industry?
2 Outline what the report states as the reasons for poor growth in manufacturing. Can you think of any other reasons?

Europe's best?

How do we measure which are the most successful firms in Europe? There are a number of possible criteria: they could be determined by greatest sales, or highest profitability, or largest number of employees. Each measure however has its own problems. If we use the highest number of sales this would disadvantage the services industries. Some would argue profits are more important, but this measure is biased against trading companies. Given the state of unemployment in Europe, it may be that the largest employer should be seen as very important. Other measures of success could also be used, such as changes in profits or growth of sales, and these would highlight companies not seen in the other measures. How to judge success is therefore very debatable.

Furthermore it must be remembered that the data is far from perfect. There are differences in data collection within countries, and changes in this can affect the figures vastly; for example recent changes in Japanese accounting rules have adversely affected the sales revenue for the large Japanese trading firms and therefore reduced their standing in the world's top companies. The figures are also all denominated in US dollars and it can be argued that for comparison of European companies only (with no Japanese and US companies involved), the euro is a better currency for comparison.

With the above in mind we now look at which are arguably the most successful European businesses. *Fortune* magazine sets out the top 500 companies in the world in August each year, and ranks them in terms of sales revenues, profits, assets, stockholders' equity and employees. It also notes the changes in sales revenue and profits from the previous year. The criteria this chapter will concentrate on are sales, profits and employment.

According to sales revenues, in 2003 153 of the top 500 world corporations were from the European Union, compared with 189 US firms and 82 Japanese. In Europe, France and Britain had the most in the top 500, with 35 each, followed by Germany with 34. It is interesting to compare this with figures for 1996. In that year 171 companies in the world top 500 came from the European Union, 162 from United States and 126 from Japan. This shows that the US companies have been becoming more dominant in the list, but it also shows how the Japanese recession in recent years has hit sales revenue for its firms.

Within Europe, Britain's figures have remained almost the same, with 34 in 1996, but France and Germany have lost firms from the list, having had 42 and 41 in the 1996 list. It must be said that some firms leave the list through merger or acquisition, so it is not always a negative sign for the figures to change downwards. It is also interesting to note the increasing presence of the newly industrialising countries (NICs) in world MNEs. South Korea had 13 companies in the list in 1996, and still has 11, but more interestingly in 1996 China only had three companies in the list, and now there are 15.

Taking a closer look at Europe, Table 1.8 gives the top 10 European companies ranked according to sales.

BP is the largest European company, with US$232.5 billion in sales (in 1996 it was Shell with US$128.2 billion in sales). It is noticeable that the tenth European company is only ranked 22nd in the world (although in 1996 it was only 36th), and that many of these companies are connected to the oil, petrol and car industries, although increasingly insurance is appearing in the list.

If however profits were seen as a measure of success, we can see that most of the companies in the sales list would fare much worse: for example DaimlerChrysler would only rank 298th in the world list in 2003. The most profitable European companies are listed in Table 1.9, and it can be seen that petroleum refining ranks highly, but so does banking (which was not strong on the lists for sales).

If we look at the biggest increase in profits (the percentage change from 2002 to 2003), we get totally different organisations listed, with the highest European company ranked at 4, Tui from Germany (928.7 per cent), followed by Banca Intesa from Italy (626.6 per cent), and La Post from France (611.2 per cent).

In terms of the biggest employers in Europe, Carrefour ranks highest (as the sixth largest employer in the world), followed by Siemens (eighth) and Compass Group, a British food service company, ranked ninth. Unilever and Nestlé, which appeared in the top ten in 1996, now only rank 39th and 34th respectively.

Obviously these are not the only measures we could use to judge success. Others could be biggest increases in sales revenues, highest returns on revenues or highest returns on assets. All would give differing rankings and lists. Therefore it is impossible to say which are the top companies in Europe, because it depends on what measurement is used.

Table 1.8 Europe's largest companies, ranked according to sales (2003)

Company (country/ industry)	Sales revenue US$ million (world ranking according to sales)	Profits US$ million (world ranking according to profits)	Employees (world ranking according to employment)
British Petroleum (Britain/petroleum refining)	232,571.0 (2)	10,267.0 (8)	103,700 (128)
Royal Dutch/Shell Group (Britain/NL/petroleum refining)	201,728.0 (4)	12,496.0 (5)	119,000 (109)
DaimlerChrysler (Germany/motor vehicles and parts)	156,602.2 (7)	507.0 (298)	362,063 (13)
Total (France/petroleum refining)	118,441.4 (10)	7,950.6 (16)	110,783 (119)
Allianz (Germany/ insurance)	114,949.9 (11)	1,828.9 (131)	173,750 (59)
AXA (France/insurance)	111,912.2 (13)	1,137.4 (187)	74,584 (195)
Volkswagen (Germany/ motor vehicles and parts)	98,636.6 (15)	1,239.3 (176)	336,843 (15)
ING Group (Netherlands/ insurance)	95,893.3 (17)	4,575.7 (43)	115,200 (115)
Siemens (Germany/ electronics/electrical equipment)	80,501.0 (21)	2,651.4 (91)	417,000 (8)
Carrefour (France/food and drugstores)	79,773.8 (22)	1,843.8 (128)	419,040 (6)

Source: *Fortune* (2004: F1).

However, it is important to look not just at the best but at in which industrial sectors Europe is most competitive. Where do these large firms have a substantial presence, and where does the rest of the world dominate? Table 1.10 gives us some indication of areas of strength in Europe.

The table shows that Europe has strong presence compared with Japan or the United States in banking, chemicals, food, general merchandisers, insurance (health and life stock), motor vehicles, petrol refining, pharmaceuticals, telecommunications and utilities. However Europe has no presence in the top 500 in the areas of computer services and software, computer equipment, diversified financials or healthcare (all US-dominated), and little presence in electronics, the energy sector, life and health care (mutual), metals, speciality retailers (dominated by the United States) and trading (dominated by Japan).

Table 1.9 Europe's ten largest companies ranked by profits (2003)

Profit rank	Sales rank	Company name (country/industry)	Profits US$ million
5	4	Royal Dutch/Shell (Britain/Netherlands/petroleum refining)	12,496.0
8	2	BP (Britain/petroleum refining)	10,267.0
13	47	HSBC Holdings (Britain/bank)	8,774.0
16	10	Total (France/petroleum refining)	7,950.6
19	114	GlaxoSmithKline (Britain/pharmaceuticals)	7,349.9
24	84	Royal Bank of Scotland (Britain/bank)	6,602.8
27	43	ENI (Italy/petroleum refining)	6,320.9
33	188	Lloyds TSB Group (Britain/bank)	5,319.5
34	66	E.on (Germany/ trading)	5,259.3

Source: *Fortune* (2004: F14).

Table 1.10 Ranking within industries (2003)

Industry	Total in world top 500	Total in EU & Switzerland/ Norway	Total in USA	Total in Japan
Banking	58	29	10	4
Chemicals	8	3	2	2
Food	6	3	3	0
General merchandisers	12	4	7	1
Insurance (health and life/stock)	21	10	3	1
Motor vehicles	32	10	7	10
Petrol refining	32	7	7	4
Pharmaceuticals	12	5	7	0
Telecoms	24	8	9	2
Utilities	23	9	7	4

Source: *Fortune* (2004: F16–F22).

Conclusion

There have been both internal and external forces in play that have led to the growth of international business. Markets have become increasing dominated by fewer major organisations. However, the size of organisations is not necessarily correlated with performance, and the last decade has witnessed a number of organisations divesting themselves of areas that do not fit in with their core philosophy or portfolio.

During the 1970s and 1980s few changes occurred in the make-up of the top 20 or top 50 firms, but the business world has become more dynamic during the 1990s and into the new millennium. Mergers and acquisitions, changes in technology, the emergence of companies from new industrial countries and the impact of the SEM have led to continual change in the ranking of dominant companies. There are concerns about the degree to which the European Union is falling behind some of its main competitors, and an indication of this is the gradual and long-term increase in the levels of unemployment the European Union has experienced relative to the United States.

Now we have had an overview of European business, its strengths and weaknesses and its trends, the next chapter considers the particular area of trade and Europe's role in this.

Questions

1   If the CR5 concentration ratio in the UK supermarket sector is the same in 2005 as it was in 1995, does this mean that there has been no change in market power?

2   Why do companies such as the Halifax Bank prefer to grow by merger rather than by internal growth?

3   Internet groups AOL and MSN have been in talks regarding cooperation in their search and advertising network businesses (*Financial Times*, 2005). Why is this a popular route to organisational growth?

4   Why did some companies, such as IBM, seek to reduce their size during the 1990s? What are the problems with this strategy?

5   Using the case studies in this chapter, consider the ways in which organisations have strategically reduced in size.

6   List the sectors where Europe has a large presence in the world market. Consider why Europe appears to have an advantage in these sectors compared with the United States and Japan.

7   Similarly look at where Japan and the United States dominate, and consider why they appear to have an advantage in these sectors.

8   Bearing in mind your answers to (1) and (2) above, consider the sectors where the NICs are likely make the biggest impact on the world market and why.

Note

1   Cyprus, Lithuania and Latvia are exceptions to the general level of industrial employment in accession countries.

References

Dicken, P. (2003) *Global Shift: Industrial Change in a Turbulent World*, 4th edn, Paul Chapman, London.

Economist (1991) 'Riding the wave', 28 September, p.104.

European Commission (1996) 'Economic evaluation of the internal market', *European Economy*, No. 4.

European Commission (1996b) 'The world's top 200 companies', *Panorama of EC Industry*.

European Commission (1996c) 'Small firms in Europe', *Panorama of EC Industry*.

European Commission (2001a) Mergers and acquisitions, *European Economy*, Supplement A, Economic trends, No. 12, December.

European Commission (2001b) *European Integration and the Functioning of Product Markets*, European Commission, Brussels.

European Commission (2004) *Mergers and Acquisitions Note*, No. 1, October, Brussels.

Financial Times (2005) 'AOL and MSN in link-up talks', 16 September, p. 29.

Fontagné, L., Fouquin, M., Gaulier, G., Herzog, C. and Zignago, S. (2004) *European Industry's Place in the International Division of Labour: Situation and Prospects*, CEPII Report for the European Commission, DG Trade.

Fortune (1997) 'The top 500 corporations in the world', 4 August.

Fortune (2004) 'Fortune Global 500', 26 July.

Lau, J. (2005) 'Domestic wines hit the spot: Changing tastes have opened up the market for western-style wines', *Financial Times*, 19 January, p. 9.

Veugelers, R. and Rommens, K. (2002) 'Persistence in dominance in European Economy, European Integration and the functioning of product markets', Special Report No. 2, European Commission, Brussels.

Wassener, B. (2005) 'Karstadt chief launches 100-day plan', *Financial Times*, 13 May, p. 28.

Williamson, O. E. (1985) *The Economic Institutions of Capitalism*, Free Press, New York.

2 International trade

Judith Piggott

Objectives   This chapter will:

- explain why trade takes place
- examine trade patterns in the European Union and the world
- outline the explanations and theories for these patterns, both old and new
- critically assess the growing concept of fair trade and why it is considered necessary.

Introduction

Why do firms trade? Domestic producers gain in many ways from trading. Raw materials and semi-manufactured goods can be obtained at lower cost, and exporting brings higher profits and larger-scale production, reducing costs again. Further exports and imports can smooth demand fluctuations in the domestic economy, and growth via exports could increase competition at home.

Therefore basically trade allows firms to escape the confines of the domestic market, so reducing costs, improving quality and hopefully leading to higher sales and profits. As the advantages have become increasingly obvious, and transport and distribution have improved markedly, so trade has grown.

Given the importance of trade to businesses, this chapter will look at how trade theory attempts to explain why countries trade, in which goods and with whom. It will consider both 'traditional' and newer theories, and look at how their predictions relate to trade in practice. The real beginning of trade theory is usually seen as Adam Smith's basic principle of exchange, but the mercantilist theory of trade predates this, and is important to consider it as it is still often discussed. Furthermore it was the theory to which Smith was reacting, when he set up the **absolute advantage** theory.

Mercantilism

The major school of thought in Europe from the 16th to the mid-18th century was called **mercantilism**. Mercantilists believed that the more gold and silver a country had, the richer and more powerful it was. Exports were seen as 'good' since they brought in gold/silver (that is, wealth), and stimulated industry to produce more. Imports, on the other hand, were 'bad' since they reduced demand at home and led to gold and silver flowing out of the country. Basically the mercantilists wanted to encourage countries to export more than they imported. It was proposed, therefore, that exports should be increased using such things as state subsidies, and imports decreased by means of **tariffs** and **quotas**.

Under this theory, trade could be advantageous to one party alone. As the supply of precious metals was relatively fixed, a nation could only increase its stock of gold at the expense of other nations. Moreover, it was impossible for all countries to possess trade surpluses.

The mercantilist theory did little to explain the basic questions of international trade – such questions as which goods are exported and imported, and by whom. There was also no consideration of what determines the prices at which exchange of exports and imports takes place – the terms of trade. Adam Smith was the first to address these questions, and in doing so he attacked the mercantilist view of trade. Taking the arguments he had formulated regarding **specialisation** and **division of labour**, he applied them to international trade, producing the principle of absolute advantage.

Absolute advantage

In essence, the principle of absolute advantage suggests that some countries are better, or more efficient, at producing certain commodities, and less efficient at producing other goods, when compared with other countries. In theory all will gain if they specialise in the product that they produce efficiently (in which they have an absolute advantage), and trade for the other products (in which they have an absolute disadvantage).

For example, if we assume Belgium is more efficient at producing chocolates than the United Kingdom but the United Kingdom is more efficient in the production of cheese, then Belgium should produce chocolates and trade these with the United Kingdom in exchange for cheese; similarly the United Kingdom should produce and trade cheese for chocolates. Such international specialisation and exchange will increase the output of both chocolates and cheese, thereby allowing both countries to enjoy a higher standard of living.

Smith also stressed that the greater resources achieved would be allocated efficiently by the market. Any interference in this process would reduce these gains. Accordingly, therefore, all countries would benefit from free trade and a policy of **laissez faire**.

At the root of Smith's theory of trade can be found the **labour theory of value**. In a closed economy, with labour the only factor of production, goods are exchanged according to the relative amounts of labour embodied in them. If it takes twice as much labour to make a television as to make a vacuum cleaner, then one television should exchange for two vacuum cleaners.

Obviously this is an oversimplification; labour is not homogeneous because there are different labour skills, and it is not the only relevant factor of production. However to discard this assumption has little effect on the conclusion of the theory; it is merely a simplifying factor. Bearing this assumption in mind, therefore, how does Smith's theory actually work?

Let us assume there are only two countries (France and Denmark), two goods (beer and clothing), perfect competition, and one factor of production (labour). As it is homogeneous, labour can be used to produce either clothing or beer in both countries. Let us assume both countries can produce clothing or beer in the quantities shown in Table 2.1. From this table we can see that Denmark has an absolute advantage over France in producing beer, but France has an absolute advantage in clothing. Without international trade, one unit of beer will exchange for two units of clothing in Denmark and one unit of beer for six units of clothing in France.

Table 2.1 Example of absolute advantage
(Output per unit of labour per day)

	Beer (B)	Clothing (C)
France	2	12
Denmark	4	8

It can also be seen that beer is relatively cheap in Denmark (1B = 2C) and expensive in France (1B = 6C). The opposite exists for clothing: in Denmark 1C = ½B, but in France 1C = 1/6B. So it would be profitable to buy at a low price and sell at a high one. Therefore it pays to buy Danish beer and sell it in France, and to buy French clothing and sell it in Denmark. Let us assume the terms of trade settle at 1B = 3C. If Denmark exports two units of beer to France, it will receive in exchange six units of clothing. Domestically Denmark can only exchange 2B for 4C, therefore it gains 2C. Similarly, France gains 1B because domestically 6C can only exchange for 1B, not 2B. Both countries benefit from trade.

Absolute advantage, however, can really explain only a small proportion of world trade today. Even at the beginning of the 19th century problems with the theory were becoming obvious, and out of these grew Ricardo's theory of comparative advantage.

Comparative advantage

This theory showed that, even if absolute advantage does not always exist, all countries can benefit from trading as long as a **comparative advantage** exists. Suppose we have the situation shown in Table 2.2.

Denmark has an absolute advantage in both commodities. Without trade, 1B will again exchange for 2C in Denmark and for 6C in France. Would trade still

Table 2.2 Example of comparative advantage
(Output per unit of labour per day)

	Beer (B)	Clothing (C)
France	2	12
Denmark	8	16

benefit both countries now? According to Ricardo, yes. Comparative advantage is all that is necessary for both to benefit.

A country has a comparative advantage in a commodity when it has a *higher degree of superiority* in its production, and it has a **comparative disadvantage** in a commodity when its *degree of superiority is lower*, relative to another country. The parts in italics are important: it is all relative, and the degrees of superiority or inferiority are vital. In our example, Denmark's degree of superiority in beer is 8B:2B and is greater than its superiority in clothing, 16C:12C. Denmark thus has a comparative advantage in beer and comparative disadvantage in clothing. France has a comparative advantage in clothing because 12C:16C is greater than 2B:8B.

So we get the law of comparative advantage. Each country should specialise in producing the good in which it has a comparative advantage. All countries will gain.

How does this work? Let us say the terms of trade equals 1B = 3C, then Denmark sells 4B for 12C. Denmark gains 4C as it would only get 8C at home; France gains 2B because it would only get 2B, not 4B, for 12C at home. So as long as comparative advantage exists, free trade will benefit all. On the very rare occasion when a comparative advantage does not exist, then there is no gain from trade.

The above system, however, is based on **barter**. How does this change when we bring in money? World trade is then determined not by differences in labour costs but by differences in money prices. We now need to transform these labour cost differences into money price differences.

We have seen above how France has a comparative advantage in clothing, but the problem we face now is, if Denmark is more efficient absolutely, how can the cost of clothing be lower in France than in Denmark in money terms? Wages are the key. When French wages are sufficiently below those of Denmark, this is a possibility. For example, if the Danish wage is DK120 per day, the average cost of producing one unit of beer will be DK15 (DK120/8 units) and the average cost of clothing per unit, DK7.5 (DK 120/16 units). If we also assume the French wage is €180 per day, the average cost of production in France is €90 per unit of beer (180/2) and €15 per unit of clothing (180/12). Is beer cheaper in Denmark or France?

To consider this we need to express prices in terms of the same currency – we need the exchange rate. Table 2.3 assumes DK1 = €3. Beer is cheaper in Denmark in both currencies (DK15 < DK 30 or €45 < €90) but clothing is cheaper in France (€15 < €22.5 or DK5 < DK7.5). As we have seen above, each country will specialise accordingly, and relative prices determine trade.

Table 2.3 Example of comparative advantage – money prices 1
(DK1 = €3)

| | Denmark | | France | |
	DK	Euro	DK	Euro
Beer	15	45	30	90
Clothing	7.5	22.5	5	15

Given the wage rates of DK120 and €180, this pattern of specialisation will remain, provided the exchange rate remains favourable (between DK1 = €2 and DK1 = €6). Above DK1 = €6, both commodities are cheaper in France. For example if DK1 = €7, we get the situation shown in Table 2.4.

Table 2.4 Example of comparative advantage – money prices 2
(DK1 = €7)

| | Denmark | | France | |
	DK	Euro	DK	Euro
Beer	15	105	12.9	90
Clothing	7.5	52.5	2.1	15

Both commodities are cheaper in France, so there is no basis for trade. If the exchange rate was DK1 = €1.5 the situation shown in Table 2.5 would result. Both commodities are cheaper in Denmark, so there would be no gain for Denmark in trading. Obviously, the nearer the exchange rate is to DK1 = €6, the more Denmark will gain from exchange, and the nearer to DK1 = €2, the more France will gain.

Table 2.5 Example of comparative advantage – money prices 3
(DK1 = €1.5)

| | Denmark | | France | |
	DK	Euro	DK	Euro
Beer	15	22.5	60	90
Clothing	7.5	11.25	10	15

The gains from trading can be shown easily by using simple demand and supply graphs. Let us take the example above, where DK1 = €3, to illustrate what Denmark gains as an importer of clothing from France. In this simple two-country model, Denmark would import clothing from France, and France import beer from Denmark (see Figure 2.1).

The price of clothing imported from France would be DK5 compared with the price for Danish-made clothing of DK7.5 (which is represented by the point where the Danish demand curve cuts the Danish supply curve on the graph). As there are only two countries in this model, the French supply curve at P_f represents the world supply. So what are the effects of opening up to trade? First, Danish consumers can buy clothing much cheaper and so buy more of it, QD_{ft} compared to Q_{dk}, and they gain a consumer surplus of $P_{dk}ABP_f$. However the Danish producers will lose sales (because the French are undercutting them), and Danish supply falls from A to C or QS_{ft}. They will therefore lose the area $P_{dk}ACP_f$. Overall Denmark has gained because the consumer gains here exceed the producer losses ($P_{dk}ABP_f$ is larger than $P_{dk}ACP_f$) (adapted from Coughlin 2002).

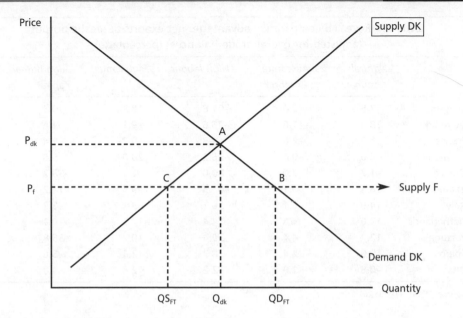

Figure 2.1 Gains from trade to Denmark as an importer – exchange rate DK1 = €3 – market for clothing

Source: adapted from Coughlin (2002).

This of course is based on the assumption that French prices do not change as a result of the increased demand from Denmark (and that Danish costs are not cut in response to the competition), whereas in reality a move to free trade would bring numerous price changes (Coughlin 2002).

An empirical study of comparative advantage

As part of his study into the potential gains and losses from the SEM, Neven (1990) calculated the revealed comparative advantage (CA) between EC countries for products using various **factors of production**: labour, capital, human capital and natural resources. Table 2.6 shows that the CA of Portugal and Greece lies in labour-intensive goods, and these are exchanged for goods intensive in human capital. Italy also has a CA in labour-intensive goods but does not have a comparative disadvantage (CD) in goods using human capital intensively, as do Portugal and Greece.

A CA in natural-resource-based industries seems to exist in Ireland, Denmark and to a lesser extent in Portugal, the Netherlands and Belgium. Germany and France seem to have some CA in industries using human capital. Furthermore Belgium, and to a lesser extent Italy, have a CA in capital-intensive products.

Finally, the figures suggest that the United Kingdom, and to a slightly lesser extent France, have no clear CA or CD in any category of products within the European Community. This suggests their stocks of factors of production probably are in line with the Community average. 'They are not particularly good at anything but they are not particularly bad either, relative to their EC partners' (Neven 1990: 27).

Table 2.6 Revealed comparative advantage: net exports/domestic output (adjusted for overall trade balances) (percentage)

	Natural resources	Av. capital/ av. labour	High labour	High capital	High human capital
Belgium	7.5	8.4	−91.8	18.3	−10.3
Denmark	28.5	−11.6	−26.5	−9.1	N/A
France	1.7	−2.6	−9.8	0.2	1.4
Germany	−4.0	−0.4	−26.2	−20.0	5.8
Greece	−1.7	7.0	80.0	−1.3	−98.7
Ireland	16.5	−9.1	−61.3	−9.5	11.2
Italy	−14.9	6.1	36.1	3.1	−5.2
Netherlands	12.0	N/A	−74.4	−17.2	−10.1
Portugal	12.2	4.4	79.4	10.2	−35.8
Spain	0.6	2.4	8.7	2.4	−6.6
UK	−0.8	1.0	−2.2	2.8	−4.8

Source: Neven (1990: 26).

Neven concludes, therefore, that specialisation within the EC occurs between north and south, not north and north, and the factors of production which appear to give strong advantage and disadvantage are labour and human capital respectively; physical capital appears to give little CA.

Criticisms of the comparative advantage theory

Criticisms mainly surround the sweeping assumptions on which the theory is based, especially those regarding technology. For example CA assumes perfect substitutability of labour and capital, yet this is not always possible. There is a limit to the transferability of factors of production from one use to another; eventually the costs will outweigh the benefits of specialisation. For example, if highly skilled agricultural workers were transferred to high-technology computer industries, it is likely that efficiency would decline quite quickly. Ricardo and Smith also ignored transport costs, yet high transport costs could rule out theoretical comparative advantage. A further, and more obvious, criticism concerns full employment – obviously not a very realistic assumption.

Apart from the assumptions, there are further problems in applying the theory to reality. First, does one country really specialise in one good and trade for another? As we will see below, this is far from reality for most countries. It also completely ignores the idea of **economies of scale**, and how these will change cost differences and affect specialisation. Further, trade will affect income distribution in the world and within the country, yet this is not considered. Finally, a more basic problem is that comparative advantage suggests that trade is based on different costs, but it does not explain what leads to these differences in comparative costs. A suggested solution to this question came about a century afterwards in the **Heckscher-Ohlin theorem** (Chacholiades 1990).

The Heckscher-Ohlin theorem

The Heckscher-Ohlin theorem assumes that not only is there more than one factor of production (for example, land, labour, capital, and you could now add enterprise), but different goods require different proportions of the various factors of production. Basically, some goods are labour intensive, some land intensive and some capital intensive.

Furthermore different countries have different amounts of factors of production (or endowments) and these result in different relative factor prices. This means that if a country has a great deal of land, land-intensive goods (that is, agricultural goods) should be relatively cheap to produce, and the country will have a comparative advantage in land-intensive products. According to this theory Argentina, Australia and Canada, with plenty of land, should export land-intensive goods such as meat, wheat and wool. The same can be argued for labour-intensive and capital-intensive countries. For example labour-abundant countries such as India, Korea and Taiwan should export labour-intensive goods such as footwear, rugs and textiles, whereas capital-intensive countries such as Germany and Japan should export capital-intensive goods such as computers and cameras. This leads to the basic Heckscher-Ohlin conclusion, that countries should specialise in goods that use intensively the factor of production that they have in abundance. So Heckscher-Ohlin basically says that trade is determined by relative amounts of factors of production, which determine the costs of trade.

The Heckscher-Ohlin theorem is based on a number of assumptions. It is a two factors of production, two goods, two countries model. There is no product differentiation, only that one good is capital intensive and the other is labour intensive, and production functions are assumed to be identical in each country. In addition there are constant returns to scale, and all countries are assumed to have access to the same technology. Factors of production are perfectly mobile inter-country, but they are immobile outside countries. All consumers have the same tastes, and all product and factor markets are assumed to be perfectly competitive, with no transport costs nor barriers to trade. Finally, neither country, it is assumed, will specialise completely in the production of one commodity: each will produce both to some extent. Many criticisms surround these assumptions, but the biggest problem for the Heckscher-Ohlin theory came with the Leontief paradox (Chacholiades 1990).

The Leontief paradox

In 1954 Leontief tried to apply the Heckscher-Ohlin theorem to reality. He used US data for 1947, at which date the United States had higher capital per head than all its trading partners. According to the Heckscher-Ohlin theorem, therefore, the United States should export capital-intensive goods and import labour-intensive goods. Leontief attempted to prove this.

He asked if US imports were reduced by US$1 million, and US exports were reduced similarly, what changes would have to take place in production requirements. He found that that to replace US imports with domestic output would need 170 more years per worker of labour and US$3.1 million of capital. To reduce US exports by US$1 million would provide 182.3 years of labour time and $US2.6 million. So comparing the two – US$3.1 million is greater than the US$2.6 million provided by exports and 170 is less than the 182.3 years of labour – showed that exports from the United States were more labour inten-sive than imports into the United States, which is the opposite outcome to that predicted by Heckscher-Ohlin. The world's most capital-intensive country was exporting labour-intensive goods (Husted and Melvin 2004).

Why? Was the Heckscher-Ohlin theorem wrong? Perhaps **factor endowments** do not determine trade. This is one conclusion that could be drawn.

Many alternative explanations have been suggested, however. One such suggestion is that Leontief picked unrepresentative data, as 1947 was a period of post-war reconstruction. The exercise was, however, repeated in 1951 and the same results obtained. Later work has suggested that the 'paradox' disap-peared by the early 1970s, although this does not dismiss the earlier problem. There is little reason to doubt that capital-abundant countries sometimes temporarily export labour-intensive goods.

Furthermore, the United States was highly protected against trade in 1947. If these tariffs were aimed at labour-intensive goods, then the only chance of exporting to the United States would be by selling capital-intensive goods. Baldwin (1971) showed that both tariff and **non-tariff barriers** operated in the direction of the Leontief paradox, but these can only partly explain it (Appleyard and Field 2001).

An alternative explanation is **factor intensity reversal**. Heckscher-Ohlin suggests that one commodity is capital intensive (say, cars) compared with another (say, furniture) in all countries, all of the time. However cars could be capital intensive in some countries but labour intensive in others. This is referred to as factor intensity reversal. For example if cars are capital intensive in Spain, but labour intensive in Germany, then labour-abundant Spain would export furniture (its labour-intensive commodity) to Germany. To pay for it Germany would need to export cars, but cars are labour intensive in Germany. So Germany is both importing and exporting labour-intensive products, and this produces the Leontief paradox. In reality, however, there is little evidence to suggest this is commonplace.

Heckscher-Ohlin is, however, purely a supply-side theory; demand conditions are totally ignored. The Leontief paradox could therefore be explained by demand conditions in the United States. There may be strong preferences for capital-intensive goods in the United States and such demand could exceed domestic supply, therefore the country would need to import such goods. Various studies suggest, however, that there is considerable similarity in demand functions between countries, and this consumption bias cannot account for much of the Leontief paradox.

Leontief proposed his own answer to the paradox. He suggested that US workers were three times more productive than those in other countries, and therefore if this was taken into account, the United States was really a labour-abundant country. This suggestion was supported by Kreinin's study (1955) but to nowhere near the extent Leontief claimed. Kreinin found approxi-mately a 20–25 per cent superiority, which would not make the United States a labour-abundant country.

Finally, Heckscher-Ohlin ignored certain factors of production. Vanek (1963) pointed out that natural resources were not considered, yet in 1947 the United States was importing a lot of metals and minerals which it used to export (especially oil), and obtaining these resources needs considerable capital. When it began importing these products, the United States began importing a great deal of capital; hence the Leontief paradox. If natural resources are included, some of the paradox disappears but not all of it (Chacholiades 1990).

Similarly, Leontief did not include human capital in his notion of labour – all labour is taken to have the same skill. It is argued, therefore, that the United States was a skill-abundant country, with a comparative advantage in skill, not in labour-intensive commodities, so explaining the Leontief paradox.

Having looked at 'traditional' theories, and before looking at the newer theories, we should now ask what are the facts concerning international trade at the present time.

World trade flows

In 2002 there were US$6,389.2 billion worth of exports in the world. Of this US$3,994.5 billion came from the developed country sector, but, only US$2,083.1 billion came from the developing country sector. Within this only US$355.9 billion came from Latin America and US$143.5 billion from the whole of Africa. The growing sector of the world economy, Asia, accounted for US$1,319.5 billion (a massive increase from US$455.2 billion in 1990) (United Nations 2003).

Table 2.7 shows the dominance of the developed countries in world trade, and also shows who trades most with whom. For example 53.3 per cent of Latin American trade goes to the United States, and 21.5 per cent of US trade goes to Latin America. The growing trade within the Asian region is also illustrated, with 42.7 per cent of Japanese trade going to this area and 39.2 per cent of trade staying within the region (United Nations 2003).

So the developed world still dominates world trade. However there have been significant changes within these figures since 1948. Table 2.8 shows that the percentage of trade accounted for by North America has fallen to 17 per cent from 27.5 per cent in 1948 (although the absolute figure has increased), but has remained pretty stable at that point since the 1970s. The area that increased its share of trade significantly between 1948 and 1973 was western Europe, but most notable between 1973 and 2000 has been the massive increase in Asia's share of world trade (from 15 per cent in 1973 to 26.7 per cent in 2000). A more worrying trend however has been the declining percentage of world trade enjoyed by Africa and Latin America, although the latter revived a little in 2002.

It is also interesting to see in what products the differing regions dominate trade. Table 2.9 shows what percentage of world exports in various products come from the different regions. Again, not surprisingly the developed economies dominate, especially in the chemical sector but also more interestingly in the agricultural raw materials sector (something many would attribute to the high degree of protectionism in this sector by these countries: see Chapter 3). Fuels and textiles are two areas where the developing countries play more of a role, southeast Asia providing 46.1 per cent of world trade in this.

Table 2.7 Direction of world trade: exports (FOB) 2002 (percentages)

	Destination								
Source	*Developed economies*	*EU*	*US*	*Japan*	*Developing countries*	*LA*	*Africa*	*WA*	*ESA*
World	65.9	36.2	17.9	4.8	28.3	5.3	2.2	3.4	17.5
Developed economies	71.4	44.9	14.8	2.9	23.1	5.6	2.1	3.3	12.0
European Union	77.6	61.0	9.4	1.7	14.1	2.2	2.7	3.7	5.5
United States	54.9	20.8	–	7.4	44.0	21.5	1.5	3.2	17.8
Japan	48.8	14.7	29.2	–	50.5	3.6	1.1	3.1	42.7
Developing countries	56.2	17.3	25.9	9.0	40.5	5.1	2.3	3.4	29.6
Latin America (LA)	72.2	12.3	53.3	2.1	24.9	18.1	1.1	1.2	4.5
Africa	70.5	48.6	14.5	3.4	25.9	3.5	9.2	3.6	9.6
Western Asia (WA)	49.8	20.4	13.6	13.7	40.0	1.2	3.8	8.6	26.4
Eastern & southern Asia (inc. China) (ESA)	51.6	14.7	22.1	10.6	46.4	2.6	1.6	2.9	39.2

Source: United Nations (2003).

Table 2.8 Share of world trade over time

	1948	*1973*	*2000*
North America	27.5	17.2	17.1
Latin America	12.3	4.7	5.8
Western Europe	31.0	44.8	39.3
Transition economies	6.0	8.9	4.4
Africa	7.4	4.8	2.4
Middle East	2.1	4.5	4.3
Asia	13.8	15.0	26.7

Source: United Nations (2001: 155).

Table 2.9 Percentage of exports in various commodities which come from different regions

% of world exports coming from this region	Food	Agricultural raw materials	Fuels*	Textiles	Chemicals	Machinery and transport	Metals
Developed economies	66.0	62.0	31.0	36.2	80.4	69.7	66.5
Economies in transition	2.9	5.5	11.0	4.2	2.8	2.8	9.8
Africa	2.8	3.3	11.1	2.4	0.4	0.2	1.0
Latin America	14.1	11.4	9.1	6.8	2.9	4.8	8.1
S-E Asia	12.4	16.5	10.1	46.1	11.1	21.8	12.4

* 27.7% of world exports in fuel come from the Middle East.

Source: United Nations (2003).

The study by Neven (1990) mentioned earlier attempted to measure **intra-industry** EC trade. Neven worked out a Grubel-Lloyd index for 29 industries representing the whole manufacturing sector and trade flows within the European Community.[1] The results are shown in Table 2.10, which gives the average intra-industry trade indices as percentages.

Table 2.10 Average intra-industry trade indices (percentages)

	UK	Ger	Bel	Fra	Neth	Ita	Den	Spa	Ire	Por	Gre
UK		73	73	79	77	64	63	57	70	40	41
Germany	73		74	74	63	58	71	58	59	36	35
Belgium	73	74		72	77	54	55	59	50	40	36
France	79	74	72		63	63	50	63	48	39	37
Netherlands	77	63	77	63		41	67	53	52	39	44
Italy	64	58	54	63	41		46	60	47	47	31
Denmark	63	71	55	50	67	46		39	55	29	28
Spain	57	58	59	63	53	60	39		40	46	19
Ireland	70	59	50	48	52	47	55	40		25	25
Portugal	40	36	40	39	39	47	29	46	25		31
Greece	41	35	36	37	44	31	28	19	25	31	

Source: Neven (1990: 21).

It can be seen that both Greece and Portugal have lower percentages of bilateral EC trade than other EC countries. This could be because of their later entry into the European Community (although Spain seems less affected), but it also suggests that the two countries have different factor endowments, leading to the production of different goods from the other EC countries. At the other end of the spectrum, Germany, France, the United Kingdom, the Netherlands and Belgium show signs of very high levels of intra-industry trade, mainly with each other. The results for Ireland, Spain and Italy are less decisive.

Finally, in the post-war period, two other possibly contradictory features in international trade have occurred. First, there has been increasing liberalisation of trade (see Chapter 3), but second, there has also been a growth of economic integration, or intra-bloc trade (see Chapter 4).

The growth of trading blocs is shown in Figure 2.2. The number of regional agreements increased dramatically from the early 1990s. Of the 250 regional trade agreements (RTAs) notified to the General Agreement on Tariffs and Trade (GATT)/World Trade Organization (WTO) up to June 2002, 129 were registered after January 1995. Out of the 250, 170 RTAs are still in force and another 70 are 'estimated to be operational although not yet notified. By the end of 2005, if RTAs reportedly planned or already under negotiation are concluded, the total number of RTAs in force might well approach 300. Virtually every WTO member is today engaging further on the RTA track as part of its trade strategy, increasingly for defensive reasons, to protect market access' (WTO 2003: 27). The WTO suggests therefore that the fear of losing market access is one of the major reasons for all the trade agreements at present. It does however express some concern over this movement, stating that 'this is likely to give rise to regulatory confusion, distortion of regional markets, and severe implementation problems, especially where there are overlapping RTAs' (WTO 2003: 27). This topic will be looked at in further detail in Chapter 4.

This, of course, links up with our first feature of trade – the growth of trade between industrialised countries – and can be a partial explanation for it.

However, even given this fact, we can see that traditional theories have been found somewhat wanting. The result has been a plethora of new theories to explain the post-war modern 'facts' of international trade.

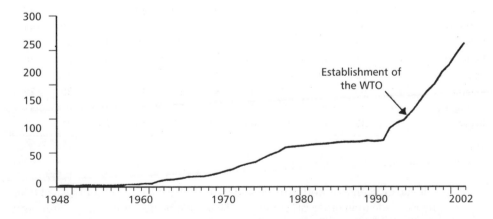

Figure 2.2 Evolution of regional trade agreements in the world, 1948–2002

Source: WTO Secretariat.

Increasing returns and imperfect competition

One explanation for the modern trade patterns has been that modern industries tend to be dominated by large industrial units and thereby gain **economies of scale**, both internal and external. This obviously means that modern industry is typified by increasing, not constant, returns to scale, which was the assumption of the previous trade theories. Previously it was assumed that if inputs doubled, output would also double. Now the assumption is that with large modern industries, if inputs double output will more than double; that as firms get larger, they get more efficient (Krugman and Obstfeld 2003).

If firms concentrate on the domestic market, there will be limited economies of scale. As we have seen already, trade allows specialisation in a narrower range of products, and production can exceed that necessary for the domestic market, thereby allowing economies of scale to be reaped through larger plants and larger production runs. A good example of this is given by a comparison of Europe before and after the formation of the European Economic Community (EEC). Before the formation, EEC industrial plants tended to be small and catered for the domestic market. The EEC allowed firms to expand and trade; they grew in size, their costs fell and brought with them an increase in efficiency (see Chapter 4).

These reduced costs from economies of scale are a reason or determinant of trade in itself. Normally however, a situation where scale economies exist will also be one of **imperfect competition**. This occurs where firms have some power over the price charged; it is not totally determined by the market. It usually occurs because the goods are made to be or thought to be different, for example via packaging or advertisements, and this differentiation prevents substitution and gives some kind of power to set the price. Alternatively we could see economies of scale which mean lower costs per unit as bringing imperfect competition, in that they give large firms an advantage over smaller firms and consequently market power.

Trade will enlarge the domestic market to an international market, so increasing the number of firms, but at the same time each can produce on a greater scale, so reducing average costs. What does this actually say about the pattern of trade, though? According to Krugman and Obstfeld (with a two-country model), 'because of economies of scale, neither country is able to produce the full range of manufactured products by itself; thus although both countries may produce some manufactures, they will be producing different things' (2003: 137). Trade in manufactures will therefore be of two types:

> manufacture for manufactures called intra-industry trade. The remainder of trade is an exchange of manufactures for food called inter-industry trade. The latter can be explained by comparative advantage, the former by economies of scale and imperfect competition. The relative importance of intra and inter industry within trade depends on the similarity of countries. If they are very similar, intra-industry trade will dominate and if very different, inter-industry trade will be the norm.

(Krugman and Obstfeld 2003)

Linder's preference similarity hypothesis

This theory is not the only explanation of post-war trade patterns. In 1961 Linder put forward another explanation. He said that a country will export the manufactured products for which it has a good domestic market. Why? Three reasons lie behind this conclusion:

- A good domestic market gives producers a greater awareness of the opportunities for profit with their product.
- Any research and development undertaken by firms is aimed at satisfying obvious needs; needs usually made obvious through the domestic market.
- Even if a firm recognises the profitable opportunities within the foreign market, it is often expensive to develop or adapt a product to fit an unfamiliar market.

According to Linder therefore, the range of products a country exports will be a subset of the range supplied and consumed in the domestic market. Similarly the products a country imports will have a close resemblance to the products it already consumes. Whether these products are imported or produced domestically depends on the relative prices of imports and domestic goods. This suggests that trade will take place between similar countries in similar products (Chacholiades 1990).

Linder also asked what determines the demand structure. The most important influence is per capita income. The higher per capita income, the higher the demand for high-quality and luxury consumer goods and more sophisticated capital goods. Lower per capita income means more demand for necessary consumer goods and less sophisticated capital goods. So if a country is rich, it will have a comparative advantage in quality goods for the above reasons, and therefore export them to other rich countries which make up its big export markets (due to their overlapping demand structure).

There will be some overlapping demand in some poor countries and rich ones because of unequal distribution of income within each country. So those who are comparatively rich in less-developed countries (LDCs) buy luxury goods from developed countries, and those who are comparatively poor in developed countries will buy more basic goods. Therefore income, taste and demand patterns generally determine trade. This leads to the conclusion that the closer the overlap between two countries' consumption patterns, the higher the potential for trade.

It should perhaps be stressed at this point that Linder's theory is an attempt to explain the trade in manufactured goods; it does not cover primary product trade. For this, Linder suggested that the basic nature of primary products ensures the export potential is easily recognisable. However, it is often foreign entrepreneurs who provide the initial impetus to these exports, possibly because they are more aware of the demand for these products in their home country.

Linder's theory therefore explains intra-industry trade from a demand-side point of view. It does ignore the supply side, however (the opposite problem to the Heckscher-Ohlin theory). We must also question whether it is realistic to assume that countries cannot appreciate foreign demand and respond to it, or that a country's natural advantages in some goods will not be exploited because of limited demand from the home market. There are also cases that do not fit. For example China produces Christmas crackers, yet not only is there no home demand, there is not even an obvious Chinese word for the product.[2] Similarly Linder's theory has problems with the idea of outsourcing; although it could be said that home demand has prompted multinational companies (MNCs) to supply that product, but from a low-cost source.

Two other models attempting to explain empirical evidence on trade are based on the question of technology. The first theory really paves the way for the second; however they both attempt to make traditional theory more dynamic.

Posner's technological gap theory

Posner's technological gap theory, put forward in 1961 (and sometimes known as the imitation lag hypothesis) suggests that innovation and imitation are especially important for exports, and that technology is not the same everywhere. New products are developed, they become profitable, thereby giving firms a temporary monopoly, and this leads to easy access to foreign markets. Initially the level of exports grows, but growing profits bring imitation elsewhere, gradually eroding the comparative advantage. Once this has been lost the firm or industry will search for another new product, and so a new cycle of innovation and imitation begins. The innovating country will continue to develop new products and to have temporary absolute advantage in these, but eventually other countries will produce them more efficiently. Therefore Posner's explanation of patterns of trade is based around different innovations occurring through time.

Posner's theory fails to explain why this technological gap exists, however, and the size of the gap. A generalised version of this theory was suggested by Vernon in 1970, in the context of a product's life cycle.

Vernon's product cycle model

Vernon similarly stressed how some countries have better access to technology than others; they have a comparative advantage in 'high-tech' goods. Without such technology a country could not compete in this market.

Vernon suggests that a product goes through three stages: it starts off as a new product, then becomes a maturing one and finally a standardised one. In the new product stage the product is invented by a country with high-tech advantage (hence there is a link to Posner) in response to domestic demand, and marketed in the domestic market, thereby allowing the production techniques and the product itself to be tested. This links to Linder's theory in the first stage, as the producers become more aware of using technology through its possible use in the home market. There is also a need for more skilled labour in this development stage in order to test and adjust the product.

In the maturing stage the product gradually becomes standardised and mass production begins to take place; here economies of scale begin to play a part (so there is a link to Krugman). Less skilled labour is necessary, and capital becomes more important. At this stage the product is marketed internationally, so producers look for similar markets in other similar countries as export markets. As exports increase, producers then start to look at the possibility of locating nearer, or in, these markets.

The final stage is one of more advanced standardisation. Factors such as production and location costs are more important in location decisions, and it is more likely that the product will be made in other countries and imported to the original producing country. Gradually production in, and export from, the original market ceases and production is shifted elsewhere, often to LDCs. It should be pointed out at this stage that this process will vary according to the product considered (Appleyard and Field 2001).

The conclusions reached by this theory are that different countries will export different products over time. Alternatively we could say that different countries will export the same good as it moves through its lifecycle.

An example of Vernon's theory is seen in the market for colour television receivers (Baker 1990). The market started in 1954 in the United States, and in the early years the market for receivers was dominated by domestic producers. In 1967 imports were 6 per cent of the market, but only three years later these amounted to 19 per cent (over 90 per cent of which were from Japan). Later, as the technology spread to other countries, imports from Taiwan and Korea began to challenge the Japanese imports, and these fell to 80 per cent of the imports by 1977 and 50 per cent a year later. A further, more long-term example of the product lifecycle theory is the textile industry. Britain at first had a technological advantage (at the time of the industrial revolution), but gradually the technology spread to the United States and production moved accordingly. Then as production became increasingly standardised, costs became more important and production of textiles moved towards LDCs, especially in Asia. Even within Asia production is now shifting from the higher-wage centres of Hong Kong and Singapore towards the lower-wage centres of the Philippines and China (Yarbrough and Yarbrough 1997).

The usefulness of Vernon's theory to modern times has, however, been questioned. It sees producers as operating in their home markets and responding initially to this market, which is separate from other national markets. The growth of multinational companies catering for a global market has brought the relevance of the theory into question. It does, however, still have relevance for inventive and innovative small firms. These may begin by concentrating on the home market, but they eventually begin to export to find new markets for their goods. Similarly we can also relate LDC trade to this theory. Moreover it does have important points to make: that it is unwise for countries to attempt always to remain competitive in products in which they initially had an advantage, and that an element of a country's success in international trade could be how mobile its resources are between sectors: the more mobile it is, the more successful.

Porter's competitive advantage theory and Porter's diamond

Porter in 1990 did not so much question Heckscher-Ohlin as ask why some nations succeed and others fail in international trade. For example, why are the Swiss so good at producing pharmaceuticals? CA theory and the Heckscher-Ohlin model have never really got to grips with this question. They argue that the Swiss use the resources they have very well in these industries, but why don't the Spanish or the British do similarly?

Porter suggested there were four attributes of a nation that shape the environment in which local firms compete, and can help or hinder the creation of a competitive advantage through which the nation can trade. This came to be known as Porter's diamond (see Figure 2.3).

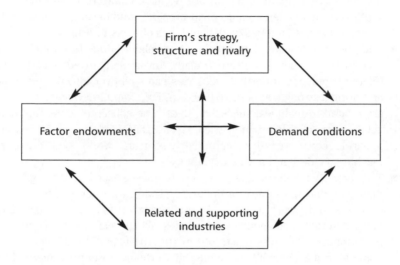

Figure 2.3 Porter's diamond

Source: Hill (2005).

Porter argued a country will succeed if the diamond is favourable. So what are these four attributes?

● The nation's position regarding factor endowments. This links to the Heckscher-Ohlin theory, but Porter analyses them much more closely, seeing a type of hierarchy among factors of production. There are basic factors such as natural resources, climate, location and population, and advanced factors such as communications, infrastructure, skilled labour, research and technological knowledge. These advanced factors are the most significant for competitive advantage, Porter argues. Furthermore they are often created through investment by individual companies and governments rather than natural endowments. Therefore, for example, government investment in education could lead to higher skills, and more research would upgrade advanced factors. The relationship between the advanced and basic factors is complex. Basic factors can provide initial advantage, which is reinforced and increased by the advanced factors. Similarly disadvantages in basic factors can create pressure to invest in advanced factors instead. For example Japan lacks basic minerals but has invested elsewhere, and has built up an endowment of advanced factors.
● The nature of the home market demand for the product. Home demand is the impetus for high-grade competitive advantage, according to Porter. Firms

are sensitive to the needs of home customers, so their demand will shape domestic-made products and bring pressure for innovation and quality (see Linder earlier). If there are sophisticated and demanding consumers, then there will be higher standards, better quality and more innovation. Similarly in cellular phones, one of the reasons why the Finnish company Nokia and the Swedish company Ericsson are dominant players in the market is the sophisticated and demanding consumers in Scandinavia who pushed them to invest in phones long before demand was obvious to others.

● The presence or nature of suppliers and related industries which are necessary to be competitive internationally. Investment in advanced factors by related suppliers/supporting industries can spill over into the main industry and bring a strong competitive position. For example Swiss pharmaceuticals are related to technical success in dyes. The consequence is that countries get clusters of related industries – for example the German textiles and apparel sector includes high-quality cotton, wool, synthetics, sewing machine needles and textile machinery.

● The conditions governing how companies are created, organised and managed, and the nature of domestic rivalry: in other words, the strategy, structure and rivalry of firms. With strategy, for example, different nations have different management ideologies which can help or hinder their performance. This was illustrated in the 1970s and 1980s when engineers dominated management in Japan and Germany, so improvements in manufacturing process and design occurred there, whereas in United States there was more a finance background for management, which meant a lack of attention to production and design processes and more emphasis on short-term financial returns, which reduced competitiveness in engineering industries. There is also a strong association between vigorous domestic rivalry and persistent competitive advantage. Rivalry means that competition increases, which leads to more efficiency, innovation, higher quality, lower costs and investment to upgrade advanced factors.

Porter argued that countries will succeed if the diamond is favourable. The factors in the diamond are also mutually reinforcing. One attribute can affect the others: for example favourable demand conditions will not bring competitive advantage unless there is rivalry to which firms can respond.

Two other variables can influence competitive advantage according to this model – chance and the government. Chance events such as major innovations can lead to discontinuities which can reshape industry structure and allow one nation's firms to supplant another's. Similarly government choice of policy can help or hinder national advantage; for example education policy investment can change factor endowments. So the government can influence in a positive or negative way by such things as subsidies, capital market policies, education and so on, and shape demand via product standards and regulations; it can support related industries and so on, and change competition via tax and competition polices.

If Porter's diamond model is correct, then countries will export products from industries where the four points of the diamond are favourable and import from where they are not (Hill 2005). How this works in practice is shown in the case study below.

PORTER'S DIAMOND: KEY FACTORS OF SUCCESS FOR CASE STUDY REGIONS

The EU's *Competitiveness Report 2003* undertook five case studies of a mixture of differing EU regions, all of which were considered successful as they had above-average productivity growth over the period 1987–2000. These regions ranged 'from the urbanised Ile de France region, the hub of the French economy, to the sparsely populated Greek region of Sterea Ellada' (European Commission 2003: 162). The aim of the case studies was to identify the reasons for these regions' success. The results are summarised for each region in Table 2.11.

Table 2.11 Five case studies

Region	Factors for success
Oberbayern, Germany (dominated by Munich)	Good transport links, particularly the airport. High level of firm creation, linked to strong entrepreneurial culture. Immigration supplying skilled labour to support growth in high-tech areas. Very modern manufacturing base and a rapidly expanding services sector. Policy to retain manufacturing through provision of specially designed industrial sites. Strong public support through energy supply, transport infrastructure and educational facilities. Clusters in ICT, media and biotechnology likely to lead to large spillover effects.
Darmstadt, Germany (contains Frankfurt)	Immigration of skilled, multi-lingual workforce, from within and outside the country, to support growth in employment. Leading financial centre, together with strength in telecommunications and pharmaceuticals. Well-developed public transport system (road, rail, water and air) and modern telecommunications structure. Cluster of life science research institutes. Strong links between university and business reinforced by public authority support. Active policy to promote the region and city in an enlarging Europe.
Sterea Ellada Greece (borders Athens)	Presence of large, high-productivity companies with high levels of innovation created via high R&D spend. Agencies and institutions supporting innovation and technology transfer in medium-sized and large companies. A regional innovation system in part supported by European funding. Vocational training in relevant applied technologies. Proximity to the capital city and good communications.

Table 2.11 continued

Region	Factors for success
Ile de France, France (Paris area)	Cultural hub of French economy – history of centralist policy making. Centre of national transport network – well served by TGV and regional train lines, motorways and international airports. Shift to high-tech industries supported by network of research centres offset problems of de-industrialisation in early 1980s. Policy to locate clusters (particularly bio-tech, electronics and engineering) in modern towns outside the central city region. National leader in defence manufacturing, with resulting network of support companies. Strong presence of foreign-owned companies, particularly in pharmaceuticals, chemicals and plastics.
Niederosterreich Austria (near Vienna)	A critical mass of untraded interdependencies (networking, common vision and spillovers). Economic development governance and the presence of a regional innovation system. An emphasis on internationalisation. An economically embedded and networked research and educational base with an emphasis on industrial collaboration. Innovation and technology upgrading being seen as the solution to labour cost pressures. Geographic position, proximity to Central and Eastern Europe.

Source: EU (2003: 162–3).

Questions

1 How well do these success factors fit Porter's diamond analysis?

2 What could other regions learn from this?

Fair and ethical trade

As we have seen earlier, trade is still very much dominated by the developed countries (DCs), and income distribution in the world today is very unequal. An example often used to illustrate this is the comparison of the world to a village. If we see the world as a village of 100 inhabitants:

- 57 would be Asian, 21 European, 14 American, 8 African
- 51 would be women and 49 men
- 45 would be under the age of 25
- 20 would have well-equipped houses
- 75 would be living on less than US$1 a day
- 33 would have no electricity

- 1 would have a university degree
- 17 would not have purified water
- 50 would be suffering from malnutrition
- nobody would have a computer
- and 6 people would own 50 per cent of the wealth (Smith 2003).

One of the basic problems is that the world trading system is stacked against the LDCs. Many LDCs have a comparative advantage in terms of low costs, usually in labour. Therefore it is not surprising that often MNCs from DCs locate in LDCs for these low-cost reasons; low wages, low rent, low level of unionisation, low standards concerning environment and labour factors, and exploitation of natural resources. However these large MNCs gain a great deal of power, as there is little alternative for a poor country eager to increase employment, and gain foreign exchange and an entry into world trade.

The world trade system is dominated by the DCs, and often the goods that LDCs produce suffer from poor terms of trade. Africa, for example, is still heavily dependent on production and export of just a few primary products. These tend to have very volatile prices (see the coffee case study below), something not helped by the power of MNCs. For example if there is one or a few major buyers, they have a monopsony and can practically determine the price that suits them. To take products like tea, cocoa and coffee, these are all produced in LDCs but their prices have changed little in real terms for the past 40 years. Furthermore falling commodity prices can have dramatic consequences for LDC producers, often forcing them into debt, with the loss of land and homes (again see the coffee example below).

Development agencies and charities, seeing what was happening in world trade, decided to use the power of the consumer to improve the situation.[3] They felt that many consumers would be willing to buy at a slightly higher price if they felt they were aiding the producers in the LDCs and enabling them to work under fairer conditions. The Fairtrade foundation and Fairtrade mark was therefore established. 'As long as manufacturers agreed to buy from registered suppliers according to Fairtrade criteria their products could carry the Fairtrade seal of approval' (Fairtrade no date). Such criteria mean that traders must be paying a price that 'covers the costs of sustainable production and living; pay a "premium" that producers can invest in development; make partial advance payments when requested by producers; sign contracts that allow for long-term planning and sustainable production practices' (Fairtrade no date). Basically the aim has been to pressurise retailers to stock Fairtrade-label products, and provide proof that the workers and environment have not been exploited or badly treated, so changing the balance of power.

The country to launch the first fair-trade label was the Netherlands, launching the Max Havelaar label in 1989. The Fairtrade label now has initiatives in 18 countries and covers a range of products from orange juice to tea and bananas. Fairtrade products now achieve something like 15 per cent of national market share in the UK (Fairtrade no date).

An alternative way of improving conditions in LDCs has often been put forward, especially by the Clinton regime in the United States in the 1990s. It was suggested that what was needed was a set of international standards

THE COFFEE MARKET

Millions of people rely on coffee to make a living. There are 25 million coffee producers around the world, and in many cases coffee is grown as a cash crop. Although some is grown on plantations, it is one of the few internationally traded commodities that is still grown on small holdings in the main.

The coffee market is very much controlled by the four big coffee companies, called the roasters: Kraft Foods, Nestlé, Procter & Gamble and Sara Lee. They control the big brands of Maxwell House, Nescafé, Folgers and Douwe Egberts. In 2001 Kraft made profits of over US$1 billion on sales of beverages, cereals and desserts. Nestlé instant coffee (3,900 cups of which are drunk every second) makes such healthy profits that one investment analyst called it the commercial equivalent of heaven. But the situation is not so happy for the others at the growing end of the scale.

When the price of coffee is low, the small farmer gets poorer. Many countries are also highly reliant on coffee: in Ethiopia coffee accounts for 50 per cent of export revenues, in Burundi 80 per cent. So when the price of coffee falls, the economy of the whole country suffers. The governments cannot afford to provide publicly funded health and education, and the people cannot buy these services, as they do not get enough from their only source of money – coffee.

What has happened to the price of coffee recently? The price of both robusta and arabica coffee has fallen.[4] It started to fall dramatically in 1997 and hit a 30-year low in 2001. After inflation has been taken into account the price of coffee beans is one quarter of what it was in 1960. So the money the farmer makes is only worth a quarter of what it was 40 years ago. This does not cover the costs of the producers; for example in Viet Nam (one of the lowest-cost producers) it covered around 60 per cent of the production costs.

So why has the price fallen so dramatically? Many have pointed to the end of the managed market. Until 1989 the coffee market was managed by the International Coffee Agreement (ICA), whereby producer and consumer nations agreed supply levels via export quotas for producers, and the aim was to keep price high and stable inside a band or corset. This agreement went the way of most such international commodity agreements and broke down. Prices are now determined on the two big futures markets in London and New York.

Others have pointed to oversupply. There have been new entrants to the market such as Viet Nam, and increased supply by traditional producers such as Brazil. However some have said maybe it is not so much a supply side problem as a demand one. So many alternatives now exist to coffee that it is a very competitive market.

Sources: Oxfam (2002), *Financial Times* (2002).

Questions

1 Show in terms of supply and demand why coffee has fallen so much in price recently.

2 Why would the ending of the ICA lead to a drop in price?

3 What would happen if producers produced less coffee?

4 What are the alternatives for coffee producers?

setting up a 'level playing field' for trade. There should be a certain minimum level of labour standards set internationally, for example a minimum working age, no slavery, no restrictions on trade unions, and collective bargaining as a right. Some also argue for minimum wages to be set internationally. These ideas were put forward very strongly in the abandoned WTO meeting in Seattle in 1999 (see Chapter 3). Others argue that there should be minimum environment standards: for example there should be limits on the level of pollutants, and environment and wildlife protection.

LDCs however have been strongly opposed to this view, arguing that international standards are unlikely to raise their welfare and more likely to destroy their comparative advantage in low-wage labour. If they are allowed to develop and trade fairly, then this will automatically bring in higher standards. They also point out that most DCs industrialised by exploiting workers and the environment. They are just following the same path to industrialisation, so preventing exploitation could also prevent industrialisation. Finally they argue if standards are imposed, alternatives must be provided. For example if children are stopped from working, this could mean condemning the whole family to desperate poverty and forcing them into unregulated jobs that are much worse than their current ones.

The whole idea of setting international standards has faded somewhat since the Seattle meeting, and the United States now no longer pushes this view in the same way. The fair-trade label and 'consumer power' in this respect have however gone from strength to strength.

Conclusion

Trade is a vital part of all EU economies, and also vital for companies. Various theories have attempted to explain why trade occurs between which countries and in which goods. The more traditional, older theories of absolute and comparative advantage and the Heckscher-Ohlin theory have provided a base for the newer trade theories of increasing returns and imperfect competition, preference similarity, product lifecycle and Porter's diamond. The newer trade theories have concentrated much more on explaining the changing patterns of trade: intra-industry trade and the dominance of the developed world. Each theory however stresses that free trade is preferable to protecting firms from competition, which leaves the question, why then do countries protect their industries?

?? Questions

1 In the past, companies within differing countries have been seen to have an absolute advantage 'in everything'. In the early 19th century this applied to the United Kingdom, then it shifted to the United States, Japan in the 1960s/1970s and now China. What gives them this advantage, and what

problems does it bring with it? Use the example of China now, to illustrate your answer.

2 If the production capacity of the Netherlands and Belgium in two goods. cheese and chocolates, is as follows, per unit of labour per day:

	Chocolates boxes	Cheese rounds
Netherlands	20	50
Belgium	100	80

(a) Which country has a comparative advantage in which product? Explain your conclusion.
(b) What rate of exchange would Belgium prefer and why?
(c) What rate of exchange would the Netherlands prefer and why?
(d) What rate of exchange is likely?
(e) Prove both will gain if they follow the principle of comparative advantage. Use the example of Belgium selling 30 boxes of chocolates and a rate of exchange (or terms of trade) of 1 box of chocolates = 1.5 cheeses.

3 The Netherlands exports Heineken beer and imports Löwenbräu. What sort of trade is this an example of?

4 In the chapter we showed that one of the major influences on world trade is, and has been, the growth of regional trade agreements (see also Chapter 4). Imagine you are the manager of an EU electronics company attempting to sell your product to a customer in the NAFTA trading block, what problems do you think you might encounter?

5 In the chapter, the example given of Vernon's product lifecycle is the market in colour televisions. Can you think of another product where you could trace the trading lifecycle in this way?

6 The figures in the chapter show how important trade is becoming for most nations and companies. What factors do you think could stop the growth of trade continuing? Choose a particular country and particular company, and analyse how a slowdown in world trade growth would impact on them.

7 In the chapter we looked at fair trade and the case study examined the case of coffee. However there have been other examples like this in the press in recent years, sugar and cotton being just two. How could fair trade help the LDC producers and DC consumers in these two areas? Can you think of any other areas where fair trade is 'long overdue'?

Notes

1 The Grubel-Lloyd index considers trade between countries in a certain industry.
2 With thanks to students on module 52039 International Economics at Oxford Brookes University who spent time and imagination trying to think of 'an example that didn't fit'. Special thanks to Dan Liu who came up with the Chinese crackers example!

3 In the United Kingdom the Fairtrade Foundation was established by CAFOD, Christian Aid, New Consumer, Oxfam, Traidcraft and the World Development Movement (www.fairtrade.org.uk).
4 There are two types of coffee. Robusta, as it sounds, is a hardy plant, used for strong roasts and soluble coffee. Arabica is better quality, milder and grown at high attitudes, but harder to grow and more vulnerable to disease, so it commands a higher price.

References

Appleyard, D. R. and Field, A. J. (2001) *International Economics*, 4th edn, McGraw Hill, Boston, Mass.

Baker, S. A. (1990) *An Introduction to International Economics*, Harcourt Brace Jovanovich, San Diego, Calif.

Baldwin, P. E. (1971) 'Determinants of the commodity structure of US trade', *American Economic Review*, vol. 56 (June), pp. 466–73.

Chacholiades, M. (1990) *International Economics*, McGraw Hill, New York/London.

Coughlin, C. C. (2002) 'The controversy over free trade: the gap between economists and the general public', The Federal Reserve Bank of St. Louis *Review*, January/February, vol. 84, no. 1, pp. 1–21.

European Commission (2003) *The EU's Competitiveness Report*, Commission Staff Working Document.

Fairtrade Foundation (no date). Information on www.fairtrade.org.uk, accessed 10 July 2004.

Financial Times (2002) 'Campaigners target collapsing coffee price', 18 September.

Fontagne, L. (2004) 'European industry's place in the international division of labour: situation and prospects', Summary. *Report for the European Commission Directorate of Trade*.

Hill, C. W. L. (2005) *International Business: Competing in the global marketplace*, 5th edn, McGraw Hill, Boston, Mass./London.

Husted, S. and Melvin, M. (2004) *International Economics*, 6th edn, Pearson Addison Wesley, Boston, Mass./London.

Kreinin, M. E. (1965) 'Comparative labour effectiveness and the Leontief scarce factor paradox', *American Economic Review*, vol. 55 (March), pp. 131–40.

Krugman, P. R. and Obstfeld, F. (2003) *International Economics: Theory and policy*, 6th edn, Addison Wesley, Boston, Mass./London.

Neven, D. J. (1990) 'Gains and losses from 1992', *Economic Policy*, April, pp.13–62.

Oxfam (2002) 'Mugged: Poverty in your coffee cup', http://www.oxfamamerica.org/newsand publications/publications/research_reports/mugged

Smith, D. J. (2003) *If the World Were a Village*, Allen and Unwin, London.

United Nations (UN) (2001) *World Economic and Social Survey 2001*, UN, New York.

UN (2003) *World Economic and Social Survey Survey*, UN, New York.

Vanek, J. (1963) *The Natural Resource Content of Foreign Trade, 1870–1955*, MIT Press, Cambridge, Mass.

WTO (2003) *Annual Report*, WTO, Geneva.

Yarbrough, B. V. and Yarbrough, R. M. (1997) *The World Economy*, 4th edn, Dryden Press, Forth Worth/London.

3 The protection of trade

Judith Piggott

Objectives

This chapter will:

- consider the reasons that countries undertake protectionist measures
- outline the differing types of protection
- show how this protectionism affects the differing economic agents
- give an overview of the World Trade Organization (WTO) and its history.

Introduction

Despite being members of the General Agreement on Tariffs and Trade (GATT)/World Trade Organization (WTO), European nations have always used a number of protectionist measures, relying historically on **tariffs**, and more recently on **non-tariff barriers** to trade. This chapter examines the effects of tariffs on trade, charts the growth of non-tariff barriers, discusses the role of the GATT/WTO in reducing barriers, and looks at the new issue of fair trade.

Arguments for protectionism

As was seen in Chapter 2, a country that engages in international trade enjoys benefits in the form of both immediate improvements in standards of living and economic growth. The standard of living that can be obtained exceeds that which would be available to a competitive economy that operates without trade (**autarky**). In addition, there may be political and economic benefits, in that as countries become more economically independent, they are less likely to undertake hostile actions. Nevertheless, countries still apply a variety of measures aimed at controlling the amount of free trade. Why then do countries ignore the obvious benefits of free trade policies?

There are many arguments put forward for intervention in free trade. The following are some of the major reasons.

Infant industry

This is an argument mainly for temporary protection, and one of the oldest arguments: it was first put forward by Alexander Hamilton in 1791. The basis of the argument is that young industries need protection from international competition, and that while protected they will make the necessary invest-ments, build up human capital through training and 'learning by doing', and so become more efficient. Once this has been achieved, the protection will be removed. Examples of the 'successful' use of the infant industry argument in practice can be found in the automobile industry in Korea, the production of commuter airplanes in Brazil, and the European Union's protection of its video and compact disc markets. But such successes are rare, as there are also problems with the infant industry argument.

First, the main beneficiaries of this in developing countries have often been foreign firms, which locate behind tariff walls, rather than indigenous firms. Second, this argument is for temporary protection, but many such industries do not 'grow up' and are content to hide behind protective tariffs – so it becomes permanent protection. We further have to ask: if the industry is likely to become profitable in the future, why isn't private industry willing to support it? If the government has superior information to potential investors, then it should surely share it. If however there are external benefits that private investors would be unlikely to take account of, for example, new technology which could benefit other industries or society, then it would be better to use subsidies for this particular area (see later).

Strategic argument

This argument suggests that there may be social benefits which exceed private benefits. The argument is that all countries need a defence industry for security purposes, or that all need to have an agricultural industry, so they can feed their population in times of war. These are obviously based around value judgements, and examples in the past show how this can be misused. For example the defence argument has been put for gloves, pens, pottery, peanuts, umbrella frames, paper, candles and drawing pins, and the case argued for the protection of fishing nets because of their potential as camouflage nets in times of war. It is ironic that often imports of things like mittens, socks and handkerchiefs are more controlled than imports of pistols, rifles and nuclear reactor parts (Husted and Melvin 2004).

Revenue reasons

Tariffs provide revenue for the government (see later), and any method of collecting revenue will incur distortions and costs such as administrative costs and the distortion of consumption decisions. For some countries, such as less-developed countries (LDCs), tariffs may be the least distortionary way of collecting revenue because they involve a few ports/airports and a handful of bureaucrats. However as countries develop and the ability to use other taxes grows, the case for tariffs declines. For example Uganda collects approximately 70 per cent of its government revenue from tariffs, whereas the corresponding figure for the United Kingdom is 0.02 per cent (Husted and Melvin 2004).

Unfair competition

This argument usually takes two forms.

Dumping

This is when a country's exports are priced below cost as a result of either government subsidy or an attempt to take over the market (known as predatory **dumping**). In neither case will the lower price be permanent, but once the competition has be pushed out of the market, the price will be increased to at least cover costs (if not more). Competition is destroyed and consumers suffer ultimately through a higher price. To counter this, anti-dumping legislation is used in many countries. For example the European Union has its own legislation against this type of practice, and if the rules are not applied fairly, there is the ultimate sanction of reporting it to the WTO.

The problem with anti-dumping legislation is that it is hard to distinguish between dumping and normal international competition. Should dumping be proven, the usual situation is that countries are allowed to impose countervailing duties on the products: in other words, duties which counter the price cut. Often the threat of this is sufficient to bring about an increase in price without any further action being taken.

It has been noted however that the number of anti-dumping investigations notified to the WTO has been rising: 157 cases were initiated in 1995 but this had risen to 347 in 2001.[1] The sectors where most cases occurred were metals, especially steel (38 per cent of 2001 cases), chemicals (17 per cent), plastics and rubber (14.4 per cent). The largest users of anti-dumping provisions since 1995 have been the United States (257), India (248), the European Union (247) and Argentina (166), while the countries who have been accused most of dumping products onto the market have been China (261), the Republic of Korea (139), the United States (103) and Chinese Taipei (96). Of the cases notified, about half have resulted in some sort of countermeasure being imposed (WTO 2003). The question has to be asked whether this increase is due to these countries dumping goods onto the market, or whether they have suddenly become competitive on the world market.

Cheap labour argument

The argument is that workers need to be protected from cheap foreign labour elsewhere, and that it is not possible to compete against such cheap wages and costs, so jobs are jeopardised. However the law of **comparative advantage** (CA) (see Chapter 2) states the trade is based on such cost differences, and that all benefit from free trade. As pointed out earlier, CA does not however take account of changes in income distribution, and it is true that some sectors will be hurt by free trade. For example the textile and shipbuilding industries in the north of the United Kingdom were largely destroyed by cheap imports in the 1970s and 1980s. In theory the portion of society who gain from free trade should aid those who suffer, but unfortunately this rarely happens. The government could step in, and for example subsidise retraining to help those who lose their jobs to cheap overseas competition, but the point is that there is no economic argument for a tariff. The only time this might be put forward is if the lower wage country's government were proven to be subsidising the wages, so acting unfairly, and then a countervailing tariff could equalise matters.

Terms of trade/optimal tariff argument

This applies mainly to a large country with power in the market. Increasingly this could be applied not by a country but by a group of countries in a trading bloc like the European Union or North American Free Trade Area (NAFTA) (see Chapter 4). The argument is that such a country could impose a tariff which so reduces world demand that the world price falls, possibly sufficiently to counter the effect of the tariff. Such an event would mean that there would be no effect on domestic consumers and producers (see later), and the government would collect revenue, but who would pay it? The answer is that the importer absorbs the tariff. This is referred to as an optimum tariff because it increases welfare in the imposing country more than it loses in protectionism. Obviously it only applies to a limited (but possibly growing) number of situations.

Strategic trade policy

The basis of this argument lies in the new trade theories, especially Krugman's increasing returns to scale concept (see Chapter 2), and it also has strong links with the earlier infant industry argument. The idea is that certain high-rent industries that have strong externalities with regard to other industries (for example telecommunications, aerospace, pharmaceuticals) should be protected in order to strengthen them against foreign rivals and gain economies of scale. The main example of this has been Japan's strategic trade policy of the 1970s, which protected its computing and automobile industries. However, as Japan discovered, other countries began to resent this and started to retaliate to counter this advantage (see VERs below). There are further problems: in Krugman's words, 'even if you understand an industry well enough to devise an activist policy, or are willing to assume that your model is really good enough, estimates of the gains from strategic trade policies are almost always very small' (Krugman 1996: 24).

The balance of trade effect

This is often quoted as a good reason for protection. Basically the idea is that protection reduces imports and therefore improves the balance of trade. This cannot really be argued with, especially in the short term, but in the long term a country imposing barriers is quite likely to face retaliatory actions from those who can no longer export into that country. Therefore the protectionist country is likely to face tariffs on its own exports, and in the end the balance of trade deteriorates again.

Protectionism is not a costless approach (as has already been seen) but in monetary terms the costs of protection are not always obvious. For example, the quotas on clothing and world textile trade are reported to cost US$200,000 (£109,000) for each US textile worker annually (*Financial Times* 2004a). So who bears these costs? Basically who gains and loses through protectionist devices? The answer to these questions varies according to the type of protection.

Tariffs as a barrier to trade

Historically the main form of trade protection has been the tariff. This can be levied as an **ad valorem** percentage of the value of imports (for example 10 per cent) or as a **specific duty** (for example €10 per tonne), or a mix of both (€10 per tonne + 10 per cent).

Most of the time when people refer to tariffs, they are referring to import tariffs. However export tariffs do exist. These push up the price of exports and raise revenue for governments. However it is a risky strategy, and in order not to reduce export sales, demand for the good on which the export tariff is imposed would need to be relatively price inelastic.

The more common tariff however is a tariff on imports. The effect of this is to push up the price of the goods, and usually to reduce demand for them. The effects of an import tariff are illustrated in Figure 3.1.

In Figure 3.1 the domestic demand and supply curves for the market when there is no international trade are shown as D and S respectively. If the economy indulged in international trade and is assumed to be small relative to the rest of the world, then it would face a horizontal, or perfectly price-elastic, world supply curve for products (in other words it could buy or sell all it wanted

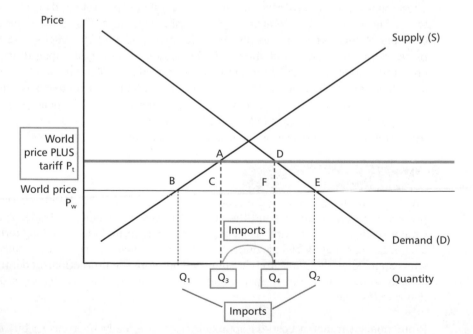

Figure 3.1 Effect of import tariff on output and price

at the world price without causing the world price to change). At world price, domestic supply would be Q_1 and domestic demand Q_2. The difference would be made up of imports – the distance $Q_1 - Q_2$. If this is seen as too great (for reasons given above), it may force the government to impose a tariff on imports.

The effect of a tariff (t) is to raise the world price to P_t. Domestic consumers therefore reduce their demand from Q_2 to Q_4 and this reduces consumer surplus by P_tDEP_w. Domestic producers can expand their output (as they can now charge a higher price) from Q_1 to Q_4, and the producers' surplus is increased by the area P_tABP_w. The government gains revenue in the shape of the area ADFC. The resource misallocation costs of the tariff (called the deadweight loss of the tariff) are shown by the triangles ABC and DEF; ABC is the cost of supporting inefficient domestic industry which could not compete at the world price, and DEF is the cost to consumers who have left the market because the price is too high now.

There are however other effects of tariffs that cannot be shown in the diagram. Briefly, there may well be a competitive effect because competition has been reduced at the margin. There will also be a redistribution effect. Employers domestically will gain, output will rise, and income and employment may also increase. However those who have the tariff imposed on them (foreign producers) will be experiencing the opposite, which is why it is often referred to as a '**beggar thy neighbour**' policy. Finally there may be a positive effect on the balance of payments, as imports are reduced, but as seen above, in the longer term as retaliation sets in, this could be countered by falling exports.

Table 3.1 gives a list of average tariffs for a variety of WTO member countries. It is notable that the average rates are low in many countries, the highest being in the medium-developed countries (MDCs) and less-developed countries (LDCs), for example India and many of the African countries. However it should be noted that the rates do vary considerably across products. For example the highest tariffs (referred to as **tariff peaks**) are to be found on agricultural products, textiles and footwear. It is noticeable that many of the products in these sectors are of interest to the LDCs in terms of exports. Furthermore tariffs tend to increase as the product is refined, a process called **tariff escalation**, and noticeably this tends to affect the same sectors as tariff peaks. This is illustrated in Table 3.2.

For example the WTO in its 2003 *Annual Review* summed up the situation by saying:

> tariffs in developed countries are low, [but] tariff 'peaks' and escalation can constitute major impediments to poorer countries' development and industrialisation, for example, through exports; they tend to be concentrated in agricultural products, textiles and clothing and other manufactures in which developing countries have a potential comparative advantage. Since agricultural products and textiles and clothing account for more than 70 per cent of poor countries' exports, the potential benefits from the reduction/elimination of peaks and escalation are large.
>
> (WTO 2003:10)

The problem with the analysis outlined above is that the impact of a tariff has been discussed under rather strict assumptions. Two such assumptions are

Table 3.1 Tariff rates internationally

Country	Average applied tariff rate	Year
North America		
Canada	4.2	2002
United States	4.4	2001
Mexico	15.6	2001
Latin America		
Argentina	13.4	2000
Brazil	13.8	2000
Chile	9.0	2000
Colombia	11.2	2000
Costa Rica	4.7	2000
Europe		
EU (15)*	4.1	2002
Switzerland	2.3	2000
Middle East		
Bahrain	7.7	2000
Asia		
Bangladesh	21.9	1999/00
Hong Kong, China	0.0	2000
India	31.0	2001/02
Japan	3.9	2002/03
Korea, Rep. of	7.5	2000
Malaysia	9.9	2001
Pakistan	20.1	2001/02
Singapore	0.0	2000
Oceania		
Australia	4.7	2001/02
Africa		
Cameroon	17.6	2000
Gabon	17.5	2000
Ghana	12.5	2000
Madagascar	6.1	2000
Mauritania	10.4	2001
Mauritius	19.8	2001
Mozambique	13.1	2000
South Africa	10.9	2002

* This now applies to all the new entrants to the EU that have taken the common external tariff.

Source: WTO (2003: 13).

Table 3.2 Tariff escalation in the 'Quad'*

		United States 2001	Canada 2002	EU (15) 2002	Japan 2002/03
Food	First stage of processing	3.2	7.9	12.4	25.4
beverages	Semi-processed	9.0	6.8	19.1	30.3
and tobacco	Fully processed	13.1	34.3	18.8	22.6
Textiles and	First stage of processing	2.2	1.0	0.9	9.8
leather	Semi-processed	9.8	7.0	6.7	6.8
	Fully processed	10.3	13.5	9.7	12.0
Chemicals	First stage of processing	2.0	1.5	1.7	2.5
	Semi-processed	4.6	2.9	4.5	2.8
	Fully processed	4.1	4.7	3.8	2.0
All sectors	First stage of processing	2.2	3.9	7.3	14.6
	Semi-processed	5.2	3.9	4.9	4.9
	Fully processed	5.7	8.9	7.0	7.8

* The Quad is the United States, the European Union, Japan and Canada.

Source: WTO (2003: 37).

those of the 'small country' and perfectly competitive markets. Krugman (1997) has argued that because trade occurs not in perfect markets, but in markets where imperfections and possible increasing returns to scale exist, it is possible for governments to intervene in free trade via a tariff to increase the welfare of that country (see strategic trade policy earlier).

Non-tariff barriers to trade

As shall be seen later, as GATT became increasingly successful in reducing tariffs, countries have looked to other ways to protect their industries. **Non-tariff barriers (NTBs)**, the so-called '**new protectionism**', have rapidly been replacing tariffs as instruments of commercial policy. NTBs basically are any barriers to trade that are not tariffs. Some of these and their effects are considered below.

Quotas

An import **quota** is a limit on the number of goods imported into a country. This will create a shortage and thereby raise the price. The economic effects of quotas for a small open economy are shown in Figure 3.2.

The demand and supply curve are those of the domestic market, and P_w represents world price (again assuming perfect elasticity of supply). At world price the level of imports would be Q_1 to Q_2. However if a country now imposes a quota which restricts the quantity of imports of this product to $Q_3 - Q_4$, then the price will rise to P_q. This will reduce consumer surplus by P_qDEP_w and

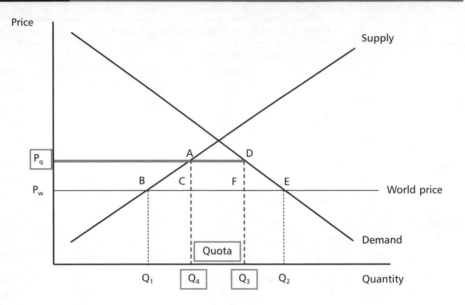

Figure 3.2 Effect of quotas for a small economy

increase producer surplus P_qABP_w (as with a tariff). But who gets the extra revenue from the quota? This depends on how the **quota licences** are allocated. They can be allocated by bureaucrats, based on such things as historic market share, or they could be allocated more efficiently by auction (the market decides). In the latter case, it is usually assumed that the whole of the revenue section ADFC will go to the government imposing the tariff. Again there are deadweight losses – ABC and DEF – for similar reasons to the tariff.

So what are the differences between quotas and tariffs? First, as we have seen above, the government will only collect the revenue section if it auctions the licences. Second, there is a different reaction to changes in supply and demand conditions. For example if demand for say imported US baseball caps rose, and these had a tariff imposed on them, it would be easy to just import some more; the quantity would rise. If there was a quota instead, the effect would be an increase in price, as no further caps could be imported. Nowadays there are fewer quotas in practice. However they still do exist. For example there is a quota for garlic and mushrooms imported into the European Union from China (*China Daily* 2004a).

There are also export quotas. These restrict the amount of exports that leave the country, again creating a shortage, and increasing the price abroad this time. However they also increase the quantity kept at home, thereby reducing the price. As with export tariffs, this will only work if the product exported has very inelastic demand (perhaps because only one country produces the product or there are few substitutes), otherwise purchasers will just buy from other countries. Recently, for example, the European Union asked China to remove its export quota on coking coal, which is a vital raw material for steel making. The quota was cut from 12 million tons in 2003 to 9 million in 2004, and this had the effect of reducing world supply and increasing world price. However

China's growing steel industry also needs this raw material to meet its home demand, and claims this is the reason for the quota. China also claims that to remove the quota would cause a sharp drop in price and could bring a price war amongst its local producers (DTI South Africa 2004). This looked like it could become the one of the first dispute cases to be brought against China since it joined the WTO in 2001, but in May 2004 the European Union and China reached a compromise agreeing that the European steel industry will get at least 4.5 million tons from China in 2004 (the same as in 2003) and that 'export licences will be delivered without cost or delay' (*China Daily* 2004b).

Furthermore sometimes a tariff and quota can be combined. The famous case of this was the European Union's banana regime, under which ex-EU colonies (Asian, Caribbean and Pacific (ACP) countries) were protected by a quota on Latin American bananas, If the quota was exceeded, a tariff of 170 per cent was imposed. After many years of arguing, and the WTO declaring the regime illegal, it was announced that the banana regime would be replaced by a simple tariff-only regime in 2006 (Piggott 1999).

Quotas are officially outlawed under the GATT, but certain exceptions are allowed, for example with agricultural products and in cases where governments need to impose temporary protection to aid locally distressed industries, or when a country has a balance of payments problem. Whereas global quotas are relatively uncommon, country to country quotas are more common. In addition, countries have found ways of imposing quotas indirectly on others by obtaining agreements from exporting countries to 'voluntarily' limit exports.

Voluntary export restraints (VERs)

The **voluntary export restraint** (VER) or orderly marketing agreement (OMA) is a form of quantitative restriction also now outlawed by the WTO, but such agreements were prolific in the 1990s. In 1994 for example, there were 26 VERs on textiles, 14 on agricultural products, ten on steel, ten on footwear, five in electronics and 79 in total. Of the 79, 46 were imposed by the European Union (Salvatore 2001). Here the exporting firm or country agrees with the importing country to restrict the volume of its exports to a specified amount, over a given period of time. VERs have been negotiated on such things as footwear, steel, electronics, textiles and agricultural products for example, but the most famous VERs were those imposed on Japanese cars by the United States, United Kingdom and finally the European Union (see below).

A VER is very similar to a quota in effect, except the restriction is voluntary and administered by the exporter. So, as with a quota, consumers will lose, domestic producers will gain, and there will be two deadweight losses. The main difference between a VER and a quota, however, is in the revenue area ADFC on Figure 3.2. With a quota, this goes to the government if it sell licences, but with a VER, it goes to the foreign producer (as a higher price for its goods). In other words, foreign producers gain an economic rent, a net transfer from domestic consumers to overseas producers. Of course offsetting the impact of this loss to the domestic consumer is the impact of increased employment and output in the domestic economy, although whether this is the most efficient way of achieving these gains is debatable.

VERs tend to be less effective than quotas in restricting trade because it is easier to control imports than exports. In addition VERs usually cover only major suppliers, so suppliers from other countries can still gain access to the market. VERs are therefore discriminatory and a violation of the non-discrimination rule embodied in GATT's/WTO's most-favoured nation (MFN) principle.

As an illustration of the level and impact in reality, the example of the VERs on Japanese cars is a good one. From the United Kingdom's point of view the VER arranged with Japan over car imports during the early 1980s appears to have made little difference to overall car imports, as Japanese cars were merely replaced by imports from the European Union which were not restricted. Yet a National Consumer Council survey of the effect suggested that losses to the consumer exceeded gains for producers by around £9 billion (National Consumer Council 1993). This translated into consumers paying £700 more for each imported Japanese car.

In the United States a study by Berry, Levinsohn and Pakes in 1999 showed the impact of the VER on the US market. It was shown that prices for Japanese cars increased by 14 per cent above what their level would have been without the restraint. This led to some customers deferring purchase and others switching to US-produced cars. However the 'switchers' were very price-sensitive, and this meant the home producers could only raise prices by about 1 per cent, but they did sell far more than they might otherwise have done, as fewer Japanese cars were available. As a result it was estimated that profits for US car producers were US$2 billion higher due to the VER. But again consumers were the biggest loser, especially those who liked to buy Japanese cars, losing something like US$13 billion. Taking account of the producer gains and other gains to the US economy, it was estimated that the welfare losses in total from the VER were approximately US$3 billion (Benjamin 1999).

So why the proliferation of VERs? For the government a VER shows that it is proactive on behalf of industry, but the real impact is hidden (particularly from consumers) and the budgetary implications are minimised. For foreign producers the VER may be the least bad of a number of measures that could be taken against them, and they do of course gain economic rent on the amount they do sell.

Production subsidies

Here domestic producers are encouraged by a **production subsidy** from the government which reduces costs (rather than raises the price of the good).

The impact of the subsidy can be seen in Figure 3.3. The subsidy shifts the domestic supply curve down from S_0 to S_{sub}. Domestic suppliers now supply Q_3 and imports are reduced from Q_1Q_2 to Q_3Q_2, but domestic consumers still pay P_w. Since domestic demand is unaltered, there are no losses in consumer surplus, but area a is again the increase in producer surplus and area b is the deadweight production loss, or the net loss to the economy. However as there is only one deadweight loss, in economic welfare terms this is seen as preferable to both a tariff and quota. Finally it should be pointed out that unlike a tariff, where there is a revenue gain to the government, here there is a revenue loss.

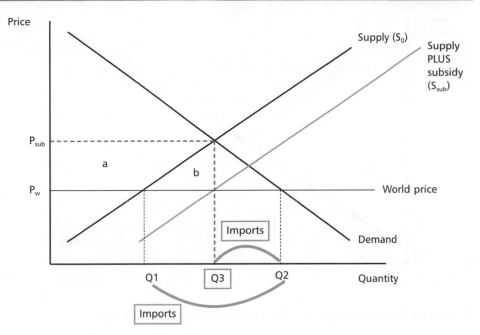

Figure 3.3 Effect of production subsidies

Export subsidies

With an export subsidy, the government subsidy pushes the domestic price of exports below the world price. This is considered to be a form of **dumping**, and countries who believe that the price of the exported good is lower than the price of the good in the exporter's domestic economy often impose penalties such as countervailing tariffs to remove any advantages that these goods may obtain.

The effect of an export subsidy can be seen from two perspectives, that of the importing country and that of the exporting country. See Figures 3.4 and 3.5.

The effect on the importing country is to cut the price of imports from P_0 to P_1, thereby shifting the world supply curve down by the amount of the subsidy (those from the outside world will also have to cut their prices to compete with the subsidised country). This means the amount of imports will increase from Q_1Q_2 to Q_3Q_4. The consumers gain from lower prices (area a+b+c+d), the producers in the importing country lose (area a), but there is a net transfer from the exporting country to the importing country of area c. A countervailing duty can be imposed to counter the effect on the importing country's producers, and this would push the supply curve back up towards P_0; the effect on the consumer and producer would be countered but the transfer to the exporting country would not be eliminated.

From the exporting country point of view, the world price is set at P_0 (this is above the domestic price equilibrium, otherwise the country would not be exporting but would sell all production at home) and Q_1Q_2 worth of exports are sold. If exports are now subsidised, the price the exporters receive will be P_0 + subsidy, which is P_1 on the diagram. The higher price raises production to Q_4

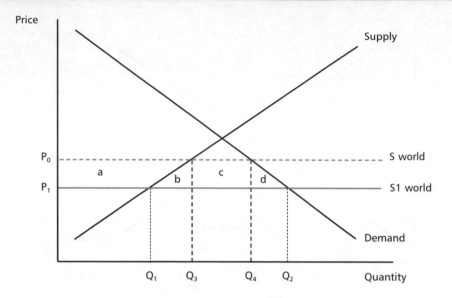

Figure 3.4 Effect of export subsidy from importing country's view

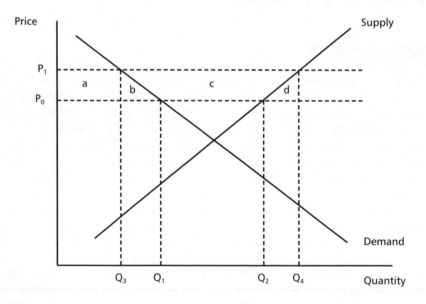

Figure 3.5 Effect of export subsidy from exporting country's view

but means that less will be sold domestically, so increasing the price to P_1 and reducing the quantity to Q_3. Domestic consumer surplus falls by $a+b$, the exporter surplus rises by $a+b+c$, and taxpayers pay $b+c+d$ for the subsidy. Area b is lost twice (to consumer and taxpayer) and gained once (by the exporter), and area d is lost by the taxpayer and gained by no one; therefore the deadweight losses are area b and d. In total welfare terms the exporting country has lost but it has gained an export market for its goods in the process (Yarbrough and Yarbrough 1997).

Not all export subsidies are easy to recognise, however. For example, it is possible to give exporting companies preferential low rates of interest on any money borrowed, or for these companies to offset more items against tax, or it is possible for governments to subsidise wages through increased transfer payments so that the workforce keep their wage demands low, leading to competitive export prices. All these are forms of export subsidy.

As with quotas, export subsidies on manufactured goods are not allowed under the GATT/WTO as can be seen with the FSC trade dispute (see case study 3.2).

Case study 3.1

THE SUGAR INDUSTRY

A World Bank report stated that sugar was 'the most policy distorted of all commodities' (Alden and Buckley 2004: 17) and that global welfare could rise by US$4.7 billion (£2.5 billion, €3.7 billion) a year if there was reform of trade in sugar.

The United States started protecting its sugar industry by the Sugar Act of 1934, which was intended to stabilise the sugar price. The effect has been to stabilise the price over the last decade at three times the world price. It has also been estimated that in 2000 US users paid £2 billion in higher prices as a result of the sugar programme.

The European Union also supports its sugar industry to a massive extent. The European Union does not have the climate to produce sugar cane, but it does produce sugar beet. An Oxfam report in 2004 showed how relatively inefficient sugar production is in the European Union. For example the cost of producing a pound of sugar in the European Union is 25 cents per pound, while in Brazil it is 4 cents. Yet the European Union protects its industry from Brazilian sugar by imposing tariffs. It also subsidises its sugar farmers (via levies) to the tune of US$1.3 billion, plus, Oxfam claims, hidden subsidies of €833 million in addition. Brussels sets the price sugar processors pay to the farmers, plus the price they gain for the processed sugar, and the EU consumer pays three times the

world price. These generous prices for European sugar farmers have meant oversupply, and 5 million tonnes of subsidised EU sugar is dumped on the markets each year. The effect on the more efficient producers is devastating. It is claimed that Brazil loses around US$500 million a year and Thailand US$151 million. Other less efficient and poorer countries such as Mozambique were estimated to lose US$38 million in 2004.

This system is however facing increasing threats. Brazil, Australia and Thailand have jointly brought a dispute case to the WTO, stating that the levies represent illegal subsidies, and the WTO has ruled in favour of them. This ruling is at present in appeal.

In the United States the protection of the sugar producers is also under threat from trade liberalisation, although there is a powerful lobby group supporting the industry. But the industry is also under threat from the World Health Organization's (WHO's) campaign against obesity and reduction of sugar in diets. This is a long-term threat to sugar consumption and therefore sugar producers, and it is not surprising that the validity of the scientific evidence of the WHO is being questioned by the lobbying groups supporting sugar.

Not all LDCs will gain from such dismantling of trade barriers. Although at present export subsidies by the richer nations have driven down world prices, the removal of such subsidies will mean prices rising. Those countries that import food products will therefore be hurt by removal of these barriers and 'as many as 45 of the world's least developed countries are net food importers' (Panagariya 2004: 17).

Furthermore while the most efficient exporters, such as Brazil and Argentina, will gain, some of the poorer and most vulnerable LDCs will lose. Many of these have preferential access to rich-country markets, and taking away this privileged access could expose them to potentially harmful competition. For example the Everything But Arms (EBA) initiative gives LDCs 'duty and quota free access to the EU market for all products except rice, sugar and bananas' (Panagariya 2004: 17). But as was stated in a *Financial Times* editorial in 2004:

> it is a delusion to think such special trade arrangements can survive much longer. The [WTO] sugar ruling is only one of many forces conspiring to undermine them. Trade preferences have in any case often had undesirable consequences, preserving

inefficient production and penalising economic diversification. Weak economies need generous and carefully targeted international assistance to help them adjust to freer trade. How the US and EU respond will test the strength of their commitments to promoting global development.

(*Financial Times* 2004b: 16)

Sources: Alden and Buckley (2004), Denny and Moore (2004), *Economist* (2004), *Financial Times* (2004b),Panagariya (2004).

Questions

1 Explain, using graphs, the effect of such subsidies and tariffs on the United States and European Union, and the effect on the more efficient world producers (for example Brazil and Thailand) of the dumping of excess sugar production.

2 Identify the effects on the differing economic agents, for example consumers and producers, on these diagrams. Are there any other effects?

3 What do you think is the economic justification for the United States and European Union undertaking such protectionism?

Discriminatory government procurement

Most governments discriminate in favour of their domestic producers, perhaps for strategic and employment reasons, but this can also be a form of trade protection. The government may show a bias in the issuing of contracts to home producers, or instruct certain industries in the home economy to buy their raw materials or semi-manufactured goods from other companies in the domestic economy. In fact things like the 'Buy British' campaign or 'Buy American' are the government trying to influence consumers to buy domestic goods, and so would fall under this heading.

This barrier was discussed in the Cecchini Report on the Single European Market (SEM), which stated that public procurement accounted for 11.5 per cent of EU GDP but only 0.14 per cent went outside the individual EU states. In fact 100 per cent of Italian government purchases went to Italian firms, while the figures for France, Germany and the United Kingdom were 99.9 per cent, 99.7 per cent and 98.3 per cent respectively (Cecchini 1988 – see also Chapter 4).

EXPORT SUBSIDIES – THE FOREIGN SALES CORPORATION (FSC) DISPUTE

In July 1998 the European Union filed a complaint with the WTO that the United States was subsidising the exports of many US companies through its taxation system. This was effectively distorting trade and giving the companies an unfair competitive advantage in world markets. It is estimated for example that it involved more than 6,000 US exporting companies such as Boeing, Microsoft and Procter & Gamble. The European Union claimed that about half of all US exports, worth US$125 billion, were via FSCs.

The US scheme allowed US exporters to avoid US tax on foreign income by using tax havens and subsidiaries. (If US companies establish subsidiaries to process export sales in US-controlled tax-free zones in the Virgin Islands or Guam, for example, they would pay no tax on these.) This was achieved originally through the Domestic International Sales Corporation (Disc) scheme, but in 1976 this was condemned by GATT and replaced by the Foreign Sales Corporation (FSC) Act. In 1981 the United States claimed that the GATT agreed this was an acceptable regime, but it did not appear in the GATT/WTO Subsidies Code of 1994, and therefore the European Union claimed it could not be seen as legal.

The WTO set up a dispute panel in 1999 to consider the EU complaint, and eventually in August 2001 ruled that the US FSC tax system violated its rules. The United States appealed, but in August 2002 the WTO rejected this and gave permission for the European Union to place sanctions worth US$4 billion on US exports to counter this unfair advantage. The European Union gave the United States until March 2004 to repeal the law or face tariffs, but the United States did not meet this deadline, and therefore the European Union began gradually to impose counter-measures in March 2004, despite the fact that the US Trade Representative warned in 2001 that to impose such sanctions would be like detonating a nuclear bomb on the trade system, and would hurt the European Union as much as the United States.

In May 2004 the US Senate adopted the JOBS act which repeals the FSC Act. The European Union has said it considers this an important step in the direction of settling the dispute, and that 'the moment WTO-compliant legislation becomes law, the European Union will immediately repeal the countermeasures' (Europa 2004).

Sources: Castle (2002), de Jonquieres (1999, 2000), Europa (2004), European Union (2003), Williams (2002).

Questions

1 Illustrate the effect of such a subsidy for the EU and US producers.
2 Illustrate the effect of sanctions on US imports to the EU market.
3 What are the motives for this action by the European Union? Are there any hidden motives?

This type of discrimination is really a subsidy paid to domestic firms, who could be undercut by foreign firms in a free market situation.

In 1979 the GATT was amended to incorporate restrictions on local preferences by government purchasing agents. It was agreed that countries would grant each other equal access to government contracts, though countries would be free to exclude certain agencies from the agreement. The Uruguay Round expanded the procurement code to include services as well as goods, and central, local and government-owned enterprises. Most governments exclude part, if not all, of contracts for defence, energy, postal services and telecommunications (Husted and Melvin 2004).

Multiple exchange rates

Monetary authorities may sell foreign currency at different rates of exchange depending on the use to which the currency is being put. For example, if a firm is exporting rather than wanting the foreign exchange for importing, it could get a more favourable exchange rate than the market rate. So exports are being effectively subsidised and imports discriminated against. A real-life example of multiple exchange rates can be found in Zambia, where the general manager of Zimbabwe Electricity Supply Authority (Zesa) has been quoted as saying:

> The many exchange rates used are affecting us. We have the rate used by Zimra [Zimbabwe Revenue Authority] which is $3.875. Then we have the official rate which depends on the auction rate of the day, and then we have the parallel market rate which is used when we source spares from other players in the industry.
>
> (Chanakira 2004)

He claims this has acted as a serious constraint to efficiency, and priority should be given to Zesa as it provides an essential service.

Indirect non-tariff barriers

The previous types of direct NTBs or new protectionism have advantages over the indirect methods that follow, in that it is possible to illustrate the burden of these, whereas the effects of indirect NTBs, it is argued, are far more pervasive and more difficult to identify. They still raise costs and reduce competitiveness. Such indirect barriers include bureaucracy or 'red tape', as well as less obvious examples where health and safety and environmental rules have been used to obstruct importers. It is also possible for tax regimes to deter the entry of some goods into a market. The French domestic tax on cars is positively related to a car's horsepower; as such, it raises the prices of US-produced cars relative to French cars, since US cars have more horsepower, and can be regarded as discriminatory. The UK and Italian governments have sometimes required importers to deposit a sum equal to half the value of the import of a commodity at their government's treasury for six months at no interest.

A good example of bureaucracy being used to protect domestic producers is customs valuation procedures which are made sufficiently complex to add to the uncertainty of importers. For example, in the 1980s the French system for the importation of video cassette recorders (VCRs) required that they were all brought into the country through Poitiers airport, a small airport with eight people working in customs, who insisted on unpacking and checking every VCR. As can be imagined, the delays were very long, and this discouraged imports to France of VCRs. Complaints were made to WTO/GATT and eventually the restrictions were removed, but the developing French VCR industry had been protected in the meantime.

Many examples can also be found where health and safety legislation has been used to protect industries from products. In recent years Japan has announced that foreign-made skis will not be allowed into the country because they are unsafe, citing the reason that the snow in Japan differed from the snow in Europe and the United States. Small cherry tomatoes were banned from the United States as they were claimed to be dangerous to eat.

A classic example of using health and safety legislation to protect producers (or is it consumers?) is the case of beef, and specifically the beef hormone dispute between the United States and European Union in the case study below.

Case study 3.3

HEALTH AND SAFETY AS A MEANS OF TRADE PROTECTION? THE BEEF HORMONE DISPUTE

The beef hormone dispute is now the longest trade dispute with the WTO/GATT, lasting over 16 years. In 1989 the European Union banned the use of six growth hormones in the production of beef. This ban was apparently non-discriminatory as it included farmers worldwide, including EU farmers. The reason given for the ban was it was felt these hormones were not safe for human health. The effect of this however was to dramatically reduce US exports, since most US beef producers use the hormones, by US$20 million per annum. The United States saw it therefore as a protective device, or at best a way of stabilising the EU beef market after so many food scares and so much consumer pressure. The immediate reaction of the United States was to impose trade sanctions on EU exports worth US$100 million, effectively doubling the price of canned tomatoes, coffee, pet food and drinks in the United States.

In 1996 the United States (jointly with Canada, Australia, New Zealand and Norway) took the case to the WTO disputes settlement system, claiming that it violated the SPS (Sanitary and Phytosanitary Measures) Agreement as there was no scientific proof that the hormones were dangerous to justify the ban. The WTO panel ruled in favour of the United States. The European Union claimed that the burden of proof of safety lay with the United States (as with other products), and that the WTO had exceeded its rights and become a health legislator. It therefore appealed in January 1998, but the WTO upheld the ruling that it had still breached the rules. However the WTO did allow 15 months for more proof to be found, until May 1999. Finally in July 1999 the WTO ruled that no new scientific proof had been found, and gave the United States the right to impose sanctions of US$116 million and Canada of C$75 million by applying 100 per cent duties on EU-produced beef and pork. The European Union had not lifted the ban at the time of writing.

Source: Piggott (2003).

Questions

1 The European Union claims there is still a potential risk, but has little scientific proof. Does it have the right therefore to protect its consumers in this way? Should consumers have the right to choose (for example, if the beef was labelled as containing growth hormones, consumers could refuse to buy it)?

2 Is this really a means of protecting the EU farmer?

3 Ultimately, what is the dispute really about?

Differences in indirect taxes

Excise duties differ between countries, often discriminating against the country of origin on imported goods. For example, the United Kingdom has a greater duty on wine than on beer, and the Italians charge a greater duty on imported spirits than on home-produced ones. These differences in indirect taxation can cause distortions in the market.

Why there was a growth in non-tariff arrangements

All these NTBs may be difficult to quantify, but why were they introduced in the first place? It is not sufficient to say that they have simply replaced tariff barriers which have been reduced under the GATT/WTO regime. We need to look more at the conditions under which tariffs were cut.

The period up to the mid-1970s was one of general world expansion, and in this sense it was easier for the developed nations to reduce tariffs. Since then we have seen three world recessions, from 1974–5, 1980–1 and 1990–2. When economies experience the effects of slowdowns in world growth, they are more loath to reduce tariffs, and they may also seek to further protect their domestic economies through non-tariff barriers.

The 1980s also witnessed the growth of some of the LDCs into newly industrialised countries (NICs); thus the western developed nations felt threatened in their traditional export markets and domestic markets. A response was to protect these through non-tariff barriers. There is also evidence that products that face a high incidence of NTBs also tend to be products that face high tariffs: that is, NTBs and tariffs are complements rather than substitutes. To make matters worse, NTBs are often not imposed singly but piled upon a single commodity. Thus a country that faces an NTB such as a quota on a particular product may also face health and safety restrictions on the same product.

The prevalence of tariffs in the 1930s led to the setting up of GATT after the Second World War, and the continued protectionism today has led to the setting up of the WTO to extend its work.

GATT

The GATT was formed in 1947 in Geneva by 23 nations. Its charter contains 38 articles with three over-riding aims:

- to provide a framework for the conduct of orderly trading relations
- to encourage free trade and reduce the possibility of countries taking unilateral action against others
- to reduce tariffs and quantitative restrictions.

Although GATT may not have appeared to have affected individual countries directly, it had a number of indirect effects. In particular by encouraging countries to lower their trade restrictions with other member countries of the GATT, it enabled some organisations to achieve greater cost-competitiveness and widened their markets.

The GATT agreement embodied three main principles: **non-discrimination**, **reciprocity** and **transparency**.

- **Non-discrimination:** this says that countries should treat all their trading partners the same way. For example, if the United Kingdom puts a tariff of 40 per cent on an Australian import, it should not put a higher tariff on a similar good imported from India. This is known as non-discrimination or most-favoured nation (MFN) treatment. Similarly, if the UK agrees a tariff reduction with Australia, bilaterally, then this tariff concession should be extended to all other countries. Any tariff reduction gained can almost certainly be expected to be permanent. Therefore, the advantages of the MFN treatment is that two countries, in bargaining for tariff reductions, know that a later deal between one of the countries and a third party will be passed on. The process also helps small countries who may have little bargaining power.
- **Reciprocity:** if country A makes a 10 per cent reduction in tariffs on an import from country B, country B should make a corresponding reduction in tariffs on imports from country A. The MFN rule would then enable these reductions to be transmitted between all GATT nations. Reciprocity recognises the existence of the 'free-rider' problem inherent with trade liberalisation.
- **Transparency:** countries should replace disguised and less quantifiable protectionism with more visible tariffs. NTBs generate uncertainty which then acts as further non-tariff barrier.

GATT also realises that there may be occasions, such as temporary balance of payments problems and the need to protect a domestic industry, when short-term trade measures might be allowed. Additionally, discrimination is allowed against countries that 'dump' goods onto another country's home market.

There is a special place within GATT for LDCs, which may benefit from MFN tariff reductions without the necessity of reciprocation. Nevertheless the extent to which an LDC remains an LDC or becomes an NIC, and thereby loses some of its tariff protection, has come under close scrutiny by the developed nations.

The GATT rounds

The first four rounds of trade negotiations in Geneva 1947, Annecy 1949, Torquay 1950–1, and Geneva 1955 achieved little. The Dillon Round which followed in 1959–62, and the Kennedy Round in 1963–7, were almost exclusively concerned with tariff liberalisation. Following the conclusions of the Kennedy Round the tariff cuts affected around US$40 billion worth of world trade – approximately 75 per cent of total trade, with an average reduction of 36–39 per cent (Greenaway 1991).

Three factors were important in the outcome of the first six rounds. First, tariff reductions applied mainly to industrial goods; the developed economies still protected their agricultural sectors. Second, one important sector of manufacturing – textiles – was exempted. Finally, industrialised countries tended to reduce tariffs on primary commodities and raw materials to a greater extent than those on finished goods.

The major difference between the Tokyo Round (1973–9) and the previous rounds was that it examined a much wider set of issues, such as NTBs (subsidies and quotas) and trade in agricultural goods. Still the main result of the Tokyo Round was average tariff reductions of between 33–38 per cent, with higher average tariff countries conceding higher than average cuts. Altogether around US$112 billion of trade in industrialised products (at 1976 prices), or around 20 per cent of the value of trade in industrial products, was affected (Greenaway 1991).

The Uruguay Round

As can be seen above, GATT was particularly successful in dealing with tariff barriers to trade, especially those associated with industrial products, but as this chapter has shown, as tariffs declined, NTBs increased in popularity. The situation gradually grew worse. More and more the European Union and the United States for example resorted to other measures to keep out imports. Moreover, the slowdown in the growth of world trade and the move by many industrialised countries towards more of a service-oriented economy, and the role of agriculture within trade relationships, meant that the last round of GATT talks had a much wider range of issues with which to deal.

The eighth round of GATT talks began in Uruguay in 1986 and finished in Marrakesh in 1993. It had a much wider portfolio to consider, and as Table 3.3 shows, achieved agreement in a wide variety of areas.

Table 3.3 Uruguay Round details

Area	Agreed change	Main impact
1. Industrial tariffs	Tariffs on industrial goods cut by rich countries by more than a third. Over 40 per cent of imports enter duty free. Key traders scrap duties for pharmaceuticals, construction equipment, medical equipment, steel, beer, furniture, farm equipment, spirits, wood, paper and toys.	Easier access to world markets for exporters of industrial goods. Lower prices for consumers. Higher-paying jobs through promotion of competitive industries.
2. Agriculture	Trade-distorting subsidies and import barriers cut over six years. Domestic farm supports reduced 20 per cent. Subsidised exports sliced 36 per cent in value and 21 per cent in volume. All import barriers converted to tariffs and cut 36 per cent. Japan's and South Korea's closed rice markets gradually open. Tariffs on tropical products cut by over 40 per cent.	Restraint of farm subsidies war. Lower food prices for consumers in currently protected countries. Better market opportunities for efficient producers. Special treatment for developing countries, though higher world prices could hurt poor food importers.

Table 3.3 continued

Area	Agreed change	Main impact
3. Services	Rules framework for basic fair trade principles such as non-discrimination. Special provisions for financial services, telecommunications, air transport and labour movement. Individual countries pledge market opening in a wide range of sectors. Further talks on telecommunications and financial services.	Boost for trade in services, currently worth US$900 billion in business of foreign subsidies. Further liberalisation to be negotiated.
4. Textiles and clothing	Multi-fibre agreement (MFA) quotas progressively dismantled over ten years and tariffs reduced. Developing countries reduce trade barriers. Normal GATT rules apply at the end of ten years.	Developing countries able to sell more textiles and clothing abroad. Reduced prices for consumers worldwide because of fairer textiles and clothing trade (worth US$248 billion in 1992).
5. World Trade Organization	GATT becomes permanent world trade body covering goods, services and intellectual property rights with a common disputes procedure. World Trade Organization implements results of Uruguay Round.	Boost to the status of international trading rules and more effective advocacy and policing of the open trading system.
6. Others: intellectual property and anti-dumping	Extensive agreement on patents. Clearer rules for conduct of investigations and criteria for determining dumping.	Boost for foreign investment. Harder to use anti-dumping action for trade harassment.

Source: Jones (1994).

At the same time as the Uruguay Round was being finalised, the members of GATT agreed to establish a new trade body, the **World Trade Organization** (WTO), which came into operation on 1 January 1995. This new body is in charge of administering the new global trade rules agreed in the Uruguay Round, and reflects a widespread desire to operate in a fairer and more open multilateral trading system for the benefit and welfare of all countries.

The WTO is different from GATT in a number of respects:

● The WTO is more global in its membership than GATT. Its membership in December 2005 consisted of 149 countries and territories, with many more considering accession (WTO 2005).
● It has far wider scope than GATT, bringing into the multinational trading system for the first time trade in services, intellectual property protection and investment.

- It is a fully fledged international organisation in its own right, while GATT was basically a provisional treaty administered by an ad hoc secretariat.
- It administers a unified package of agreements to which all members are committed, while GATT included a number of side-issues, such as anti-dumping measures and subsidies, whose membership was limited to a few countries.
- It reverses policies of protection in certain 'sensitive' areas which had become tolerated under the old GATT system, such as export restraints on textiles and clothing, and voluntary export restraints.
- The WTO's objectives are to oversee the implementation of decisions made in the various rounds and in the ministerial meetings. It is the guardian of international trade, examining on a regular basis the trade regimes of individual members, and examines proposed trade measures and proposals by countries which could lead to trade conflicts. Members of the WTO are also required to supply a range of trade statistics which will be kept on the WTO database.
- The WTO provides a whole range of conciliation services and also a disputes settlement mechanism (the Dispute Settlement System (DSS)) for finding a solution to problems. If trade disputes cannot be solved through bilateral talks, then the dispute is adjudicated under the WTO dispute settlement body (DSB). Here panels of independent experts are established to examine disputes in the light of WTO rules and provide rulings. This tougher, streamlined procedure aims at ensuring equal treatment for all trading partners, and encourages members to honour their obligations. The whole programme of dispute settlements is far more streamlined than the old GATT system, and the aim is to encourage parties to seek independent jurisdiction of their case rather than resort to individual pieces of domestic legislation. Up to the end of November 2005 335 cases had been reported to the DSB. Of the 335 reported, 130 cases were taken to the panel stage and 54 taken to the appeal stage (Piggott 2003, WTOc no date). The WTO claims that 'One of the main successes in the operation of the WTO dispute settlement mechanism has been that in every single case where a panel or an Appellate Body recommendation has been adopted to date by the DSB, Members have either already complied with such recommendations or have expressed their intention to comply' (WTO 2003: 5). However as we have seen in the case study on the beef hormone dispute, it sometimes takes a very long time!

It is also interesting to see who are the main complainants and main respondents, shown in Figure 3.6. It can be seen that the United States dominates the number of cases brought, with 23 per cent (73 cases), but the European Union is not far behind, with 20 per cent (62 cases). Similarly in terms of respondents the United States tops the list, being cited in 28 per cent of cases (83), followed by the European Union in 20 per cent (62 cases). Interestingly though, the leading role since 2001 has been taken over by the next biggest 'complainer' in total, after the United States and European Union, Latin America with 21 per cent (66 cases), and in respondent terms 21 per cent (66 cases), putting the European Union into third place in both categories. In terms of products it is noticeable that one of the biggest areas of the Uruguay Round and subsequent ministerial meetings has been agriculture and agricultural products, and these figure largely in the disputes (see Figure 3.7) (adapted from Piggott 2003).

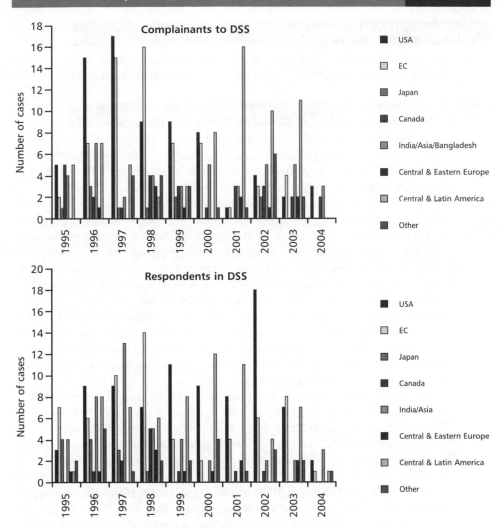

Figure 3.6 Complainants and respondents in WTO dispute cases

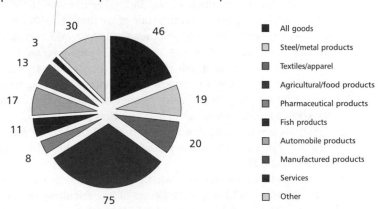

Figure 3.7 Products involved in WTO dispute cases 1995–2001

Since the Uruguay Round: the WTO in practice

We have seen above one element of the WTO, the dispute mechanism, working in practice, but what else has been happening since the Uruguay Round?

Ministerial meetings and the Doha Development Agenda

It was agreed when the WTO was set up there would be a ministerial conference where all members would meet at least once every two years (article IV of the Marrakesh Agreement which set up the WTO). The first such conference was held in Singapore in December 1996 (WTOd no date).

The second, which celebrated the 50th Anniversary of GATT/WTO in 1998, was held in Geneva, but it was the third ministerial conference held in Seattle in December 1999 which really hit the headlines. Before the conference there was a great deal of talk about a new round being set up, but even before the meeting started there were problems. Many felt there was too little time to tackle the agenda, that the agenda was poorly prepared and that there were two major items on the agenda which would bring about the collapse of the talks: labour standards and agriculture. LDCs also felt marginalised, and the WTO was felt to have procedures which were unworkable. None of this was helped by the atmosphere created by the massive scale of the rioting going on in the streets outside. Not surprisingly the Seattle meeting closed suddenly, with chaos and recriminations and no decisions made.

The fourth ministerial conference took place in Doha, Qatar, in November 2001 and it was from this meeting that the Doha Development Agenda (DDA) emerged. Some call it a new round of talks, but it is interesting that the WTO only referred to it as an agenda (WTOd no date) The DDA identified 21 issues for negotiation, including reducing barriers in agriculture, liberalising trade in services, cutting tariffs on non-industrial goods, amending the **Trade-Related Aspects of Intellectual Property Rights (TRIPS)** agreement and aid implementation of agreements in LDCs (Husted and Melvin 2004). Also coming from the Doha meeting were the 'Singapore Issues', which involved changing global rules on competition, investment, transparency in government procurement and trade facilitation.

To consider the progress of the Doha Agenda was the main reason for the fifth and latest conference (at the time of writing), the Cancun ministerial meeting in September 2003. The Cancun agenda followed very much that of Doha – clarifying the TRIPS agreement and giving cheaper access to medicines, reducing farm support, cutting industrial tariffs – especially in areas such as textiles where many LDCs have a comparative advantage – freeing trade in services, and considering the Singapore Issues (something developed countries (DCs) were very keen on introducing, especially the European Union).

Prior to the meeting it was agreed that LDCs could have access to cheap medicine, but the rest of the agenda was lost when the Cancun talks folded. What happened?

What the LDCs wanted most was agricultural reform. One of the major problems for many LDCs has been protectionism of its agriculture by the developed world. In fact two-thirds of the benefits from Doha were to come from freeing up farm trade. At present the rich spend over US$320 billion in subsidies (six times the

value of aid to LDCs and equal to the annual GDP of Africa), and Japanese and western farmers gain massive rents from this support. This costs each OECD household
in the region of US$1,000 per annum which they pay as higher prices and higher
taxes (BBC 2003). There is also overproduction and selling of surpluses at below
cost, which drives LDC farmers (with little or no subsidies) out of business. Three-
quarters of the world's poor live in rural areas, and most are dependent on agriculture. Oxfam states, 'To put the figures in context, the support provided to
agricultural producers in rich countries is equivalent to more than the total income
of the 1.2 billion people in the world living on less than $1 a day' (2003: 12). Agri-
culture has been on the agenda since the Tokyo Round, but very little has occurred
to open up trade in its products; in fact in 2002 the United States announced a new
Farm Bill, effectively protecting US agriculture even more.

The problem of tariff escalation (see earlier) was also of concern to LDCs.
They felt little was being done to tackle this.

The DCs' emphasis was however more on the Singapore Issues, but these
were seen by many LDCs as a threat. The fear was that the DCs could use these
rules to dictate things like foreign direct investment in their countries. There
was also concern that LDC negotiators did not have the technical expertise to
be able to negotiate on such issues. In fact the LDCs' main fear revolved around
competition and investment policy but the other two areas, transparency in
government procurement and trade facilitation, could be seen as very beneficial
to LDCs. However the European Union refused to allow the four issues to be
split – until it was too late to save the talks.

If the DDA had collapsed at Cancun, the LDCs would have been the biggest
victims. A Doha Development Round, according to the World Bank, could
increase global income by US$290–520 billion per annum by 2015, and over 60
per cent of gain would be to the poor (144 million people) (World Bank 2003).
Many people felt that one of the major positive moves that came from Cancun was
the G21 group of LDCs. Led by Brazil, China and India they became a powerful
voice, representing half the world's population and two-thirds of the world's farmers. They were well organised and professional, and although they spanned
diverse interests they stood together, pointing out that the OECD countries had
hardly changed the level of agricultural support over the previous 15 years, and
more was needed to open up markets to LDCs. For the first time, the LDCs
worked together as a group to negotiate with the more developed countries.

The latest event in the Doha Agenda occurred in August 2004, when an agreement was reached in Geneva between trade ministers of WTO countries which
marked 'The end of talks about talks and set broad guidelines for the conduct of
future negotiations' (de Jonquieres 2004: 5). This agreement managed to get EU
commitment to eliminate its agricultural subsidies, and the United States also
agreed in principle to reduce its food aid and export credit programmes. But more
worryingly no date was fixed for these changes to take place. The plans for reducing agricultural and industrial tariffs are also sketchy and the liberalisation of services is very vague. However on the Singapore Issues, it was agreed that they would
remain in the work programme but not part of the negotiations, apart from the
issue of trade facilitation. So the Doha talks have been put back on track – just!

What next? The next meeting is due to be in Hong Kong at the end of 2005.
So far the G21 has shown no sign of disintegrating as was anticipated. There have

however been worrying signs. The number of **bilateral trade deals** has increased dramatically (see Chapter 4). These deals effectively bypass the WTO multilateral negotiations and tend to leave out the poorest countries. Furthermore the DDA has already missed its original deadline of January 2005, but then the Uruguay Round went way over schedule as well, so it is not that surprising.

Green trade issues

The move towards free trade has led both markets and organisations to become increasingly globalised. But what is the relationship between international trade and the environment? Many proponents of free trade argue that environmental regulations are often used as new barriers to trade, reducing the efficiency of the global economy and slowing down the process of technological change. Those who support the protectionist view of limiting trade argue that free trade enables multinational enterprises to shift their polluting activities to less well-regulated countries, thereby perpetuating the use of inefficient technologies and harming the world's poor.

Both sides of the argument can be seen in the use of the European Union's **eco-labelling** system. Eco-labels indicate the most environmentally friendly way of producing a product. The eco-label for tissue paper, for example, is intended as a means of informing European consumers which tissue products are environmentally friendly. It sets standards for air and water emissions and for resource usage. These standards are consistent with the conditions that exist within Europe, but they are not necessarily consistent with the conditions in Brazil, the United States and Canada, so this eco-label discriminates against products from the Americas. Thus the governments of the Americas see it as a means of protecting the European producers of tissue paper, while the European governments see it as a method of environmental protection. Furthermore as Morris (1996) notes, since governments are beginning to include environmental considerations in their procurement policies, eco-labels are becoming an important new form of protectionism. The WTO has noted that 'The use of eco-labels by governments, industry and non-governmental organisations is increasing. Moreover, the growing complexity and diversity of environmental labelling schemes raise difficulties for developing countries, and particularly SMEs in export markets' (WTOa no date).

However, there are other environmental regulations that clearly impede free trade, but most would not object to them. For example there are the Convention on International Trade in Endangered Species (CITES) which prohibits the importation of ivory, and the Basel Convention on Transboundary Movements of Hazardous Wastes and their Disposal, which rules out trade in certain substances. The Montreal Protocol added a further twist. This protocol is concerned with ozone depletion, and initiated the phasing out of chlorofluorocarbons (CFCs). However, the treaty also allowed member countries to implement trade sanctions against non-member countries. In addition, the convention prohibits imports of all products that use CFCs in their production processes, such as computer components cleaned with CFC-based solvents. Other examples of the use of environmental protection to restrict trade include the United States' efforts to protect dolphins by banning Mexican tuna, which tended to be caught in nets which also caught dolphins, and Denmark's efforts to protect its refillable bottle system by requiring all beer and soft drinks to be sold in refillable bottles.[2]

The problem for the WTO is that multilateral environmental agreements such as the Basel Convention or the Montreal Protocol state that countries can restrict trade on environmental grounds, whereas the WTO is trying to remove all trade restrictions. Therefore there is a conflict between the two. The WTO states that 'The WTO's role is to continue to liberalise trade, as well as to ensure that environmental policies do not act as obstacles to trade, and that trade rules do not stand in the way of adequate domestic environmental protection' (WTOb no date). Efforts are under way, however, to 'green' the WTO. The tension between **multinational enterprises**, governments and free trade therefore needs to be reconciled, and at the first Ministerial Conference of the WTO in December 1996, the WTO Committee on Trade and the Environment attempted to move this issue forward, through bringing together environmentalists and those who believe in free trade. Since then the Doha Ministerial Conference agreed to include in its negotiations the link between trade and the environment.

But are free trade and the environment in conflict? It is possible to argue that free trade is a prerequisite for environmental improvement rather than a threat. Free trade can improve economic growth and wealth, and Grossman and Kreuger (1991) have indicated that economic growth begins to alleviate air pollution when per capita income reaches US$4,000–5,000 per year. Material poverty, not economic trade, is the single greatest threat to environmental quality.

Conclusion

Trade barriers will always exist. The questions are how hidden these are and how far countries wish to reduce them. Historically trade barriers took the form of tariffs, but GATT and now the WTO have been successful in reducing these. However, as tariff barriers have fallen they have been replaced by other forms of new protectionism. Included here are quotas, VERs, health and safety regulations and bureaucracy. The Uruguay Round of trade talks took seven years to complete, and indicated the growing complexity of matters in the international trade arena. There are now more countries, more issues, and a wider variety of trade barriers to consider.

The Uruguay Round highlighted that the GATT, which may have been the appropriate organisation for discussing trading relations in the three decades after the Second World War, needed changing. Its development into the WTO has heralded a new approach to trade. The arrival of the WTO has added impetus to trade negotiations and the belief in free trade, as can be seen from the rise in membership. Moreover it has a much more appropriate and speedy disputes mechanism which has encouraged countries to seek help from the WTO rather than take their own direct reprisals. The world is unlikely to get less complex, and the WTO faces some interesting times ahead.

Questions

1 In 2005 the European Union imposed a quota on Chinese textiles – why? Outline the effect of such a quota on EU consumers, EU producers and the economy as a whole. What effect would it have on other non-EU producers? (See the companion website for this book for a case study in this area.)

2 Taking the above example, would the Chinese textile importers have preferred to have been facing a tariff? Why didn't the European Union choose this option?

3 Explain, using examples, how restrictions on public procurement effectively block trade. Which companies gain and which lose? How could companies avoid such restrictions?

4 The case study on the beef hormones dispute between the United States and the European Union shows how health and safety legislation could possibly be used as a means of trade protectionism. Can you identify similar examples where legislation is apparently being used to protect consumers but could also be seen as really protecting producers from trade?

5 In the Doha Development Agenda negotiations, one of the areas of dispute was cotton, or more specifically the way the United States protects its cotton producers. Show diagrammatically how the United States protects its producers and the effect of this on LDCs. (Also see companion website for case study.)

6 What is now happening about the Doha Development Round? Go to the WTO website – www.WTO.org – and see what progress (or not) has been made and what has been the impact on DC and LDC companies.

Notes

1 It should be noted that the WTO does not hear actual cases of whether dumping has occurred but is limited to 'considering whether the facts have been properly established and evaluated by the countries imposing the duty' (Piggott 2003).

2 Six cases of environmentally related disputes were held under GATT: US–Canada tuna, Canada–US salmon and herring, Thailand–US cigarettes, Mexico–US tuna, US–EEC tuna, US–EEC automobiles. Under WTO there have been three: US–Venezuela and Brazil gasoline, US–India, Malaysia, Pakistan and Thailand shrimps, US–Malaysia, shrimp/turtles (arguing the United States had not properly implemented findings in the previous case) (WTOc no date).

References

Alden, E. and Buckley, N. (2004) 'Sweet deals: 'Big Sugar' fights threats from free trade and global drive to limit consumption', *Financial Times*, 27 February, p. 17.

BBC (2003) *Today* programme 'Report on Cancun', 15 September.

Benjamin, D. K. (1999) 'Voluntary export restraints on automobiles', www.perc.org/publications, accessed 2 July 2004.

Berry, S., Levinsohn, J. and Pakes, A. (1999) 'Voluntary export restraints on automobiles: evaluating a trade policy', *American Economic Review,* vol. 89 no. 3, pp. 400–30.

Castle, S. (2002) 'EU threatens Washington with $4bn trade tariffs', *Independent,* 14 September.

Cecchini, P. (1988) *1992: The European Challenge,* Gower, Aldershot.

Chanakira, N. (2004) 'Multiple exchange rates hurt Zes', *Zimbabwe Independent,* 28 May, www.theindependent.co.zw, accessed 2 July 2004.

China Daily (2004a) 'EU plans new import quotas for China', 3 March.

China Daily (2004b) 'EU, China reach deal on coke supply', 31 May.

De Jonquieres, G. (1999) 'EU claims initial victory over US in trade dispute', *Financial Times,* 24 July.

De Jonquieres, G. (2000) 'Bananas, beef and now export subsidies', *Financial Times,* 18 February.

De Jonquieres, G. (2004) 'Trade deal marks end to talks about talks but the real negotiations lie ahead', *Financial Times,* 2 August.

Denny, C. and Moore, C. (2004) 'Family's £25m sugar bonanza', *Guardian,* 14 April, p. 16.

DTI South Africa (2004) 'End of export quotas would be disastrous for coke', 21 May, www.dti.gov.za, media releases, accessed 2 July 2004.

Economist (2004) 'Oh, sweet reason', 17 April, p. 17.

Europa (2004) 'USA Foreign Sales Corporation: Pascal Lamy welcomes US Senate vote', 19 May.

European Union (2003) 'WTO dispute settlement', *Trade Issues,* 5 November, www.europa.eu.int, accessed 6 November 2005.

Financial Times (2004a) 'A threadbare plea for protection', 21 June.

Financial Times (2004b) 'Sweet justice for EU sugar' , 6 August, p. 16.

Greenaway, D. (1991) 'GATT and multilateral trade liberalization: knocked out in the eighth round', *Economics,* Autumn.

Greenaway, D. (1994) 'The Uruguay Round of trade negotiations', *Economic Review,* November.

Griffiths, A. and Wall, S. (2004) *Applied Economics,* 10th edn, Financial Times/Prentice Hall, Harlow.

Grossman, G. and Kreuger, A. (1991) *Environmental Impacts of a North American Free Trade Agreement,* Princetown University, November.

Hitiris, T. (1991) *European Community Economics,* 2nd edn, Harvester Wheatsheaf, Hemel Hempstead.

Husted, S. and Melvin, H. (2004) *International Economics,* 6th edn, Pearson Addison Wesley, Boston, Mass./London.

Jones, R. (1994) 'Completion of the Uruguay Round', *British Economy Survey,* vol. 23 no. 2, Spring.

Krugman, P. (1996) 'Making sense of the competitiveness debate', *Oxford Review of Economic Policy,* vol. 12, no. 3, pp. 17–25.

Krugman, P. (1997) 'Is free trade passé?', *Economic Perspectives,* vol. 1, no. 2.

Morris, J. (1996) *Green Goods? Consumers, product label and the environment,* Institute of Economic Affairs, London.

National Consumer Council (1993) *International Trade: The Consumer Agenda,* London.

Oxfam (2003) *Running into the sand: why failure at the Cancun trade talks threatens the world's poorest people,* Oxfam Briefing Paper 53.

Panagariya, A. (2004) 'The tide of free trade will not float all boats', *Financial Times,* 3 August, p. 17.

Piggott, J. (1999) 'Anatomy of a trade dispute: the banana trade war', *Teaching Business and Economics,* vol. 1, no. 3, Autumn.

Piggott, J. (2003) 'How well is the WTO Dispute Settlement working?' Chapter 4 in P. Arestis,

M. Baddeley and J. McCombie, *Globalisation, Regionalism and Economic Activity*, Edward Elgar, Cheltenham.

Salvatore, D. (2001) *International Economics*, 7th edn, Prentice Hall, New York/Chichester.

Williams, F. (2002) 'WTO arms Europeans with weight weapon', *Financial Times*, 31 August.

World Bank (2003) *Global Economic Prospects and Developing Countries: Investing to unlock global opportunities*, Washington, DC.

World Trade Organization (WTO) (2003) *Annual Report 2003*, WTO.

WTO (2005) 'Understanding the WTO: the organization', www.wto.org/english/thewto_e/whatis_e/tif_e/org6_e.htm, accessed 21 December 2005.

WTOa (no date) 'Labelling requirements for environmental purposes', www.wto.org – trade and environment section, accessed 17 August 2004.

WTOb (no date) 'Parameters of the discussion in the WTO', www.wto.org – trade and environment section, accessed 17 August 2004.

WTOc (no date) 'Disputes chronologically', www.wto.org – trade and environment section, accessed 17 August 2004.

WTOd (no date) 'Ministerial conferences', www.wto.org – introduction; the mandate, accessed 17 August 2004.

Yarbrough, B. V. and Yarbrough, R. M. (1997) *The World Economy*, 4th edn, Dryden Press, Forth Worth/London.

4 Economic integration

Haluk Sezer and Judith Piggott

Objectives

This chapter will:

- outline the subtle differences between the different types of economic integration
- examine the rationale for regional trading agreements (RTA)
- evaluate the benefits and economic impact of regional integration.

Introduction

Economic integration is a term which is subject to different interpretations. In its wider sense it means closer economic cooperation and interdependence among different nations. However, in the field of international economics it has a more specific meaning, namely, the process by which different economies combine together into larger free trading regions (El-Agraa 2004). For this reason it is sometimes referred to as regional integration.

Economic integration encompasses different forms of economic cooperation among the independent nations of a particular region, such as the North American Free Trade Area (NAFTA) or the European Union. These forms range from the minimum cooperation, that is, free trade areas, to the maximum, which is economic and political unions. A typical taxonomy of economic integration would include the following categories of cooperation: **free trade areas (FTAs), customs unions (CUs), common markets (CMs), economic union (EU)** and complete **political unions (PUs)**.

Forms of economic integration

FTAs involve the elimination of **tariffs** among the member countries but each country applies its own tariff policy to non-member countries. In a FTA members remove trade impediments among themselves but retain the freedom to determine policies with respect to the outside world (non-participants). An example of an FTA is the European Free Trade Area (EFTA), which was originally created by the United Kingdom as a reaction to de Gaulle's veto of the United Kingdom's application to join the European Economic Community in 1960. It has included at various points in time Austria, Portugal, Norway, Sweden, Switzerland, Denmark and the United Kingdom, but recently only

Norway, Switzerland, Iceland and Liechtenstein have been members. Other examples are the Latin American Free Trade Area (LAFTA) and NAFTA. FTAs tend to be partial rather than complete; they cover only certain products, and tariffs are cut to varying extents. Within EFTA for example the United Kingdom followed a policy of giving preference to the Commonwealth. Finland also gave the USSR preferential terms for trading.

One of the consequences of an FTA is the possibility of '**trade deflection**'. This is the phenomenon that goods in an FTA may enter the area through a country with the lowest external tariff and then circulate through members. The importers of a particular commodity naturally wish to incur the lowest possible tariff, and thus import the good into the country with the lowest tariff and redistribute it through the area free of import duty. This, however, could have implications for the distribution of production, consumption, income, investment and welfare of the members of the FTA.

CUs are similar to FTAs except that members must have a set of common tariff barriers called a **common external tariff** (CET) against non-members. Thus a CU is an area where tariffs and quotas on goods are removed for all intra-union trade, and there is a common tariff and quota system for all extra-union trade; therefore the possibility of trade deflection is removed in a CU. An early example of a CU is Benelux, which was formed by Belgium, Luxemburg and the Netherlands in 1948 as a CU in industrial goods (later converted into an EU in 1960). The European Coal and Steel Community (ECSC) was established by the Treaty of Paris among the original six EEC members (the Benelux countries plus France, Germany and Italy) in 1953, which created a CU in coal and steel. In fact, the present European Union was a CU until the Single European Market (SEM) legislation.

A CM is a CU with free **factor mobility** across frontiers. Capital, labour and enterprise can move unhindered between participants. For example, a British citizen can go to Germany and work; someone from Spain can come to the United Kingdom to work; students pay the same fees as locals in EU universities; anyone can set up a company in the Netherlands if he or she is from another EU country, and so on. CMs tend to need to be geographically close to allow this; an example is Mercosur (see later).

An EU is a CM but in addition it involves a high degree of integration of fiscal, monetary and commercial policies. In fact a complete economic integration would mean the unification of such economic policies. This is required in order to ensure effective free movement of factors of production, and harmonisation of macroeconomic policies as well to prevent any distortions to trade flows. An EU will have a central authority to exercise control of matters, for example the European Central Bank. However, the euro-zone as it stands is only a partial EU since economic policies such as fiscal policies are not completely harmonised.

A complete PU would imply a federal state. A central authority controls monetary and fiscal policies. It is also responsible to a central parliament, with loss of sovereignty for each member's government. That is, defence and the foreign policy matters fall within the jurisdiction of the federal government as well as important legislative, judicial and administrative functions. However, member states retain a considerable amount of power regarding legislative, administrative and financial matters. Examples are the United States and Spain.

Whatever the eventual outcome, the European Union currently is, of course, a long way from this kind of arrangement.

Table 4.1 indicates the degree of cooperation for each category.

Table 4.1 Taxonomy of economic integration

Policies	FTA	CU	CM	EU	PU
Removal of tariffs and quotas	Yes	Yes	Yes	Yes	Yes
CET	No	Yes	Yes	Yes	Yes
Factor mobility	No	No	Yes	Yes	Yes
Harmonisation of economic policies	No	No	No	Yes	Yes
Federal structure	No	No	No	No	Yes

Economic cooperation beyond an FTA requires policy compatibility, which involves the imposition of constraints on policy objectives, and ultimately the creation of supranational institutions. Progress towards integration depends on the willingness of national governments to relinquish some of the traditional national legislative and executive powers in favour of these supranational authorities. If this is lacking, it is conceivable that the economic cooperation between all or some of the members may cease to exist altogether.

Many suggest that economic integration has its own dynamics. A CU would be under pressure to progress to higher forms of economic integration. This arises from the increasing political and economic interdependence among the participants, which tends to create policy conflicts among the members, which in turn necessitates either a forward step towards deeper integration or a backward step towards a looser form of international cooperation. Others point to historical examples where such moves have not occurred. The European Union has gradually moved towards closer integration within Europe. It never really was an FTA, but certainly was a CU until the establishment of the Single European Market in 1992. The SEM legislation made it more of a CM as it established the principle of the free movement of goods and services, people and capital across frontiers. Further elements of an economic and monetary union were put in place in the Maastricht Treaty, which eventually led to the establishment of the single European currency among the participating nations. By March 2002 the euro, the European currency, was firmly established as the only legal tender among 12 members of the then 15 states of the European Union.

The theory of customs unions

Although the literature on the subject goes back to the classical economists, it has generally been accepted that the real theory of CUs only developed in 1950, with Jacob Viner's theory. The pre-Vinerian view was that since free trade maximises world welfare and a CU is a move towards free trade from protectionism, then a CU would increase world welfare, even if it does not maximise it. Viner showed that this was not necessarily the case. He suggested that CUs combine elements of free trade with greater protectionism, so it is not clear whether such arrangements increase or decrease welfare.

CUs have two opposing tendencies: they increase trade within the union but reduce trade with the rest of the world. This is the basis of Viner's central concepts, **trade creation** and **trade diversion**.

Trade creation (TC) is when a country starts to import a good previously produced at home, because it is now cheaper to import it from inside the union. Basically the nation is changing from a higher-cost domestic producer which was protected by a tariff, to a lower-cost producer from within the union/FTA with no tariff. This represents a positive welfare effect on the economy, as the price is now lower and a more efficient producer is being used.

Trade diversion (TD) occurs when a country starts to import from a member of the union/FTA a good that had previously been imported from outside the union. So a switch is made from a lower-cost producer outside the union (but with a tariff imposed) to a higher-cost producer inside the union (without tariff), giving a negative welfare effect, as a less efficient producer is being used.

To illustrate this, a fictional example can be used. Assume the home country is France and the product concerned is digital cameras. The free trade price of such cameras is €200 for France. Other producers and traders are Germany and Japan which have free trade prices of €160 and €120 respectively. These prices reflect the costs of production and therefore show the level of economic efficiency. Say France, to protect its industry, places a 100 per cent tariff on cameras. In these circumstances France would produce cameras domestically as indicated by (a) in Table 4.2.

If France then forms a customs union with Germany, it will drop the tariff from German cameras, with the result that Germany is now the cheaper producer, and France will now import from Germany at the price of €160 rather than produce at home for €200 (as indicated by (b) in Table 4.2). This is an example of trade creation. Trade has occurred where previously it did not, and production is being undertaken by a more efficient producer (Germany's prices and costs are lower than those of France). It should be noted however that Germany is not the lowest cost producer – Japan is. Therefore although a positive move has been made towards more efficiency, it is not as good as free trade would be.

However if the tariff were originally set at 50 per cent instead of 100 per cent, the picture would be different. The cheapest producer would now be Japan, and France would therefore import from there (as indicated by (c) in

Table 4.2 Trade creation and trade diversion

Price of cameras (€)	FR	GR	JP
Price without tariffs	200	160	120
a) Price with 100% tariff	200	320	240
b) Then France forms CU with Germany	200	160	180
c) Price with 50% tariff	200	240	180
d) Then France forms CU with Germany	200	160	180

Table 4.2). If France then forms a CU with Germany, the result is that Germany again becomes cheaper, and France will import from Germany (as indicated by (d) in Table 4.2). However, this time trade will be diverted from Japan to Germany; an example of trade diversion. Trade has been diverted from the most efficient producer to a less efficient producer, and the effect is negative on world welfare (as indicated by the dotted line in Table 4.2).

Thus trade creation occurs when the formation of a CU means that the country in question starts trading from a lower-cost union partner and produces less domestically; trade diversion occurs when the formation of the CU means that the country starts to trade with a higher-cost partner within the union and stops trading with a lower-cost (but tariff-affected) country outside the union.

The economic welfare effects of a CU can be neutral, detrimental or beneficial. In short, trade creation is good as it tends to increase welfare, while trade diversion is bad because it decreases welfare. The net effect depends on whether TD is greater than TC (a fall in world welfare would result) or TC is greater than TD (representing an increase in world welfare).

Partial equilibrium theory of customs unions

Using the example above, let us start from the idea that France is the home country and has a common tariff of 50 per cent on both Germany and Japan (see Figure 4.1). At this point the price of Japanese cameras with a tariff ($P_{JP}^* = 180$) is lower than the French price without tariff ($P_{FR} = 200$).

France will import Q_1–Q2 from Japan and produce 0–Q_1 at home, and nothing is imported from Germany. Then France forms a customs union with Germany. The price of cameras falls to €160 = P_{GR} and the level of imports increases to Q_3–Q_4. Both trade creation and trade diversion can be seen here:

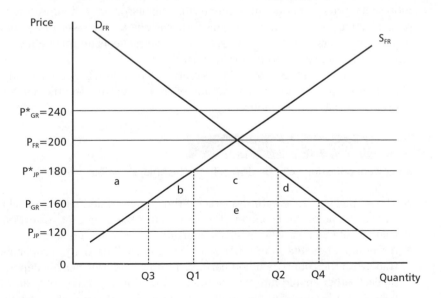

Figure 4.1 Welfare effects of a customs union on home country (FR)

- Trade has been diverted from Japan to Germany of Q_1 to Q_2.
- However, the price has fallen, which has encouraged domestic consumption but discouraged domestic production. Trade creation of Q_3–Q_1 has occurred (and production has moved from France to Germany).
- The quantity Q_2 to Q_4 is not strictly trade creation as this amount did not previously exist before the price reduction, it is more **trade expansion** which is an increase in trade due to lower prices.

Thus, the price is reduced due to the formation of the CU, but it is still not as low as the free trade price. It is good news for the consumer (but not as good as free trade) but bad news for the inefficient domestic producer which was previously protected by tariff barriers. The net effect on the world economy however depends on the extent of trade creation compared with trade diversion.

The welfare effects can also be shown in Figure 4.1. The welfare effect of the CU on France is clearly positive since consumer surplus has increased by [a + b + c + d]; a is a transfer from producer surplus and c is a transfer from government, which was formerly tariff revenue that now accrues to consumers. Thus the net welfare gain for the country is [b + d].

However, there are also other welfare effects. One is that there is no revenue accruing to the government since there is no tariff. The lost tariff revenue is measured by the rectangles c and e. Rectangle c represents the transfer of welfare to domestic consumers in terms of lower price. As for rectangle e, it represents the difference in price between Japan and Germany (the union partner) and thus is the cost of moving from the low-cost source to the high-cost source, in other words trade diversion in value terms.

Areas b and d represent, as before, the gain in consumer surplus that is not transferred from domestic producers and the government. Area b actually represents trade creation in value terms. Similarly, area d represents the remaining part of the gain in consumer surplus due to the lower price enjoyed by the consumers of France, that is, the non-Vinerian consumption effect, or in other words trade expansion in value terms.

The net impact of this economic integration depends on the sum (b + d – e). Since there is no guarantee that the sum of (b + d) will exceed the area e, the impact of the CU is ambiguous.

Conclusions from Viner's analysis

Some generalisations can be drawn from the analysis so far:

- The scope for trade creation is larger if the foreign trade sector is small relative to the domestic economy. This is because the scope for distortions in trade would be relatively small and a chance for creation greater.
- A country's benefits from a CU will be larger, the higher the proportion of trade with the country's union partner. That is, countries heavily dependent on each other should integrate with each other. If the trade between countries A and B constitutes a small proportion of total trade of A, it will not bring many gains for A to form a CU with B.

● A CU is more likely to bring gains, the higher the initial tariffs between the union partners. Conversely, the lower the tariffs with the rest of the world, the smaller the welfare losses arising from trade diversion.

Although still the basis of CU theory, Viner's analysis has been extended in certain vital areas, the **terms of trade** effects and **dynamic effects** of economic integration.

The terms of trade effects

An important assumption made above was that the home country is small in relation to both its partners and the rest of the world, and the formation of a CU would not have any effect on the terms of trade. Clearly, this is not always a very realistic assumption. A large CU like the European Union must have some effect on the terms of trade. Once the assumption is dropped, the welfare effects are harder to distinguish in simple TD and TC terms; the welfare of the CU and the rest of the world will not necessarily move in the same direction.

The terms of trade effect also focuses attention on the importance of a CU in enhancing the bargaining power of its members in negotiations with the rest of the world. Thus, the higher the number of member countries in the union, the stronger the bargaining position of the union will be. However, the greater the membership, the less likely the union is to achieve consensus on the precise nature of the concessions desired from the rest of the world.

Dynamic consequences of economic integration

We have so far focused on the static consequences of economic integration. However, the dynamic effects must also be considered. Positive dynamic effects could be sufficient to outweigh some negative trade diversion. Dynamic effects embrace a whole category of factors that influence growth and improve efficiency, and include external **economies of scale**, 'learning by doing', capital accumulation, technical progress, training and **market concentration** (the idea of competition level). These are difficult to analyse within a conventional economic framework, with the exception of external economies of scale. However, they can be discussed in general terms.

One of the possible dynamic consequences is economies of scale. Balassa (1961) suggested that CUs expand the market facing domestic producers, and present further opportunities for gaining economies of scale. A movement to a CM, with its removal of internal barriers, will have a similar effect (see later). These economies of scale could and should result in higher growth which will lead to possibly more investment and technical progress. Such growth could also reduce uncertainty and improve expectations, so boosting investment again – a virtuous circle.

Another possible effect of economic integration is its impact on market concentration. The removal of barriers through a FTA, CU or CM should lead, initially or at least potentially, to greater competition. Monopolistic and oligopolistic structures within the domestic economies become exposed to much greater outside competition. This should bring greater efficiency and possibly higher levels of research and development, and technical change. Again this should bring higher investment and economic growth. This, of course, assumes that a domestic monopoly does not become a union monopoly!

Empirical studies

The economic theories above have suggested various factors which lie behind the emergence of FTAs and CU formation, such as trade flows, income effects, balance of payments effects and the growth effect. Empirical studies try to identify these factors and their relative importance, as well as to quantify possible benefits from a specific example of economic integration. Many of the empirical studies attempt to estimate the trade creation and trade diversion effects resulting from changing patterns of trade flows. There are two major categories of empirical studies differing in the methods they adopt. One category contains simulation models trying to estimate potential gains from economic integration (World Bank 2004). Such models set up an anti-monde position, which shows what would have happened if an economy were not part of a regional trading agreement, and then compare it with the actual situation. These models, also called *ex ante* studies or residual models, suffer from the deficiency that it is rather difficult to estimate what the trade flows would have been in a hypothetical situation. Studies by Balassa, Truman and Kreinin (in El-Agraa 2004) and perhaps a more sophisticated study by Winters (1987) are examples of this method.

The second category of studies consists of econometric studies using the **gravity model**, which illustrates trade flows between two countries in proportion to their economic mass. These models try to predict the impact of economic integration on trade flows. The gravity model is often criticised for lacking rigorous theoretical foundation and for being an ad hoc model (World Bank 2004). A 1972 study by Verdoorn and Schwarts (in El Agraa 2004) and the famous Cecchini Report regarding the effects of the European Single Market (see later) are based on the gravity model (McDonald and Dearden 2005).

The studies by Balassa, Truman and Kreinin mentioned above relate to the European Community, and show that trade creation exceeds trade diversion, indicating a net positive welfare effect. The Balassa study used the changes in the ratio of the average annual change in imports to the gross national product (GNP), as an indicator of the effect of integration. The assumption is that the ratio will remain constant if there is no integration, so an increase in the ratio for intra-area trade is supposed to indicate gross trade creation. The same increase in trade with all sources of supply would point to net trade creation. Conversely, a decrease in the ratio for extra-area trade would mean trade diversion. Balassa found evidence of trade creation and external trade creation, but not of trade diversion for manufactured commodities within the European Community in the early years.

The welfare implications in terms of income gains of these studies were also similar, but they were rather small, varying between 0.15–1.0 per cent of combined GNP. However, the method of estimating the welfare effect was rather crude, and involved multiplying the volume of trade created or diverted by half the tariff.

A later, similar but more sophisticated study by Winters (1987) found that, on average, external trade creation outweighed trade diversion within the European Community, that trade creation internal to the United Kingdom was substantial, and that UK exports to EC countries increased considerably at the expense of exports elsewhere. However, although UK imports from the European Community increased even faster, with the result that the United Kingdom incurred a considerable deficit in manufacturing trade with the European Community, the increase was not at the expense of imports from elsewhere, which indicated that there was no trade diversion as a result of British accession to the European Community.

The overall picture appears to be that the European Community has had a considerable impact on the pattern of trade in Europe in general, but the welfare effects of the European Community have not seemed significantly large. However, it should be noted that these studies are concerned mainly with the static, resource-allocation effects of integration. Studies on the dynamic effects are less easy to find, but the theoretical analysis suggests that the dynamic effects would be much more beneficial to the European Community, although the distribution of these benefits might be less than desirable. The Cecchini Report of 1988 stated that the benefits from the establishment of the SEM would be considerable – as high as more than 5 per cent of the combined GDP of the European Community – mainly arising from the removal of physical and technical barriers, economies of scale, and increases in **X-efficiency** due to competition (McDonald and Dearden 2005; also see later in this chapter).

There was also a large-scale review of the SEM in 1996 by the European Commission, which included a survey of 20,000 enterprises among other things. The aim of the review was to focus on three economic aspects of the SEM programme: the allocation (efficiency) effects, the growth effects and the location effects. The review concluded that the allocation effects have been positive due to increased intra-EU trade, improved competition and a reduction in price differentials. Its findings were also positive regarding the growth effects, since it estimated an additional growth of up to 1.5 per cent of GDP arising from the SEM programme. The review concluded that the SEM encouraged intra-industry trade, which led to geographically based specialisation. The review was unable to confirm the estimates given in the Cecchini Report (McDonald and Dearden 2005).

It should be stated that nearly all the studies are based on the assumption that the main objective of integration in western Europe is to remove discriminatory tariffs. This is unsatisfactory since the European Union has been guilty of discrimination in its tariff policy, for example regarding textiles from Turkey, India and Pakistan, and by forcing Japan to adopt **voluntary export restraints** (see Chapter 3). Furthermore, at the time of the formation of the European Community and EFTA, certain changes in the pattern of trade were already beginning to emerge, such as a reduction in discrimination against the United States. Such developments are also bound to have influenced trade patterns.

Furthermore the impact of integration on only the manufacturing sector has been considered. Economic integration may have had a negative impact on the member economies apart from the trade diversion effects on welfare. These negative effects include the influence that a CU might have on, say, regional and interpersonal inequalities (see Chapter 11). It should be remembered that a CU is only one form of economic integration. Higher forms of integration might bring far more benefits than a CU at relatively low costs. Finally, the *World Trade Report* (2003) by the World Trade Organization (WTO) indicates that recent regional groupings have resulted in a slight amount of trade creation and no trade diversion on a global scale.

We should perhaps remind ourselves that the advantages and disadvantages of CUs and economic integration cannot be evaluated simply by examining the theory of integration. It is also necessary to look at the experience of movements towards regional integration in practice.

The adjustment costs of integration and implications for distribution

Clearly the impact of economic integration will not be felt equally by all groups or individuals within a particular country. There are two main issues to be considered here: first the long-run effect of integration, and second the adjustment costs of integration. These are the costs involved in moving from one situation, for example high tariff barriers, to another, such as an FTA, which are associated with the process of transition rather than the final outcome.

With regard to the first issue, the distributional effect of integration can be measured in a number of ways. One approach is to concentrate on factors of production such as land, labour and capital, and look at the impact of changes in trading arrangements on these. This involves, for example, asking whether the move to integration favours workers more than the owners of companies, or vice versa. Alternatively, we can look at the impact of integration on sectors or industries, defined more or less broadly. A general approach would be to look at the relative impact of FTAs or CUs on agriculture, manufacturing and services. More specifically, the effect of integration on particular industries could be examined within these broader categories. A third approach is to look at the way in which integration changes the relative position of particular regions, either within country boundaries or spanning borders. More recently, feminist writers have looked at the effect of the European Union on the relative position of women. It is possible to extend this list of approaches to distribution to encompass a wide range of other categorisations.

Clearly, the approaches listed above are not independent of each other, although they are distinct. The decline or rise of certain industries, for example, can have pronounced regional impacts and also alter the industrial relations climate.

In addition to looking at the long-run effect of integration it is also important to look at the transition process between different stages of integration, and the associated costs. In a textbook example of a freely adjusting market such costs are relatively minor. As openness to trade causes industries to decline where there is a comparative disadvantage, new industries open up. Similarly, if regions experience economic difficulties, labour and other costs will tend to fall, making investment more attractive and attracting new flows of capital. In practice, however, there may be significant costs if either labour or capital is immobile. Such a situation might arise if there are difficulties for workers in moving geographically or between sectors requiring differing skills, or if there are problems for companies in raising the finance to move into new areas of production.

The number of different issues involved make it impossible to formulate a general theory covering the adjustment costs and distributional implications of the formation of the European Union, or a similar regional arrangement. It is necessary to analyse these questions concretely, by focusing on the experience of particular groups, industries or regions. One example of this is Milward's detailed study of the impact of the European Economic Community on the Belgian coal industry in the 1950s and 1960s (Milward 1992). Milward shows both how the particular position of the industry affected the negotiations that led up to the Treaty of Rome in 1957, and how in turn the process of integration affected the industry and the region, the Borinage, where it was primarily located.

The advantages and disadvantages of CUs and economic integration cannot be evaluated simply by examining the theory of integration. In the remainder of this chapter we shall be focusing on the growth of the European Union but also comparing the European Union with other regional groupings, in order to see how integration works in reality.

Economic integration in practice

A historical background

Economic integration and customs unions are not a new development in historical terms. In the 19th century, for example, there were the Austro-Hungarian CU and the 'Zollverein', and the Prussian-led CU beginning in 1834 which helped to begin the process of German unification. However, regional integration declined in the period between the two world wars, as both European and Latin American countries responded to recession by imposing tariffs and other controls on trade. Further, the idea of regional blocs was put into question by, on the one hand, the use of colonial possessions as an alternative trading area by Britain and France, and on the other, the attempt to impose regional domination through force by Germany and Japan. Finally, the inter-war period was typified by an isolationist mood in the United States which weakened the interest of that country in forms of economic integration.

The period since 1945 however has seen a resurgence of regional blocs, and virtually every member of the WTO is involved in a regional trade agreement of some kind (see Chapter 2 for details). Among these various groupings the European Union is unique in the level of integration that has been achieved, in terms of unifying trading policies with the rest of the world, dismantling non-tariff barriers, enforcing common policies in areas like competition and agriculture, and setting up a common currency. The European Union has also been in existence for considerably longer than many of the newer trading arrangements. In order to understand the process of economic integration, then, it is necessary to look at the European Union, and why it has taken integration so much further than other groups of countries. Is this likely to continue? Also, what sort of model does it provide for other **trading blocs**?

Origins and nature of the European Union

The European Economic Community (EEC) and the European Atomic Energy Community (Euratom) came into being with the signing of the Rome Treaties in March 1957. The countries involved at this stage were Belgium, France, Luxemburg, Italy, the Netherlands and West Germany. The combination of the EEC and Euratom brought about the European Community (EC), which became the European Union (EU) on 1 January 1994, following the ratification of the Maastricht Treaty. By January 1973 Denmark, Ireland and the United Kingdom expanded the Community to nine members, and these were joined by Greece in January 1981 and by Spain and Portugal in January 1986. In October 1990 the five Eastern *lander* of the newly united Germany became part of the EC. Austria, Sweden and Finland joined the European Union in January 1995, yielding a total of 15 members. In May 2004 ten further states joined. Estonia, Latvia, Lithuania, the Czech Republic, Slovakia, Slovenia, Hungary, Poland, Cyprus and Malta completed a union of 25 member states.

The process of the formation of the EEC is quite controversial, because of what it tells us about the nature of the grouping and the intentions of its founders. The Treaty of Rome followed some ten years of discussions concerning various forms of closer cooperation in western Europe.[1] The immediate predecessor of the EEC was the ECSC, which was set up by the Treaty of Paris in March 1951. The proposal for the ECSC (often referred to as the 'Schuman plan' after Robert Schuman, the French foreign minister who originally proposed it) was prepared within the French Planning Commission by staff under the direction of Jean Monnet, and it is on the basis of this that Monnet and Schuman are sometimes regarded as the originators of the European Union. The ECSC was never simply a free trade area. Proposals for liberalising trade went together with a supranational arrangement for regulating the market under a 'high authority', including rules for pricing, subsidies for firms hurt by the new trading arrangements, and funds for retraining workers. In this way the ECSC foreshadowed a number of later developments in the European Union.

Some writers have seen the formation of the EEC as the culmination of this period of increasing interest in integration, and as the launching pad for future developments in this area after 1958. In this way the Treaty of Rome became part of a gradual movement towards closer and closer integration.

This whole approach to economic integration and the formation of the EEC has been questioned by Milward, who has presented a very different account of the developments (1984, 1992). For Milward, the EEC and the ECSC were not the end-point of the discussions of integration that had taken place in the 1940s. He suggested the attempts at integration in the 1940s were largely encouraged by the United States, and linked to the programme of 'Marshall Aid' for western Europe. The aim of the United States in these discussions was to encourage a form of integration which would weaken the nation-state in western Europe, and eventually lead to a United States of Europe, which would be a global ally for the United States of America. According to Milward, this concept of integration was successfully resisted by the western European countries, and the institutions created in the 1950s were designed to promote a very different approach and to strengthen rather than weaken the nation-state. The importance of the approach to integration proposed by Milward is that, if it is correct, there is no reason to suppose that integration has an inherent tendency to increase and deepen (Milward 1984).

This 'neo-realist' view of integration has been challenged, notably by Anderson (1996a). Anderson states that:

> a customs union, even equipped with an agrarian fund, did not require a supranational Commission, a High Court capable of striking down national legislation, a Parliament with nominal rights of amendment or revocation. The limited domestic goals Milward sees as the driving-force behind integration could have been realised inside a much plainer framework.
>
> (Anderson 1996a:14)

He claims that it is also necessary to consider a number of other factors driving integration: the federalist views of Monnet and others, the desire of the United States to create a strong west European counterweight to the Soviet Union, the aim of the French government to limit German power, and the German objective of returning to the established community of nations and keeping open the possibility of eventual reunification. These international issues, for Anderson, have to be linked with the domestic concerns emphasised by Milward, in order to explain European integration.

Anderson however does not state explicitly the extent to which he sees European integration as a process that has an inbuilt tendency to deepen. To analyse this would require looking also at developments since 1958, as well as attempts at integration elsewhere.

The development of the European Union

The development of the European Union has often been divided into four main periods. The first, from 1958 to 1973, saw the removal of internal tariffs and the accession of three new members. The relatively optimistic atmosphere of this period saw a number of new proposals for further developing the Community, such as in the area of monetary union. The second period, from 1973 to the early 1980s, was a less happy period for the Community. Economic crisis and internal disagreement led to something of a paralysis of decision making within the Community, and the ambitious schemes of the late 1960s were not carried out. However, the early 1980s saw the opening of a more positive third period in the Community's development, leading up to the Single European Act of 1986 and the preparations for the Single European Market, involving renewed interest in monetary union. The fourth period began with the Maastricht Treaty of 1991 and has involved a move towards monetary union (for most) and an expansion to the east of Europe. But there has been increasing public disquiet with further integration.

In order to explain why the European Union has taken the process of integration further than other regional groupings in the world it is especially important to analyse the developments in the 1980s.

The 1980s

At the start of that decade it appeared quite possible that the European Union would remain simply as a customs union. There were recurrent disagreements over the EC budget. The British and German governments wanted budgetary restraint, but the French and German agreement to maintain the Common Agricultural Policy (CAP) escalated the costs of farm support, and the budget was progressively squeezed. This limited the effectiveness of other areas of Community expenditure such as the Social Fund, European Investment Bank and the European Regional Development Fund (Swann 1988).

The attempt to formulate a common monetary policy was equally problematic. The Hague summit of December 1969 endorsed the idea of Economic and Monetary Union (EMU) and set up the Werner Group to report on the matter. The Werner Report of October 1970 called for complete and irreversible convertibility of currencies, closely aligned exchange rates, full liberalisation of capital movements and a common central banking system within a decade. As a result, the EC members formed the 'snake' in 1972, where EC currencies were to be kept within a margin of fluctuation of 2.25 per cent on either side of the dollar's value. However, the snake was a victim of the increased instability in world exchange rates after the floating of the dollar in 1971. A number of currencies left the snake, and by the end of 1977 only five EC members remained.[2] Further, the hoped-for effect of exchange rate discipline encouraging more coordination of EC members economic policies had not happened (Swann 1988, Middlemas 1985).

Given this scenario, why did the 1980s see a resurgence of interest in integration? Various reasons have been put forward for this development.

First, western Europe faced serious economic problems. In particular, it appeared to be falling behind one of its major competitors, the United States. The European Union lost ground in a number of key industries with high rates of growth. The European share of the output of the world's 12 largest companies in the dynamic industry of computers and office equipment between 1980 and 1990 was just 7 per cent (Wolf 1994). This relative economic failure was often attributed to institutional problems in the European economies and called 'Eurosclerosis'. Economic integration was widely seen as a potential cure.

A second factor was the influence of the European Commission, and in particular its President, Jacques Delors. Business leaders in Europe had widely differing views on integration, and the Commission played a key role in unifying different perspectives and outlining a way forward: 'in the mid 1980s it was the decisive action of the European Commission that pointed Europe in new directions' (Ross 1992: 56).

A third approach stresses the growing convergence of ideas among the European governments and policy makers in the 1980s. Dyson (1994) has traced the importance of ideas about 'sound money' in creating the movement towards EMU in the late 1980s. Such ideas provided a framework within which the governments could move towards integration. A further key development in terms of ideas was a growing scepticism about whether an individual European country could maintain an effective independent economic policy. The experience of the French Socialist government in the early 1980s shed doubt on this.[3]

The final set of reasons for increased movement towards integration centres on institutional developments within the Community. First, it expanded with the joining of Greece, Spain and Portugal. This showed the Community could complete negotiations concerning the accession of relatively poor countries with substantial agricultural sectors. Second, it began to have more success in the area of exchange rate policy with the formation of the European Monetary System (EMS) in 1979. The first few years of the EMS were fairly cautious, with frequent realignments of currencies. However after 1983 realignments became fewer, and from 1987 until 1992 there were no realignments (Gros and Thygesen 1992). The convergence of European inflation rates in the 1980s was widely attributed to the effect of the EMS. The success of the EMS played a large role in encouraging the movement towards monetary union. The third development was the decision in 1976 to institute direct elections to the European Parliament. The first such elections took place in 1979. The powers of the Parliament remain limited, but direct election has played a role in increasing popular interest in, and involvement with, the European Union. Finally, the June 1984 Fontainebleau Summit provided agreement both on budgetary reform and on a commitment to reform the CAP. Again, this did not solve all the problems in these areas, but it did lessen the previous arguments over the budget.

These four reasons for increased interest in economic integration within Europe were not mutually exclusive, but to a large extent reinforced one another. Many of the converging ideas in Europe about policy resulted from the economic difficulties the European Union was facing. The ability of the European Commission to play an active role depended on the institutional context within the Community. The desire of the Commission to play this role was in turn influenced by high unemployment and slow growth in Europe, and so on.

The result of this greater interest in further integration was the move in 1987 towards the SEM and the Maastricht Treaty.

The Single European Market

The Single European Act (SEA) came into force on 1 January 1993, although preparations started from 1987 onwards. Its base was the original Treaty of Rome, which spelled out the four freedoms: the free movement of goods, services, people and capital. In effect, it was an attempt to extend national freedoms to the whole of the European Union. But what exact benefits were anticipated?

Essentially the European Community was trying to bring freer trade by removing trade barriers, so reducing costs and thereby prices. It was also hoped that the elimination of barriers would bring greater competition and new patterns of competition, as markets were no longer so protected by national barriers. Old cartels would be threatened, and ossified industries 'woken up' by new forces of competition. Rationalisation would then occur and costs be reduced. Firms would also be encouraged to go out and attack the European market, and more innovation in processes and production would occur. Firms would grow and gain greater efficiency, through the exploitation of potential **economies of scale** by serving a much greater 'domestic' EC market. Costs would again fall, prices follow, and both consumers and producers gain.

To summarise, the constraints of the non-unified market were preventing companies from achieving their full potential. To remove these constraints would improve the competitive environment and allow exploitation of new opportunities. This would then make EC industries more competitive and better equipped to compete against the United States, Japan and the newly industrialised countries.

The Cecchini Report of 1988 into the costs of a non-united Europe suggested that such a supply-side shock to the European economy could trigger a boost to economic activity in the medium term of, on average, 4.5 per cent to the European Community's GDP, and that the cost of maintaining the barriers to free movement of people and capital could be in the region of ECU200 billion (at constant 1988 prices). It was also estimated that prices to consumers could be deflated by an average of 6.1 per cent, and some 1.8 million new jobs could be created.

The gains in output, competitiveness and the reduction of inflation, it was suggested, would ease the pressure on governments, allowing more space for action on growth. So if the EC governments pursued relevant macroeconomic policies, in the long run it was estimated the EC economy could grow by up to 7.5 per cent in GDP and gain approximately 5 million new jobs, without the risk of higher inflation (Cecchini 1988).

Some criticisms of Cecchini's conclusions and figures should be noted, however:

● They were very optimistic. It was assumed that all the proposals would be carried out on time, and in a world and European economy which was expanding, not one of recession and unemployment.
● They also assumed labour made redundant by rationalisation due to restructuring would be successfully re-employed; again, a very optimistic view.
● They ignored the distributional aspect by not looking at the possible detrimental effects on some states compared with others. No account was made of the adjustment costs of firms, regions and even governments to the single market.
● It was assumed states would adopt similar economic policies and trade policies.
● The estimates were only approximate.
● It was a report commissioned by the European Commission and one has to question its neutrality.

This said, however, the possible gains could also have been underestimated as certain dynamic consequences were ignored. For example:

● There is evidence to suggest that technical innovation increases with the presence of competition. Therefore a more open, integrated market would increase such innovation.
● Also ignored were learning economies of scale, which are especially important in high-tech industries.
● No account was made for the changes of business strategies which could occur, and these could boost the potential gains.

These gains could therefore be achieved by removing barriers to a unified Europe. The barriers were summarised as physical, fiscal and technical, and are discussed in Chapter 3. The SEA was aimed at dealing with these barriers, and it has had great success in many areas. In October 2003 the European Commission, in a paper by Pascal Fountaine, outlined what had been achieved and was left to be achieved by the SEA as follows:

- The national public contract market has been opened up.
- Disparities between national tax systems have been sorted out through common rules on indirect tax, VAT and excise duties.
- The money market and financial services have been liberalised.
- There has been harmonisation of national laws on safety and pollution, especially agreed recognition of laws and certificates from other EU countries.
- Obstacles concerning movement of people have been removed. Passport checks at internal borders no longer exist and there is recognition of professional qualifications.
- Company law has been harmonised in the European Union and intellectual property rights laws brought into line.

But there are still things to do:

- There are still obstacles hindering the movement between countries and doing certain types of work; for example educational qualifications/job qualifications still need total recognition

And to this could also be added:

- There is still no European company law
- The adoption, implementation and enforcement of legislation is patchy. Coverage of indirect taxes has been harmonised but not the rates, and this has caused problems (see Chapter 3 for the problems of lack of harmonisation in rates for alcohol and tobacco).

So what has been the effect of the SEA on European business, for which it was mainly designed? The case study on the following page shows the effects highlighted by two main studies in 2002.

The Maastricht Treaty 1993/enlargement of the European Union

The setting up of the SEM, and the movement of the European Union into social, environmental and regional areas, added momentum to the European Union. Furthermore the reunification of Germany and collapse of communism 'swept away the post war economic and political order of Europe' (McDonald and Dearden 1999: 10), so leading to greater pressures towards further integration, especially from Germany and France. Therefore the European Commission set up two Inter-Governmental Conferences (IGC): one to investigate EMU and the other, political union. These led to the negotiations which established the Maastricht Treaty (more formally known as the Treaty of

Case study 4.1

SEM EFFECTS ON BUSINESS

In 2002 the European Commission asked EOS Gallup Europe to undertake a survey of European businesses ten years after the start of the SEM, and to find out what changes in the general business environment had occurred. Nearly 6,000 managers from all the EU15 countries took part in the survey. Generally the majority interviewed felt that there had been no perceptible impact on their business in terms of sales and productivity, but that the advantages of the SEM exceeded the disadvantages to the SEM. Firms were particularly positive about the elimination of administrative tasks of customs and VAT procedures at EU borders, and furthermore a third of those interviewed felt there had been a positive effect on their pricing and purchasing policies within the European Union.

However certain barriers remained. It was felt there was still little labour mobility inside the European Union to aid labour shortages, and most large and small companies wanted further harmonisation of regulations, procedures and tax regimes to ensure fairer competition. Further, 80 per cent wanted to see the SEM further developed in the future, especially with the opportunities available since the recent EU enlargement.

Figure 4.2 summarises the firms' views of the effect of the SEM on their businesses.

A further survey of small and medium-sized enterprises (SMEs) was carried out by Grant Thornton at the same time. This pointed out that the SEM was seen as a success in terms of opening borders and aiding expansion, distribution and marketing but many felt the European Union had

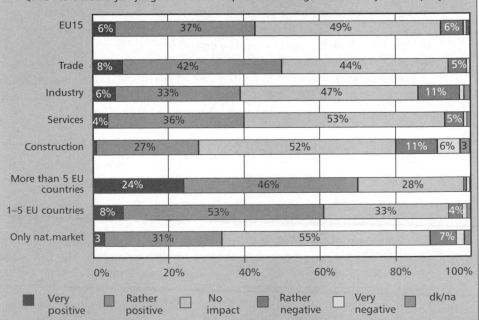

Q. 15 How would you judge the overall impact of the Single Market on your company?

Figure 4.2 Summary of firms' views

Source: Eurobarometer 130 (2002): Flash EB, Fig. 27.

become more demanding and costs of administration were rising. For example 26 per cent of companies in the European Union felt costs had risen and 1 per cent felt administrative burdens had increased. Furthermore 45 per cent felt they had suffered from greater competition.

However the study also showed that SMEs had become more ambitious over the ten years: 67 per cent said they wanted to develop new markets, 51 per cent wanted to diversify their product ranges and 24 per cent planned to enter joint ventures and strategic alliances. Finally in terms of short-term constraints on SMEs in the previous ten years, the shortage of skilled labour was highlighted as a growing constraint but the cost of finance was seen as a lessening one (Grant Thornton 2001).

These two surveys suggest that the SEM has had a major impact on European businesses and international business. All have been forced, some more reluctantly than others, to face the opportunities and threats the SEM has posed.

There are still gaps in the legislation, the SEM is far from complete, but further significant legislation is unlikely in the near future.

Source: EOS Gallup Europe (2002), Grant Thornton (2001).

Questions

1 Highlight what have been the major effects of the SEM on businesses. Are there any surprises?

2 Do you feel the European Union is right in the last statement above? Is there any way it can be more proactive?

Economy Union) (McDonald and Dearden 1999). However these negotiations exposed the fact that there was little consensus as to what the European Community's next step would be, and the Maastricht Treaty was famous for its long, fractious negotiations.

The treaty established new separate structures for justice and home affairs, and a common foreign and security policy, so establishing the three pillars of the European Union.[4] It gave citizenship to the population of the then 12 states, allowing them to move and live in any EU state and vote in European and local elections in any EU country. Social and employment issues were also dealt with in the Social Chapter, a protocol added to the treaty, covering things like workers' pay and health and safety. The United Kingdom opted out of this initially but this 'opt out' was later removed in the Amsterdam Treaty of 2000.

However the Maastricht Treaty is probably most famous for setting out the blueprint for EMU, by defining its stages and criteria (see Chapter 5 for further details on the single currency). Finally it set up the idea of subsidiarity. This is where the Union agrees not to take action except in areas which fall within its exclusive competence, or unless it will be more effective than action at national, regional and local level. Some saw this as clearly setting out the rights of national and local governments, and a welcome move, and others viewed it as giving more power to the European Union.

Although the Treaty of Economic Union was signed on 7 February 1992, it struggled to be ratified by the various countries, thereby highlighting the lack of consensus about how the European Union would develop in the future. Denmark voted against ratifying the treaty in June 1992, and it took a second referendum in 1993 to secure a small majority in favour. France narrowly voted 'yes' and the United Kingdom had major problems in processing its ratification via Parliament. In Germany it was claimed the government had no constitutional right to transfer sovereignty to non-German institutions, and the question of ratification was taken to a constitutional court for a decision. This ruled it could ratify the treaty but ironically Germany, one of keenest countries to deepen integration, was the last to ratify the treaty (McDonald and Dearden 1999).

At about the same time as the ratification of the Maastricht Treaty, a second agreement was achieved in 1993, setting up the European Economic Area (EEA), which extended the Single European Market to EFTA states, allowing free movement of goods, services, capital and labour across the whole area. Switzerland however voted against membership of the EEA, but for many of the others it represented a springboard to full membership, with Sweden, Finland and Austria joining in 1995 (a Norwegian referendum rejected membership of the European Union at that time) (McDonald and Dearden 1999).

The further enlargement of the European Union was also discussed in the Madrid Council of December 1995, when it asked the Commission to prepare 'opinions' on the suitability of allowing some of the central and eastern European countries (CEECs) to join the European Union. Agenda 2000 recommended in July 1997 that negotiations begin with Poland, Hungary, the Czech Republic, Slovenia and Estonia, together with Malta and Cyprus. In 1999 it further recommended negotiations with Bulgaria, Romania, Latvia, Lithuania and Slovakia. The presumption was that all would not join at the same time, the 'regatta principle'. In December 1999 the Helsinki Council agreed, and negotiations started in February 2000 (Kilmister 2001). In October 2002 the Commission agreed the expansion of the European Union to 10 further member countries.[5] These had met the 'Copenhagen Criteria' which list things like 'institutional stability, democracy, market economies, and adherence to the aims of political, economic and monetary union' (Griffiths and Wall 2004: 604) and it so was agreed they could join the European Union in 2004. The membership of Bulgaria and Rumania was delayed until 2007.

This represented the biggest expansion of the European Union ever seen, although in terms of population and GDP, the 1973 enlargement was actually bigger. The average GDP per head of these new accession countries, however, was only 46 per cent of the EU15 average, and it has been estimated, for example, that it will take Poland 59 years to catch up in terms of GDP per head (*Economist* 2004d). But what effect will these new accession countries have?

The Centre for Policy Research (CEPR) estimated the enlargement of the European Union could lead to gains of €10 billion (£7 billion) for the EU15 and €23 billion (£16 billion) to new members. The European Commission also estimated it could bring greater growth of in the region of 1.3–2.1 per cent to the accession countries. Finally in 2002 the European Round Table of Industrialists calculated the 2004 enlargement of the Union could create 300,000 jobs in the EU15 (Griffiths and Wall 2004).

In terms of trade creation and trade diversion (see earlier), Gros and Steinherr (1995) showed that trade creation would probably exceed trade diversion in any customs union (CU) if the following conditions were met:

1 Applicants had higher tariffs than those in the CU.
2 The common external tariff (CET) of the CU was low.
3 Tariffs against the rest of the world were high.
4 The CU was large.
5 The trade structure was complementary and competitive with the rest of the CU.

Although the European Union is no longer a customs union, we can apply this to the new enlargement situation. Conditions 1 and 2 were satisfied, 4 was met well, 3 was true, but non-tariff barriers (NTBs) were high against CEECs. Condition 5 was too difficult to judge, as it relates to how trade might develop. This would seem to suggest the recent expansion of the European Union will bring more trade creation than diversion. However it has to be said that to some extent some of the gains have already occurred through the **Europe Agreements**, but it also has to be remembered that this is a static analysis and ignores the dynamic consequences of this expansion (Kilmister 2001), which are likely to be very positive.[6]

For businesses, however, further benefits can be identified. **Foreign direct investment (FDI)** has poured into the region, and Hungary, Poland and the Czech Republic have seen per capita levels of FDI similar to many EU states (Kilmister 2001). Furthermore the transition arrangements, whereby many of the richer EU countries have either banned or limited inflows of cheap workers for between two and seven years, have forced other businesses to consider establishing in the new accession countries in order to take advantage of the low wages inside the European Union. These countries have the advantage over other low-wage countries, such as China and India, as they have higher productivity, tariffs and border problems are removed, shipping costs are lower and the business environment is more familiar. This is especially important for medium-sized firms who tend to be put off by more exotic business environments and lack the funds to set up further afield. Furthermore with low average incomes, most multinational companies (MNCs) will retain separate divisions and strategies for western and eastern Europe despite the accession, so increasing FDI more (*Economist* 2004b).

Two big concerns about the CEEC accession countries, however have dominated the headlines: the cost to the Social and Cohesion Funds of the European Union (see Chapter 11) and the CAP and the migration of labour (see Chapter 9). Agenda 2000 recommended that between 2002–06 the new EU countries should receive ECU53.8 billion (38 billion from structural and cohesion funds and 15.8 billion from the CAP and other agricultural support) and proposed a five-year transition period where budgetary transfers would rise gradually. to a full level. Similarly the level of CAP was kept much lower than if it was to be just extended (Kilmister 2001). However the problem with agriculture still exists. For example, 'According to estimates from the Polish Peasants' party, only 600,000 of the country's 2m farms will survive the process of joining the EU' (Patterson 2000 in Kilmister 2001). There is also the fear the that the already strong farming lobby of the European Union will be further boosted by the huge number of farmers in some new accession countries (*Economist* 2004c).

Concerning migration, the CEPR has suggested that a movement of 5 per cent of the population of the CEECs into the European Union would only mean a movement of 5.7 million people, or 1.5 per cent of EU population over several years. This movement would be likely to occur (legally or illegally) even without these countries being members of the European Union, and is small in comparison with past migrations into Europe (Kilmister 2001).[7] However this fear of mass migration into the European Union seemed to strengthen amongst the EU15 population as 1 May 2004 approached, and many countries imposed transition arrangements to limit migration.

Finally some have pointed out that in fact the enlargement to the east is exactly what the European Union needed. Many suggest the European Union is undergoing further Eurosclerosis (similar to the 1970s). Growth is sluggish, unemployment high and most EU companies are failing to compete effectively with US/Asian equivalents. This has led to disillusionment with EU governments and Union itself. The arrival of the new countries in the European Union, it is argued, should change this. Most of their economies are growing faster, bringing bigger and more dynamic markets. The lower wages, benefits and taxes are seen as a potentially powerful stimulus to existing members to become more competitive. Finally they have a much more optimistic attitude to the European Union, which might help others think similarly (*Economist* 2004c).

The single currency and enlargement completes the work put in hand in the 1990s. Little in the way of inspiring ambitions is now on the horizon. Future enlargements are possible: Romania and Bulgaria are hopeful of joining in 2007, Croatia is likely to start talks soon, Macedonia has applied recently. Turkey also hopes to start accession talks now it has been agreed it has met the Copenhagen Criteria. The only other major new event in the offing is the new constitution (*Economist* 2004d).

The new EU constitution

On 18 June 2004 a constitution for the European Union was agreed, bringing together many of the various treaties and agreements which form the basis of the European Union. Basically the constitution defines what powers the European Union has, and where it can act. It states that the European Union is subsidiary to the nation-state and will only act if 'the objectives of the intended action cannot be sufficiently achieved by the member states but can rather … be better achieved at Union level' (EU constitution quoted in BBC 2004a). This basically extends the concept of subsidiarity, and so for some this represents a necessary curb to the European Union's powers, whereas to others, given the European Union can act in so many areas (for example monetary policy, customs policy, the internal market, agriculture and fisheries), this is pretty meaningless. It also expands its powers into new areas, especially justice policy, so covering things like asylum and immigration.

Other changes are:

1 The new constitution extends the principle of **qualified majority voting**, arguing that without this, a union of 25 member states would never agree on

anything.[8] Vetos however will still exist in the areas of foreign policy, defence and taxation. A country that is outvoted on an issue it feels strongly about can take its case to the European Council (referred to as the 'emergency brake') for consideration.

2 There is a new post of president of the European Council. This used to rotate every six months but now a more permanent post for a term of two and a half years has been created.

3 Similarly a minister of foreign affairs will be appointed (by qualified majority) to speak on behalf of the European Union on foreign and security matters.

4 The new constitution suggests a reform of the Commission. From November 2004 for five years, there will be one commissioner for each member state. After that, the number of commissioners will be reduced, with two-thirds of the states having a commissioner (at present that would mean 18 commissioners).

5 The constitution acknowledges the greater powers that the European Parliament has gradually acquired. Now if the Parliament disagrees with some legislation, it can stop it. Given the Parliament is the only EU institution where the public can directly influence its composition, this effectively boosts democracy in the European Union.

6 A charter of 'fundamental rights, freedoms and principles', including such things as the right to life and the right to strike, has been included. The status of this is rather vague and it will probably require testing in the courts before it is clarified.

7 The new constitution sets up a legal personality for the European Union, and its laws will supersede the laws of member nation-states, something which basically confirms what already happens.

8 Finally the constitution sets up a formal procedure of how a member state could leave the Union, showing that the European Union is a voluntary association (BBC 2004a).

The new constitution needed agreement by each member state either via parliamentary vote or public referendum. However when 55 per cent of the French voted 'no' in May 2005, and a more resounding 61.6 per cent of the Dutch, the whole thing seemed derailed. Many postponed ratification indefinitely and little further movement is imminently expected.

Now we have studied in depth the recent changes in the European Union, we need briefly to consider what has happened to economic integration elsewhere.

Economic integration outside the European Union

Until recently, regional trading agreements took two main forms. First, there were arrangements which were mainly responses to European developments and the formation of the European Union. EFTA and the Council for Mutual Economic Assistance (Comecon) (which involved the old communist states of eastern Europe and the USSR) were examples of this. These agreements did not lead to any more general moves towards integration. Comecon was dissolved in 1991, while the majority of EFTA members have joined the

European Union and the remaining countries are linked to it through the EEA, with the exception of Switzerland.

The second kind of arrangement has been that between groups of developing economies: for example, the Andean Pact and Mercosur in South America, the ASEAN Free Trade Area in south-east Asia, the Caribbean Community and numerous African arrangements (see later case study). The extent to which such groupings could become truly integrated was rather limited, since trade relations with dominant partners from the industrialised countries (the United States, France, Japan) tended to take precedence over regional objectives.

The recent rebirth of widespread interest in regional integration began with NAFTA.

NAFTA

The North American Free Trade Area (NAFTA) agreement was signed in August 1992 by Canada, Mexico and the United States, and took effect from 1 January 1994. This agreement built on the earlier free trade agreement between Canada and the United States implemented in 1989, and on a decade of trade liberalisation between the United States and Mexico. It is estimated the GDP of the NAFTA area is around US$12.9 trillion and it covers 372 million people.

NAFTA is simply a free trade area at present with no common external tariff. The idea of the NAFTA was to eliminate tariffs over a 15-year period and reduce NTBs. Most tariffs on industrial goods have already been eliminated, and tariffs on agricultural products are due to end in 2008. But there are so many exclusions and exemptions that it far from removes all trade restrictions. There are also sectoral agreements on automobiles, textiles, apparel, agriculture, energy, petrochemicals and financial services.

So what has been the effect of NAFTA ten years on? Most trade economists suggest that trade within the region has expanded dramatically; in 1990 US exports to Mexico and Canada represented approximately 25 per cent of its trade, now it is more like 33 per cent. Similarly US exports to Mexico doubled between 1993 and 2001 to US$91 billion but imports from Mexico have tripled to US$131 billion. US trade outside NAFTA has also grown strongly, which suggests most of this switch has been in the form of trade creation rather than diversion (Husted and Melvin 2004).

One of the United States's biggest concerns when NAFTA was set up was that it would destroy US jobs, with US companies shifting to Mexico which had a comparative advantage with its cheaper labour and more lax labour and environmental laws. Hufbauer and Schott however have pointed out that between 1994 and 2000 the United States gained more than 2 million jobs a year. Manufacturing jobs did fall but other areas more than made up for the fall. Also they suggested that most of the new jobs have been at higher than average wages (*Economist* 2004a). Further, US firms have benefited from lower labour costs and have increased funds available for new technology, and this has also released US labour for higher-skilled jobs (Husted and Melvin 2004).

Canadian unemployment similarly fell over the period, but Canada's main fear was that its social welfare model (with its generous minimum wage, for example) would be threatened. However despite some reductions in public spending, this has not happened (*Economist* 2004a).

There were also fears from environmentalists that if production moved to Mexico with its lower environmental standards and enforcement, then US firms could do more damage to the environment. There has been no conclusive evidence of this, although it is often said that if you go over the border, just breathing in proves it (*Economist* 2004a). However there has been increased cooperation in this area, and the environmental laws have been improved.

But the country that was supposed to gain most from NAFTA was Mexico: how has it fared? It is difficult to disentangle the effect of NAFTA from the effect of the Tequila crisis of 1994–5 when the Mexican peso dropped in value by 53 per cent and money flowed out of the country. The effect was a collapse of the financial system, and the government was forced to bail out the weakened banks at huge cost. The system has still not recovered, and the lower level of credit and financial services have affected the domestic economy considerably. For example the effect on wages in dollar terms was to cut them by 20 per cent, yet productivity rose, so real wages have in fact only just reached the same level as before the crisis (*Economist* 2004a). On the positive side, Mexico has recovered from the crisis more quickly than from previous crises in 1982 and 1986. Mexico was also less affected by the recent Brazilian and Argentinean crises than it probably would have been pre-NAFTA.

As to Mexican trade, as already seen, this has increased, especially with the United States, with which it has had a trade surplus throughout its NAFTA membership. FDI has also increased and jobs in the export businesses have tended to pay more than in the rest of the economy (*Economist* 2004a).

However there are still things that NAFTA has not solved for Mexico. The continuing outflow of people to the United States – legally and illegally – and the loss of people from the countryside is still a problem. The US farm policy still highly subsidises its farmers, despite NAFTA pledging to deal with this. One outcome of the US policy is excess supply of corn, which some have accused the United States of **dumping** onto the Mexican market. Mexico also still has problems with poor education, bureaucracy, poor infrastructure, lack of credit, a high level of corruption and a weak tax base, which all together have perhaps prevented it from gaining as much as it could have from NAFTA (*Economist* 2004a).

It has to be said that NAFTA is still a rather imbalanced trading bloc, strongly dominated by the United States, and the fear is that any decline in the United States will drag down both of the other partners very quickly.

The formation of NAFTA influenced a number of other regional agreements in the first half of the 1990s, and one of these was the setting up of Mercosur.

Mercosur

Mercosur (Mercado Comun del Sur) was set up in 1991 by the Treaty of Asuncion, with Argentina, Brazil, Paraguay and Uruguay as members. In 2004 they had a combined population of over 230 million and GDP of over US$1 trillion. Chile and Bolivia became associate members in 1996 and in 1998 joined the common mechanism for political consultations called 'Political Mercosur' (Europa no date).

Officially Mercosur is a customs union; it eliminates tariffs on goods and services and sets a CET for the group. In fact tariffs and NTBs have mostly disappeared, with the exception of sugar and automobiles. The CET is between 0–20 per cent on most products (but with some exceptions such as computers, telecommunications, leather and arms). There are also some elements that go beyond a customs union definition, moving towards a common market-type status. For example there is a reciprocal investment promotion and protection agreement (set up in January 1994, and called the Colonia Protocol) which guarantees non-discriminatory treatment. In August 1995 intellectual property rules were set up (FTAA no date).

What are the advantages and disadvantages of the bloc (for those inside and outside)? Mercosur has appeared to be strikingly successful in a number of ways. It has been estimated that there has been substantial trade creation since its inception. Trade expanded rapidly to start with; many have suggested too rapidly. Between 1990 and 1996 members' imports rose 314 per cent to US$171.1 billion, and non-members' imports rose 185 per cent to US$66.7 billion, with exports to non-members rising 37 per cent to US$57.9 billion. Some have suggested that this represents substantial trade diversion, as the areas that have grown the most are those with the highest tariff barriers against non-members, and in industries where Mercosur countries would not be expected to have a comparative advantage (Dunn and Mutti 2004). However a number of agreements have been drawn up to try to cut this element; for example Mercosur has been talking to the European Union about setting up a free trade deal for many years now. The deal could embrace 'nearly 680m Europe and Latin American consumers, and $11.6 trillion of GDP, could be signed by October' (*Economist* 2004c). There is also the possibility of the FTAA (see below). Finally Mercosur has given Latin America a voice to counter the overwhelming US voice in the area.

However Mercosur also faces a number of problems. First, a major problem with Mercosur is the imbalance between country size. It consists of two big countries and two small ones. If the two large countries – Brazil and Argentina – flounder, so does Mercosur. This is something that has happened recently. Mercosur suffered a shock when Brazil devalued in 1999, and then the Argentinean crisis of December 2001 hit trade and output in the area. It has also left many questioning the stability of the group, and has slowed the progress of Mercosur. This instability has affected FDI. A recent UN report on FDI in Latin America and the Caribbean stated that this region had seen FDI flows fall over the period 1999–2003, and FDI was sharply down in Mercosur (UNCTAD 2004).

Furthermore there are areas in which Mercosur has been slow in making decisions. There is no dispute settlement procedure, little has been achieved in freeing trade in services and government purchases, and there are still many exceptions to the CET (*Economist* 2001).

The success of NAFTA and Mercosur is one of the reasons the United States has been talking of extending the idea to the whole of the Americas in the shape of the Free Trade Area of the Americas (FTAA).

FTAA

In 1994 the Summit of the Americas in Miami agreed to a free trade area of the Americas (from Alaska to Tierra del Fuego) to incorporate 34 nations (Catan

2002, FTAA no date). The original aim was to complete negotiations by 2005, so bringing free trade to over approximately 800 million people, and a trade boom over 34 countries. The negotiations were formally launched in Santiago, Chile in 1998 (FTAA no date). But things have not gone smoothly, and at a Monterrey conference in January 2004, the group only 'pledged themselves to the FTAA, but not to a specific date' (*Economist* 2004b).

Other regional groupings have formed outside the American and European continents. In Asia there has been APEC and ASEAN, and in Africa there are numerous trading blocs.

ASEAN

ASEAN was founded in 1967 and aimed to be a free trade area between Brunei, Indonesia, Malaysia, the Philippines, Singapore and Thailand. These countries have a population of approximately 500 million, a combined GDP of US$737 billion and total trade of US$720 billion (ASEAN no date). There have been four additional members since 1967: Vietnam, Cambodia, Laos and Mynamar. In 1993 it was agreed that the Asian Free Trade Area (AFTA) would be set up by 2008, but this was later shortened to 2003. However progress towards a free trade area has been slow, mainly because negotiations have been on a product-by-product basis (Husted and Melvin 2004). However, in the first three years after the agreement, exports among ASEAN countries grew from US$43 billion in 1993 to US$80 billion in 1996, and the share of intra-regional trade rose from 20 to 25 per cent (ASEAN no date). Seven members of ASEAN are also members of APEC.

APEC

Asia-Pacific Economic Cooperation (APEC) was founded in 1989. It currently has 21 members. These are seven of the ASEAN countries, the three NAFTA countries (the United States, Canada and Mexico), Australia, Japan, New Zealand, Papua New Guinea, Chile, Taiwan, South Korea, China, Hong Kong (which maintains a separate membership of APEC) and more recently in 1998 Peru and Russia.[9] The area has a population of 2.5 billion, a combined GDP of US$19 trillion, and accounts for 47 per cent of world trade (APEC no date).

APEC is clearly a much larger grouping, in terms of both population and numbers of countries, than NAFTA or Mercosur, or even the European Union. Consequently, it is more loosely structured than these groupings. While it is concerned with intra-regional issues, APEC also attempts to act as a pressure group in global trade negotiations. It states it is working towards the goals of 'free and open trade and investment in the Asia-Pacific by 2010 for developed economies and 2020 for developing economies' (APEC no date), and has specified three specific areas crucial to achieve these: trade and investment liberalisation, business facilitation, and economic and technical cooperation (APEC no date).[10]

Funabashi states emphatically that:

> APEC was born out of fear – fear of a unilateralist or isolationist America, fear of a balkanisation of the world into competing economic blocs, and fear of the potential death of the GATT-centred world trading system. It

was no coincidence that the strongest initiatives for APEC's founding came from Japan and Australia. Both countries faced similar threats from the emerging forces at the end of the Cold War. Both nations also traditionally relied politically, militarily and economically on the United States, making them especially vulnerable to an aggressive or inward-focused America.

(Funabashi 1995: 105)

APEC has also been successful in heading off the proposal that individual countries in the Asia–Pacific might join NAFTA. This caused great concern in Asia at the time, because of the possibility that trade would be diverted away from non-member countries and because of the pressure this would cause for a countervailing east Asian regional bloc.

However, while APEC has had some success in promoting these more general objectives, there is some concern about what are the most appropriate concrete measures that can be taken by such a large and potentially unwieldy grouping.

Conclusion

This chapter has suggested the means by which one of the most important developments in world trade today, the growth of trading blocs, can be analysed. The theoretical analysis of the effect of such blocs on differing economic actors has been outlined, and empirical work following from this has been briefly considered. We continued by showing the development of the European Union and the forces behind that development. The European Union has been a major force in encouraging the development of other trading blocs, partly from being a good example and partly through being seen as a threat. These new blocs have not reached the same degree of integration as the European Union and in some cases (for example the FTAA, APEC and African blocs) this is not really an option in the near future.

 ## Questions

1   Assume that Austria, Hungary and Turkey all produce refrigerators and the domestic price per refrigerator in Austria is £600, in Hungary £500 and in Turkey £360.

a) Suppose Austria imposes a 100 per cent tariff on refrigerators. What are the trading options open for Austria?

b) If Austria then formed a CU with Hungary with a common external tariff of 100 per cent, how would Austria's options change?

c) How would you describe the situation in (b)?

d) If the tariff rate in Austria in (a) were 50 per cent instead of 100 per cent, how different would your answers be to (a), (b) and (c)?

AFRICA'S ECONOMIC INTEGRATION

Regional integration is very popular in Africa. There are 14 differing regional economic communities in Africa which cover most countries (see Appendix 4.1). The types of integration range from the Central African Economic and Monetary Community, to the Common Market for Eastern and Southern Africa, to the Southern African Customs Union, indicating the varying types of integration in their names. It has been suggested that the impulse for regionalism in Africa dates as far back as the 18th century, with its base in colonialism (when colonial administrators set up federations in west, central and eastern Africa). Attempts to increase integration from the 1960s to 1980s struggled, and new blocs were imposed on existing blocs, meaning that many countries belonged to too many entities. From the late 1980s onwards, however, the ideals of pan-Africanism through regional cooperation have emerged, and the Constitutive Act of African Union is now seen as the next stage for African trading cooperation.

Why have attempts at regional integration in Africa been so unsuccessful? A number of reasons have been put forward. Most regionalism was economic, and ignored the political aspect. As Adedeji asks, 'How can you disagree politically and cooperate economically?' (Economic Commission for Africa 2002: 9). So basically there has been little in the way of 'shared political vision, values and stability' (Economic Commission for Africa 2002: 9). Furthermore this is a south–south integration and involves mainly economies with little in the way of industrial bases, very reliant on agriculture and with not much intra-regional trade. Therefore the integration has had little on which to build. There was also far too much concentration on the institutions and their structure rather than the real substantive issues, and these institutions proliferated and overlapped in terms of tasks and mandates.

As a result any external shock tended to topple them:

> Africa's balance sheet demonstrates such problems as lack of political will, lack of sanctions against non-performers, and overlapping memberships. Others are the over-reliance of governments on tariff revenues, inequitable sharing of costs and benefits of integration, an unrealistic timetable, the practice by member states of signing protocols and not implementing them, and low private sector and civil society participation.
>
> (Economic Commission for Africa 2002: 9)

Finally El-Agraa (in Economic Commission for Africa 2002) has pointed out that an African union would cover 800 million people but the GDP of this union would be less than that of France. Economic activity in Africa is concentrated in certain areas, and this would also need to be dealt with. Europe dealt with this problem by setting up structural funds, and it was pointed out that Africa would probably have to do something similar. This would probably prove too expensive for Africa, and it has therefore been suggested that an African Union would have to try to strongly encourage FDI to help bring about more cohesion. In order to do this, strong institutions would be needed to inspire confidence in investors.

Source: Economic Commission for Africa (2002).

Questions

1 What reasons are listed for the proliferation of trading blocs in Africa? Consider these and can you think of any other reasons?
2 What is the prospect of building an Africa-wide trading bloc?

2 Turkey is in a CU arrangement with Germany but not with Iran. Why would such a CU be better economically for Turkey?

3 Using the example in Table 4.2 (page 92), explain the likely impact of trade creation and trade diversion on the French, German and Japanese businesses.

4 Which business sectors of which economies would have lost most by the United Kingdom's membership of the European Community in 1973?

5 How would you account for the relatively poor economic performance in western Europe in the 1970s and 1980s? In what ways might the revival of European integration help this performance?

6 Do you think US businesses would view NAFTA as a success? Would Canadian and Mexican businesses think likewise? Why or why not?

7 If Asian business executives were asked which has had the most effect on their business, ASEAN or APEC, which do you think they would choose and why?

Notes

1 For example the Benelux customs union of Belgium, the Netherlands and Luxemburg which was founded in October 1947, the Organisation of European Economic Cooperation (OEEC) (later to become the Organization for Economic Cooperation and Development or OECD with the addition of the United States and Canada) in April 1948, the Council of Europe in April 1949 and the European Payments Union in September 1950.
2 Sterling left the Snake in June 1972, the Italian lira in February 1973 and the French franc in January 1974.
3 After its election in 1981 the Mitterrand government tried a policy of economic expansion, but this triggered a balance of payments crisis and the devaluation of the franc, and was abandoned in 1983.
4 Community, Justice and Home Affairs, and Foreign and Security Pillar.
5 These were Estonia, Latvia, Lithuania, the Czech Republic, Slovakia, Slovenia, Hungary, Poland, Cyprus and Malta.
6 The Europe Agreements were set up in 1992 with the aim of creating a free trade area between the countries of central and eastern Europe and the European Union (Dyker 1999).
7 For example post-war migration into West Germany and the movement of Algerians into France after their war of independence (Kilmister 2001).
8 Qualified majority voting means that at least 55 per cent of the Council members representing 65 per cent of the population of the Union must approve a decision, and the Council needs at least 15 members to be quorate.
9 The seven ASEAN members do not include Cambodia, Laos and Mynamar.
10 These goals are called the Bogor goals.

References

Anderson, P. (1996a) 'Under the sign of the interim', *London Review of Books*, 4 January.
Anderson, P. (1996b) 'The Europe to come', *London Review of Books*, 25 January.

Anderson, P. and Gowan, P. (eds) (1997) *The Debate on Europe*, Verso, London.

APEC (no date) Website information, www.apecsec.org.sg.html, accessed 16 August 2004.

Artis, M. J. and Lee, N. (eds) (1994) T*he Economics of the European Union*, Oxford University Press, Oxford.

Artis, M. and Nixson, F. (2001) *The Economics of the European Union*, 3rd edn, Oxford University Press, Oxford.

ASEAN (no date) Overview of the Association of SouthEast Asian Nations. www.aseansec.org.html, accessed 18 August 2004.

Balassa, B. (1961) *The Theory of Economic Integration*, Allen and Unwin, London.

Baldwin, R. and Wyplosz, C. (2004) *The Economics of European Integration*, McGraw-Hill, London.

BBC (2004a) 'What the EU constitution says', 22 June, www.news.bbc.co.uk, accessed 10 August 2004.

BBC (2004b) 'France plans EU constitution poll', 14 July, www.news.bbc.co.uk, accessed 10 August 2004.

Catan, T. (2002) 'Mercosur seeks to build ties with Mexico', *Financial Times*, 6 July.

Cecchini, P. (1988) *1992: The European challenge*, Gower, Aldershot.

Chacholiades, M. (1990) *International Trade Theory and Policy*, McGraw-Hill, New York/London.

De Jonquieres, G. (1996) 'Mercosur trade group under fire', *Financial Times*, 24 October.

Dunn, R. M. and Mutti, J. H. (2004) *International Economics*, 5th edn, Routledge, London.

Dyker, D. A. (1999) *The European Economy*, 2nd edn, Longman, Harlow.

Dyson, K. (1994) *Elusive Union: The process of economic and monetary union in Europe*, Longman, Harlow.

Economic Commission for Africa (2002) *Defining Priorities for Regional Integration*, proceedings of Third African Development Forum, 3–8 March, Addis Ababa, Ethiopia (includes contributions from Adedeji and El Agraa).

Economist (1995) 'Trade in the Pacific: no action, no agenda', 25 November.

Economist (1996) 'Survey on Mercosur', 12 October.

Economist (2001) 'Another blow to Mercosur', 31 March.

Economist (2004a) 'Free trade on trial: 10 years of NAFTA', 3 January.

Economist (2004b) 'Loveless brothers', 17 January.

Economist (2004c) 'Still prickly', 1 May.

Economist (2004d) 'A club in need of a new vision', 1 May.

El-Agraa, A. (2004) *The European Union: Economics and policies*, 7th edn, Financial Times/Prentice Hall, London.

EOS Gallup Europe (2002) *Internal Market Business Survey*, flash Eurobarometer 130, October.

Europa (no date) *The EU's relations with Mercosur*, http:europa.eu.int/comm/external_relations/Mercosur/intro, accessed 13 August 2004.

FTAA (no date) *About the FTAA*, www.ftaa-alca.org, accessed 4 October 2004.

Funabashi, Y. (1995) Chapter 6 in *Asia Pacific Fusion: Japan's role in APEC*, Institute for International Economics, Washington, DC.

Gerber, J. (2004) *International Economics*, 3rd edn, Pearson Addison Wesley, Reading, Mass.

Glyn, A. (1992) 'The costs of stability: the advanced capitalist countries in the 1980s', *New Left Review*, no. 195, September/October.

Grant Thornton (2001) 'Single market has a positive effect on expansion of European businesses', 3 December, www.gti.org/marketsurvey, accessed 9 July 2004.

Griffiths, A. and Wall, S. (eds) (2004) *Applied Economics*, 10th edn, Financial Times/Prentice Hall, London.

Gros, D. and Steinherr, A. (1995) *Winds of Change: Economic transition in central and eastern Europe*, Longman, Harlow.

Gros, D. and Thygesen, N. (1992) *European Monetary Integration: From the European Monetary System towards monetary union,* Longman, Harlow.

Haas, E. (1968) *The Uniting of Europe: Political, social and economic forces 1950–1957,* Stanford University Press, Stanford.

Hudsted, S. and Melvin, M. (2004) *International Economics,* 6th edn, Pearson, Boston, Mass./London.

Lawrence, R. and Schultze, C. (1989) 'Barriers to European growth: an overview' in A. Jacquemin and A. Sapir (eds), *The European Internal Market,* Oxford University Press, Oxford.

Kilmister, A. (2001) 'Enlarging the European Union to the east: issues and problems, *Business Update,* Spring.

Krugman, P. R. and Obstfeld, M. (2003) *International Economics: Theory and policy,* 6th edn, Addison Wesley, Boston, Mass./London.

McDonald, F. and Dearden, S. (eds) (1999) *European Economic Integration,* 3rd edn, Longman, Harlow.

McDonald, F. and Dearden, S. (2005) *European Economic Integration,* 4th edn, Financial Times/Prentice Hall

Middlemas, K. (1985) *Orchestrating Europe: The informal politics of the European Union 1973–95,* Fontana, London.

Milward, A. (1984) *The Reconstruction of Western Europe 1945–51,* Methuen, London.

Milward, A. (1992) *The European Rescue of the Nation State,* Routledge, London.

Rosamond, B. (2000) *Theories of European Integration,* Palgrave, Basingstoke.

Ross, G. (1992) 'Confronting the new Europe', *New Left Review,* no. 191, January/February.

Ross, G. (1995) *Jacques Delors and European Integration,* Polity, Cambridge.

Swann, D. (1988) *The Economics of the Common Market,* 6th edn, Penguin, London.

Tsoukalis, L. (1997) *The New European Economy Revisited,* Oxford University Press, Oxford.

UNCTAD (2004) *Trade and Development Report 2004,* United Nations, 16 September.

Winters, A. L. (1987) 'Britain in Europe: A survey of quantitative grade studies', *Journal of Common Market Studies,* vol. 24, no.4, pp. 315–35.

Wolf, M. (1994) 'A relapse into Eurosclerosis', *Financial Times,* 24 February.

World Bank (2004) *Global Economic Prospects 2005: Trade, regionalism, and development,* World Bank, Washington, DC, November.

World Trade Organization (WTO) (2003) *World Trade Report,* WTO, Geneva.

Appendix 4.1 Regional trading blocs in the world

Europe

	Year	Members	Aim
European Free Trade Association (EFTA)	1960	Iceland, Liechtenstein, Norway, Switzerland (most of original members left to join the EU). All but Switzerland are part of the European Economic Area (EEA) which is a free trade area linking to the EU.	Free trade area
European Union	1957	1957: Belgium, Netherlands, Luxemburg, France, Germany, Italy. 1973: Denmark, United Kingdom, Ireland. 1981: Greece. 1985: Spain and Portugal. 1995: Sweden, Finland and Austria 2004: Estonia, Latvia, Lithuania, Hungary, Poland, Slovenia, Czech Republic, Slovakia, Cyprus, Malta.	Common market and for some in 'Euroland' economic union

Asia

	Year	Members	Aim
Association of South East Asian Nations (ASEAN)	1967	Brunei, Indonesia, Malaysia, Philippines, Singapore and Thailand	Free trade area
Australia–New Zealand Closer Economic Relations Trade Agreement (ANZCERT)	1990	Australia and New Zealand	Free trade area

Source: Husted and Melvin (2004).

Latin America and North America

	Year	Members	Aim
Andean Community	1969	Bolivia, Colombia Ecuador, Peru, Venezuela	Common market
Caribbean Community	1973	Antigua and Barbuda, Bahamas, Barbados, Belize, Dominica, Guyana, Grenada, Jamaica, Montserrat, St Kitts and Nevis, St Lucia, St Vincent and the Grenadines, Suriname, Trinidad and Tobago	Common market
Central American Common Market	1961	Costa Rica, El Salvador, Guatemala, Honduras, Nicaragua	Customs union
Mercosur	1994	Argentina, Brazil, Paraguay, Uruguay	Common market
NAFTA	1994	Canada, Mexico, United States	Free trade area

Source: Gerber (2004: 378).

Africa

	Year	Members	Aim
Central African Economic and Monetary Community (CEMAC)		Cameroon, Central African Republic, Chad, Dem. Rep. of Congo, Equatorial Guinea, Gabon	Economic and monetary union
Community of Sahel-Saharan States (CEN-SAD)		Burkina Faso, Central African Republic, Chad, Djibouti, Egypt, Eritrea, The Gambia, Libya, Mali, Morocco, Niger, Nigeria, Senegal, Somalia, Sudan, Tunisia	
Economic Community of Great Lake Countries (CEPGL)		Burundi, Dem. Rep. of Congo, Rwanda	
Common Market for Eastern and Southern Africa (COMESA)		Angola, Burundi, Comoros, Dem. Rep. of Congo, Djibouti, Egypt, Eritrea, Ethiopia, Kenya, Madagascar, Malawi, Mauritius, Namibia, Rwanda, Seychelles, Sudan, Swaziland, Uganda, Zambia, Zimbabwe	Common market
East African Community (EAC)		Kenya, Tanzania, Uganda	

Africa – *continued*

	Year	Members	Aim
Economic Community of Central African States (ECCAS)	1981	Angola, Burundi, Cameroon, Central African Republic, Chad, Dem. Rep. of Congo, Equatorial Guinea, Gabon, Republic of Congo, Rwanda, Sao Tome and Principe	Customs union
Economic Community of West African States (ECOWAS)	1975	Benin, Burkina Faso, Cape Verde, Côte d'Ivoire, The Gambia, Ghana, Guinea, Guinea-Bissau, Liberia, Mali, Niger, Nigeria, Senegal, Sierra Leone, Togo	Customs union
Intern-Governmental Authority on Development (IGAD)		Djibouti, Eritrea, Ethiopia, Kenya, Somalia, Sudan, Uganda	
Indian Ocean Commission (IOC)		Comoros, France (Reunion) Madagascar, Mauritius, Seychelles	
Mano River Union (MRU)		Guinea, Liberia, Sierra Leone	
Southern African Customs Union (SACU)		Botswana, Lesotho, Namibia, South Africa, Swaziland	
Southern African Development Community (SADC)		Angola, Botswana, Dem. Rep. of Congo, Lesotho, Malawi, Mauritius, Mozambique, Namibia, South Africa, Swaziland, Tanzania, Zambia, Zimbabwe	
West African Economic and Monetary Union (UEMOA)		Benin, Burkina Faso, Côte d'Ivoire, Guinea-Bissau, Mali, Niger, Senegal, Togo	
Arab Maghreb Union	1989	Algeria, Libya, Mauritania, Morocco, Tunisia	Customs union

Sources: Husted and Melvin (2004: 66–7) and Economic Commission for Africa (2002: 5–6).

5 Foreign exchange markets

Judith Piggott and Andy Kilmister

Objectives

This chapter will:

- outline the various types of exchange rate definition
- illustrate these by considering movements of certain currencies
- critically assess the various theories explaining exchange rate movements
- outline the concept of optimal currency areas and analyse the case of the single European currency.

Introduction

Exchange rates are often referred to in the press and on television, and a changing exchange rate can have a massive impact on business decisions, especially concerning pricing and export profitability. For example Europe and the United States recently have been complaining that the Chinese yuan has been undervalued, so making Chinese exports very cheap and forcing other companies' goods off international markets. (The Big Mac Index would support this, suggesting that in 2004 the yuan was 57 per cent undervalued (*Economist* 2005b).[1]) Similarly in the case study below, the effect of the weak dollar on consumer behaviour at the start of 2004 is shown.

Before we proceed with the body of the chapter, however, it is important to clarify a point which often causes confusion. The convention of expressing exchange rates as the amount of foreign currency that can be purchased with one unit of domestic currency is commonly used in Britain. If you watch the news, the exchange rate will be expressed as £1 equals a certain number of dollars or euros. However most other countries and international institutions define the exchange rate as the amount of domestic currency needed to purchase one unit of foreign currency; in other words the number of pounds needed to buy one dollar or euro. For example on 9 August 2004 the *Financial Times* quoted a sterling/dollar exchange rate for the UK of £0.5422 (the amount needed to purchase US$1), whereas the television would have quoted this as £1 = $1.8442. In this chapter we use both conventions, choosing the one that makes the material simplest at the time. It is important to check that you are clear about how the exchange rate is being defined.

The foreign exchange market

The foreign exchange market is a market in which large volumes of mainly bank deposits denominated in one currency are bought and sold in exchange for bank deposits denominated in other currencies. Most individuals' contact with the foreign exchange market occurs when they are buying foreign bank notes and coins for the purpose of a holiday or a business trip. In fact, the transactions in currency amount to fairly trivial sums compared with the transactions in bank deposits. For most individuals and firms the main agents in the transfer of money are the banks, and it is really the banks authorised to deal in foreign currency that comprise the foreign exchange market.

The foreign exchange market is in fact a worldwide market. Banks in the major financial centres are able to buy and sell foreign currency virtually throughout 24 hours. Thus, when the Hong Kong foreign exchange market has just closed at 9.00 GMT the London foreign exchange market has been open for half an hour, and by the time the London market has closed at 16.30 GMT the San Francisco market has also been open for half an hour. Obviously, the eastern markets are operating in the early part of the day (by GMT) and as the day progresses, Frankfurt, London, New York and so on are opening and closing. London, Frankfurt and New York account for most of the trade in foreign currencies. Clearly there is no single location for the foreign exchange market, and it is really a global market united by efficient telecommunications and computer systems. Since the bulk of transactions in foreign currency involve the US dollar it is hardly surprising that large US banks are important operators.

The daily turnover in foreign currency deposits, converted to US dollars as a standard measure, was approximately US$1.2 trillion in 2001. In 1998 it was a staggering US$1.49 trillion, which given it was only US$590 billion in 1989, represents a growth rate of 10 per cent a year. The most traded currency was the US dollar, which was involved with 90.4 per cent of total trades (either as currency sold or bought), followed by the euro with 37.6 per cent and the Japanese yen and British pound with 22.7 per cent and 13.2 per cent respectively.[2] However the United Kingdom dealt with 31.1 per cent of all trading, compared with 15.7 per cent in the United States and 9.1 per cent in Japan. In fact more dollars were traded in London than New York, and 82 per cent of trades in London did not involve the pound. This is perhaps not surprising in view of the large number of foreign banks operating from London (Gerber 2005).

How the exchange rate is measured

When buying or selling foreign currencies the bank will quote two prices, one at which it will sell and one at which it will buy. Indeed this is one of the most familiar ways in which foreign currency prices are quoted. For example, on 9 August 2004 the average price quoted during that day for the euro against the pound sterling was £1 = €1.5045. Banks buy currency at a lower price and sell for a higher price, so the selling rate for the euro on that day was €1.4358 for £1 and the buying rate was €1.5992 for £1.[3] The difference between the two prices is called the **spread**, and in the example above it was 0.1634: or as a percentage of the selling price:

$$(0.1634/1.4358) \times 100 = 11.38\%$$

The difference between the two prices is required to provide the banks with a profit on their dealings as well as cover them for their administrative costs and any risks they may run in such transactions.

Nominal exchange rates

There are actually several ways in which exchange rates might be expressed. The example above represents a bilateral rate: that is, the price of one currency expressed in terms of one other currency. Since foreign currency deposits are traded freely in several financial centres simultaneously during each working day, once the quoted rate of exchange of the pound is known, for example against the US dollar and against the euro, the exchange rate of the US dollar against the euro can be worked out. The average exchange rates for the pound on 9 August 2004 in London were:

£1 = US$1.8442   £1 = €1.5045

Therefore the exchange rate of the US dollar against the euro must have been 1.8442 /1.5045, making €1 = $1.2258. If this were not the situation on that day, it would have been possible to switch from one currency to another to make a profit based on the inconsistency between their prices. Suppose the exchange rates had been:

US$1 = €1.22 (in New York)

£1 = US$1.8442 (in London)

£1 = €1.5045 (in Frankfurt)

A bank in London with £10 million could buy US$18.44 million, transfer this into €22.49 million in New York, then exchange this back into £14.9 million in Frankfurt – so making £4.9 million in profit for a few minutes' work. Obviously, such profitable opportunities would be visible to all banks operating in foreign currency markets, and this would lead immediately to changes that make the exchange rate consistent – with a rate of €1 = US$1.2258 in New York. The mechanism that ensures that these various cross-rates (the price of one currency in terms of several other currencies) are consistent, and which is described above, is called **arbitrage**.

The exchange rates above are called **spot rates**. This is because they are prices quoted for the delivery of foreign currency immediately or 'on the spot'; the deal is done then and there and the currency is expected to be available after the transaction. Some 64 per cent of transactions on any one day are spot (Griffiths and Wall 2004). It is also possible to buy and sell foreign currency in the future. This can be via the forward market which allows business (and individuals) to purchase a currency at a set price for future delivery one month or three months (or more) in the future. These rates of exchange are called

forward rates. Alternatively it is possible to purchase a **futures** contract. Like the forward rates, this represents an agreement to buy a currency at a future date, but this contract is resellable up to the time it matures, so if the business no longer needs the currency, it can sell it. The contract also has specific maturity dates, so standardising the transaction, and the broker negotiates a contract at the best rate, thereby allowing an element of competition into the market. Finally these are dealt with in the UK via LIFFE (the London International Financial Futures Exchange) which centralises the deal. The costs however are usually higher than the forward market.

Finally it is possible to buy currency **options**. These represent a contract giving the right to buy a currency at a set exchange rate at a given future date. However the option need not necessarily be exercised at that date. An option will involve a fee but this is the maximum loss if the option is not exercised.

Effective exchange rates (EER)

An average foreign currency value, of, say, the pound or euro against several other currencies is computed for all major currencies. These 'average exchange rates' are termed effective exchange rates, and are calculated as an index. Table 5.1 shows the recent movement in the effective exchange rates for the United Kingdom, euro area, United States and Japan. It can be seen that the effective exchange rate for the US dollar rose to a peak of 134.8 in 2002 but it has since declined in value. The yen however has declined since 2000 but appeared to be starting a recovery in 2003. Similarly the EER shows the strength of sterling and the weakness, especially in the early stages, of the euro.

Table 5.1 Effective exchange rates (1995 = 100)

	1996	1997	1998	1999	2000	2001	2002	2003*	2004*
US$	105.6	113.1	124.8	124.4	127.5	134.3	134.8	126.5	121.8
Yen	87.2	83.3	96.6	99.3	108.1	99.7	95.5	98.6	103
£sterling	102.3	119.2	127	127.5	130.9	129.6	131.1	126.4	132.7
Euro	102	95.5	100.7	99	90.1	92.4	95.5	106.9	109.2

* Estimated

Source: OECD (2004: 251).

Real exchange rates (RER)

Both nominal and effective exchange rates try to measure the rate at which one currency exchanges for another. For a country that relies heavily on trade to maintain living standards (as most EU countries do) it is arguable that the exchange rate that is important is not the rate at which its currency exchanges for another, but the rate at which its goods exchange in international trade. This is referred to as the real exchange rate (RER). It relates the effective exchange rate to the price of domestic goods relative to the price of foreign goods.

The real exchange rate for, say, Italian goods compared with UK goods, is calculated from the following formula

RER = price index of Italian goods / (price index of UK goods x effective exchange rate)

This allows us to judge the competitiveness of Italian goods.

Table 5.2 Real exchange rate example

	Price index UK	Price index Italy	EER	Real ER for Italy – $P_i/(P_{uk} \times EER)$
Year 0	100	100	100	100.0
Year 1	105	115	100	109.5
Year 2	110	130	100	118.2
Year 2A	110	130	90	106.3

Table 5.2 provides a simple illustration of how this works. Say we have two price indices which give a representative bundle of the same goods in two countries, the United Kingdom and Italy, and illustrate the rate of inflation in these countries. At the start (which we call year 0) both indices are set at 100. However at the end of the first year prices in the United Kingdom have risen by only 5 per cent, but in Italy they have risen by 15 per cent. The real exchange rate for Italy would be 109.5, showing Italian goods as being 9.5 per cent more expensive by comparison with UK goods. If the same inflation rates continue in year 2, the RER will deteriorate even further, showing an increase of 18.2 per cent. However we are assuming that the EER stays the same – but the EER is likely to change in this situation. So if the EER falls (example 2A in Table 5.2), this could counter some of these inflationary effects and the RER would only be 6.3 per cent of the year 0 rate (better than the year 1 rate). Therefore we can see that a rise in the index suggests an reduction in competitiveness, and a fall in the index, an increase in competitiveness.

To illustrate the significance of the RER we can see in Table 5.3 the RER data for the United States, Japan and the euro between 1995 and 2003. This, together with Figure 5.1, clearly illustrates the decline in the yen since 1994,

Table 5.3 Real exchange rates, 1995–2003 (2000 = 100)

	1995	1996	1997	1998	1999	2000	2001	2002	2003
UK	85.3	87.1	99.4	103.8	102.2	100	97.2	98.3	95.6
US	85.2	86.9	90.9	99.0	98.9	100	106.2	106.2	98.1
Japan	109.7	93.1	88.1	88.4	96.9	100	89.7	83.8	83.0
Eurozone	120.2	119.3	109.1	112.2	109.3	100	101.4	105.2	117.3

Source: UN (2004) World Economic and Social Survey p. 151 (Table A12).

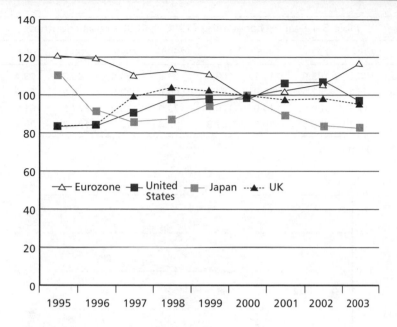

Figure 5.1 Real exchange rates 1994–2002 (2000 =100)

with the Japanese recession reducing prices and the yen rates, especially in the latter period. The initial problems with the euro, and its fall in 1999 and 2000, are also clear. The strength of the dollar over the period is also shown (although it has since declined – see the case study below).

It is also interesting to compare Figure 5.2 and Table 5.4, which show some currencies that have had significant problems over the period. They show what has happened to the Malaysian, Mexican, Korean and Argentinean currencies over the period, and it is very clear when their currency crises occurred and the subsequent recovery.

Who buys and sells foreign currencies?

The answer to this question is businesses, individuals and governments. Business demand and supply is from two sources;

- non-financial companies such as BP, Gillette, Remy Cointreau and Volkswagen which need foreign currency to buy raw materials, semi-manufactured goods or equipment from foreign firms
- financial companies, mainly banks, which buy and sell foreign currencies for their clients and also for their main business of lending.

Individuals buy and sell foreign currencies for business reasons but also for purposes of foreign travel, and immigrants often send money back to their country of origin. Table 5.5 provides an approximate summary of these various reasons for buying and selling foreign currencies from a UK perspective.

Table 5.4 Real exchange rates (1990 = 100) – crisis countries

	1994	1995	1996	1997	1998	1999	2000	2001	2002
Malaysia	106.1	105.9	111.1	108.5	83.3	84.8	86.8	93.4	95.5
Korea (S)	85.8	87.5	89.9	84.4	65.9	72.9	78.9	73.9	77.3
Argentina	111.4	109.0	113.0	120.5	123.0	125.0	127.5	131.8	70.5
Mexico	112.2	78.9	89.8	102.8	102.4	112.7	126.2	133.1	133.4

Source:UN (2004, table A12).

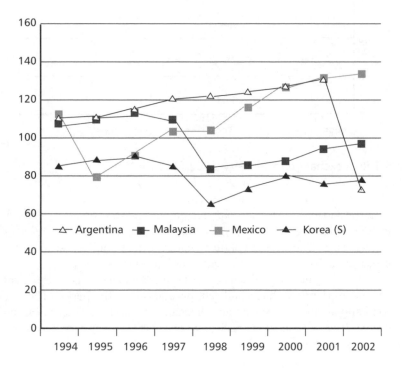

Figure 5.2 Real exchange rates 1994–2002 – crisis currencies

Many of the items in the table are self-evident: 42 per cent of the demand for foreign currency in 2002 was for the purchase of such tangible items as basic materials, manufactured goods and food. Almost as important, UK residents and businesses bought 'invisible' items of various kinds such as services (like tourism, shipping, insurance and banking) as well as buying foreign currency in order to transfer funds abroad. Most of these 'transfers' take the form of budgetary contributions to the European Union and the repatriation of funds by private individuals, for example UK citizens who have relatives living abroad. By far the largest single item under the heading of invisibles is 'investment income', and the largest item in this is caused by the payment of interest to foreigners and foreign financial institutions such as banks that have placed

Table 5.5 UK purchases of foreign currency, 2002 (£ million)

Import of goods		232,712	(42%)
Finished manufactured goods	143,571		
Semi-manufactured goods	52,572		
Food, drink and tobacco	19,324		
Basic materials	5,950		
Oil and oil products	8,838		
Coal, gas and electricity	1,005		
Unclassified	1,452		
Purchases of foreign 'invisibles'		193,758	(35%)
Services	71,304		
Transfers	20,498		
Investment income	100,902		
Compensation for employees	1,054		
Purchases of foreign assets		125,084	(23%)
Direct investment	27,812		
Portfolio investment	609		
Other investment abroad	98,123		
Financial derivatives	− 1,001		
Reserve assets	− 459		
Total		551,554	

Source: UK Balance of Payments Pink Book 2003, various tables.

funds on deposit with banks in the United Kingdom. It is also clear from Table 5.5 that UK residents buy substantial amounts of foreign currency in order to buy foreign assets. These can be in the following forms:

● direct investment by UK companies in their overseas branches, subsidiaries or associated companies, including not only the purchase of fixed assets but also additions to working capital
● portfolio investment, which represents the purchase of financial assets in the form of securities issued by overseas registered companies or securities issued by overseas governments
● other investment abroad, which is mainly deposits by UK banks in foreign currency.

It can be seen that in 2002 the last of these dominated the figures. However transactions in this area in recent years have been very volatile. In 1997 UK banks deposited £113.5 billion, and in 2000 a record £131.2 billion, but in 2002 the figure was £98.123 billion. However if we look back over past years we can see volatility in the figures of both direct and portfolio investment. In 2000 outward direct investment from the United Kingdom peaked at £155 billion as a result of massive merger and acquisition activity, but by 2002 this had declined to £27.8 billion. Portfolio investment in 2001 was £86.5 billion but by

2002 it was only £0.6 billion – reflecting the collapse of the equity markets in 2002 (UK government 2003).

Obviously the other side of the coin is the foreign demand for UK currency, which would be reflected in export figures of goods and services, investment income coming back to the United Kingdom, and demand for UK assets of varying kinds.

Having seen the various types of exchange rates and the source of demand for currency, we next have to ask what determines foreign exchange movements.

Factors that determine foreign exchange movements

One of the major factors that determine what movements take place in exchange rates is the exchange rate system which is in force in the country. A variety of systems exist but they all have elements of the two extremes of the spectrum: fixed and floating exchange rates. These two will therefore be considered first.

Fixed and floating exchange rates

What determines the exchange rate under a floating exchange rate system is supply and demand for the currency, whereas under a fixed system it is the government that decides the rate of exchange. It has to be said that supply and demand still play a significant role under a fixed system, as if these are ignored and the currency becomes seriously out of line with the rate the market would determine, this would bring major problems for the government.

Taking floating exchange rates first; as stated above, the exchange rate is determined by the market, and how this works can be shown using a supply and demand diagram for the currency. Figure 5.3 shows demand for sterling in euroland. It needs to be noted that the exchange rate used on the vertical axis is expressed as the amount of foreign currency that can be purchased with one unit of domestic currency. So a movement down the axis suggests a reduction in the price of pounds (a depreciation of the pound), and a movement upward represents an appreciation in the value of the pound. For Europeans British goods are less expensive when the pound is weak and the euro is strong; in other words you get more pounds for your euros. So at a rate of £1 = €1 British goods are less expensive than at, say, £1 = €2. To take an example, if someone in Spain wanted to buy a car from a dealer in Oxford, UK, worth £6,000 and the exchange rate was €1 = £1, the car would cost the Spaniard €6,000. If however the rate was €1 = £2, it would only cost €3,000, so we would anticipate more cars and more sterling would be demanded. The demand curve would slope downwards.

The supply of sterling however comes from those wanting to sell sterling in exchange for euros; in other words UK businesses/individuals who want to buy cars from Spain will need to sell sterling in order to buy euros, therefore supplying the market. A Spanish car valued at €6,000 will cost £3,000 at £1 = €2 but will be much more expensive to UK consumers at £1 = €1, £6,000, because to buy every euro you would have to pay £1. So at the lower rates, there would be

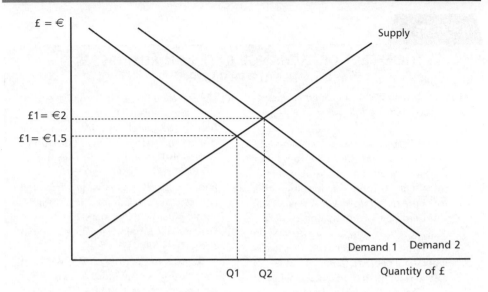

Figure 5.3 Floating exchange rates

less demand from the United Kingdom for euros and correspondingly less supply of sterling, and at a higher rate the exact opposite. The point where supply equals demand gives the exchange rate (see Figure 5.3).

Should there suddenly be an increase in demand for sterling (for example suddenly it becomes fashionable to own a new-style mini car), the demand curve will shift to the right and the exchange rate will change to £1 = €2 in Figure 5.3. Similarly if something should change the supply of sterling (or the demand for euros by sterling holders), then the supply curve will shift and change the exchange rate.

The exact size of the movements in the exchange rate will however depend on how responsive or sensitive UK and Spanish business are to changes in prices. If, for example, a small change in the exchange rate brings about a massive increase in demand for Spanish cars by UK consumers and a corresponding demand for euros, then this will affect the elasticity (and slope) of the supply curve. Similarly if Spanish consumers are responsive to changes in prices of UK cars as a result of exchange rate changes, this will change the elasticity of the demand for sterling; so a small change in the exchange rate can bring a massive change in demand for sterling. This is illustrated in the case study below.

With a fixed exchange rate system, this would be more complex. Under a fixed exchange rate system, the rate is set by the government and will not automatically adjust to changes in supply and demand. So taking the earlier pound/euro example, if we assume initially that the government sets the exchange rate where supply equals demand at the rate of £1 = €1.5, this will be fine until something happens to change the demand or supply of the currency. Let us say demand for sterling increased. The government would be forced to intervene in the market and to meet the excess demand (AB on Figure 5.4).

THE EFFECT OF EXCHANGE RATES ON BUSINESSES – THE US DOLLAR

On 20 February 2004, the *Guardian* newspaper reported the following:

> Carrie Bradshaw, the shopaholic heroine of *Sex and the City*, buys her Jimmy Choos on Madison Avenue. Now it is no longer a ridiculous idea for Britains to follow her lead. The standard pair of Jimmy Choo stilettos costs £360 in London. In New York, the same shoes retail at $575. At the wonderful new exchange rate of $1.90 to the pound, that's £302, a saving of £58. Buy a couple of pairs, throw in a handful of CDs, and maybe pick up an Apple iPod (£249 in UK, £158 in the US) and you've saved enough to pay for your flight and a couple of nights in a Manhattan hotel. These bargains on offer across the pond may be good news for shoppers, but firms in Britain and the eurozone watching their exports become more expensive for the American buyers are not so thrilled. The dollar's 20 per cent decline over the past year is causing alarm in European capitals.
>
> Not that these concerns appear to be weighing on the mind of the great British consumer. ... Lastminute.com ... sold 70 per cent more flights to New York in January [2004] than in December [2003]. ...Many of those making the trip say the chief appeal is bargains, even if they are 3,500 miles away. ... Virgin is feeling the beneficial effect of a weak dollar in many of its operations. Although the profits it earns in the US are worth less when translated into sterling, it thinks it is a net winner from the process. In recent weeks, for example, Virgin Atlantic's four daily flights from Orlando to Britain have been almost completely full. ...
>
> Of course the process also works in reverse – it is now more expensive for Americans to visit Britain. The fact is alarming the British tourist industry but Mr Whitehorn [a director of Virgin Group] thinks there is little reason to worry. 'Nobody in the US is in the least bit bothered about this', he says. 'Only 11 per cent of adult Americans have a passport after all. It's only rich Americans who go abroad and they are rich enough not to be too affected by this.'

Source: adapted from Pratley (2004).

Questions

1　Identify the differing effects the low dollar has had on US and UK businesses.
2　What does the article suggest about the elasticity of supply and demand for sterling and dollars?

It would do this by entering the market, buying euros with sterling, thereby supplying more sterling to meet the demand. Obviously the government could only do this for a limited time, and should the demand shift prove permanent it would have to consider changing the rate upwards, which is called **revaluation** of the pound, or revaluation of the exchange rate. If the demand or supply shift caused excess supply of pounds, then the government would in the short term intervene by buying sterling with its reserves of euros, but should this continue into the longer term, it would have to consider reducing the exchange rate, called **devaluation** of the pound, or devaluation of the exchange rate.

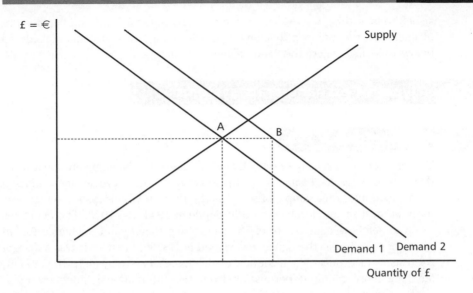

Figure 5.4 Fixed exchange rates

Advantages and disadvantages of floating and fixed exchange rates

The advantage of the floating exchange rate system is that the exchange rate continually adjusts to changes in the market. The government does not intervene and does not have to make decisions about what rate to set. It also allows countries to have differing rates of inflation and yet still remain competitive, as the exchange rate changes in order to counter these (see purchasing power parity later). Finally nowadays the problem of uncertainty can be overcome, at a small price, through the forward and **futures** markets.

Floating exchange rates are however much more volatile, partly as a result of speculative activity, and so lack the stability of fixed exchange rates. With fixed exchange rates the rate is known over a period of time, so providing businesses and individuals with stability and security in their dealings on the foreign exchange markets. This also means that domestic prices are less influenced by the variability of import prices and inflation is more a domestic policy issue. Further, fixed exchange rates force more discipline on government policy, as the government cannot undertake too radical or extreme policies as this may cause speculators to lose confidence in the currency, so reducing demand and forcing the government to either devalue or change course. This also means that it would be difficult to undertake substantially differing monetary or fiscal policies from other countries without the risk of a speculative run on the currency, which could be a problem for a country in real need of significant change.

Fixed exchange rate systems do require the government to keep substantial reserves in order to support their currency in the market (as seen above), and often even these cannot prevent a speculative run on the currency (see example on page 130). The other problem with fixed exchange rates are that they are often fixed for far too long. Therefore as a country changes in its economic structure over time, the exchange rate may not adjust for this and become out of line. This can be seen in many of the exchange rate systems considered below, especially where the fixed element dominates.

Other types of exchange rate systems

Adjustable peg system

This is when the exchange rate is fixed but allowed to be adjusted upwards or downwards when the balance of payments of the country proves unsustainable at the fixed rate. An example of this was the Bretton Woods system which was used by most of the developed world between 1944 and 1973. The countries involved set how many units of their currency they would exchange for an ounce of gold, but as the ounce was valued at US$35, in effect it was a system fixed against the dollar. Each country could change its rate by up to 10 per cent, anything more required permission from the International Monetary Fund (IMF), which required proof of some fundamental problem, mainly with the balance of payments. In the Bretton Woods system, the exchange rate was also allowed a small movement from the set, or 'par' value of +/– 1 per cent in any one year without permission. However the system in effect was very much fixed and lacked flexibility. In fact there were only six adjustments to the rates between 1947 and 1971, meaning the United Kingdom had the same set exchange rate between 1949 and 1967 while the economy changed radically (so reflecting the problem of structural change mentioned above) (Griffiths and Wall 2004).

Target zones

In target zone systems the exchange rate is fixed but allowed to fluctuate within certain bands around the fixed rate. A classic example of this was the Exchange Rate Mechanism (ERM) of the European Community, where the rates were set against the ECU (which gained its value from a weighted basket of EC currencies). Originally this set a target zone or divergence limit of +/–2.25 per cent for most currencies (although some more volatile ones were allowed a +/–6 per cent movement). Once the currency was within 75 per cent of the allowed movement (called the **divergence threshold**) the government had to intervene in the market (as described above) to prevent the rate moving outside the target.

The ERM was set up in 1979 and lasted until the single currency took over in 1999. It also provides a good example of one of the other problems of the fixed system, the need to support the currencies with reserves. In September 1992, sterling and the Italian lira came under severe speculative pressure to devalue their rates (and other countries such as Sweden, Finland and France also suffered strong pressure). The UK government was forced to borrow £7.25 billion in foreign currency, and on 16 September raised its interest rates by 2 per cent, followed by a further 3 per cent (to 15 per cent) to try to curb the pressure. However it was eventually forced to withdraw from the system (along with the lira) as the speculative pressure was too strong. The Bundesbank announced that it had used more than DM92 billion trying to defend sterling, the lira and the franc over the period (of approximately two weeks) (Griffiths and Wall 2004).

Currency boards

Here an institution is set up (but is distinct from the government) which exchanges domestic currency for foreign currency at fixed exchange rates. This is usually done for confidence reasons, taking the responsibility for the exchange rate out of the hands of the government and giving it to an independent currency board. It usually occurs in less-developed countries (LDCs), when the government is seen as unlikely to undertake policies that ensure currency stability. A potential difficulty with a currency board arises when the commitment to defend the fixed exchange rate means that the money supply has to be cut back, leading to a potential recession. This happened in Hong Kong in 1997 and Argentina in 2001. In Hong Kong the economic situation was sufficiently stable to allow the board to be maintained, but in Argentina problems were so severe that the currency board had to be abandoned.

Managed floating (sometimes called dirty floating)

Here ostensibly the exchange rate is left to float on the market, but the government sometimes chooses to intervene to 'manage' the rate and prevent it falling or rising unacceptably. Often this form of floating is adopted because the government wants to push the exchange rate in a particular direction for policy reasons or wants it to move in a more orderly fashion, preventing too much volatility.

Now we have considered the relative movements of fixed and floating systems, we need to consider what lies behind changes in exchange rates.

Theories of exchange rate determination

Purchasing power parity

The simplest theory of what determines the nominal exchange rate is known as **purchasing power parity (PPP)**. This starts from the principle that, measured in a common currency, traded goods should cost the same wherever they are bought across the world. So if a camera costs US$100 in New York and €80 in Paris, then the dollar–euro exchange rate (E) must be 1.25 (note that we are defining (E) here as the home country price of a unit of foreign currency and taking USA to be the home country). In this case a French citizen can either buy the camera for €80 at home, or convert his or her funds into US$100, since 0.8 euros are required to buy one dollar, and buy the camera for the same amount of money in the United States. If a camera were to cost €100 in Paris, everyone in France would import their cameras from the United States, since they can buy a camera there by converting just €80 and so save €20 on each transaction.

If such a situation were to arise then France would run a trade deficit in cameras with the United States. Consequently, if cameras represent a significant enough part of the trade between the two countries, then this deficit would increase the supply of euros on the foreign exchange markets, as French people sold euros for dollars to buy imported cameras. An increase in the supply of euros would lower the value of euros relative to dollars. Given the way we have defined the exchange rate, such a lowering of the value of the euro would raise (E), until it reached a rate of 1, at which point the cameras would again be equal in price, measured in a single currency. So the exchange rate will change to keep prices the same. Figure 5.5 shows the effect of such an increase in the supply of euros.

Clearly, we need to extend this argument beyond the case of just one good, so the PPP hypothesis is normally stated in terms of a representative basket of goods. We say that absolute PPP holds if such a basket costs the same across different countries (again when measured in a common currency). This is sometimes referred to as the 'Law of one price'. In the real world prices may not be brought exactly into line in this way because of transport costs, and so the argument above is generally taken to lead to the approximate equality of prices rather than exact equality.

If we take P to be the price of such a basket of goods in the home country and P* to be the price of the basket abroad (measured in foreign currency), then absolute PPP says that $P = E.P^*$ or alternatively $E = P/P^*$. However, extending the model to a basket of goods leads to a number of complications. Two of these are especially important. First, when the relative prices of goods in the basket move in opposite directions then the exchange rate between two countries may change even though the overall price level remains constant in each country. Generally, the currency of the country where the

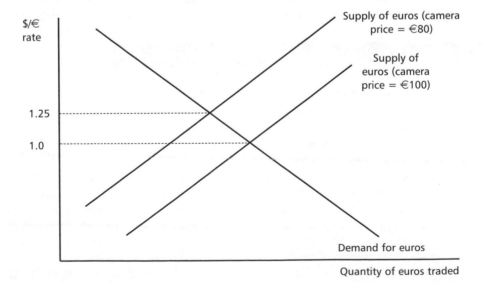

Figure 5.5 The market for euros

goods which are increasing in price are consumed most heavily will tend to rise in value.[4] Second, consumers not only consume goods traded across national boundaries, they also consume services which cannot be exported or imported, for example haircuts or music lessons. If the relative productivity in the traded goods sector between two countries differs more than the relative productivity in the production of non-traded services, then the exchange rate will appear to differ from its PPP value.

This result is known as the Balassa-Samuelson effect. The reasoning behind it is as follows. For two countries like the United States and China the exchange rate, if it is allowed to float, will be determined by the relative prices of traded goods, predominantly manufactured goods. However, non-traded services will be much cheaper in comparison to traded goods in China than in the United States, because productivity is relatively higher in that sector (it takes the same amount of time to cut someone's hair or give them a lesson in both countries), while wages are assumed to be the same across both sectors, and to be lower in both in China than in the United States. Consequently, a unit of Chinese currency will buy more goods and services in China than the equivalent amount of US currency will buy in the United States. The purchasing power of the Chinese yuan will exceed that of the dollar, and so the yuan will appear to be undervalued relative to its PPP value.

Such issues mean that absolute PPP is rarely used in empirical studies, and such studies focus more on relative PPP. The relative PPP hypothesis is that changes in the exchange rate are determined by relative inflation rates, so that if Δp is the home inflation rate and Δp^* is the foreign inflation rate, then $\Delta e = \Delta p - \Delta p^*$. So the change in the exchange rate Δe will equal the difference in inflation rates, $\Delta p - \Delta p^*$. Empirical work using relative PPP normally measures the values of these variables in logarithms, and this is why they have been written in lower case. The advantage of doing this is that the change in the logarithm of a particular variable is the same as the proportional or percentage change in the variable itself, so that by looking, say, at the change in the logarithm of the price level, we obtain the inflation rate.

When testing whether relative PPP holds empirically or not, economists have tended to focus on the RER. This is because the RER as defined above equals P/P.*E, and since relative PPP says that any changes in P* relative to P (for example if there is a faster or slower inflation rate abroad than at home) will induce exactly offsetting changes in E, it must be the case that if relative PPP holds, the RER will be constant (if absolute PPP holds, then since E = P/P*, the RER has to equal 1). Consequently, we can test for relative PPP by looking at the stability of the RER.

There have been a very large number of such tests, from the early years of the widespread adoption of floating exchange rates in 1973 onwards.[5] Initial tests were unable to reject the hypothesis that RERs followed a '**random walk**'. This is a time series where the best estimate of any future value of the relevant variable at any point is that it should remain at its current level. In other words, far from remaining constant, or reverting back to the PPP level after some kind of shock (for example changes in demand or supply conditions), as relative PPP predicts, RERs showed no tendency at all to 'recover' from such shocks. Once the RER has changed there appear to be no forces pushing it back to its previous level, and so over time it would be likely to diverge continuously from that level as a result of various economic developments.

Later studies, however, have found that RERs do tend to revert back to their mean (average) values, but only slowly. These tests are seen as superior to previous studies because they either use longer runs of data (up to two centuries in some cases) or test several exchange rates simultaneously in what are known as 'panel data' studies (as opposed to the earlier 'bivariate' tests which just looked at two currencies at any one time). Repeated testing along these lines saw economists in the 1990s arrive at a consensus that if a shock results in the exchange rate moving away from its PPP value, half of the divergence will be eliminated in three to five years through reversion back towards the mean.

While these results were more encouraging for the PPP hypothesis than the previous studies, writers like Rogoff (1996) pointed out that the very slow response to shocks indicated by such figures did not sit easily with the tremendous volatility of RERs in the short run. Given the speed with which rates adjust from day to day it is not clear why they are so slow to move back to their PPP levels. In addition, the long-run tests mentioned above have been questioned because they use data from both fixed and floating-rate periods in the international monetary system, while the panel data tests are somewhat restrictive in that they reject the random walk model if only one of the several exchange rate series involved in the test does not follow such a pattern, leaving open the possibility that all the rest may be plausibly described in that way.

Rogoff concludes his study by suggesting that PPP does not hold, except perhaps in the very long run, because of barriers to the integration of international markets:

> One is left with a conclusion that would certainly make the godfather of purchasing power parity, Gustav Cassel, roll over in his grave. It is simply this: international goods markets, though becoming more integrated all the time, remain quite segmented, with large trading frictions across a broad range of goods. … [I]nternational goods markets are highly integrated, but not yet nearly as integrated as domestic goods markets. This is not an entirely comfortable conclusion, but for now there is no really satisfactory alternative explanation to the purchasing power parity puzzle.
>
> (Rogoff 1996: 665)

Taylor and Taylor argue that one possible resolution of the puzzle lies in allowing the RER to adjust in a non-linear way. Rather than assuming a constant speed of adjustment back towards the PPP level, they argue that the rapidity of movement of the rate will depend very much on how large the deviation from that level is. If the deviation is large enough to allow profits from **arbitrage** in trading goods, then movement back towards PPP may be quite fast, but if the deviation is smaller there may be little or no movement because trading costs make arbitrage unprofitable. Tests using this kind of approach (known as 'threshold autoregressive' models) generally find much shorter half-lives for movement back towards PPP than conventional tests (Taylor and Taylor 2004).

However, as Taylor and Taylor point out, even if PPP does appear plausible on this basis as a theory governing exchange rates in the medium run, the large short-run movements in both nominal and real rates remain an issue demanding explanation.

Monetary models of the exchange rate

The issue of short-run exchange rate volatility was also taken up soon after the move to floating rates, since movements in rates from the late 1970s onwards were much larger than had been expected by those influenced by writers like Milton Friedman, who had argued that floating rate systems would be essentially stable (Friedman 1953). At this time a dominant influence in macroeconomics generally was monetarism, and the models used to explain the exchange rate tended to adopt a monetarist framework of analysis. In particular, they added a theory of what determined prices to the PPP hypothesis that exchange rates depended on relative price levels. This theory was based on the quantity theory of money, which saw prices as dependent on the money supply, with output fixed in the short and medium run, and only changing slowly over time in response to supply-side factors. The monetarists also added a new emphasis on the capital or financial account of the balance of payments in affecting exchange rates, and so laid considerable stress on the importance of interest rates in exchange rate determination.

Early monetarist models assumed that prices adjusted immediately to changes in the money supply and that exchange rates followed suit, through the PPP mechanism, and so these models were unable to explain the short-run divergences from PPP that occurred in the late 1970s. However, a more influential approach was adopted by Dornbusch in his 'overshooting' model (Dornbusch 1976), which has been seen as the most important model in international finance of the last 30 years.[6] In order to understand the Dornbusch model however, it is necessary to look a bit more closely at the conditions for equilibrium in the international capital markets, and in particular at what are known as interest parity conditions.

Interest parity conditions

In the simplest monetary models of exchange rates, it is assumed that capital mobility creates a common world interest rate. Clearly though, in reality different countries have different interest rates, and so it becomes necessary to look at the impact of this on flows of capital across national boundaries. Three equilibrium conditions have been derived as ways of describing this impact.

The first of these is covered interest parity (CIP). This starts from the insight that someone needing a particular sum, say €1 million, at a definite point in time, for example next year, has two ways of ensuring that he or she will have access to the necessary funds. The person could invest a sufficient number of euros now at the ruling rate of interest to ensure he or she will have the money next year. If the interest rate is 10 per cent then it will be necessary to set aside €909,000. An alternative is to convert the euros currently held into a foreign currency, for example dollars, and sell sufficient dollars in the forward market at the forward exchange rate (F) to ensure that they will produce €1 million the next year.

If capital markets are competitive both strategies must give the same return and so must require the same initial sum of money. For example if the second strategy offers higher returns, everyone will start following it and selling dollars forward, so pushing the price of euros in the forward market up until the two approaches are brought into line. In a similar way, if the first strategy offers higher returns the supply of dollars in the forward market will decline, pushing the forward price of euros down and again equalising returns across the two strategies. The money obtained from the first strategy is $(1+i).909,000$ euros where i is the home (European) interest rate. The money obtained from the second strategy is $F/E.(1+i^*)909,000$ where i^* is the foreign (US) interest rate. Thus, the CIP condition is that $(1+i)=F/E.(1+i^*)$.

The second condition is that of uncovered interest parity (UIP), according to which any interest rate differential must be balanced by an offsetting expected change in the exchange rate; so that $\Delta e = i - i^*$. Consequently UIP does not require analysis of the forward or futures markets. The reasoning behind UIP is that foreign exchange traders will take returns in the form of either income or capital gains, and if, say, euro interest rates are higher than foreign interest rates, then it must be the case that the euro is expected to go down in value (that is, that e is expected to rise). If this is not so, everyone will start to buy euros, pushing up the value of the currency until it has reached the point at which it is expected to fall by an amount equivalent to the interest rate differential, at which time no further arbitrage profits can be made.

A third condition is real interest parity (RIP). This begins from the definition of the real interest rate (r) as being equal to the nominal interest rate (i) minus the expected rate of inflation Δp^e. Rearranging this we find that for the home country, $i = r + \Delta p^e$. Correspondingly for a foreign country (or more broadly for the rest of the world), $i^* = r^* + \Delta p^{e*}$ and so $(i - i^*) = (r - r^*) + (\Delta p^e - \Delta p^{e*})$. If we then assume that real interest rates are equal across countries, it follows that $(i - i^*) = (\Delta p^e - \Delta p^{e*})$, and if we then combine this with UIP, we obtain $\Delta e = (\Delta p^e - \Delta p^{e*})$, which is the RIP condition.

An immense amount of effort has gone into testing these various parity conditions. CIP appears to be quite well supported by the data, although it is possible that this result only emerges because forward traders set their prices by reference to CIP, so that it does not actually tell us very much about capital mobility.[7] On the other hand UIP and RIP do not seem to be confirmed by empirical evidence.[8] Three possible reasons have been put forward for this, with special reference to UIP. First, capital movements may not simply be determined by income and the prospect of capital gains, but may also depend upon the perceived risk of particular currencies (so that a risk premium is demanded for holding them). Second, tests of UIP always depend on some kind of hypothesis about how expectations are formed. The most commonly used approach has been to assume 'rational expectations', in which expectations are on average correct, but this may not in fact be the case. Third, if speculative 'noise' traders are active in the currency markets, their trades may influence capital movements away from levels consistent with UIP.

With these interest parity conditions in mind it is now possible to return to considering Dornbusch's extension to monetary models of the exchange rate.

The Dornbusch 'overshooting' model

Dornbusch added two things to the monetarist model of the exchange rate. First he assumed that, while asset prices adjust instantaneously to ensure equilibrium, goods prices only move slowly; in other words goods markets are typified by 'sticky prices'. These are a result of long-run contracts, informational problems and related matters. Second, Dornbusch adopted the hypothesis of 'rational expectations', according to which, on average, the expectations formed by economic agents correspond to the 'true' economic model governing the markets in which they participate. The consequence of this hypothesis is that agents never systematically over-predict or under-predict the levels of variables. In fact, for simplicity, Dornbusch went further than this and assumed 'perfect foresight' so that market participants always expect the correct result, not just on average. This however is not essential for his result.

Dornbusch's argument was as follows. Suppose the government cuts the money supply in order to damp down demand. In the medium run this will lower prices, leaving all other variables unchanged. However, in the short run prices do not adjust, so the real money supply (M/P) falls, and this leads to a rise in interest rates.

Dornbusch assumes that PPP will hold in the long run, so the cut in the money supply, which will eventually cut prices, will lower (e) and strengthen the currency. However in the short run, since interest rates at home exceed those abroad, (e) must be expected to rise in order to maintain UIP. We appear to have a paradoxical situation in which (e) must fall in the long run but rise in the short run. The solution to the paradox is that (e) will initially fall very sharply, 'overshooting' its new equilibrium value, and will then rise gradually up to that new value as domestic prices adjust to the new level of the money supply. The time-path of the exchange rate in the overshooting model is shown in Figure 5.6.

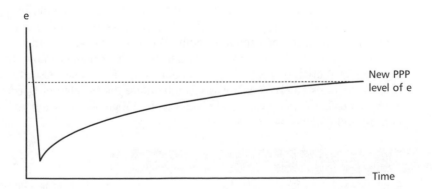

Figure 5.6 Time path of the exchange rate in the Dornbusch overshooting model

At every point UIP holds, since as prices gradually fall, the real money supply expands and so interest rates drop back to their original level. As interest rates decline, the rise in (e) required to ensure that UIP obtains becomes less and less. Eventually, when (e) has reached the PPP value, interest rates will be back at their original point and there will be no further requirement for the exchange rate to change. Of course in the real world we actually observe cuts in the rate of growth of the money supply and in the inflation rate, rather than cuts in the level of money and prices. However the overshooting model can easily accommodate this with a slight increase in complexity.[9]

Dornbusch's model was extremely attractive in general terms as an explanation for the short-run movements in exchange rates. It was able to explain both the volatility of rates around a long-run equilibrium PPP value and the fact that, for much of the time, rates seemed to move in the opposite direction to that predicted by PPP, with (e) rising at the same time as the inflation rate was falling. More specifically, the model was able to explain the dramatic rises in the value of sterling in 1979 and in the value of the dollar in 1981 as a result of the monetarist policies of the Thatcher and Reagan governments, which led to high interest rates and consequent recessions, partly as a result of currency appreciation.

However, the model has fared much less well empirically since that period.[10] In particular, it is hard to explain the continuing rise in the value of the dollar through the four years from 1981 to 1985, which occurred at a time of record US current account deficits, as a consequence of overshooting. This is because exchange rates that have risen through overshooting are supposed to drop back to their new equilibrium value, not to continue gradually rising for several years.

In addition, the overshooting hypothesis is vulnerable to a number of theoretical objections. It relies on the assumption of UIP, but as we have seen most empirical tests of UIP show it to be conclusively rejected by the data. As a related point the hypothesis uses only a very limited menu of assets. Since UIP is deemed to hold, so that the choice between home and foreign bonds depends only on interest rate differentials and there is no risk premium attached to investing in a particular country, Dornbusch is implicitly assuming that all bonds are perfect substitutes. This means that the model looks at just two assets, money and bonds. In addition, the model goes to the other extreme from PPP with regard to the balance of payments. While PPP analyses just flows of goods through the current account, Dornbusch just looks at flows of investment through the financial or capital account. Yet, it can be argued that long-run current account deficits or surpluses will in turn affect financial flows by altering the distribution of wealth between countries.[11] For these reasons portfolio balance theories emerged as a way of embedding the insights of Dornbusch's work in a broader framework, including a wider range of assets and linking the current and financial accounts.

Portfolio balance and currency substitution

Currency substitution models start from the premise that individuals do not just hold one currency as an asset, but hold a portfolio of currencies between which they can shift quite quickly in response to economic variables.[12] As a result currencies can overshoot their long-term PPP values but for a different reason than in the Dornbusch model. Suppose the European Central Bank increases the money supply. The long-run effect of this will be a rise in prices and so a rise in the euro exchange rate (in other words a weakening of the euro). In the short run, however, those holding the euro will switch rapidly to holding their wealth in foreign currencies, say dollars, because they will anticipate a capital gain in the future when the euro's value has gone down and they can sell these dollars back for euros. The result of this will be a rapid decline in the value of the euro and a current account surplus for the euro-zone countries as their goods become more competitive. The current account surplus will gradually push up the value of the euro until it reaches its long-run equilibrium. This will be at a higher exchange rate than the original position, but not at such a high one as that reached immediately after the money supply increase.

Portfolio balance models can be seen as the mirror image of currency substitution models. While currency substitution considers choices between a single type of bond and two kinds of money, foreign and domestic, portfolio balance looks at the situation where households and firms hold only domestic money but can hold both domestic and foreign bonds (see Dornbusch and Fischer 1980). These models look at a variety of possible policy decisions, and again show how overshooting results can arise for very different reasons than in the original Dornbusch model.

One commonly cited example is an 'open-market operation' where the central bank purchases bonds from the public, thereby increasing the money supply. The immediate effect of this will be that there is more money in the economy than households wish to hold. Consequently, at any given interest rate there will have to be an increase in the price level to persuade them to hold the extra money, since it is generally assumed that higher prices raise money demand proportionately. This can be brought about by an increase in the exchange rate, which raises import prices. The mechanism that brings about this increase in the exchange rate is increased demand for foreign bonds, as households try to rebalance their asset portfolios. The rise in the rate leads to a current account surplus. The transfer of wealth as a result of the surplus boosts the demand for money and brings the exchange rate back down, but again not as far as the original level before the money supply increase.

Portfolio balance and currency substitution models are thus able to explain the volatility of short-run exchange rates around their longer-term PPP values. In addition, they tend to show currencies strengthening in value when a current account surplus is being achieved. This was attractive in explaining the trends of the 1960s and 1970s when countries like Japan and West Germany, which had such surpluses, also had strong currencies. However, both kinds of model were less successful in explaining later developments, in particular the rise of the dollar in the first half of the 1980s. In addition, the quantitative significance of foreign currency holdings has been questioned, although it has also been suggested that if the euro comes to challenge the dollar as an international reserve currency, then currency substitution might come to be an important and potentially destabilising feature of a world with two such currencies rather than one (Portes and Rey 1998).

Empirical challenges and new developments

In 1983 the monetary and portfolio balance models of the exchange rate and the Dornbusch model were all dealt a severe blow by the empirical tests of Meese and Rogoff (1983). Meese and Rogoff estimated coefficients for variants of each of these three kinds of model on data from 1973 to 1980, and then used the estimated equations to forecast exchange rates for 1981 and 1982. (Of course the actual values of the rates for those years were known and could be compared against the forecasts.) They compared the forecasts obtained from these 'sophisticated' exchange rate models with those generated by a simple random walk model, and found that in almost every case the theoretical models did significantly worse than the random walk. The implication was that no short-run or medium-run theory of exchange rate determination could claim to be supported by the evidence.

There have been three main responses to the Meese–Rogoff critique of exchange rate modelling. First, it has been pointed out in subsequent studies that over a time horizon of more than three years, theoretical models do outperform a random walk. However, this is not terribly encouraging if such models aspire to be useful practically, since in practice foreign exchange traders will be operating over much shorter time periods than three years. Second, some writers have argued that recent developments in econometric techniques invalidate the Meese–Rogoff results (Hallwood and MacDonald 2000). Third, there have been various attempts to develop alternative theoretical models of exchange rates. Examples here include models of 'rational speculative bubbles' (Hallwood and MacDonald 2000), De Grauwe's attempt to use a model of 'near-rationality' in exchange rate expectations and to bring this together with approaches based on chaos theory (De Grauwe 1996), and general equilibrium models of the exchange rate. These last start from the presumption that, instead of looking at the foreign trade sector and the exchange rate from the basis of a pre-existing level of domestic output and prices, we should construct models in which exchange rates and output are determined simultaneously. Two important approaches here are the flexible price models of Stockman (1980) and Lucas (1982) and the 'redux' model of Obstfeld and Rogoff (1995), which allows more of a role for sticky prices and market frictions (Copeland 2005).

European monetary union

Optimum currency areas and the rationale for a single currency

The unexpected volatility of exchange rates after the shift to floating rates in 1973 led to a revival of interest in fixed rate systems of various kinds, including the European Monetary System (EMS) which was initiated in 1979. The project of European monetary union (EMU) is the most developed example of this. In order to analyse the rationale for EMU, it is necessary to look at both the costs and benefits of monetary union.

The main cost of monetary union for a participating country is the loss of the exchange rate as a policy instrument. If a country, say France, has its own currency, it can respond to an economic 'shock', such as an unexpected decline in demand for its exports in foreign markets, by devaluing the currency in order to make those exports cheaper and so more attractive. If devaluation is ruled out by a common currency, either France will have to take domestic policy measures to rectify the situation (for example anti-inflationary policies) or its trading partners will have to help out (say by boosting demand in their economies), or French workers in export industries will risk losing their jobs. In such circumstances the most problematic shocks are so-called 'asymmetric shocks' which affect different countries unequally. For example, if there is a generalised decline in demand in both France and Germany which lowers demand for French exports to Germany, the German government is likely to take action to boost demand at home which will help French exporters among others. However, if the decline in demand only affects French goods, so that German consumers shift their preferences away from such goods towards other products without lowering the overall level of demand in Germany, then the German government is much less likely to be prepared to reflate the economy.

The theory of '**optimal currency areas**' (OCAs) was developed by Mundell (1961), Kenen (1969) and McKinnon (1963) to analyse the costs arising from currency unions. An OCA exists if the structure of the participating countries is such as to make the loss of the exchange rate as a policy instrument relatively unproblematic. Four main conditions have been put forward for this to be the case.[13] First, the higher the degree of labour and capital mobility in response to asymmetric shocks, the more likely it is that an OCA will exist. For example, in the simplest case, if demand for French exports goes down but French people are quite happy to migrate to Germany and work there, then the costs of currency union will be minimised. Second, the more open the participating countries are and the more diversified their trade structures, the greater the chance of an OCA existing. The more varied the exports of a country are, the lower the chance that a significant proportion of them will be hit by a particular shock. Third, the existence of an OCA is aided by similar policy preferences among participating countries. If one country is highly reluctant to boost demand owing to a strongly anti-inflationary policy bias while another sees avoiding unemployment as its chief priority, then the chances of asymmetric economic outcomes are magnified. Finally, fiscal transfers between countries, so that declines in demand can be mitigated by increased public spending, will aid the development of an OCA.

There is general agreement that neither at the time of the Maastricht Treaty in 1991 nor at the launch of the euro in 1999, did the euro-zone constitute an optimum currency area. While the countries involved were relatively open economies and there is considerable evidence of convergence on common economic policies over the 1980s and 1990s (partly in fact because of preparations for EMU), fiscal transfers in response to differential shocks remain minimal compared with those within national economies, and there is much less labour mobility between euro-zone countries than there is within each country. Indeed, since the euro has been established there have been quite wide divergences in the economic performance of the participating countries, which in the absence of the possibility of exchange rate changes have led to considerable economic pressures, as shown in the case study below. The argument for EMU, then, has to involve either the view that the conditions for an OCA will arise as a result of monetary union rather than pre-exist as a condition for it (in other words they are 'endogenous' to the monetary union process) or the view that the relatively high costs of EMU are outweighed by even greater benefits.

The first of these views could be justified by a number of arguments. One claim might be that EMU, by deepening the general process of European integration, will in turn increase labour mobility across Europe – and indeed the preparations for EMU did involve dismantling of capital controls and so the creation of conditions for capital mobility. Another might be that increased trade will reduce the likelihood of asymmetric shocks as the economies of the various countries become more intertwined. However, a counter-argument to this could point to the possibility of trade encouraging specialisation in particular products by countries, and leading to an increased vulnerability to shocks affecting those products. More generally, it may be that some of those proposing EMU did so partly in the belief that the difficulties caused by monetary union without fiscal transfers would in turn spur later movement towards a common European fiscal policy, in the same way as the Single European Act of 1986 encouraged subsequent moves towards a common currency to 'complete the single market'.

There are a number of important benefits to monetary union which can be set against the costs (de Grauwe 2003). First, a common currency reduces transaction costs, especially for households. Second, by creating price transparency it will increase competition and so potentially benefit consumers. Third, the elimination of exchange rate risk can benefit both providers and users of funds, lowering the cost of capital and allowing businesses to plan for the long term. Larger companies may already have obtained at least some of these benefits through the use of hedging instruments, but such instruments are often expensive or unobtainable for smaller firms. Fourth, it has increasingly been argued that monetary union (or, in the case of developing economies, adoption of the currency of a larger economy, as in so-called 'dollarisation'), now represents the only realistic alternative to floating exchange rates, so that if floating exchange rates are seen as undesirable, monetary union becomes consequently more attractive.

The argument here is that fixed exchange rates provide important benefits in terms both of economic stability and the credibility of anti-inflationary policies, especially if the currency is tied to the currency of another country with a strong record of keeping prices down. In the case of the European Union the relevant example is the role of Germany within the European monetary system, where fixing exchange rates (with a certain amount of movement up or down allowed) against the Deutschmark allowed other countries to benefit from the record of the Bundesbank in limiting inflationary pressures. However, as was seen in the crises of the ERM in 1992 and 1993 (referred to above), fixed exchange rates can become a one-way bet for speculators. If a currency is fixed against, say, the mark, but a devaluation is expected, then there is no incentive whatsoever for speculators to hold that currency, since the worst that can happen if they sell is that the devaluation will not take place and they will lose the transaction costs associated with the sale. On the other hand, if devaluation does occur they will make a profit. Consequently, it appears that in a world of highly mobile capital a small loss of confidence in a currency in a fixed exchange rate system can easily turn into a fully fledged crisis. As a result, after 1993 many European policy makers came to feel that the only way to ensure the benefits of fixed rates was to ensure that the market would not believe in the possibility of rates changing under any circumstances, and that monetary union was the only way to do this.

A subsidiary reason for adopting monetary union, which was linked with this, was the desire to have a more 'equal' relationship between the various currencies, rather than a system dominated by the mark. The EMS was effectively a set of bilateral exchange rates, in which each currency was pegged against the mark, so that, given the size and credibility of the German economy and central bank, all other countries ended up adjusting their monetary policies to keep in step with German policies. EMU provided a framework within which monetary policy would, at least in principle, be decided jointly by all participants. This caused some concern to the Bundesbank, which was instrumental in ensuring that the operation of EMU was governed by strict limits on government borrowing by individual countries, set down first in the 'convergence critieria' of the Maastricht Treaty and later in the 1997 Stability and Growth Pact. Ironically, Germany has turned out to be one of those countries participating in EMU that has had most trouble in meeting these limits.

Case study 5.2

REAL EXCHANGE RATES IN THE EURO-ZONE

The introduction of the euro has permanently fixed the nominal or money exchange rates of the 12 participating countries against each other. However, their real exchange rates can still vary. The *Economist* (in February 2005) reported on the changes in European real exchange rates since 1999. The European Commission calculates real effective exchange rates for euro-area countries against other member countries and against a basket of external currencies on a quarterly basis. The difficult issue is choosing which index of prices or costs to use. The Commission actually publishes five indices, based on consumer prices, the GDP deflator, export prices, unit wage costs in manufacturing, and unit labour costs across the whole economy. Most economists believe that there are problems in using export prices and consumer prices, and that relative unit labour costs provide the best measure of underlying international competitiveness.

At the time of the launch of the single currency, Germany's unit labour costs were the highest in the euro area, but from 1999 to 2005 they fell by 10 per cent relative to the average. However, the relative unit labour costs of Italy, Spain and the Netherlands rose by 9 per cent over the same period. Ireland and Portugal also saw rises in labour costs which exceeded the average. In addition to this Germany has boasted faster growth in labour productivity than the euro-area average.

We have also seen considerable variation in the effective exchange rate of individual euro-zone economies against the rest of the world. These reflect differences in both inflation and the geographic spread of trade, which affects the relative weight of particular currencies in the basket used to calculate the effective rate for each country. From early 2002 to early 2005 the US dollar fell by 50 per cent against the euro. However, the euro's real trade-weighted exchange rate only rose by 18 per cent, based on relative unit labour costs. (Note that the figures used in the article are based on defining the nominal exchange rate as the foreign currency price of a unit of home currency, so that a rise in the real exchange rate indicates a loss of competitiveness.) Germany's RER has risen by only 4 per cent since early 2002, France's by 9 per cent and those of Italy and Ireland by 17 per cent. In fact each individual European country has seen a smaller rise in the RER than the euro-zone has experienced as a whole. This is because the rates for individual countries are calculated by including trade with other euro-zone countries in the basket, while the rate for the euro-zone as a whole just uses trade with external countries, and so the declining dollar has a higher weight in the aggregate figure.

These figures have interesting implications for the theory that the declining dollar will weaken European business. In fact, from 2000 to 2005 German exports held up strongly, growing by almost 40 per cent in volume terms. As of spring 2005 Germany was the only G7 country to have increased its share of world exports over the previous five years. The *Economist* concludes by

commenting that 'the popular notion that high wage costs have left Germany uncompetitive no longer seems to be true. Alas, it could take some time before the gains feed through to household incomes and spending, and spur the German economy to grow again' (2005a: 82).

Source: *Economist* (2005a: 82).

Questions

1 Why do you think German labour costs grew more slowly over this time period than those in other European countries?

2 What do the changes described in the case study imply about the relationship of the nominal exchange rate of the euro to its PPP value? Are the developments in the article consistent with the theory of PPP?

3 On the basis of what happened to the real exchange rate of the euro over the time period described in the case study, what would you expect to have happened to the nominal value of the euro from spring 2005 onwards? Do your predictions coincide with what did actually happen?

The international role of the euro

Another reason for EMU was the desire to create a new international currency to rival the dollar. Indeed, writing in 1999, Wyplosz observed that:

> The international role of the euro is the hidden agenda of Europe's long-planned adoption of a single currency. Some Europeans long to regain monetary leadership, either for political symbolism or because they believe that it is financially profitable. Some in the USA are concerned for exactly symmetric reasons.
>
> (Wyplosz 1999: 76)

In order to assess the realism of this objective, it is first necessary to look at what an international currency is. One approach to this (Krugman 1991) is to start from the three basic functions of money: as a means of payment, store of value and unit of account. An international currency will have a private role corresponding to these functions, which is similar to the private use of a national currency; it will be used in the settlement of international transactions, it will be held by companies, households and financial institutions as an asset, and financial and other markets will make quotations in that currency. However, an international currency will also have a distinctive official role: it will be used for official interventions in the foreign exchange markets, other currencies will have their values pegged against it, and it will form an important component of official reserves.

It is not at all clear exactly how large the benefits of having an international currency are for the issuing region. Portes and Rey (1998) quote a number of authors who believe that such a development confers significant political power. Wyplosz (1999) sees the main benefit as being decreased transaction costs for domestic residents in their international dealings. A more vexed question is that of 'seigniorage'. There is a common view that the United States has derived benefits from having an international currency insofar as this has allowed it to run a deficit on the current account of the balance of payments through printing money in order to pay for imports. As dollars are treated as an acceptable international means of payment, the United States is not subject to the same foreign exchange constraints as other countries. However, the situation is not quite as simple as this. While other countries do hold foreign exchange reserves denominated in dollars, allowing US import purchases as described above, these reserves mainly take the form of treasury bills on which the US government has to pay interest. Wyplosz also makes the point that, while the stock of dollars held abroad amounts to some US$250 billion, or 3.3 per cent of US GDP, this has accumulated over a long period of time. Annual seigniorage revenues amount to some 0.2 per cent of GDP (Wyplosz 1999).

The role of an international currency also carries with it some disadvantages, notably potential instability of money demand owing to currency substitution (as described above) and also the danger of banking and financial problems involving the currency arising outside the area of home country supervision.

Assuming for the moment that the role of an international currency is a desirable one, the next question is, what determines whether a currency assumes this role or not? One possible determinant is the share of the issuing region in world trade. Here the euro-zone is roughly comparable to the United States. The value of international loans and foreign bank holdings as a percentage of GDP was again approximately comparable for the Deutschmark and the dollar in the mid-1990s. However, the main influence on whether a currency becomes international or not, according to Portes and Rey, is the level of transaction costs in the financial markets. This argument is based on what is known as the 'vehicle currency hypothesis'. This states that currencies assume an international role when it becomes cheaper for trade between two other countries to take place using the international currency as a medium than through direct currency exchange. For example, if transaction costs for sterling–euro exchanges and for euro–Swiss franc exchanges are each lower than for sterling–Swiss franc exchanges, trade between the United Kingdom and Switzerland may be settled in euros. The complicating factor here is that such transaction costs themselves depend on the volume of trade in particular currencies, which in turn depends upon the international status or otherwise of those currencies. In this way this status can become 'history dependent' or subject to 'hysteresis', with an international currency exhibiting low transaction costs which in turn reinforce its international role. Shifts between currencies then come to depend on significant external factors such as the two world wars, which led to the replacement of sterling by the dollar as international money.

Using this framework, Portes and Rey (1998) derived a number of different estimates of the euro's international role based on varying assumptions about the elasticity of transaction costs with respect to trading volumes, and about the degree of financial market integration within Europe. They concluded that the euro was quite likely to become a serious international challenger to the dollar, and to be the main currency for US–Europe and Asia–Europe exchanges, but not for US–Asia exchanges. They also argued that this would generate significant welfare gains for Europe, mainly through increased efficiency and decreasing costs in the bond markets.

The first major study of international trading activity following the introduction of the euro was carried out by Hau, Killeen and Moore (2002). They looked at the difference between buying and selling prices for the euro (the 'bid–ask **spread**') as a measure of transaction costs, and at trading volumes, and compared these with previous figures for the Deutschmark. Their study was based on triennial survey data from the Bank for International Settlements (BIS) for April 1998 and April 2001, and on more frequent data from the Electronic Broking System (EBS) and Reuters for the 1998 and 1999 calendar years.

The findings of the Hau, Killeen and Moore study were very striking. According to their data, trading volumes for the euro were not as high as for the mark and transaction costs were higher. For example in April 1998 the mark had 26.7 per cent of global forex (foreign exchange) turnover, and the other 'legacy' currencies (in other words those currencies later unified within the euro) had 17.6 per cent, making a total of 44.3 per cent, but three years later the euro had a share of just 37.5 per cent. The explanation put forward by Hau and colleagues was that forex traders actually preferred to operate in a multiplicity of currencies because currency unification increases market **transparency.** This in turn raises the possibility of other traders correctly anticipating the future trades of their competitors and opportunistically trying to exploit this knowledge to make profits. Such behaviour will raise inventory costs for traders in general.

These results appear at first sight to constitute a significant challenge to those like Portes and Rey who see the euro as a potential international currency. Consequently, they have been heavily criticised by Portes and others (Honohan 2002, Franks 2002, Portes 2002). Three main points have been raised. First, EBS data only covers a small part of the foreign exchange market. Second, the BIS data is not reliable because it includes derivatives trades (see Chapter 8) which may be determined by different factors than spot trading in foreign exchange. Third, the decline in trading volume when the euro was introduced appears to have been a temporary phenomenon which has now been reversed. As a result the question of the scope of the euro's future international role remains open.

A final important question concerns the relationship between the possible international role of the euro and the potential strength of the euro, especially with regard to its value against the US dollar and the yen. On the one hand Portes and Rey suggest that if the euro becomes an international currency, this is likely to increase demand for it, and that a consequent rise in its value might be a problem in terms of the likely effect on European exporters. Wyplosz argues that, while stability of the euro's value is more important than strength for acquiring an international role, a strong currency is more likely to become acceptable in international payments than a weak one. De Grauwe, however, points out that while euro-denominated assets will rise if the euro becomes international money, so too will euro-denominated liabilities, leaving the impact on currency value indeterminate. In his view, the questions of the strength of a currency and its international role are conceptually quite separate (de Grauwe 1998). Certainly it is true that for most of the period since 1973 when the US dollar has been the sole international currency, unchallenged by gold or by sterling, it has also been falling in value and has been relatively weak compared with the yen and to the mark.

Conclusion

This chapter may seem to have left us with a large number of unanswered questions. There is still a great deal of controversy about exactly what determines exchange rate movements. We do not yet know whether the costs outweigh the benefits of EMU or not. It is also not yet clear what international role, if any, the euro will have. However, the concepts and distinctions we have examined during the course of the chapter, for example the distinctions between nominal and real exchange rates and between various kinds of exchange rate systems, and the concepts of optimum currency areas and vehicle currencies, are likely to prove the foundation for investigating these important questions in the future, as new data which might answer them becomes available.

Questions

1   The following exchange rates were quoted for 2 August 2004.
    £1 = US$1.8184
    £1 = SF2.3264
    US$1 = SK13.9546
    (SF: Swiss franc; SK Swedish krona)
    Calculate: (i)   the sterling/krona exchange rate
                (ii) the US dollar/Swiss franc exchange rate
                (iii) the Swiss franc/krona exchange rate.

2   What might be the effect on the exchange rate, within a flexible exchange rate system, of:
    (i)   income and spending within a country rising faster than that in the rest of the world?

(ii)   a government choosing to tighten monetary policy by raising interest rates?

(iii) a government choosing to relax fiscal policy by permitting a growth in government spending financed by sales of government bonds?

(iv)   a country experiencing a sharp and sustained increase in the growth rate of productivity compared with the rest of the world?

3   What might be the consequences of such changes for a country that is part of a fixed exchange rate system?

Using the data below:

(i)   Construct a purchasing power parity adjusted sterling/mark exchange rate.

(ii)   Calculate a real exchange rate for sterling against the mark.

(iii) Assess your results in relation to data (from, say, the Monthly Digest of Statistics) of the value and volume of exports and imports from Germany during the period.

4   In recent years the United States has argued strongly that China should revalue its currency upwards. One piece of evidence that has been put forward for this is that the purchasing power of the yuan appears to be higher than that of the dollar – in other words the yuan appears to be under-valued relative to its PPP. In the light of the discussion of PPP, in this chapter how convincing do you find this argument to be?

5   Dornbusch bases his overshooting model on the view that goods market prices adjust more slowly than asset market prices. Why do you think that he believed this? Do you think this is a realistic assumption?

6   How convincing do you think the explanations put forward in the text are for the failure of UIP to hold in practice? Can you think of any alternative explanations?

7   You are the financial manager of a company which operates internationally, receiving funds and making payments in a variety of currencies. Your deputy has just completed an MBA and she tells you that the Meese–Rogoff results mean the company should simply abandon the attempt to explain exchange rate behaviour and adopt the random walk view that the best estimate of the exchange rate tomorrow is simply that it will stay the same as it is today. What would be the implications for such a company of adopting this view? Do you think it would be sensible for you as a financial manager to follow your deputy's advice?

8   What current developments in the European Union might encourage or discourage movement towards the euro-zone countries becoming an optimal currency area? Do you think such a development is likely in the short or medium term?

9   What are the arguments for and against the euro becoming an international currency which could rival the dollar from the point of view of (a) the euro-zone countries and (b) the international financial system as a whole? Would such a development be one that European businesses should welcome?

Notes

1 The Big Mac Index uses the concept of PPP (see later in the chapter) to calculate what the exchange rate would be if all Big Mac burgers cost the same the world over (with US Big Macs representing the base cost).
2 Note the total is 200 per cent, as the currency could be involved on either side of the transaction.
3 Rates quoted by UK Post Office on 9 August 2004.
4 See Melvin (2004: 131–4) for an explanation of why this happens.
5 See Rogoff (1996) and Taylor and Taylor (2004) for surveys of this work.
6 See Rogoff 2002 for an argument to this effect
7 See Aliber (1973), Frenkel and Levich (1975), Clinton (1988), Taylor (1989).
8 See Froot and Thaler (1990) for a review of studies of UIP.
9 See Buiter and Miller (1981).
10 See de Grauwe (1996, ch. 7) for a review.
11 See for example Lane and Milesi-Ferretti (2002).
12 See McKinnon (1982).
13 See De Grauwe (2003, ch. 1).

References

Aliber, R. (1973) 'The interest rate parity theorem: a reinterpretation', *Journal of Political Economy*, November/December.

BIS website www.bis.org.

Buiter, W. and Miller, M. (1981) 'Monetary policy and international competitiveness: the problem of adjustment', in P. Sinclair and W. Eltis (eds), *The Money Supply and the Exchange Rate*, Oxford University Press, Oxford.

Clinton, K. (1988) 'Transactions costs and covered interest arbitrage: theory and evidence', *Journal of Political Economy*, April.

Copeland, L. (2005) *Exchange Rates and International Finance*, 4th edn, FT-Prentice Hall, Harlow.

De Grauwe, P. (1996) *International Money*, 2nd edn, Oxford University Press, Oxford.

De Grauwe, P. (1998) 'Comment on Portes and Rey', *Economic Policy*, no. 26.

De Grauwe, P. (2003) *Economics of Monetary Union*, 5th edn, Oxford University Press, Oxford.

Dornbusch, R. (1976) 'Expectations and exchange rate dynamics', *Journal of Political Economy*, December.

Dornbusch, R. and Fischer, S. (1980) 'Exchange rates and the current account', *American Economic Review*, December.

Economist (2005a) 'Economics focus: The real picture', 19 February.

Economist (2005b) 'The Big Mac Index: food for thought', 22 April.

Franks, J. (2002) 'Comment on Hau, Killeen and Moore', *Economic Policy*, no. 34.

Frenkel, J. and Levich, R. (1975) 'Covered interest arbitrage: unexploited profits?', *Journal of Political Economy*, April.

Friedman, M. (1953) 'The case for flexible exchange rates', in *Essays in Positive Economics*, University of Chicago Press, Chicago.

Froot, K. and Thaler, R. (1990) 'Anomalies: foreign exchange', *Journal of Economic Perspectives*, Summer.

Gerber, J. (2005) *International Economics*, 3rd edn, Pearson/Addison Wesley, Boston/London.

Griffiths, A. and Wall, S. (eds) (2004) *Applied Economics*, 10th edn, FT/Prentice Hall, Harlow.

Hallwood, C. and MacDonald, R. (2000) *International Money and Finance*, 3rd edn, Blackwell, Oxford.

Hau, H., Killeen, W. and Moore, M. (2002) 'How has the euro changed the foreign exchange market?', *Economic Policy*, no. 34.

Honohan, P. (2002) 'Comment on Hau, Killeen and Moore', *Economic Policy*, no. 34.

Kenen, P. (1969) 'The theory of optimum currency areas: an eclectic view', in R. Mundell and A. Swoboda (eds), *Monetary Problems of the International Economy*, University of Chicago Press, Chicago.

Krugman, P. (1991) *Currencies and Crises*, MIT Press, Boston, Mass.

Lane, P. and Milesi-Ferretti, G. (2002) 'External wealth, the trade balance and the real exchange rate', *European Economic Review*, June.

Lucas, R. (1982) 'Interest rates and currency prices in a two-country world', *Journal of Monetary Economics*, November.

McKinnon, R. (1963) 'Optimum currency areas', *American Economic Review*, September.

McKinnon, R. (1982) 'Currency substitution and instability in the world dollar standard', *American Economic Review*, June.

Meese, R. and Rogoff, K. (1983) 'Empirical exchange rate models of the seventies: do they fit out of sample?', *Journal of International Economics*, February.

Melvin, M. (2004) *International Money and Finance*, 7th edn, Pearson Addison Wesley, Boston/London.

Mundell, R. (1961) 'A theory of optimal currency areas', *American Economic Review*, September.

Obstfeld, M. and Rogoff, K. (1995) 'Exchange rate dynamics redux', *Journal of Political Economy*, June.

OECD (2004) *Economic Outlook*, 1, no. 75, June.

Portes, R (2002) 'Comment on Hau, Killeen and Moore', *Economic Policy*, no. 34.

Portes, R. and Rey, H. (1998) 'The emergence of the euro as an international currency', *Economic Policy*, no. 26.

Pratley, N. (2004) 'How the sickly dollar has spawned a shopping bonanza, New York style', *Guardian*, 20 February.

Rogoff, K. (1996) 'The purchasing power parity puzzle', *Journal of Economic Literature*, June.

Rogoff, K. (2002) *Dornbusch's Overshooting Model after Twenty-Five Years*, IMF Staff Papers, special issue.

Stockman, A. (1980) 'A theory of exchange rate determination', *Journal of Political Economy*, August.

Taylor, A. and Taylor, M. (2004) 'The purchasing power parity debate', *Journal of Economic Perspectives*, Fall.

Taylor, M. (1989) 'Covered interest arbitrage and market turbulence', *Economic Journal*, June.

UK government (2003) *UK Balance of Payments*, HMSO, London.

United Nations (2004) *World Economic and Social Survey*, UN, New York.

Wyplosz, C. (1999) 'An international role for the euro?', in J. Dermine and P. Hillion (eds), *European Capital Markets with a Single Currency*, Oxford University Press, Oxford.

6 Multinational corporations or MNCs

Alan Jarman

Objectives

This chapter will:

- outline the definitions of multinational companies (MNCs), transnational companies (TNCs) and globalisation
- examine the size and importance of some MNCs
- discuss the concept of the transnationality index (TNI) and its meaning
- assess some of the difficulties in conducting research into the performance of MNCs
- set out the positive and negative effects of MNCs
- debate the desirability of rules of governance for MNCs
- critically assess the possible forms of regulation of MNCs.

Introduction

This chapter considers first the definition and meaning of the term multinational company (MNC). The size and growth of MNCs are then commented on, leading to aspects of the debate about the effects of MNCs in the modern world. Arguments suggesting that the MNC is a benign influence spreading knowledge, transferring technology, increasing employment opportunities and raising living standards around the world are contrasted with the view that sees MNCs as agents of control rather than of change, exploiting markets, governments and employees in home and host societies to the benefit of the MNC alone. Different explanations of the phenomenon of globalisation are discussed, and finally we encounter differing opinions on the desirability and efficacy of attempts to regulate the activities of MNCs.

Other parts of this book discuss globalisation (Chapter 1) and **foreign direct investment (FDI)** (Chapter 7). These three areas – MNCS, globalisation and FDI – are closely interrelated, and could be argued to be broadly all part of one discussion. Globalisation, as it is most commonly described, means the rapid spread of firms' production and sales around the world, viewing all of the world as both potential markets and potential production or sourcing centres, together with the growth of international trade that goes with this international expansion of businesses. MNCs are the business form that carries globalisation around the world, and FDI is an important method that firms employ to engage in their globalised growth strategies. But these views of MNCs, of globalisation and of FDI are too narrow and rather simplistic. There is debate about the meanings of all three terms, and we next look at some of them.

What are MNCs?

Some commentators would treat the terms multinational company and transnational company (TNC) as interchangeable, while others would assign different meanings to them. Those who would distinguish between TNCs and MNCs would typically argue that MNCs are simply firms that operate in more than one country, whereas a TNC is a firm that not only operates in two or more countries but also sees these countries, and indeed the whole world, as its possible sphere of operation, favouring no one country over another purely on nationalistic grounds. Seen from this perspective the TNC is the true inhabitor of what Ohmae has memorably called the 'borderless world' (Ohmae 1994), and the MNC is simply a firm doing international business.

Drucker, 'the father of modern management' (*Fortune* 2004: 36) would agree. Drucker refers to TNCs, making the MNC/TNC distinction as above, arguing that 'traditional multinationals used to set up subsidiaries in foreign countries that operated essentially as marketing outposts' whereas in the modern transnational company 'foreign operations are an integral part of how [they] actually run. Without them, many corporations couldn't function or be competitive ... [and internet technology] makes every supplier appear "local", even if it is half a world away' (*Fortune* 2004: 36).

This difference of view of TNCs and MNCs also reflects differences of opinion on the meaning of globalisation. There is a wide-ranging debate about what globalisation means, and indeed whether it is a real and/or new phenomenon at all. Ohmae argues that the world is now, and has been for some time, a borderless place to do business. Companies are essentially footloose in search of production opportunities and efficiencies, and this is a thoroughly good, and now unstoppable, process (Ohmae 1994). Others might argue that treating globalisation as an inevitable and unstoppable process is simply wrong, as it denies the possibility for governments or for people and popular movements to restrict or even halt the expansion of international business. Treating globalisation as inevitable in this way can become a justification for the rich countries of the world to impose 'northern' solutions through institutions like the International Monetary Fund (IMF), World Bank and World Trade Organization (WTO) on poorer countries; 'the powerful countries of the North are able to exercise their power by pleading powerlessness in the face of the supposed globalizing market forces' (Brah, Hickman and Mac an Ghaill 1999: 8). Thus we can see that there is debate and disagreement over how properly to define and distinguish between MNCs and TNCs, which will be returned to later in the chapter. Unless it is clearly specified otherwise, MNC and TNC will be treated here as interchangeable terms, and MNC will be used as our standard term.

Most usually a MNC is defined as a firm that operates in more than one country and engages in those countries in its main lines of business; it is not merely selling abroad. Some however prefer a broader definition that covers all income-generating assets, and which would therefore include foreign sales subsidiaries, or operations that might be merely selling abroad. Dicken has taken this broader view of MNCs a stage further, and suggested that we should consider as an MNC any firm that 'has the power to coordinate and control operations in more than one country, even if it does not own them' (Dicken 2003: 198). This suggestion is interesting as it looks not just at business locations but at the power companies may exercise, and in particular power to integrate business activities across national borders.

Why are MNCs important?

Nearly a decade ago Dunning and Sauvant stated that:

> It is not difficult to understand why so much attention has been given to TNCs and their activities:
>
> - At least 37,000 TNCs operate more than 200,000 affiliates in virtually all countries of the world.
> - The value of the production of these affiliates exceeds that of world exports.
> - For most of the past three decades, FDI flows have been increasing at a higher rate than both the world's GNP and world exports.
> - TNCs account for between 25 per cent and 30 per cent of the world's GNP, about three-fifths of non-agricultural trade and around three-quarters of the world's stock of privately generated innovatory capacity.
> - TNCs employ directly some 73 million people or 10 per cent of employment in non-agricultural activities world wide.
>
> (Dunning and Sauvant 1996: 11)

Since this was written TNCs have become even more numerous, and more significant within the global economy. Recent data indicate that there are now 65,000 MNCs rather than 37,000, and that they have 850,000 foreign affiliates rather than 200,000. FDI has also been growing at twice the rate of expansion of exports (UNCTAD 2002). These enormous commercial organisations are clearly factors of some significance in modern life, not just in business, but for society at large. Dominating world culture as well as world commerce, MNCs are a remarkable and significant feature of our lives. Of these corporations operating worldwide, very many have EU-based operations. They include for example British American Tobacco (BAT), Philips Electronics, AstraZeneca, Electrolux and Interbrew. Giving an historical view of *The Rise of the Corporate Economy*, Hannah (1983) discussed the seemingly irresistible trend towards larger and larger business units, looking back at business growth and amalgamations since the early 1900s. He points out that not only has British industry become increasingly concentrated over the last hundred years, but that 'large corporations have been no respecters of national boundaries, but have expanded overseas as well as in the domestic economy' (Hannah 1983: 2). These firms are the MNCs of today. But how big are these organisations and where are they based?

The largest companies in the world

In Chapter 1 the largest EU companies were considered. Table 6.1 shows the world's 50 largest corporations in 2003, size here being measured by annual sales revenue in US dollars. This information has been taken from the 'Fortune 500' which is a list published annually by *Fortune* magazine, and from some commentaries in the same edition of the magazine.

Table 6.1 The world's largest corporations

Rank 2003	Rank 2002			REVENUES $ 000 million	% change from 2002	PROFITS $ 000 million	Rank	% change from 2002	EMPLOYEES No. 000s	Rank
1	1	Wal-Mart stores	US	263	6.7	9.0	12	12.6	1,500	1
2	5	BP	Britain	232	30.1	10.2	8	50.0	103	128
3	3	Exxon Mobil	US	222	22.2	21.5	2	87.7	88	157
4	4	Royal Dutch/ Shell Group	Britain/ Netherlands	201	12.4	12.4	5	32.7	119	109
5	2	General Motors	US	195	4.6	3.8	59	120.2	326	19
6	6	Ford Motor	US	164	0.4	0.5	300	–	327	17
7	7	DaimlerChrysler	Germany	156	10.7	0.5	298	(88.6)	362	13
8	8	Toyota Motor	Japan	153	20.4	10.2	7	66.9	264	30
9	9	General Electric	US	134	1.9	15.0	4	6.3	305	24
10	14	Total	France	118	22.2	7.9	16	41.6	110	119
11	12	Allianz	Germany	114	12.8	1.8	131	–	173	59
12	15	ChevronTexaco	US	112	22.7	7.2	20	538	61	242
13	31	Axa	France	111	80.4	1.1	187	26.8	74	195
14	36	ConocoPhillips	US	99	70.4	4.7	41	–	39	337
15	20	Volkswagen	Germany	98	20.0	1.2	176	(49.3)	336	15
16	16	Nippon Telegraph & Telephone	Japan	98	9.6	5.7	30	197.6	205	46
17	17	ING Group	Netherlands	95	8.8	4.5	43	7.6	115	115
18	13	Citigroup	US	94	(6.0)	17.8	3	16.9	256	33
19	19	International Business Machines	US	89	7.2	7.5	18	111.9	319	20
20	25	American International Group	US	81	20.5	9.2	10	68.0	86	165
21	21	Siemens	Germany	80	4.3	2.6	91	11.1	417	8
22	29	Carrefour	France	79	22.8	1.8	128	41.9	419	6
23	26	Hitachi	Japan	76	13.7	0.14	410	(38.5)	326	18
24	40	Hewlett-Packard	US	73	29.1	2.5	97	–	142	84
25	28	Honda Motor	Japan	72	10.5	4.1	51	17.4	131	93
26	39	Mckesson	US	69	21.7	0.64	275	16.4	24	398

Table 6.1 *continued*

Rank 2003	Rank 2002			REVENUES $ 000 million	% change from 2002	PROFITS $ 000 million	Rank	% change from 2002	EMPLOYEES No. 000s	Rank
27	27	US Postal Service	US	68	3.1	3.8	58	–	826	4
28	24	Verizon Communications	US	67	0.2	3.0	77	(24.6)	203	48
29	44	Assicurazioni Generali	Italy	66	24.5	1.1	186	–	60	251
30	32	Sony	Japan	66	8.2	0.78	241	(17.3)	162	70
31	34	Matsushita Electric Industrial	Japan	66	9.0	0.37	332	–	290	27
32	41	Nissan Motor	Japan	65	17.4	4.4	46	9.7	123	102
33	38	Nestlé	Switzerland	65	14.2	4.6	42	(4.9)	253	34
34	37	Home Depot	US	64	11.3	4.3	48	17.5	300	25
35	78	Berkshire Hathaway	US	63	50.8	8.1	15	90.2	172	61
36	33	Nippon Life Insurance	Japan	63	4.4	1.7	133	89.7	70	208
37	35	Royal Ahold	Netherlands	63	7.1	(0.001)	444	–	257	32
38	55	Deutsche Telekom	Germany	63	24.5	1.4	160	–	248	36
39	52	Peugeot	France	61	19.3	1.6	139	6.0	199	50
40	30	Altria Group	US	60	(2.4)	9.2	11	(17.1)	165	66
41	58	Metro	Germany	60	24.5	0.56	289	34.0	198	51
42	57	Aviva	Britain	59	20.6	1.5	149	–	60	250
43	63	ENI	Italy	59	28.0	6.3	27	45.6	76	188
44	49	Munich Re Group	Germany	59	13.7	(0.5)	459	(148.1)	41	332
45	48	Credit Suisse	Switzerland	58	13.1	3.7	63	–	60	248
46	_	State Grid	China	58	–	0.26	374	–	75	193
47	89	HSBC Holdings	Britain	57	40.0	8.7	13	40.6	218	43
48	54	BNP Paribas	France	57	12.0	4.2	50	36.6	89	155
49	60	Vodafone	Britain	56	21.0	(15.2)	499	–	60	254
50	53	Cardinal Health	US	56	11.1	1.4	163	33.1	50	290

Notes: figures in brackets () are losses, or negative changes.
Some numbers have been rounded.

Source: *Fortune* July 26, 2004

Judged by annual sales revenues Wal-Mart, the giant US supermarket chain, is now the largest business enterprise on earth. Apart from this retailer, it can be seen that oil companies and vehicle manufacturers, with eight of the largest ten, are the absolutely dominant companies in global commercial terms. And these firms are truly huge, the average turnover of the five largest being approximately US$200 billion. By way of comparison the UK gross national product (GNP) in 2003 was about US$1,500 billion. That is to say the UK economy in GNP terms is about seven times larger than these firms; the US economy is about 50 times larger. When they are compared with smaller countries the figures are truly dramatic. The annual sales revenues of these giant firms are about 50 times that of the GNP of Zambia, and more than 100 times as large as the 70 smallest and poorest countries in the world.

These figures tell us only of the size of MNCs' revenues and countries' GNPs; they do not tell us about their power or how it might be used. They do however suggest something of the bargaining imbalance that might exist if one of these corporate behemoths was in discussion with a small developing country about, for example, locating a new production facility in that country. To the MNC the choice of location may be between one of many possibilities, and might depend upon the terms the 'host' country is willing to offer, perhaps including a tax holiday or other incentives. Thus the location decision for the MNC might be almost trivial, whereas to the potential host the decision could be one with massive employment and income-generating implications. The negotiations will not be conducted on equal terms.

These MNC revenue and GNP comparisons are often made. However it is sometimes pointed out that we are not comparing like with like here. GNP measures value added, whereas MNC sales adds up all revenues, and would be deemed as double counting if used when measuring GNP. This is a valid point. Nonetheless the dramatic differences in sizes of countries and MNCs indicated by these data, even if they are not strictly comparable, do give us an idea of MNCs' potential economic power.

The total revenues of the 35 UK MNCs in the 500 list for 2003 were over US$1,000 billion, and in the US nearly US$6,000 billion. For Switzerland the figures show that their 14 MNCs in the 500 list had sales revenues in 2003 almost exactly equal to Swiss GNP. The MNCs are huge, and getting bigger. In 2003:

> the world's largest 500 companies rebounded with a vengeance, posting their highest profits and revenues ever. Even with a war in Iraq, a jobless recovery in the US, and anemic growth in Europe, the Fortune Global 500 companies reported revenues last year of $14.9 trillion – higher than the $14.1 trillion at the height of the tech boom in 2000 – as well as record profits of $731 billion.
>
> (*Fortune* 2004: 37)

There is little doubt, then, that MNCs are here to stay, and they seem to be going from strength to strength.

The 500 list first appeared in its current format in 1995. In 2004 *Fortune* asked:

> The decade's biggest winner? The US. Ten years ago it had 151 companies on the list, accounting for 29 per cent of the Global 500's revenues; this year the 189 US companies had 39 per cent of the revenues. Over the same period the number of Japanese companies dropped from 149 to 82 while the number of Chinese companies rose from three to 15.
>
> (*Fortune* 2004: 36)

Over this decade the number of EU-based MNCs on the 500 list dropped from over 150 to nearer 140. Five 'poorer' countries, Mexico, Venezuela, Brazil, Turkey and India, had seven MNCs between them on the 500 list for 1994, and in 2003 there were eight MNCs representing these five countries. Thus the pattern seems fairly clear. The United States has dominated, and continues to dominate, the global MNC picture. The European Union is losing some ground and Japan is struggling. The less rich countries are hardly represented at all, and then only by some of the very largest of the developing economies. The rich economies are very clearly dominant in this vital commercial sphere.

This dominance of the rich north in the MNC sales revenue tables opens up a further question: that is: to what extent are the MNCs of today, as Ohmae argues, inhabiting a 'borderless world' in which 'Country of origin does not matter [and] Location of headquarters does not matter' (Ohmae 1994: 94). Dicken uses two approaches to try to evaluate the extent to which MNCs are really becoming more and more placeless. First there is the transnationality index (TNI). The TNI is a measure designed to indicate the extent to which firms that engage in international business are dependent on and integrated with their foreign operations. The TNI is made up of the average of foreign assets to total assets, foreign sales to total sales and foreign employment to total employment. In Table 6.2 we see MNCs listed by their TNI rankings.

From Table 6.2 we can see that only five of the top 35 MNCs ranked by the TNI are from the United States or Japan, whereas in Table 6.1, ranking MNCs by sales, 22 of the top 35 are from the United States or Japan. Many of the firms that top the TNI rankings are based in relatively small economies such as Switzerland, the Netherlands and Canada. From this evidence Dicken concludes that 'there is little evidence of TNCs having the share of their activities outside their home countries that might be expected' (Dicken 2003: 224).

Furthermore the TNI approach is augmented by qualitative evidence about the extent to which MNCs adopt the culture or business styles of the foreign countries they operate in. US, Japanese and German firms are all said to retain their distinctive national management styles when abroad to a very large extent. Similarly, in cultural adoption terms, we can see two recent examples which, by exception, may prove the rule that MNCs typically stay close to home in cultural terms. In March 2005 it was announced by Sony that a Welshman, Sir Howard Stringer, had been appointed as the first non-Japanese head of the electronics and entertainment company. In 1999, Brazilian-born Carlos Ghosn became the first non-Japanese head of Nissan, and this was also seen as an exceptional appointment.

MNC research

Much research and empirical work has been undertaken in relation to the performance of multinational, transnational and international businesses. The research and results are not always easy to interpret, however. This is hardly surprising, given some of the parameters of this area of research, and not least the political aspects of any such studies. This area is inherently a very complex and 'untidy' one for research: MNCs come from a very wide variety of countries

Table 6.2 Transnationality of the biggest MNCs

Rank	TNI Index	Company	Country	Industry	Foreign share of Assets (%)	Empl. (%)
1	95.4	Thomson Corp.	Canada	Publ'g and printing	98.6	92.5
2	95.2	Nestlé	Switzerland	Food/beverages	89.9	97.2
3	94.1	ABB	Switzerland	Electrical equip.	88.2	96.3
4	93.2	Electrolux	Sweden	Electrical	92.9	90.4
5	91.8	Holcim	Switzerland	Constr. materials	91.9	93.4
6	91.5	Roche Group	Switzerland	Pharmaceuticals	90.4	85.6
7	90.7	BAT	UK	Food/tobacco	84.0	96.8
8	89.3	Unilever	UK/Neths	Food/beverages	90.4	90.5
9	88.6	Seagram Company	Canada	Beverages/media	73.1	–
10	82.6	Akzo Nobel	Netherlands	Chemicals	85.0	81.0
11	82.4	Nippon Oil Co.	Japan	Petroleum	88.7	74.5
12	81.9	Cadbury-Schweppes	UK	Food/beverages	88.8	79.7
13	79.4	Diageo	UK	Beverages	69.3	82.6
14	78.3	News Corporation	Australia	Media	61.2	72.5
15	76.9	L'Air Liquide Group	France	Chemicals	–	–
16	76.6	Glaxo Wellcome	UK	Pharmaceuticals	70.2	74.1
17	73.8	Michelin	France	Rubber/tyres	–	–
18	73.7	BP	UK	Petroleum	74.7	77.3
19	72.5	Stora Enso OYS	Finland	Paper	–	–
20	71.6	AstraZeneca	UK/Sweden	Pharmaceuticals	37.3	83.3
21	70.3	Totalfina	France	Petroleum	–	67.9
22	68.0	ExxonMobil	USA	Petroleum	68.8	63.6
23	67.8	Danone Groupe	France	Food/beverages	62.9	–
24	67.1	McDonald's Corp.	USA	Eating places	57.6	82.8
25	65.6	Alcatel	France	Electronics	52.1	74.1
26	65.2	Coca-Cola	USA	Beverages	83.3	–
27	64.7	Honda	Japan	Automobiles	58.4	–
28	63.8	Compart SpA	Italy	Food	–	68.2
29	62.2	Montedison Group	Italy	Chemicals	–	71.7
30	61.4	Volvo	Sweden	Automobiles	–	53.4
31	60.9	Ericsson	Sweden	Electronics	44.5	57.4
32	60.9	BMW	Germany	Automobiles	69.1	40.1
33	60.2	Bayer	Germany	Chemicals	58.0	53.2
34	60.2	RTZ	Australia/UK	Mining	61.2	62.5
35	59.9	Philips	Netherlands	Electronics	76.2	–
36	59.2	BASF	Germany	Chemicals	57.0	44.4
37	58.9	Bridgestone	Japan	Rubber/tyres	44.6	69.0

and cultures, industries and technologies, and operate in host situations which are similarly varied. The categorising of firms, industries, markets, cultures and so on in order to set up research studies can yield endless permutations. Therefore ambiguous results are not really surprising.

In addition we cannot ignore the nationalistically focused or country-centred perspective which may infiltrate analysis in this area. For example, in an early study Hymer and Rowthorn (1970) cited studies of European and US MNCs undertaken on both sides of the Atlantic in the 1960s, and indicated that the role of the MNCs differed from the two cultures' perspectives. During the 1960s there appeared to be a strong feeling among European commentators that US MNCs were battling vigorously to penetrate European markets. They were doing this by FDI as well as by exporting, in an attempt to gain dominant positions in some European industries, or sections of them, such as motor manufacture. American commentators, on the other hand, saw US firms taking a long-term view of their European activities, as a defensive strategies to try to maintain their share of world trade in the face of rapidly growing European firms. How did such a 'misunderstanding' arise? Hymer and Rowthorn argued that this was partly because of a conundrum in the 'evidence'. US operations in Europe typically exhibited faster growth rates than comparable European firms in the same sectors, while at the same time the European companies were growing faster than the combined (parent and subsidiaries) US firms. So both points of view can be explained in the sense that a firm can be both challenging and challenged at the same time, but the differences in explanation also surely stemmed from the different country perspectives of the commentators. Even accepting the problems of conducting this sort of empirical research, it must be said that much of the work on the scope and size of MNCs, and their impact on home and host economies, is far from conclusive.

By penetrating foreign markets, particularly if doing so by FDI, MNCs could be said to be inhibiting the growth of indigenous firms, exporting profits and thereby retarding the growth of output and employment in the affected industries. But many accounts of MNC growth rates, profit rates and impact on host industries' performance levels have given rise to indeterminate findings. As suggested above there are many possible reasons for the ambiguity of such findings; politics is one and the sheer variety and complexity of the studies is another. A further difficulty could also be the lack of consensus on an adequate theoretical framework or paradigm in which to conduct enquiries into the operations and outcomes of international business. The 'missing consensus' may reflect the varieties of situation in which MNCs act, the huge range of contexts within which, and as parts of which, they function, and the near impossibility of fitting the giant corporations into neat 'neo-classical boxes'.

Vernon (1994) commented on the nature of research into MNCs. He introduced, early on, the idea of an imbalance of power between some of the largest MNCs and some host governments (Vernon 1971). Later he discussed the failure of MNC research, in particular economic research, to deal adequately with MNCs. He describes economists as being stuck in a neo-classical paradigm and unable to break free. Thus economists often study MNCs as if they were 'ordinary' firms, and consider their conduct as cost minimising or profit seeking, in line with typical neo-classical assumptions. What is needed, Vernon suggests, is to break away from this neo-classical constraining mindset, and to think of MNCs in terms of their strategic competitive behaviour, more in line with **prisoner's dilemma** and game theory. The analysis of MNCs could then begin to take account of the fact that MNCs are not just firms in a market, but may be uniquely powerful players in a multi-faceted environment, where politics, management and organisational culture, and sheer animal spirits of the executives, may be more significant explanators than the quantifiable factors like minimising transaction costs, or elements of the ownership, location and internalisation (OLI) or eclectic paradigms (see Chapter 7).

Following on from this idea that politics can be a vital factor in determining MNCs' operating environments, strategic trade theory as developed in the 1980s has suggested that there may be times when home governments could or should support home MNCs. The theories involve analysis of how competing MNCs may engage in strategic 'games' with each other. Under certain assumptions MNCs of similar capabilities may come to find that all of a market opportunity is taken up by one, at the expense of the other, and then there may be arguments in defence of tariffs, quotas or subsidies to protect the 'home' MNC from foreign attack. Of course the next question is, how likely are foreign MNCs' own governments to retaliate? The outcome depends on the relative bargaining power of both the MNCs involved and their governments (Krugman 1987a, 1987b).

International trade theory writers also suggest that there are difficulties associated with what is sometimes called 'the theory of multinational enterprise' (Krugman and Obstfeld 2003: 172). As pointed out above, research into the performance of MNCs has not produced clear answers. 'The important question … is what difference multinationals make? With only a limited understanding of why multinationals exist, this is a hard question to answer' (Friends of the Earth 2001: 1, Krugman and Obstfeld 2003: 174). Similarly it has been argued that 'Why some firms choose to become MNCs is an interesting and unresolved question in economics' (Husted and Melvin, 2004: 295). Husted and Melvin go on to consider some of the research done on MNCs' impacts on employment levels at home and in the host economies, arguing that the results are unclear: the research 'seems to suggest that the location of overseas production by US MNCs appears to be determined more by access to markets than by access to low-wage labor or natural resources' (Husted and Melvin 2004: 296, our emphasis).

Thus there is a degree of consensus that the questions why firms choose a multinational growth route, and with what effects, have no simple clear answers. The question of 'why go multinational' is discussed in further detail in Chapter 7.

Among the many aspects of the debates and disagreements about MNCs, some areas of particular importance can be identified, particularly the positive and negative effects of MNCs, and the possible regulation of them. The theory behind some of these arguments may be rather unclear, but the arguments about the role, operation and effects of MNCs rage on.

The positive and negative effects of MNCs

The debate about the effects of MNCs is closely linked with the vigorous contemporary controversy surrounding globalisation. Our discussion of the role of and effects of MNCs will necessarily, therefore, involve some aspects of the globalisation debate. Furthermore the impact of MNCs on the host economy may be related to the extent and level of economic activity, and MNCs may have differing effects on developing economies and developed ones. It has been argued that MNCs are the ideal medium for spreading modern technology and business methods worldwide; however, it has also been suggested that MNCs have huge resources and power, and with this comes the potential abuse of that power. The question then arises of whose interest MNCs serve. Looking at the positive effects or taking an optimistic perspective, it might be argued as follows.

First, 'MNCs serve the interests of the people who work for them; they are major employers who have increased employment and real wages at home and around the world substantially faster than non-international companies' (Freeman 1981: 13–14). Employment is one of the major reasons governments try to attract MNCs into their country, and it is true that MNCs do employ millions worldwide. Wal-Mart, for example, is not only the biggest MNC in terms of sales revenue, it is also the biggest employer in the world (see Table 6.1). The amount of direct employment that MNCs bring will depend on the scale of activities and the technology employed (for example is the operation capital or labour intensive?).

Further to this direct effect, there will also be an indirect one, with employment growing in local firms. The amount will depend on the size of local linkages formed by the MNCs and also the amount of income generated and retained locally. However the MNC may also displace jobs by squeezing out local firms purely by its size and strength, for example. Therefore the net effect on employment in the host economy will be:

Number of direct jobs + indirect jobs – displaced jobs

Added to this, we have to consider the type of job created. These tend to differ according to the level of development, with more production-type jobs in less-developed countries (LDCs) and more research and decision-making-type jobs in the developed countries (DCs) (Dicken 2003).

Finally the quotation by Freeman above talks of increased real wages brought by MNCs. It has to be remembered that often the thing that draws MNCs to countries is lower wages (see Chapter 7). However UNCTAD has stated, 'Generally speaking, at the aggregate and industry levels, the workforce directly employed by foreign affiliates enjoys superior wages, conditions of work and social security benefits relative to the conditions prevailing in domestic firms' (quoted in Dicken 2003). It does have to be said, though, that although this may be positive for those working for MNCs, it can have a negative effect on local firms which not only have to try to compete with these higher wages, but see their best workers leaving to work for MNCs.

Second, MNCs serve their customers by developing mass markets which thereby increases efficiency, and lowers costs and selling prices.

Third, MNCs can serve to improve trade linkages internationally and regionally (OECD 2003) (see Chapter 2).

Fourth, 'MNCs take technology to poorer countries; they are the equivalent of workhorses for the world' (Freeman 1981: 13–14). Therefore they serve the spread of technology worldwide. When locating in a developing country, for example, an MNC will bring new technology, new working practices, more R&D, marketing skills and further training for its workers. (It has to be said, however, that the extent to which MNCs do this varies significantly.) Such technologies and improved skills can be especially beneficial when they spill over into the domestic economy through linkages between domestic firms and the foreign investor. MNCs can therefore increase technological choice and improve training not only within their own organisation but locally (Alfaro and Rodriguez-Clare 2003, Novartis 2005, Piscitello and Rabbiosi 2005).

The president of the International Chamber of Commerce, speaking at the 2002 World Economic Forum (WEF), summed up many of these arguments when he said:

> Multinationals are a powerful force for good in the world. They spread wealth, work, and technologies that raise living standards and better ways of doing business. That's why so many developing countries are competing fiercely to attract their investment. The protesters in the streets [see below] are modern day **Luddites** who want to make the world safer for stagnation. ... [T]heir resistance to globalization and their hostility to business make them an enemy of the world's poor. That's why people from developing countries are so rare in the ranks of the demonstrators.
>
> (McCormick 2002)

The discussion is shifting ground a little. The focus is still on MNCs, but the context is globalisation. The protesters being referred to by McCormick are some of the many thousands who regularly take to the streets when meetings are taking place of organisations like the IMF, G7 or **G8**, or indeed the WEF that McCormick was addressing.

Some might state the optimistic or pro-business/MNC case even more strongly. Writing about the giant modern companies like General Electric, General Motors, Microsoft and IBM, *Fortune* contends that:

> Without them and their proven ability to marshal and allocate resources, organize and harness the ingenuity of people, respond to commercial and social environments, and meet the ever more elaborate challenge of producing and distributing goods and providing services on a global scale, we would have far less innovation – and less wealth. ...[[T]hese organisations are] the latest jewel in the crown of human endeavour.
>
> (*Fortune* 2004: 36)

This is praise indeed for the giant corporations.

The opposing, and very negative and pessimistic, views of the role of MNCs and the march of globalisation are widespread. Voices raised in criticism of aspects of globalisation and the activities of some MNCs range from the long-established and mainstream like Christian Aid, Oxfam, FairTrade, Friends of the Earth, the World Development Movement (WDM) and so on, to other groups active around the world in what has come to be known as the 'anti-globalisation movement'. This anti-globalisation movement was seen in Seattle in the United

States in November 1999 at the time of the WTO Ministerial Conference there, when a huge demonstration seriously affected the meeting. Since then there have been numerous similar protests and attempts to disrupt the workings of major international institutions. In 2001, for example, about 200,000 people took part in the biggest protest so far against the 'globalisation of capitalism', at the time of the G8 summit in Genoa, Italy, and in May 2003 another G8 meeting in Evian, Switzerland was disturbed. Further disruptive actions also occurred at the G8 meeting in Gleneagles, Scotland in July 2005.

What are the anti-globalisation protestors arguing against? On almost every point they would disagree with the positive, optimistic views outlined above. Some of the negative, pessimistic arguments might include that MNCs:

- may operate in unethical and even immoral ways
- may abuse their power over both individuals and governments
- may show a lack of respect for health and safety matters
- may practise tax avoidance
- may display 'unpatriotic arrogance'
- may exhibit poor governance, even dishonesty, and need a greater awareness of corporate social responsibility (CSR).

An example of what is argued to be unethical activity is given by Nestlé, the Swiss confectionery giant, with its marketing of baby foods, especially powdered milk, in East Africa, despite the fact that the World Health Organization (WHO) and others have demonstrated that breast milk is far better than processed milk because of its disease-resistance properties. Preparation of such milk also needs regular supplies of good drinking water, sterile bottles, teats and mixing equipment, conditions unlikely to prevail in many LDCs. Yet Nestlé still continues with its sales. When the first edition of this book was published in 1993 this example of the Nestlé baby food 'scandal' was already well known; however the controversy is as active today as it ever was.

Another illustration of unethical behaviour is given by the Swiss-based pharmaceutical giant Hoffman-LaRoche. The company was brought to the attention of the European Commission for engaging in market-sharing and price-fixing activities which violated parts of the EC competition policy, and was fined DM1 million for its breaches of these rules. Hoffman-LaRoche somehow found out the identity of the man from whom the information had been obtained, and this led to his arrest under Swiss industrial secrecy laws and ultimately to prison, where he committed suicide. The questions raised by this case centre on the role played by Hoffman-LaRoche in generating huge profits from its illegal anti-competitive activities and in, apparently, pressurising EU officials to give up highly sensitive and confidential information (in this case on the informant). Deeper questions also arise. How typical is this example? Can the power, influence and financial 'muscle' of giant corporations be used not only to 'bully' individuals, like the whistleblower in this example and the EU officials, but also to circumvent or subvert the proper process of regulation? (See below on tax avoidance, 'arrogance' and CSR.)

As far as health and safety allegations are concerned, many examples could be given, including those relating to sweatshop production standards for sports goods in the developing world. Perhaps the most high-profile case is the terrible accident at the US-owned Union Carbide plant at Bhopal in India in December 1984. On the tenth anniversary of the disaster it was stated that

> as a result of slipshod management and a breakdown of safety procedure, water got into a tank of methyl isocyanate (MIC), a deadly cyanide gas, heating it and causing it to escape as a gas. It killed in the end almost 3,000 people; this was the worst ever industrial disaster.
>
> (*Economist* 1994: 78)

The tragedy of the deaths is shocking, but almost as disturbing was the behaviour of Union Carbide in its attempts to avoid legal liability. In the end a settlement with the Bhopal victims 'for $470m was reached, far less than even Carbide expected' (*Economist* 1994: 78). Now 20 years on Union Carbide has agreed to pay some compensation, but it has for 13 years totally ignored the summons of an Indian court where it faces criminal charges of culpable homicide. Today, we are told, 120,000 in Bhopal are still seriously ill from the effects of the gas, and the official death toll is now more than 20,000. The disaster site (the ruined factory) has never been cleaned up, lethal chemicals are still present and nearby drinking wells are toxic. Union Carbide says it has no responsibility for cleaning up the factory (Pesticide Action Network 2004).

As far as corporate governance is concerned, the example of US energy giant Enron is well known, and in 2004 Shell found itself in the public eye for its systematic and deliberate misleading of its shareholders, and the market at large, over the extent of its oil reserves, so as to artificially support its stock market valuation.

Transfer pricing and the inference of MNCs' tax avoidance are very serious and rather complex matters. Transfer pricing may be a perfectly standard (if rather tricky) business procedure, particularly in large decentralised companies. For example a vehicle producer might have a body plant, a paint shop, an engine division and an assembly plant amongst others. The body plant supplies the paint shop with bodies to paint; the painted bodies are then supplied to the assembly division. Similarly engines made by the company are supplied to the assembly division. If the paint shop, body plant, engine division and assembly plant are seen by the company as separate cost or profit centres, each has to allocate a price, on paper at least, that it pays the supplying division or receives from other divisional buyers, so that its performance can be monitored and evaluated. The procedures for doing this involve one division charging another a 'transfer price' for the supplies. So this is a standard business practice, even if the reality gets complicated.

To illustrate this complexity, Mansfield explains that 'At the Ford Motor Company [US] there has been a special intracompany pricing coordinator for administering transfer pricing policies, with six or seven full time employees to assist' (Mansfield, 1999: 507). When used by MNCs there is considerable potential to manipulate such internal transfer prices between divisions in different countries so as to seriously reduce tax liabilities. This is done by reversing the normal business maxim of 'buy cheap and sell dear'. The MNC may, on paper only, reverse this normal way of doing things, so that a division in country A (a high-tax country) buys [supplies] dear, from another division, and sells them on cheap to a division in low-tax country B. The country A division then registers little profit, or even losses, and the country B division may record very high profits. If country B is one like the Cayman Islands, or the Bahamas, or Liechtenstein, the division nominally based there may pay little or no tax on company profits, as the host or offshore government makes money from these foreign-registered firms by charging them annual location fees or the like, rather than levying taxes on them. Very recently the government of Liechtenstein has started to change its tax rules to try to reduce the number of companies registered there for tax-reduction purposes, in recognition of the bad press that the country gets as a result of allowing this sort of behaviour. In estimating the extent of such tax avoidance, Dicken tells us that 'A US study estimated that some $US35 billion in company taxes was being lost annually through the transfer pricing mechanism' and 'In the UK a study of 210 TNCs showed that 83 per cent had been involved in a transfer price dispute [with the tax authorities]' (Dicken 2003: 283).

Another issue might be termed 'unpatriotic arrogance'. Sampson has two interesting examples of this. At the time of the early 1970s oil crisis the chairmen of BP and Shell were specially asked by the UK prime minister to ensure adequate supplies to the UK economy; both refused. In 2000 when faced with blockades of oil refineries by people protesting at the high taxes on fuel, the (different) UK prime minister once more asked the oil companies for help, this time to break the blockades, to ensure adequate supplies to the UK economy. Again the oil companies refused, one oil executive reportedly stating, 'We are global companies with, on the whole, more influence around the world than the British government' (Sampson 2004: 298).

Finally we come to the issues of corporate governance, dishonesty and CSR. In 2004 Shell found itself in the public eye (see earlier). But the most significant recent case in this area concerns Enron, the huge US company:

> It was voted the most innovative company in America six years running, it was consistently high on lists of the best company to work for, it spent millions on literacy and community projects and was a pioneer of renewable energy. It was, of course, Enron now better known for its corporate and financial mismanagement, its culture of deceit, close ties to US politicians and alleged human rights abuses in India. This is the big problem with CSR. It has become big business for firms to invest in environmental, ethical, social and community projects. But behind the warm words and sentiments there is often a deep credibility gap.
>
> (*Guardian* 2004)

There has been a great rise in the CSR 'movement' in recent years. The Organisation for Economic Cooperation and Development (OECD), the European Union and the UK government, for example, all seem to take this idea of CSR very seriously. The clear implication is that before the recent popularity of these CSR schemes, projects and policies there was little CSR, but there should be. Nonetheless, companies by themselves cannot always be relied to behave in a socially responsible way, and governments are forced to act, as shown in the Enron case below.

SEC TO RETHINK POST-ENRON RULES

In 2002 the United States passed a new law called the Sarbanes–Oxley Act, widely known as SOX. SOX was a response to the accounting and fraud scandals of Enron, Parmalat and WorldCom, among others, which resulted in a loss of public trust in accounting and reporting practices. The SOX legislation is wide-ranging and establishes new or enhanced standards for all US public companies, including an obligation on chief executives to sign a statement taking responsibility for the accuracy of the accounts (clause 404). Firms that break the new law could face huge fines, while senior executives risk jail terms of up to 20 years.

But European firms with listings in New York have objected, arguing that the compliance costs outweigh the benefits of a secondary New York listing. The US regulator has said that foreign firms may get extra time to comply with clause 404, which came into force for foreign firms in 2005.

A delegation of European firms visited the Securities and Exchange Commission (SEC) in New York in late 2004 to press for changes in the rules. The delegation was led by Digby Jones, head of the UK Confederation of British Industry (CBI), and included representatives of BASF, Siemens and Cadbury-Schweppes. They argued that increased compliance costs are making firms wary of US listings, and cited as evidence the fact that Air China secondary listed on the London Stock Exchange in late 2004 rather than in New York as planned, with its stock market value of over US$1 billion, and is likely to be followed by other large Chinese banks which had originally planned a New York listing.

But many argue that even SOX may not be enough. 'Like you can't legislate for morality, you can't legislate for good behaviour', said Wes Rehm, head of SAS, recently. And further, the original Enron whistleblower, Lynn Brewer, argues that corporate corruption is still rife in the United States.

Sources: BBC (2005), Silicon.com and CNET Networks (no date).

Questions

1 Outline what you see as the arguments for and against foreign firms operating in the United States having more relaxed governance rules than those applying to US firms.

2 How do you think Lynn Brewer might have come by 'evidence' that corporate corruption is 'still rife' in the United States? Would you be inclined to believe her, or should she treated as a 'hostile witness', and likely to exaggerate the facts?

3 Former WorldCom chief executive Bernie Ebbers was found guilty of conspiracy and fraud (in March 2005) and faces up to 85 years in prison. (He is now 63 years old.) Do you think that 'white collar' crime like this should carry such long prison sentences? Are fraudulent executives really a danger to society?

We have seen here some of the many arguments put forward by the 'negative pessimists', but as Jarman (2005) makes clear there is a very significant gap between itemising the problems that MNC behaviour may cause and actually determining effective ways of regulating such MNC activities. This brings us to our next two sections, where we consider if there is a case for action over MNCs, and if so what action might be possible.

MNCs – a case for action?

Here we encounter two arguments. The first relates to power and its use by MNCs, the second considers different views of globalisation and how they impact on the debate about whether action is needed.

Most economists and many business commentators accept that some public policy is needed to monitor monopoly power and its potential abuse. Since 1890, when the US Congress passed the Sherman Act (the first legislation of its kind in the world), most industrialised societies have introduced some form of **anti-trust** or **competition policy (CP)** (see Chapter 10). Even Milton Friedman, a renowned advocate of minimum government, sees an important role for CP to facilitate the proper functioning of free competitive markets (Friedman 1962). To the extent that some government action is felt to be necessary to protect the public interest against potential abuse of power by 'domestic' monopolies and cartels, the argument for protection against those companies working across national economic boundaries (that is, MNCs) would seem self-evident. The advantages that it was claimed would flow from the SEM hinged to a large degree on assumptions about efficiency gains to be achieved through rationalisation, restructuring and economies of scale, which are then expected to be passed on to consumers in improved quality and/or lower prices. European markets are characterised, at least in part, by the presence of many indigenous and foreign MNCs, and because of their size, doubts have been expressed about the ability of EU CP to control them. In other words, to ensure that firms across the whole of Europe enjoy the benefits of the new, freer, single market, competition is a prerequisite.

Articles 81 and 82 of the Treaty of Rome spell out the fundamentals of the European Union's approach to promotion of competition and the regulation of anti-competitive elements (see Chapter 10). They stress that activities that would (adversely) 'affect trade between member states' are to be condemned. This adverse effect can be fairly narrowly construed, specifically to mean a reduction in the competitive conditions under which such trade is conducted, to judge whether or not such arrangements actually lead to an increase in trade or not. So a key factor in the EU policy about the conduct of businesses from the member states is that competition should not be compromised. It seems almost too obvious that some of the operations of some of the world's very largest business organisations (the MNCs) would 'affect trade' in ways which might violate the principles of EU CP.

An alternative argument relating to MNCs and CP could be that the presence of, or arrival of, foreign MNCs could be highly beneficial for competition in domestic markets previously dominated by 'home-grown' monopolists, or colluding oligopolists, and that allocative efficiency in the host economy might best be achieved by attracting in more than one foreign MNC from different countries. In contrast, Friends of the Earth argue for international CP 'to stop the mega-merger-mania that has recently been sweeping the globe and placing larger amounts of trade into the hands of a smaller and smaller number of giant transnational corporations (Friends of the Earth 2001: 1), but they are concerned that international discussion of competition rules may turn into ways of helping MNCs gain 'fair' access to new markets, to the disadvantage of indigenous firms and their customers and employees. In the context of trade talks they go on to suggest that 'liberalisation' has indeed facilitated the extension of monopolistic MNCs' circles of influence, especially in some of the LDCs. There are only about 450 MNCs of significant size in the world, but they dominate 15 or so crucial industries such as petroleum, motor vehicles, electronics, electrical engineering, computers, aerospace, soaps and cosmetics, food, tobacco, beverages, rubber and paper, and it is the potential for misuse of this power that concerns Friends of the Earth.

The debate about MNC use or abuse of power in developed countries is rather different. Moran poses an interesting question:

> What are the consequences for national power and national autonomy of allowing the globalization of the domestic market to proceed if globalization means a growing reliance on inward investment by foreign TNCs and increasing levels of outward investment by indigenous companies striving to become TNCs themselves?
>
> (Moran 1996: 426)

So we see that there is considerable support for the idea that some sort of regulation or control of MNCs may be desirable on the grounds of potential abuse of power. Next we consider some explanations of the globalisation process that may bring MNCs to foreign countries, and how these theories influence the argument about control of MNCs. Three broad theories of globalisation have been identified by some writers: the globalist view, the transformationalist view and the internationalist perspective (Kelly and Prokhovnik 2004):

> Economic globalists understand globalization as a phenomenon concerning the growing integration of the national economies of most states in the world based on five interrelated drivers of change: growing international trade, increasing FDI, increased communication via both the internet and traditional media, technological advances, and increased labour mobility.
>
> (Kelly and Prokhovnik 2004: 90–1)

Globalists would, then, include writers like Ohmae who argues that these integrating phenomena that Kelly and Prokhovnik outline are now well established, and are, indeed, a very good thing. In this Ohmae represents the positive globalist view. From this perspective globalisation is a highly desirable phenomenon, and the rise of the truly transnational TNC (not MNC, in his view) is a fact of modern life, which brings benefits to all countries and all peoples. There is also the pessimistic globalist viewpoint, broadly equivalent to the anti-globalisation movement we discussed earlier. The pessimists would generally describe the globalisation process in much the same way as the positive globalists, but see the purposes and outcomes very differently. To the pessimists globalisation represents the exercise of power in pursuit of profit, often at the expense of ordinary people (especially in LDCs), to benefit the shareholders in the rich north. To these pessimists the proper response is protest and direct action. Governments are likely to be mistrusted, and seen as partners of the MNCs in the globalisation process.

The transformationalist view is that the phenomenon of globalization can be harnessed ... [and they reject] the blanket generalizations made about the inevitability of globalization by both the positive and pessimistic globalists ... the strength of global economic forces needs to be recognized, but scope exists for states to resist these forces and to negotiate controls over them, to transform globalization.

(Kelly and Prokhovnik 2004: 105)

This is clearly a step back from the extreme 'Ohmae position', and suggests a very hands-on approach for governments and other interested bodies to try to shape the ways that MNCs work. The transformationalists would cite the very many organisations that may affect and influence MNC activities. Figures 6.1 and 6.2 would seem to support this point of view. There are quite evidently very many organisations at many levels with some input into the workings of MNCs.

The third approach is that of the so-called internationalists. Their analysis is at the opposite end of the spectrum from the positive globalists. The internationalists argue that the 'global integration' and 'borderless world' concepts of the globalists are simply wrong. There has been no revolution in the way

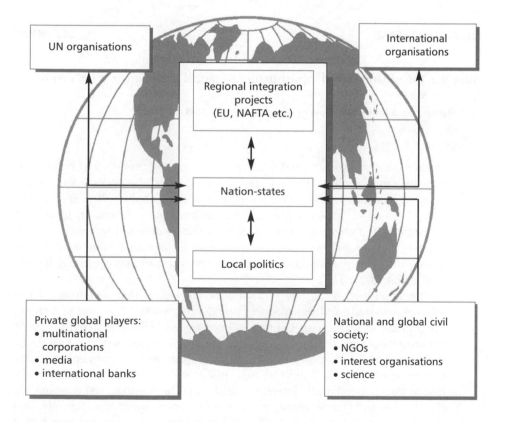

Figure 6.1 Levels in the architecture of global governance

Source: Kennedy, Messner and Nuscheler (2002), in Held and McGrew (2002: 66).

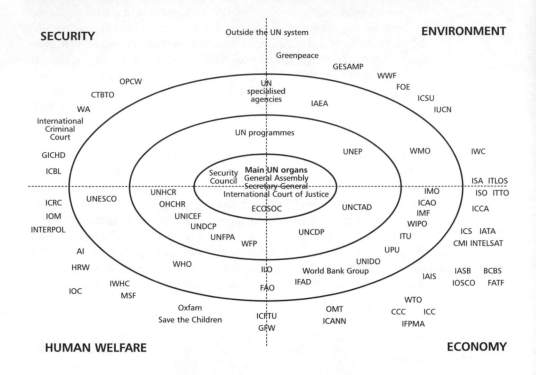

Figure 6.2 The organisational infrastructure of global governance: a UN-centric view

Source: Mathias Koenig-Archibugi, 'Mapping global governance', in Held and McGrew (2002).

world capitalism works; what we have is an ongoing evolution of businesses and business practice. The continuities in the way business operates are stressed, not the dramatic changes argued by the globalists. It is agreed that there have been 'growing and deepening international links in trade and investment [but they are] accompanied by the continual dominance of independent state-based economic units. National economies remain a viable and indeed the primary economic category in the international world' (Kelly and Prokhovnik 2004: 110).

This is an interesting line of argument, suggesting that recent growth in international trade and the speeding up of communications is part of a trend, not a break with the past. Capitalists have always looked far afield for profit opportunities from the spice trade to the China trade, and the East India Company and the Hudson's Bay Trading Company were active centuries ago. One hundred, or even 150 years ago, labour was much more internationally mobile than it is today, the internationalists say. The transnational company (in the Drucker and Ohmae sense) is still the exception rather than the rule, and the TNI data of Table 6.2 would be cited as evidence, showing that very few of the really big companies in the world are actually transnational, and that the biggest do much of their business 'at home'. Furthermore the qualitative

Figure 6.2 Key to abbreviations

AI	Amnesty International	IMO	International Maritime Organization
BCBS	Basel Committee on Banking Supervision	INTELSAT	International Telecommunications Satellites Organization
CCC	Customs Cooperation Council	NTERPOL	International Criminal Police Organization
CMI	Comité Maritime International	IOC	International Olympic Committee
CTBTO	Comprehensive Nuclear-Test-Ban Treaty Organization (not yet operational)	IOM	International Organization for Migration
		IOSCO	International Organization of Securities Commissions
ECOSOC	UN Economic and Social Council		
FAO	Food and Agriculture Organization	ISA	International Seabed Authority
FATF	Financial Action Task Force	ISO	International Organization for Standardization
FOE	Friends of the Earth	ITLOS	International Tribunal for the Law of the Sea
GESAMP	Joint Group of Experts on the Scientific Aspects of Marine Environmental Protection	ITTO	International Tropical Timber Organization
		ITU	International Telecommunication Union
		IUCN	World Conservation Union
GFW	Global Fund for Women	IWC	International Whaling Commission
GICHD	Geneva International Centre for Humanitarian Demining	IWHC	International Women's Health Coalition
		MSF	Médecins Sans Frontières
HRW	Human Rights Watch	OHCHR	Office of the High Commissioner for Human Rights
IAEA	International Atomic Energy Agency		
IAIS	International Association of Insurance Supervisors	OMT	World Tourism Organization
		OPCW	Organization for the Prohibition of Chemical Weapons
IASB	International Accounting Standards Board		
		UNCTAD	UN Conference on Trade and Development
IATA	International Association of Transport Airlines	UNDCPUN Drug Control Programme	
		UNDP	UN Development Programme
ICANN	Internet Corporation for Assigned Names andNumbers	UNEP	UN Environment Programme
		UNESCO	UN Educational, Scientific and Cultural Organization
ICAO	International Civil Aviation Organization		
ICBL	International Campaign to Ban Landmines	UNFPA	UN Population Fund
ICC	International Chamber of Commerce	UNHCR	UN High Commissioner for Refugees
ICCA	International Council of Chemical Associations	UNICEF	UN Children's Fund
		UN1DO	UN Industrial Development Organization
ICFTU	International Confederation of Free Trade Unions	UPU	Universal Postal Union
		WA	Wassenaar Arrangement on Export Controls for Conventional Arms and Dual-Use Goods and Technologies
ICRC	International Committee of the Red Cross		
ICS	International Chamber of Shipping		
ICSU	International Council for Science	WFP	World Food Programme
IFAD	International Fund for Agricultural Development	WHO	World Health Organization
		WIPO	World intellectual Property Organization
IFPMA	International Federation of Pharmaceutical Manufacturers Associations	WMO	World Meteorological Organization
		WTO	World Trade Organization
ILO	International Labour Organization	WWF	Worldwide Fund for Nature
IMF	International Monetary Fund		

evidence that Dicken also refers to (see above) suggests that the biggest companies from the United States, Japan and Germany retain strong elements of their own home cultures in their management styles.

In support of the internationalist view, Glyn refers to an interesting passage in the 1848 *Communist Manifesto* where the role of the 'bourgeoisie', or the capitalist class as we might now call them, is identified (Glyn 2004):

> The bourgeoisie has through its exploitation of the world market given a cosmopolitan character to production and consumption in every country. ... [I]t compels all nations to introduce what it calls civilisation into their midst. In a word it creates a world after its own image.
>
> (Marx and Engels 1848: 46–7)

This could almost be a pessimist globalist writing: the US MNCs giving the cosmopolitan [or US] character to every country, and creating a [US culture] world in its own image! So the internationalists trace the international growth of capitalism a long way back, and say that nothing fundamental is really changing. Similarly, Keynes famously remarked about the intensely international nature of life in London in the early 20th century, and how it was possible, with the greatest of ease, to buy goods from all around the world, and indeed to invest one's money anywhere in the world (Keynes 1919).

The internationalist analysis stresses the extent to which the rich countries dominate world trade, but points out that nonetheless most of the giant corporations conduct the majority of their business at home (see Table 6.2). By this analysis it ought to be possible to exercise some governmental control over the operations of these international companies that others call MNCs and TNCs, given the political will.

An interesting position which seems to encompass both transformationalist and internationalist analyses is seen in Singh and Thandi (1999). Here it is argued that even though LDCs may face 'the wrath of the inescapable force of globalisation' it is nonetheless the case that 'A region which is globally interactive is more influential than a region which is globally isolated [like Albania or North Korea]' (Singh and Thandi 1999: 4).

So in response to the question posed earlier of whether action is needed to 'control' or try to control MNC behaviour, we have encountered two broad types of answer. First are those answers based on analogy with the arguments for competition policy, and second are those responses related to the three theories of globalisation as outlined by Kelly.

Globalisation and MNCs – is action possible?

We can identify a number of possible responses to this question. One response, of the anti-globalisation movement, would be to support direct action and protest. We shall say no more about that here. Other reactions to the question of what can be done might include the following:

● Do nothing.
● Introduce guidelines as deemed necessary.
● Rely on public opinion.
● Use the law courts.
● Deny market access.
● Develop intergovernmental responses, for example by the European Union.

We shall briefly consider each of these possibilities.

First, from the perspective of positive globalists the reaction with respect to possible policy options to limit the activities of MNCs would be: do nothing. That is because this group argues that the growth of MNCs and the fact of globalisation are both thoroughly desirable. Indeed many countries have very actively sought to encourage inward FDI by foreign MNCs. For example the spectacular success story of the Irish economy in the 1990s owed a good deal to its long-standing policy of welcoming FDI with all sorts of incentives, not least in the boom area near Galway and Shannon Airport. In similar vein, if slightly more critical, would be some globalists with reservations. Jones (2004) for example has argued that on balance the good that MNCs does far outweighs any mistakes they might make, and that to do nothing to restrict them is the right policy. MNCs will naturally 'police' themselves, Jones argues, because reputation is a key factor in sustaining competitive advantage, and no firms, especially high-profile MNCs, will want to see their reputations damaged. The World Economic Forum (WEF) group of leaders of the rich world's nations and MNCs would similarly advocate doing little or nothing to restrict MNCs' operations. Furthermore even J. K. Galbraith, usually a stern critic of the abuse of MNC power, suggests that sometimes giant MNCs are needed: large tasks, he has argued, require large organisations to undertake them, especially in the vital area of research and development (Galbraith 1980).

The second approach to consider with respect to MNC control is the setting up of agreed standards of behaviour, or codes of practice. The OECD has published a code of practice called *The OECD Guidelines for Multi-national Enterprises.* This is a listing of what is considered to be good practice by MNCs, and is referred to as a 'key corporate responsibility tool'. Key topics covered include sustainable development, human rights, human capital formation, health and safety, good corporate governance, and abstaining from local political activities. The OECD recognises that although observance of the guidelines is voluntary for businesses, 'adhering governments are committed to promoting them and making them influential among companies operating in or from their territories' (OECD 2004). This code of practice is an important document, and gets wide publicity from the OECD itself, but also from the European Union and the UK government. The UK Department of Trade and Industry has taken the code of practice on board and has adopted the recently set-up system of national contact points (NCPs) which are designed to make it easier for citizens and businesses in all OECD countries to engage with the operation of the guidelines. (DTI 2004).

The code of practice covers many aspects of MNC operations, including recommendations about transfer pricing, about which it says that firms 'should comply with the tax laws and regulations in all countries and should act in accordance with both the letter and the spirit of those laws ... and conforming transfer pricing practices to the arm's length principle' (OECD 2004). The arm's length principle means that firms engaged in transfer pricing should use prices for their internal calculations as if dealing with outside sources (who would be 'at arm's length'). The evidence on transfer pricing, however, suggests that this particular guideline is not being followed with much enthusiasm by most MNCs. A number of states in the United States have tried to introduce so-called 'unitary' or 'unit' taxation. This involves taxing part of an MNC's profits, regardless of where they are declared, pro rata with the proportion of sales generated in the tax district. However a number of Japanese firms said that they would withdraw FDI proposals unless these states dropped their plans to set unitary taxes in this way. Consequently a number of states did indeed drop their unitary tax plans.

Another code of practice was recently established by Transparency International (TI), a non-governmental organisation (NGO) active in monitoring MNCs' and governments' activities worldwide. In January 2005 it announced that 63 MNCs had taken some steps towards implementing anti-bribery principles.

A rather more significant code of practice is the recent European Commission communication with respect to CSR (European Commission 2002). The communication brings together the need for good corporate behaviour and governance, and achievement of the goals of the Lisbon Strategy (see Chapter 10). In this detailed document the Commission, on behalf of the European Union, gives full backing to the value of and importance of CSR. However the document is more exhortation than compulsion, as is necessarily the case with codes of practice, and indeed there are no requirements indicated for CSR by any companies.

Perhaps codes of practice and statements of intent are not the most efficient ways of trying to influence MNC activities. Sometimes public opinion may bring results, if vigorously expressed or acted upon. One well-publicised incident was Shell's plan to dispose of a disused oil storage platform by dumping it the North Sea in 1995. The pressure group Greenpeace was strongly opposed to this action by Shell on environmental grounds. A consumer boycott of Shell petrol stations, in Germany in particular, led to a change of plans by Shell in a matter of days. Later Greenpeace had to admit that its estimates of likely environmental damage had been very inaccurate. Nonetheless the point is clear, that public opinion if backed by some method of causing direct commercial damage (and reputation damage, as suggested by Jones, above) may cause even one of the world's very largest MNCs to change its business plans.

Another example of public opinion taking effect in a 'one-off' way relates to the Multilateral Agreement on Investment (MAI). The MAI was a plan, put forward by representatives of some of the world's largest MNCs, which was being discussed and developed at the WTO in 2001, to deregulate FDI as much as possible, so that MNCs could actually challenge governments that sought to impose restrictions, for example on health and safety grounds. The plans were originally intended to be negotiated through the WTO, but so many objections were raised, especially by LDC governments, that the discussions moved to the OECD. Through effective campaigning, and a worldwide spate of protests largely organised via Internet networks and groupings, the MAI plans were shelved.

We consider next the use of the law courts as a means of trying to control MNCs. There are some interesting instances of MNCs being taken to court, although we saw above that Union Carbide have avoided legal actions in the Indian criminal courts for a number of years. A recent example of court action was in December 2004 when Unocal Corporation, a large California-based oil and energy company, with annual revenues of approximately US$1 billion, had to settle a compensation case brought by villagers in Myanmar who alleged rape and murder by soldiers employed by Unocal to protect an oil pipeline there. In another case in 2002 a number of retailers in the United States, including Gap, settled lawsuits by factory workers in Saipan, a Pacific island near Guam, who claimed that they had been forced to accept sweatshop conditions of employment, or have no work at all. These cases against Unocal and Gap have been seen as key test cases for human rights activists who have filed lawsuits against ChevronTexaco, Ford and IBM alleging corporate malpractice.

Thus we can see that in a variety of ways pressure can be brought to bear on some MNCs, though codes of practice may be seen to be rather feeble in some cases. Stricter systems than codes of practice may be resisted vigorously by MNCs, and as Vernon points out, 'It seems a plausible generalisation that agreements substantially affecting TNCs are unlikely to see the light of day unless they have the support of these firms themselves' (Vernon 1994: 570). If this is so what is it possible for governments, and/or the European Union, to do?

Cowling and Sugden (1987) suggested that MNCs that conduct a substantial amount of business, producing, selling or sourcing within a country could be regulated by host governments through threats to exclude the MNC from that country. Even to footloose giants this could possibly give governments very real leverage if, for example, the threat was to prohibit access to markets. The 'terms of trade' in such a relationship would depend on the volume, value and significance to the company of the operation or activity being threatened, the sort of compliance being required and the importance of the company to the host economy. For example, a confectionery manufacturer in an EU member state might be in a weak bargaining position in relation to the host government if threatened by market exclusion, as it is hardly of strategic or other key importance to the host. On the other hand an inward direct investor in a high-technology industry in a less developed or developing economy would presumably be in a much stronger bargaining position. To pull out of a country is always a possibility, but then clearly sales are lost. MNCs have however been shown to be willing to pull out. Coca-Cola for example has in the past ceased dealing in India, Nigeria and elsewhere to avoid host-country interference, and the demand to disclose its secret formula to local partners.

For EU member states acting together, this 'denial of access' could be a very powerful threat indeed. It is also, and finally, possible that the EU member states, acting in concert and with genuine commitment, could have the requisite economic and market muscle (countervailing power) to enforce appropriate MNC regulation. Establishing commitment to such a programme might however be a far from simple process, let alone achieving consensus on the policies themselves.

The European Union does not seem to have any very clear or coherent overall policy towards MNC activities, apart from the CSR projects referred to above. However, through its various economic and social programmes (including the Social Chapter and directives on the hours of the working week and so on), the European Union can, and does, greatly influence the conditions under which MNCs operate in its territory. The Commission may also affect other elements in the environment of business through consumer protection, the protection of workers' interests, the maintenance of competition, merger and acquisition rules and certain information release requirements. Nonetheless, in Europe the degree to which national governments seek to control MNCs varies, and this can be used as a mechanism to attract MNCs. The fact that there is not a level playing field in the area of MNC control in Europe has led to the development of the Bolkestein Directive, the impact of which is outlined in the case study.

A CONTROVERSIAL NEW EUROPEAN DIRECTIVE

The [UK] government is backing a European Commission initiative aimed at radically reducing the powers of national governments over MNCs. Although it has received scant media attention in the United Kingdom, the 'Bolkestein Directive' has provoked mass protests, and debate, in France, Belgium, Sweden and Denmark.

The directive, which the EU parliament voted for in February 2006 after much revision, has two main aims: to erase any national laws and standards that make it difficult for European companies to enter the markets of other member states, and to allow European companies to run businesses anywhere in the European Union according to the rules of their 'country of origin'.

The directive is controversial because it applies the same rules to healthcare and social services as it does to estate agents, fairground providers, advertising companies and private security firms. The Commission no longer sees the services provided by doctors to patients as a special public good to be enjoyed by all citizens, but as an 'economic activity', a commodity to be traded across the European Union much like any other.

Healthcare services are thought to amount to about 10 per cent of the EU's GDP, so the potential for private companies to make profits from healthcare is vast. But publicly funded healthcare systems have until now been protected by national laws. An example of this has been the UK restrictions on supermarkets dispensing NHS prescriptions except in areas of need, for fear of killing off community chemists. The Bolkestein Directive would require the United Kingdom to drop these rules.

The fact that the DTI is negotiating the UK position is a cause for worry, as the DTI is on record as saying that concerns about safety and quality standards should not be allowed to outweigh the benefits the directive might bring to British businesses.

There are also worries expressed by the Security Industry Authority, which regulates private security firms. This industry is plagued by criminal infiltration, and it could get worse if rules are relaxed. Construction companies too may be able to lower their standards relating to health and safety, and environmental campaigners fear that local planning rules, which govern where supermarkets may and may not set up, may be scrapped, as may rules allowing local regulation of the numbers of clubs and bars in city centres.

Concerns about poorly regulated foreign companies being given free rein in other EU countries fit in with arguments about the so-called 'race to the bottom' whereby MNCs can coerce economies which are competing for their business, or FDI, to competitively lower standards. Yet if EU-wide standards can be introduced to govern the quality of car tyres, why should services be exempt?

Source: *Guardian* (2005).

Questions

1   On behalf of the Commissioner for the Internal Market suggest arguments in support of the Bolkestein Directive. Which parts of your case would be most important?

2   Prepare an argument, to be put to the European Commission, that the Bolkestein Directive should be scrapped. Amongst your points should be the subsidiarity principle, and the general need for more, not less, regulation of MNCs. Outline your argument carefully, and indicate what you think the most important points to be.

3   The MAI [Multinational Agreement on Investment] was put on hold, at least, by the power of publicly stated opposition. Considering all the pros and cons, as in Questions 1 and 2, do you think the Bolkestein directive should also be put on hold?

Conclusion

This chapter has considered the size and importance of MNCs in international trade, and we have seen parts of the debate about their roles and effects. Some positive attitudes towards MNCs and globalisation have been contrasted with a more suspicious approach in which the ethics of some MNC behaviour are questioned.

Globalisation and the need for good governance generate much debate and suggestions for intervention of many types. We saw some of the many levels of global governance mapped in Figures 6.1 and 6.2. From these figures we can see, at the very least, that there are many institutions (national and international), NGOs, charities and pressure groups all with an interest in global and MNC governance.

There also seem to be grounds for suggesting that attempts should, and could, be made to regulate or control the operations of MNCs in the same way as monopolies and cartels are controlled by competition policy legislation. Individual governments or nations acting in groups (like the European Union, Mercosur, NAFTA or ASEAN, for example) may be able to exercise some countervailing power against the giant MNCs. But even if they can exercise such countervailing power they might not wish to, as Dunning reminds us. Of nearly 1,000 worldwide investment regime regulation changes in the 1990s, over 90 per cent were favourable to MNCs and FDI (Dunning 2001: 337, and see case study). Even faced with this evidence from Dunning we would add that the fact that the world economy is becoming more and more internationalised does not of itself mean that how this internationalisation happens, or the role of MNCs within the process, are all predetermined. Public opinion and governments are not necessarily powerless in the face of MNCs and globalisation.

Questions

1   What do you understand the Transnationality Index to mean? What can we learn about the process of globalisation from the TNI evidence in Table 6.2?

2   Ohmae says that we now live in a 'borderless world'. What does he mean? Do you think he is right? What impact does this have on business?

3   Explain what 'transfer pricing' means in the context of globalised business activity. Why do businesses do this and what effect does it have on governments?

4   Some people argue that globalisation has failed to rid the world of poverty and is therefore not desirable. If poverty still exists, others might reply, it is because there has not been enough globalisation yet. When MNCs are truly free to operate where and how they want to, then the benefits of free markets will be able to raise everybody's living standards. Explain these two viewpoints. Which do you think is the sounder argument?

5   It is sometimes said that MNCs limit the sovereignty of governments and nation states. Others argue that only governments can raise taxes or an army, and so governments are clearly more powerful than companies. Who is right?

6 Look at the official EU 'portal' or gateway website (http://europa.eu.int). What can you learn from this website about the EU approach to and attitude towards MNCs?

7 Look at the quotation from the *Communist Manifesto* of 1848 in this chapter. Given what is said there, and using any other relevant information you have, how surprised do you think Marx and Engels would be if they could see the levels of globalisation now, in the 21st century?

References

Alfaro, L. and Rodriguez-Clare, A. (2003) *Multinationals and Linkages: An empirical investigation*, Harvard Business School Press, Boston, Mass., September.

BBC (2005)' SEC to rethink post-Enron rules', *BBC News*, 25 January, newsvote.bbc.co.uk/mpapps/pagetools/print/news.bbc.co.uk/1/hi/business/4204, accessed March 2005.

Brah, A., Hickman, M. and Mac an Ghaill, M. (1999) *Global Futures*, Palgrave, Basingstoke.

Cowling, K. and Sugden, R. (1987) *Transnational Monopoly Capitalism*, Wheatsheaf Books, Brighton.

Dicken, P. (2003) *Global Shift*, 4th edn, Sage, London.

DTI (2004) DTI – *Europe and World Trade*, www.dti.gov.uk/ewt/ukncp.htm, accessed March 2005.

Dunning, J. H. (2001) *Global Capitalism at Bay?* Routledge, London.

Dunning, J. H. and Sauvant, K. P. (1996) 'Introduction: transnational corporations in the world economy', in UNCTAD, *Transnational Corporations and World Development*, ITB Press, New York.

Economist (1994) 'Bhopal, ten years on', 3 December, pp. 78–9.

European Commission (2002) *Communication concerning Corporate Social Responsibility; a business contribution to sustainable development*, COM 2002 (347)2002 2261 (INI).

Fortune (2004) 'The Fortune 500, Introduction', 5 April, pp. 36–8.

Freeman, O. L. (1981) *The Multinational Company: Instrument for world growth*, Praeger, New York.

Friedman, M. (1962) *Capitalism, and Freedom*, University of Chicago Press, Chicago.

Friends of the Earth (2001) *The Seattle Ministerial Conference and Beyond*, www.foei.org/trade/activistguide/millenum.htm, accessed March 2005.

Galbraith, J. K. (1974) *The New Industrial State*, 2nd edn, Penguin, London.

Galbraith, J. K. (1980) *American Capitalism*, Blackwell, Oxford.

Glyn, A. (2004) 'The assessment: how far has globalization gone?', *Oxford Review of Economic Policy*, vol. 20, no. 1, pp. 1–14.

Guardian (2004) 'A worthwhile policy or simply propaganda?', 17 July.

Guardian (2005) 'In the health trade', 20 January, p. 25.

Hannah, L. (1983) *The Rise of the Corporate Economy*, 2nd edn, Methuen, London.

Held, D. (ed.) (2004) *A Globalizing World? Culture, economics, politics*, 2nd edn, Routledge/Open University, London.

Held, D. and McGrew, A. (2002) *Globalization/Anti-Globalization*, Polity Press, Cambridge.

Hood, N. and Young, S. (1979) *The Economics of Multinational Enterprise*, Longman, London.

Husted, S. and Melvin, M. (2004) *International Economics*, 6th edn, Pearson/Addison Wesley, New York.

Hymer, S. and Rowthorn, R. (1970) 'Multinational corporations and international oligopoly: the non-American challenge', in C. P. Kindleberger (ed.), *The International Corporation*, MIT Press, Boston, Mass.

Indymedia (2003) *Summer of Resistance Europe 2001*, www.indymedia.org.uk/en/actions/2001/genoa/, accessed March 2005.

Jarman, A. F. (2005) 'Review of Madeley (1999)', *International Journal of Punjab Studies*, vol. 12, no. 1, January–June.

Jones, I. (2004) 'MNEs in third world countries – might they have a significant impact on quality of life?' Discussion paper given at Oxford Brookes University, 24 May.

Kelly, B. and Prokhovnik, R. (2004) 'Economic globalization', ch. 3 in D. Held (ed.), *A Globalizing World? Culture, economics, politics*, 2nd edn, Routledge/Open University, London.

Kennedy, P., Messner, D. and Nuscheler, F. (2002) *Global Trends and Global Governance*, Pluto Press, London, p. 143.

Keynes, J. M. (1919) *The Economic Consequences of the Peace*, Macmillan, London.

Krugman, P. R. (ed.) (1987a) *Strategic Trade Policy and the New International Economics*, MIT Press, Boston, Mass.

Krugman, P. R. (1987b) 'Is free trade passé?' *Journal of Economic Perspectives*, Fall, pp. 131–44.

Krugman, P. R. and Obstfeld, M. (2003) *International Economics: Theory and policy*, 6th edn, Addison Wesley, London/Boston, Mass.

Madeley, J. (1999) *Big Business, Poor Peoples*, Zed Books, London.

Mansfield, E. (1999), *Managerial Economics*, 4th edn, W W Norton, New York.

Marx, K. and Engels, F. (1848) *Manifesto of the Communist Party*, 1977 reprint, Progress Publishers, Moscow.

McCormick, R. D. (2002) 'Debate: globalisation – good or bad?' BBC News Online discussion, www.news.bbc.co.uk/l/low/business/1790941.stm, accessed March 2005.

Moran, T. H. (1996) 'Governments and transnational corporations', in UNCTAD, *Transnational Corporations and World Development*, ITB Press, New York.

Novartis Foundation for Sustainable Development (2005) *The Effect of Multinational Companies on Development*, Novartis, Geneva.

OECD (2003) *Incentives-based Competition for Foreign Direct Investment: The case of Brazil*, Working Papers on International Investment, no. 2003/1, OECD, Paris.

OECD (2004) *Annual Report on the Guidelines for Multinational Enterprises: 2004 edition*, www.oecd.org/document/20/0,2,en_2649_33765_34325076_1_1_1_1,00.html, accessed March 2005.

Ohmae, K. (1994) *The Borderless World*, Harper Collins, London.

Pesticide Action Network (2004) 'Elvis died in Bhopal twenty years ago', *Guardian*, 3 December.

Piscitello, L. and Rabbiosi, L (2005) 'The impact of inward FDI on local companies' labour productivity: evidence from the Italian case', *International Journal of the Economics of Business*, vol. 12, no. 1, February, pp. 35–51.

Sampson, A. (2004) *Who Runs This Place? The anatomy of Britain in the 21st century*, John Murray, London.

Silicon.com and CNET Networks (no date) *Sarbanes-Oxley: Another law to ignore?* www.silicon.com/research/special, accessed March 2005

Singh, P. and Thandi, S. S. (1999) *Punjabi Identity in a Global Context*, Oxford University Press, New Delhi.

Stiglitz, J. (2002) *Globalization and its Discontents*, Penguin, London.

Transparency International (2005) 'Press release: 63 multinational companies take first step towards implementing anti-bribery principles', www. transparency.org/pressreleases_archive/2005/2005.02.2.63%20multin_comp_implem_a_bribery.html, accessed March 2005.

UNCTAD (2002) *World Investment Report 2002*, ? publisher, Geneva.

Vernon, R. (1971) *Sovreignty at Bay: The multinational spread of US enterprises*, Basic Books, New York.

Vernon, R. (1994) 'Research on transnational corporations:. shredding old paradigms', *Transnational Corporations*, vol. 3, no 1.

World Economic Forum (WEF) (2005) *Global Competitiveness Report*, http://annualmeeting.weforum.org, accessed 7 January 2006.

7

Foreign direct investment (FDI)

Haluk Sezer

Objectives

This chapter will:

- consider recent trends in **foreign direct investment (FDI)** inflow and outflows between the European Union, North America, the Pacific rim and less-developed countries (LDCs)
- evaluate the motives and explanations of FDI
- outline intra-EU FDI flows
- appreciate the impact of FDI flows on the economies of LDCs
- consider the policy implications of FDI flows for LDCs.

Introduction

Both international trade and **FDI** are ways of obtaining market positions. A local market can be serviced by local investment, production and sales, or by imports. A foreign market can be serviced either by investing and producing domestically and then exporting; or by investing, producing and selling directly into that market. In practice international firms utilise different combinations of these two possibilities. Thus trade and FDI are sometimes competing and sometimes complementary ways of servicing a foreign market (Julius 1993). However, some researchers consider the reasons for FDI to be far more complex.

FDI by multinational companies (MNCs) is one of the most controversial subjects within economics (see Chapter 6). The LDCs seem both to oppose and to flirt with it, and the developed countries (DCs) try to limit its outflow sometimes and its inflow at other times. Some see FDI as the key to the solutions for various global problems such as famine, starvation and environmental damage; yet some researchers regard FDI as the very instrument through which these disasters are globally inflicted. This chapter looks at all these questions.

Definition

It is difficult to provide a comprehensive definition of FDI. Some authors define it in terms of its international characteristics and contrast it with **portfolio investment**; others express it in terms of the activities of MNCs (Ietto-Gillies 2005). Most definitions, however, seem to have two common elements. One is that FDI involves at least two countries. This criterion relates to the multi-national character of FDI. The other element is the issue of ownership and control, which distinguishes FDI from portfolio investment. Foreign portfolio investment is a simple transfer of financial capital, equity or loan, from one country to another, whereas FDI involves the ownership and control of production activities abroad. Needless to say what constitutes ownership and/or control itself is a controversial issue.

FDI is more complex in nature than portfolio investment since it often involves transfer of inputs such as technical know-how, and managerial and organisational ability. Moreover, when the necessary finance is raised locally there is no capital flow at all, at least not in a strict sense. Finally, FDI is embodied in the activities of MNCs. Therefore the definition of FDI cannot practically be considered in isolation from the definition of a MNC, which is also difficult to establish (see Chapter 6).

Despite these difficulties it is necessary to define FDI one way or another, partly for theoretical clarity and partly for empirical necessity. For our purpose it is sufficient to define FDI as the acquisition, establishment or increase in production facilities by a firm in a foreign country. This definition covers all three elements of FDI: '**greenfield investment**', which is when FDI enters a particular industry for the first time; **mergers and acquisitions**; and finally reinvestment, where a foreign firm that is already established reinvests its profits in the host country rather than repatriating them.

What distinguishes FDI from portfolio investment, in the case of acquisition, is that the investing firm acquires enough equity to exercise control over the capital invested (Baker 1990). What proportion of equity is needed to have control is, of course, a matter of judgment. Outward FDI implies an increase in the overseas operations of MNCs: for example, British firms investing abroad. Conversely, inward FDI means an increase in the business activities of foreign MNCs in the host country; for example, non-EU firms expanding business into the European Union.

Historical pattern of FDI

The analysis of the role of foreign investment becomes increasingly difficult as we go back in time because of data difficulties. However, despite these difficulties, it is clear that the role of foreign investment has been important since the Industrial Revolution.

Pre-First World War period

The origins of FDI go back to the Industrial Revolution. There was migration *en masse* from Europe to the Americas during the 19th century, which was accompanied by movements of large amounts of capital. As colonialisation got underway there was need for international investment, since firms were competing for markets in terms of both financing their imports of raw materials and exporting their manufactured goods. FDI in the 19th century was concentrated in natural resources and transportation, but was also found in energy and financial services. Most of this investment came from the United Kingdom, which dominated the world exports of manufactured goods (Big Picture Small World 2005).

Total world FDI stock in 1914 was more than US$14.5 billion, which constituted around 9 per cent of the total world gross domestic product (GDP) and around 35 per cent of the long-term debt in the world. This ratio of FDI to GDP was only equalled in the 1990s (see Table 7.2), a fact used by those who argue that globalisation is not a new phenomenon.

In the period before the First World War there was considerable movement of capital investment, and until recently it was thought that most of this consisted of portfolio investment. However, more recent research indicates that the role of direct investment was much more important than assumed previously.

Just before the First World War the most important capital exporting country was the United Kingdom, accounting for 45.5 per cent of all cumulative FDI outflows (amounting to approximately 7 per cent of its national income). The United States and other European countries such as France and Germany, and to a lesser extent the Netherlands, followed (see Table 7.1). A substantial amount of UK capital went into railways and government securities in the countries of the Americas and Australasia, and was mainly in portfolio investment whereas American investment was more in the form of FDI by large MNCs. However, by 1914 40 per cent of British overseas investment in the LDCs and America was direct investment (Hood and Young 1979).

The share of the European countries in world FDI, not including the United Kingdom, was over 30 per cent. Europe, including the United Kingdom, accounted for more than three-quarters of the total cumulative FDI outflows in the world in 1914. This was the heyday of European imperialism. What is not clear from Table 7.1 is that Europe concentrated on venture capital: that is, foreign production activities were controlled by acquiring sufficient equity capital. European countries were already the main source of portfolio capital outflows. In contrast, US companies used their comparative advantage in technology and management skills to establish affiliates of the home MNC overseas.

Another point worth noting is that FDI was largely concentrated in capital-intensive primary product and technology-intensive manufacturing sectors. More than 80 per cent of this investment went to what would be considered as the

Table 7.1 Percentage shares of cumulative FDI outflows by country

	1914	1938	1960	1980	1999
Developed countries	100.0	100.0	98.9	100.0	89.9
UK	45.5	39.8	16.2	15.0	14.0
Germany	10.5	1.3	1.2	8.0	8.0
France	12.2	9.5	6.1	4.0	7.2
Netherlands	5.0	7.0	10.5	7.0	6.0
Other W. Europe	5.0	10.2	8.0	10.0	19.0
Japan	2.1	3.0	0.8	8.0	6.2
United States	18.5	27.5	49.2	40.0	27.5
Rest of developed countries	1.2	4.7	8.0	8.0	2.0
Developing countries	0.0	0.0	1.1	–	9.8

Sources: adapted from Piggott and Cook (1999). O'Rourke (2002)

LDCs by contemporary criteria; by 1978 this figure was less than one-third (Dunning 1983). However, the bulk of FDI in the LDCs was in the extractive and agricultural sectors, such as rubber, tea, coffee and cocoa plantations, as well in cattle raising and meat processing. A single cash crop that dominated a country's economy was a particular favourite with the MNCs of the time: for example, sugar (Cuba), bananas (Costa Rica), tea (Ceylon) and rubber (Liberia). Thus it is possible to observe a parallel between the pattern of FDI and that of colonialism. For example 72 per cent of US investment was in the American continent, and much of British, French and Dutch investment in extractive and agricultural sectors was in their respective colonies. In contrast, the breakdown of manufacturing subsidiaries of MNCs by country of location before 1914 indicates that around 80 per cent of the subsidiaries established by US, UK and continental European-based MNCs was in the developed countries (Dunning 1983).

The inter-war period

The inter-war years witnessed a slowdown in the expansion of international business, including capital exports. Britain was still the main creditor country, but continental Europe changed from net creditor to net debtor status by the 1920s because of war debts and reconstruction costs after the First World War. Conversely, the US position was reversed from that of a debtor to that of a creditor. During the 1930s, world capital flows in general reduced drastically following the collapse of international capital markets in the late 1920s and early 1930s. Nevertheless, the FDI of the United States increased its share of the world total because it was in the form of branch plant activities by MNCs as opposed to equity capital. Thus the US share of the world capital outflows rose from 18.5 per cent in 1914 to 27.5 per cent in 1938, as can be seen from Table 7.1. In fact FDI overall increased in the inter-war period in contrast to portfolio investment.

There were also some quantitative changes. First, the LDCs increased their share of FDI inflows slightly, with Asia and Africa increasing their shares at the expense of Latin America. However the latter was still by far the largest recipient of FDI. Second, there was a noticeable amount of new MNC activity in the LDCs, in such sectors as oil (the Mexican Gulf, Dutch East Indies and Middle East), copper and iron ore (Africa), bauxite (Dutch or British Guyana), nitrate (Chile), precious metals (South Africa), and most noteworthy, non-ferrous metals (South America). Indeed according to some observers most of the mineral resources in South America were owned by US interests. Finally, FDI between the DCs was gaining importance. There was substantial flow of US capital into Canada and Europe in addition to South America. Indeed, investment from continental European firms went mainly to the other parts of Europe and the United States, and the first four Japanese manufacturing affiliates of the largest Japanese MNCs existing in 1970 appeared in this period (Dunning 1983).

The post-war period

After the Second World War, FDI dominated capital movements. The dominant position of FDI was mainly a result of the increase in the US capital outflows up to the 1960s, after which FDI from Europe, Japan and the newly industrialised countries (NICs) began to play an increasingly important role. In the 1950s and the 1960s, the Marshall Plan, the International Monetary Fund (IMF), the General Agreement on Tariffs and Trade (GATT), the formation of the European Economic Community (EEC) and the revolutionary developments in communication and transport, such as the computer and the jet aircraft, were all contributory factors for the phenomenal increase in FDI from the United States. Of about a US$40 billion increase in total FDI between 1938 and 1960, the United States accounted for about two-thirds, which increased its cumulative share of world capital stock from 27.5 per cent to 49.2 per cent, whereas the share of western Europe declined over this period (see Table 7.1).

However, some radical changes had also taken place in the composition of FDI in the aftermath of the Second World War. In 1914, nearly two-thirds of new FDI was still going to the LDCs; by 1938 this had fallen to 55 per cent, and in 1960 it was around 40 per cent. This was mainly the result of another structural change in FDI: in 1914 only 15 per cent of the US and UK accumulated investment was in manufacturing, but by 1960 this rose to 35 per cent. By contrast the proportion of UK and US FDI going to agricultural and public utility activities declined drastically between 1914 and 1960. It should be noted, however, that investment in non-ferrous metals by UK and US MNCs was an exception to this trend, since investment in, for example, copper (Chile and Peru), bauxite (in the Caribbean) and particularly oil (in the Persian Gulf), grew very rapidly (Dunning 1983).

Recent developments

Recent years have witnessed increased globalisation of the world economy, helped by technological development as well as the liberalisation and privatisation policies followed by many governments in the 1980s. In parallel MNCs have assumed an increasingly important role in the global economy, accounting for some 80 per cent of world trade and an equal proportion of the private R&D expenditure (Dunning 1993). Consequently FDI has grown dramatically reaching unprecedented levels in recent years (see Table 7.2). In addition to this quantitative increase, the composition and the geographical distribution of FDI have also changed in recent years.

One significant development regarding FDI is the increase in its relative importance in national economies in both capital-exporting and capital-importing countries. Two measures of the importance of inward FDI to an economy are the ratio of FDI to GDP and the ratio of FDI to gross fixed capital formation (GFCF). In Table 7.2 we can see that both FDI inflows and outflows have grown much faster than either GDP or GFCF, which indicates an increase in the two ratios concerned, and in turn implies an increase in the relative importance of FDI.

Table 7.3 indicates that the FDI inflows in the world increased by an incredible 122.2 per cent between the early and late 1990s. This growth continued, and between 1998 and 2000 FDI inflows doubled. However, at the beginning of the new millennium growth in the FDI inflows was negative. In fact they declined by 41.1 per cent in 2001, 17 per cent in 2002 and 17.6 per cent in 2003 (see Table 7.2). This pattern applies to the European Union as a whole although

Table 7.2 The importance of FDI

Item	Value at current prices (US$ billion)			Annual growth rate, per cent			
	1982	1990	2003	2000	2001	2002	2003
FDI inflows	59	209	560	27.7	−41.1	−17.0	−17.6
FDI outflows	28	242	612	8.7	−39.2	−17.3	2.6
FDI inward stock	796	1,950	8,245	19.1	7.4	12.7	11.8
FDI outward stock	590	1,758	8,197	18.5	5.9	13.8	13.7
Cross-border M&As	–	151	297	49.3	−48.1	−37.7	−19.7
GDP at current prices	11,737	22,588	36,163	2.7	−0.9	3.7	12.1
GFCF	2,285	4,815	7,294	3.8	−3.6	−0.6	9.9
Exports*	2,246	4,260	9,228	11.4	−3.3	4.7	16.6

GFCF   gross fixed capital formation

M&As   mergers and acquisitions

* Exports of goods and factor services.

Source: adapted from UNCTAD (2004a, ch. 1, table 1.3, p. 9).

Table 7.3 FDI inflows, 1992–2003

	1992–7 annual average		1998		2000		2002		2003	
	Value (US$ million)	% share	Value) (US$ million)	% share	Value (US$ million)	% share	Value (US$ million)	% share	Value (US$ million)	% share
World	310,879	100.0	690,905	100.0	1,387,953	100.0	678,751	100.0	559,576	100.0
DCs	180,750	58.1	472,545	68.4	1,107,987	79.8	489,907	72.2	366,573	65.5
WE	100,796	32.4	263,016	38.1	697,436	50.2	380,245	56.0	310,234	55.4
EU	95,845	30.8	249,931	36.2	671,417	48.3	374,000	55.1	295,154	52.7
OWE	4,950	1.6	13,086	1.9	26,019	1.9	6,245	0.9	15,080	3.0
USA	60,268	19.4	174,434	25.2	314,007	22.6	62,870	9.3	29,772	5.3
ODC	19,686	6.3	35,095	5.1	96,544	7.0	46,792	6.9	26,567	4.7
LDCs	118,596	38.1	194,055	28.1	252,459	18.1	157,612	23.2	172,033	30.7
CEECs	11,533	3.7	24,305	3.5	27,507	2.0	31,232	4.6	20,970	3.7

CEECs   central and east European countries

DCs   developed countries

EU   European Union

LDCs   less developed countries

ODC   other developed countries: Australia, Israel, Japan and New Zealand

OWE   other western Europe: Gibraltar, Iceland, Malta, Norway and Switzerland

WE   western Europe

Source: Adapted from UNCTAD (2004a: ch. 1, annex table B1).

there are exceptions with respect to individual countries such as Germany, Ireland and Spain. The same downward trend can also be observed for the rest of DCs as well as the United States itself. The western European countries outside the European Union, however, seem to have recovered and improved their shares in 2003, and so did the LDCs. Unfortunately, the positive outlook for LDCs is rather misleading since most of the increase in both the absolute level and the share of the LDCs is due to the strong position of China. If China is excluded from the picture, the position of LDCs with respect to FDI inflows is bleak since there has been a continuous fall since 1999.

One reason for the reduction in the FDI inflows overall is the relatively sluggish macroeconomic performance of the economies of DCs in recent years. Another reason is the substantial amount of cross-border investment in several sectors in the 1990s and 2000, which inevitably leads to a period of consolidation by the firms themselves. This particularly applies to sectors such as the new economy, where the events of recent times have resulted in investing firms moving with more caution (OECD 2004). However, UNCTAD expects an upturn in FDI inflows in coming years as growth gathers momentum in most of the developed world. In fact, a press release by UNCTAD on 11 January 2005 stated that total world FDI inflows rose by 6 per cent in 2004 according to most recent estimates, and that the outlook was positive. However, it also added that most of this increase was attributed to the LDCs and the central and eastern European countries (CEECs). The good news is that all regions of the developing world benefited from improved FDI inflows in 2004. Flows to Africa continued to rise for the second consecutive year, Asia and the Pacific saw a 55 per cent increase, and Latin America and the Caribbean achieved an increase for the first time to the tune of 37 per cent. However, FDI inflows to DCs continued to decline.

Table 7.3 also shows that around 65.5 per cent of FDI inflows were accounted for by DCs. However, the importance of DCs is decreasing and that of developing countries is increasing. This is reflected in the declining shares of DCs in both inflows and outflows, from 76 per cent and 95 per cent respectively in 1983–7 to 62 per cent and 85 per cent in 1993–5, whereas the corresponding shares of developing countries increased from 24 per cent and 5 per cent in 1983–7 to 35 per cent and 15 per cent in 1993–5. There has been a similar increase in the shares of central and eastern European countries as well. This means that there has been a widening of participation of source countries as far as outflows of FDI are concerned.

As for the outflows of FDI, there has been a decline in the performance of DCs in 2001 and 2002 but a partial recovery in 2003, except within western Europe and Japan where the decline continued. Both North America and the Pacific Rim recovered in 2003 from the decline they suffered in 2002. Thus the performance of DCs is rather uneven. This unevenness is much more apparent in the performance of the European Union. Outflows of FDI from the European Union on average declined by 4 per cent in 2003, but not from France and the United Kingdom, where they rose by 16 per cent and 57 per cent respectively. However, outflows from Germany declined by 70 per cent.

It is also clear that outflows of FDI are dominated by the DCs; not only do they account for more than 90 per cent of total world outflows of FDI, but their share has also been increasing in recent years, reaching 93 per cent in 2003 (UNCTAD 2004a).

Table 7.3 also indicates the rising importance of the CEECs as recipients of FDI flows. Inward investment into the CEECs was US$11.5 billion in the mid-1990s rising to US$31.2 billion in 2002. Despite the fall to around US$21 billion in 2003, this is a substantial increase in less than a decade. The main reason for this was the commitment by the European Union to the accession of the CEECs. The Essen Council announcement regarding enlargement eastward in 1994 resulted in substantial increase in FDI inflows into the Czech Republic, Hungary and Poland. The European Union's decision in 1997 to open negotiations with five CEECs, leaving the other five out, also led to an increase in FDI coming into the front-runners and thus widened the gap between their FDI receipts and the inflows to the other five CEECs (Bevan, Estrin and Grabbe 2001). Although all ten of the CEECs joined the European Union in May 2004 it is feared that this gap is not likely to be closed for some time.

In fact, according to the Economist Intelligence Unit (EIU), future prospects with respect to FDI inflows for the CEECs are not very bright. The EIU argues that despite the expected recovery in world FDI flows in 2005 and onwards, the sharp decline in FDI flows into the CEECs in 2003 is not temporary. The EIU expects a mild recovery in 2005/06 and then stabilisation around US$20 billion until 2008. The reasons for this relatively pessimistic forecast are first, that the market, it argues, is saturated in the CEECs, and they have already reaped all the possible benefits from FDI. Second, despite the lucrative consumer market, labour costs are relatively high in the CEECs. Thus investors, especially European investors, prefer Asian countries in general, and India and China in particular, especially where outsourcing applies (EIU 2004).

Distribution and structure of FDI

As for the geographical distribution of inward FDI worldwide, the share of DCs is expected to decline in favour of LDCs and the CEECs. Most of this decline is to be borne by the European Union, since the United States maintained its position, while Japan slightly improved its position during the first half of the present decade. However the European Union lost ground, with its share of world FDI inflows being reduced from 69.8 per cent in 2001 to 27 per cent in 2004 (UNCTAD 2005). This is mainly a result of drastic reductions in FDI inflows to Germany, Luxemburg and Spain.

Within the developing world there has been a shift away from Latin American, Caribbean and most African countries in favour of east and south Asia. While Latin America and the Caribbean slightly improved their shares between 2001 (10.8 per cent) and 2004 (11.3 per cent), Asia and the Pacific increased their share from 13.7 per cent to 27.1 per cent in the same period, with a 55 per cent growth in 2004 alone. There was also improvement in the share of the CEECs from 3.2 per cent to 5.9 per cent between 2001 and 2004.

The structure of FDI has also changed profoundly in recent years. There has been a considerable shift in FDI stock away from natural resources towards services. Only 31 per cent of the world FDI inward stock was in services (compared with 23 per cent in natural resources) in 1970. The share of services rose to 50 per cent and that of natural resources declined to 11 per cent in 1990, and today the services sector accounts for about 60 per cent of the global inward FDI stock. Traditionally, FDI in services has been concentrated in trade and finance, but recently it has been extended to the other service sectors such as electricity, water services, telecommunications, transport and storage. The combined share of the last three sectors rose from 17 per cent in 1990 to 41 per cent in 2002.

There are several factors explaining this shift to services. First, there is the ascendancy of the service sector in general in all economies. In 2001 'this sector accounted, on average, for 72 per cent of GDP in developed countries, 52 per cent in developing and 57 per cent in CEE countries' (UNCTAD 2004a: xxi). Second, most services are non-tradable and therefore necessitate FDI if MNCs are to invest in a country. Third, there has been considerable growth in the new economy sector in recent years despite several hitches; and finally, most counties have recently privatised services such as public utilities, rendering them available for foreign investment. The shift towards services also reflects itself in cross-border **mergers and acquisitions (M&A)** in recent times. At the end of the 1980s M&As in services constituted 40 per cent of all cross-border M&As whereas at the end of 1990s this figure was 60 per cent. Interestingly, up to the end of 1980s M&A activity was dominated by American MNCs, but since then EU MNCs have dominated cross-border M&A purchases, accounting for 61 per cent of world M&As during 2001–03.

An important feature of FDI in recent years has been that its pattern has started increasingly to resemble that of international trade. On the one hand many countries, particularly in the Triad (the European Union, the United States and Japan), are engaging in both inward and outward investment in a more balanced way, and on the other hand, FDI and trade are becoming more and more complements for each other rather than substitutes (Dunning 1993).

Theories of FDI

The complexities of FDI make it rather difficult to fit it into one neat theory. First there is the problem of definition, as discussed above. It is necessary to know exactly what is to be explained before a rigorously testable hypothesis can be developed. Second, any theory of FDI is almost inevitably a theory of MNCs as well, and thus inseparable from the theory of the firm. Third, the nature of FDI makes it a multidimensional subject within the sphere of economics as well as an interdisciplinary one. It involves the theory of the firm, distribution theory, capital theory, trade theory and international finance as well as the disciplines of sociology and politics. Consequently there have been many explanations of FDI, but it is not possible to identify any single theory of FDI.

Neither is it easy to classify these explanations into distinct and neat groups because there is substantial overlap between some of the explanations. Nevertheless, it is possible to group these theories into three broad categories: traditional theories, modern theories and radical theories. Traditional theories are based on neo-classical economic theory and explain FDI in terms of location-specific advantages. Modern theories emphasise the fact that product and factor markets are imperfect both domestically and internationally, and that considerable transaction costs are involved in market solutions. They also acknowledge that managerial and organisational functions play an important role in undertaking FDI. Radical theories however take a more critical view of MNCs.

Before considering the theories of FDI it is useful first to discuss ownership, location and internalisation advantages, which are sometimes referred to as the paradigm of OLI in the literature, since most modern explanations of FDI make use of one, some or all of these concepts.

The paradigm of ownership, location and internalisation (OLI)

There are three different types of advantages that are assumed by some to be necessary to explain the activities of MNCs: ownership advantage, location advantage and internalisation advantage.

Ownership-specific advantages (OSA) refer to certain types of knowledge and privileges that a firm possesses but that are not available to its competitors. These advantages arise because of the imperfections in commodity and factor markets. Such imperfections in commodity markets include product differentiation, collusion and special marketing skills, and in factor markets appear in the form of special managerial skills, differences in access to capital markets, and technology protected by patents. Imperfect markets may also arise from the existence of internal or external economies of scale or from government policies regarding taxes, interest rates or exchange rates, for example. These market imperfections give rise to certain ownership-specific advantages which can be grouped under the following headings:

- Technical advantages: these include holding production secrets such as patents, unavailable technology or management-organisational techniques.
- Industrial organisation: this relates to the advantages arising from operating in an oligopolistic market such as those associated with joint R&D and economies of scale.
- Financial and monetary advantages: these include preferential access to capital markets so as to obtain cheaper capital.
- Access to raw materials: this only applies if a firm gains privileged access to raw materials or minerals, and then this becomes an ownership-specific advantage (Hood and Young 1979).

Location-specific advantages (LSA) refer to certain advantages that the firm has because it locates its production activities in a particular area: Such advantages can come from:

- Access to raw materials or minerals: this advantage applies to all the firms established in the locality, so it is not privileged access as with ownership advantage, and is not sufficient to explain FDI in itself.
- Imperfection in international labour markets: these create real wage-cost differentials which provide an incentive for the MNC to shift production to locations where labour costs are low. An example of this is electronics component firms using south-east Asian locations for assembly production.

- Trade barriers: these provide an incentive for MNCs to set up production in certain locations. For example, Japanese MNCs may wish to produce in Europe to avoid the Common External Tariff (CET). Similarly, Canadian high tariff barriers have been used in the past to attract US direct investment.
- Government policies: a government can use its power to set economic policies, such as taxation and interest rate policies, to influence the location of FDI.

Internalisation-specific advantages (ILA) occur when international market imperfections make market solutions too costly. The idea is that the market is too costly or inefficient for undertaking for certain types of transactions, so whenever transactions can be organised and carried out more cheaply within the firm than through the market, they will be internalised and undertaken by the firm itself.

The benefits of internalisation can be grouped under three headings:

- The advantages of vertical integration cover such things as exploitation of market power through price discrimination and avoidance of government intervention by devices such as transfer pricing.
- The importance of intermediate products for research-intensive activity: the firm appropriates the returns to its investment in the production of new technology by internalising technology.
- The internalisation of human skills keeps the benefits of training and so on in the firm, particularly in high-return areas such as marketing and finance.

However, internalisation is not entirely costless. It creates communication, coordination and control problems. There is also the cost of acquiring local knowledge.

The various theories of FDI in relation to the paradigm of OLI can now be examined.

Traditional theories of FDI

Capital arbitrage theory

This theory was developed in parallel with the orthodox trade theory and eventually integrated with it by Samuelson. It states that direct investment flows from countries where its profitability is low, to countries where it is high. It follows the same pattern as portfolio investment, which flows from low-interest-rate countries to high-interest-rate ones. The theory therefore assumes that capital is mobile both nationally (across industries) and internationally (across national boundaries).

Some interesting implications follow from the above hypothesis. First, capital-abundant countries should export capital and capital-scarce countries should import capital. Second, if capital **arbitrage** were all there is to FDI, one would expect large financial intermediaries to be prominent among MNCs. Third, given the link between the long-term interest rates and return on capital, **portfolio investment** and FDI should be moving in the same direction. The reality however

Case study 7.1

GERMAN FDI IN CHINA

China was the third largest recipient of FDI in 2003 and achieved the highest growth of FDI inflows in the same year (UNCTAD 2004a). One of the countries investing in China is Germany, whose outflows of FDI to China increased from €800 million in 1995 to an estimated figure of €7.9 billion in 2003, a tenfold increase in 12 years (Deutsche Bank 2004). The following are excerpts from a publication by Deutsche Bank Research Department, which describes and analyses the German FDI in China.

Trade relations between Germany and China are expanding steadily. More than 1,500 German companies are currently represented in China. In 2002, China overtook Japan as Germany's most important trading partner in Asia: the volume of trade with China

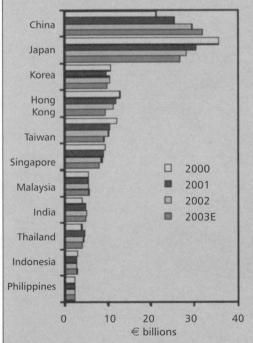

Figure 7.1 German-Asian trade

amounted to €28 billion, while the figure was slightly lower, €27 billion, for Japan. In 2003, this gap widened further (see Figure 7.1). China's accession to the World Trade Organization (WTO) in early 2002 marked the start of a process to dismantle trade barriers and significantly improve access to the Chinese market. The opening of this rapidly growing market of 1.3 billion people has lured in an enormous number of companies and investors from all over the world, including German firms. Not surprisingly, there has been a boost not only to trade relations but also to German foreign direct investment into China.

German investment in China – stylised facts

Germany is China's most important European trade partner and ranks sixth internationally. In 2003, German companies were the 7th largest investors in China and were thus the top investors from Europe.

Up to 2003, German companies had invested an estimated €7.9 billion in China. Although this constitutes a tenfold increase from 1995's figure of €800 million, German investments in China account for only 1.2 per cent of total German FDI. … In Asia, the focus of German investors rests no longer just on Japan but increasingly also on China.

Most investors are from manufacturing industry

Roughly two-thirds of all German investors are manufacturing firms, mostly from the automotive, electrical engineering, chemicals and mechanical engineering sectors. The pioneers were leading enterprises like Siemens,

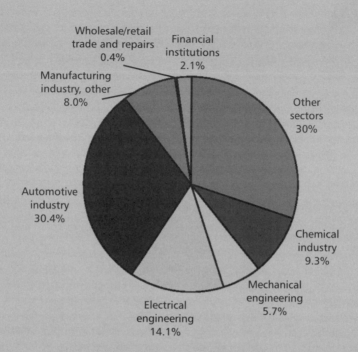

Figure 7.2 Origin of German investment (2002)

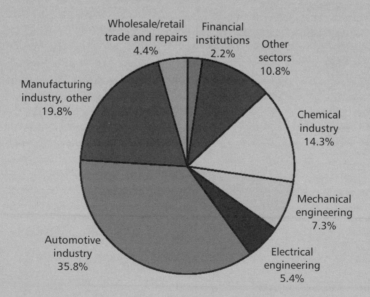

Figure 7.3 Destinations of German investment (2002)

Bayer and Volkswagen, some of which look back on over 100 years of doing business in China (see Figure 7.2).

Although the services sector accounts for only 3 per cent, the gradual opening of the Chinese services market to foreign firms since China's WTO accession in late 2001/early 2002 has seen more German firms discovering the Chinese market. Today, large services firms such as Metro (wholesale and retail trade), Allianz (insurance), Deutsche Post's DHL subsidiary (logistics), TUI (travel) and most large German banks are present in the Chinese market.

Given the industrial background of most German investors and China's reputation as the world's 'assembly line' it can hardly come as a surprise that over 80 per cent of all investment in China went to the manufacturing sector, especially the automotive, steel and chemical industries (see Figure 7.3). ... [M]any investments go towards transforming joint ventures into wholly foreign-owned enterprises (WFOE). Volkswagen is probably the largest German investor in China, followed by Siemens.

Source: Deutsche Bank (2004).

Questions

1 What happened to German-Chinese trade over the past few years?

2 What is the most important factor contributing to this development?

3 What sort of businesses seem to be keen on investing in China, and what is the most popular sector?

suggests differently. First, some countries, such as the United Kingdom, are both a source of and a host to FDI. This could be explained by the different rates of return on capital between industries within the country; that is, FDI flows into some industries and out of others. This however would require segmentation of capital markets to an unrealistic degree. Second, most MNCs are non-financial companies, and their profits do not seem to be related to the long-term rate of interest. Third, portfolio investment and FDI do not always move in the same direction. For example, the United States is well known to have been a net exporter of FDI at the same time as being a net importer of equity capital.

FDI and international trade theory

Orthodox theories of trade originally did not have much to say about FDI. In fact the theory of capital movements was developed in parallel with trade theory. For example, the **Hekscher–Ohlin (H–O) model** (see Chapter 2), does not deal with the subject of FDI in any explicit way. The model established the proposition that countries will specialise in the production of, and export, those commodities that make intensive use of the country's relatively abundant factor. One of the assumptions of the model is that factors of production are mobile across industries within the country but immobile across national boundaries. Thus FDI is ruled out in the model. Indeed, there is no need for FDI since international exchange of commodities renders international movements of capital unnecessary. It is interesting to note that if the assumption is reversed and it is assumed instead that factors are internationally mobile but commodities are not, we would be back in the realm of the capital arbitrage hypothesis.

Modern theories of FDI

Quite independently from these developments in the theory of international trade, some researchers were concentrating on FDI investment from a different perspective. Hymer's (1976) pioneering study, and others that followed, focused on particular kinds of ownership advantages. These developments took place in parallel with the dramatic increase in the activities of MNCs in the decades that followed the Second World War.

The Hymerian view

Hymer (1976) was one of the first authors to bring together both the LSAs and OSAs in an explanation of FDI. Hymer saw the MNC as a monopolist/oligopolist in product markets, investing in foreign enterprises in order to eliminate competition. The MNC was able to compete in a foreign market because it possessed an advantage over the domestic firms. Such an advantage could arise from imperfections in commodity or factor markets. The presence of OSAs to compensate for the LSAs of domestic firms explains foreign involvement, but not why it is in the form of FDI. The answer is that FDI is preferable to exports because of tariff barriers and transport costs. It is also preferable to licensing because the franchisee is a potential competitor and because the franchiser loses some control.

Hymer's approach is particularly useful in explaining the pattern of 'defensive' investment. Large companies seem to establish subsidiaries, often not so profitable, with the sole purpose of shutting out competitors. For instance Pepsi-Cola might open up factories in a country because if it does not, Coca-Cola will.

The Hymerian interpretation sees FDI as an instrument for MNCs to exercise oligopolistic power and to manipulate the market. In fact Hymer suggested that the MNC is an instrument through which wealth and power are channelled away from 'peripheral' to 'central' nations, that is, from the 'southern' to the 'northern' nations. The policy implication of this view is that the governments of host countries should take the necessary steps to prevent MNCs from such manipulation and exploitation (see Chapter 6).

The Uppsala internationalisation model

This model is based on the empirical work undertaken by a group of Scandinavian researchers in the field of international business at Uppsala University in the 1960s. It attaches a central role to organisational knowledge in the process of internationalisation of a firm's activities. Expanding into international markets requires a special type of knowledge, which accumulates as the firm's involvement in international markets increases after the initial penetration. Following the exporting stage the firm then takes its involvement one step further and establishes sales outlets in overseas markets. In the final stage, as the firm's knowledge of local markets becomes sophisticated, it eventually undertakes FDI by establishing overseas plants.

The model is criticised on grounds that it does not explain when or how the sequential process starts. It is also criticised for its inability to explain the activities of those firms that do not comply with the sequential development process.

The argument that MNCs develop from local producers to global players through sequential learning is regarded as a description of an ideal rather than reality. It is argued that sometimes only the more routine functions are transferred abroad and the important and sophisticated types of production such as R&D are kept at home (Kozul-Wright and Rowthorn 1998). Another shortcoming of the model is that the sequential process cannot be symmetrical and therefore the model cannot explain divestment, which has become an important element in investment strategies of MNCs in recent times (Lawler and Seddighi 2001). Finally, the model also fails to discuss the factors that affect the sequential process.

Aliber's theory of FDI

The extent of protective measures in the host country, macroeconomic variables such as strength of domestic currency in the **home country**, and a high growth rate in the **host country** have been put forward by Aliber as factors determining FDI flows (Lawler and Seddighi 2001). It is argued that FDI would be undertaken as a way of supplying a market that is protected by **tariff** walls. An example of this is Japanese car production companies operating in the United Kingdom in order to penetrate the EU market.

Another line of argument by Aliber is that FDI is likely to flow from strong-currency countries to weak-currency countries to take advantage of greater purchasing power. However, empirical data on FDI movements do not display an obvious correlation between the strength of currencies and flows of FDI. This is not surprising since to the extent that currency valuation influences capital movements, it would be short-term capital that is affected rather than FDI, which is more likely to be affected by long-term considerations.

There is, however, empirical evidence supporting the assertion that FDI would be attracted by high growth rates and strong demand in the host country. For example, the success of the east Asian countries in attracting FDI is attributed not only to appropriate government policies but more importantly to the rapid and sustainable economic growth achieved by these countries (Kozul-Wright and Rowthorn 1998).

The product cycle model

Another theory of FDI that shows the interactions between the OSAs and the LSAs is the product cycle theory of Vernon (1966) (see also Chapter 2). New products appear first in the most advanced economy, the United States, in response to demand conditions. The 'maturing product' stage is characterised by the product becoming more standard, increased economies of scale, high demand and low price. At this stage other advanced economies also start producing the commodity, partly via US FDI. The 'standardised product' stage is reached when the commodity is sold entirely on the basis of price. Thus the main concern is now to produce it as cheaply as possible, and this is when the production moves to the LDCs, where labour is relatively cheap.

This theory explains well the US 'offshore production' in low labour-cost countries. However, the validity of this theory has somewhat declined. One reason is that the United States no longer has the totally dominant position regarding FDI.

The MNCs of Europe, Japan and the NICs also require explanation. Moreover, MNCs are now capable of developing, maturing and standardising products almost simultaneously.

The internalisation theories of FDI

Although the concept of internalisation was first introduced by Coase in the 1930s, Buckley and Casson (1985) were the first to incorporate the ISAs into the main analysis of FDI in the 1970s. It was no coincidence that at the time FDI was growing in high-technology-intensive manufacturing industries, where the integration of R&D with production and marketing is crucial. Buckley and Casson emphasised the importance of imperfections in the intermediate product markets, particularly those of patented technical knowledge and human capital. Such imperfections provide an incentive for the firm to internalise, say, the knowledge market. The incentive to internalise depends on the relationship between four groups of factors:

● industry-specific factors, for example, economies of scale and external market structure
● region-specific factors, for example, geographical distance and cultural differences
● nation-specific factors, for example, political and fiscal conditions (leading to possible transfer pricing)
● firm-specific factors, for example, management expertise.

It should be noted that internalisation is as much a characteristic of a multi-plant uninational firm as of a multinational firm. However, the crucial point regarding internalisation is the imperfections in either the commodity markets or the input markets, or both (Hill 2005).

Another theory that makes use of the concept of internalisation is the theory of appropriability. In this theory the key firm-specific advantage that results in FDI occurs in a key input market, such as managerial excellence or a patent on an invention. Such an advantage does not provide any monopoly power in the product market, but it enables the firm to make economic gains. The firm decides to engage in FDI because the best way of appropriating the potential gains from its advantage is to keep control and ownership of the advantage to itself. This theory explains why there is a strong presence of high-technology industries among MNCs. The policy implication of the theory is that host countries should either leave FDI alone or positively encourage it.

The eclectic theory of FDI

Dunning's (1981, 1983) **eclectic theory** attempts to integrate the Hymerian view with the concept of internalisation, and claims that all three types of advantages are required for MNCs to exist. Dunning himself considers the eclectic model to be an analytical framework in which international production, including FDI activities of MNCs, can be examined (Dunning 2002). He also identifies four main motives for FDI (Dunning 1993).

- Market-seeking FDI may be motivated by a desire to dominate or penetrate a particular market. The determining factor could be the size of the market or the particular characteristics of the market, such as geographical or cultural proximity. Its effect on international trade would possibly be in the form of trade substitution, particularly in final products, but it would most likely be in the form of (intra-industry) trade creation regarding the imports of capital goods from the subsidiaries (Chesnais *et al.* 2000).
- Resource-seeking FDI would be motivated by available or cheaper resources abroad. These resources may be natural resources, for example oil, or human resources such as a particular type of (or possibility of cheaper) labour. This type of FDI is mostly in the form of 'greenfield investment', and it has a trade-creating effect, which might turn into trade destruction if disinvestment occurs.
- Efficiency-seeking FDI would be motivated by a strategic location that might enable the firm to minimise transport costs, to have easy access to ancillary services and raw materials, or to reap economies of scale and scope by supplying different markets from one centre. It could be in the form of 'greenfield investment' or M&A; it usually enhances the international division of labour and is likely to have a trade-creating effect (Chesnais *et al.* 2000).
- Strategic-asset-seeking FDI might be motivated by a desire to improve the international competitiveness or to increase the market power of the firm. It takes place through M&A and aims to acquire firms with strong market positions and advanced technology.

Many theories of FDI start with the question, why does a firm extend its activities to other countries? Dunning's answer is that there are LSAs to be enjoyed in the host country as discussed above.

However, how could a foreign firm compete with the domestic firms of the host country? Dunning's reply to this question is the OSAs. These answers inevitably lead to a third question: why should the firm choose FDI instead of exporting or licensing? The answer, of course, is the ISAs.

It is clear that the three advantages are sufficient to explain FDI. However, are they necessary? The answer seems to be no, because the LSAs and the ISAs seem to be sufficient to explain the activities of MNCs, thus rendering the OSAs redundant. In fact some people claim that the concept of internalisation alone is sufficient to explain MNC activity, and indeed the theory of internalisation is the theory of FDI (Dunning 2001).

The eclectic theory is criticised on the grounds that it is too general and includes too many variables to be of practical use; that the three legs of the paradigm are not independent from each other; and that it is not different from the internalisation theory and thus does not constitute a macro explanation of FDI. Dunning counters these criticisms by stating that the eclectic theory is not meant to be a full explanation for all activities of MNCs, but only a general framework; that there is a degree of interdependence. Nevertheless separating them out enables the identification of policy implications, and it is macro-analysis in the sense that it deals with the issue of FDI at the country level.

The radical (heterodox) explanations of FDI

Unlike orthodox economists, who view the MNC as the most efficient vehicle for both the optimal allocation of resources and the efficient distribution of products internationally, radical economists see MNCs as instruments of economic exploitation, political instability (especially in the LDCs), and environmental damage because of their relentless search for profits and enormous economic and political power (see Chapter 6). In particular, some Marxist economists regard FDI as an instrument of imperialistic expansion that is necessitated by the long-term tendency of the rate of profits to fall as a result of over-production in the domestic economy. Hobson argued that FDI is needed to counteract inadequate consumption caused by the uneven distribution of income and wealth in capitalist economies, while Lenin regarded FDI as a complementary activity to exports. Capitalistic development results in the creation of large international monopolies on the one hand and the concentration of financial and industrial capital on the other. These monopolies colonise the world and use FDI as an instrument in this process (Ietto-Gillies 2005).

Although the picture regarding FDI is rather different today than it was at the beginning of the 20th century, there are nevertheless some concerns relating to FDI and the activities of MNCs in the world today. It is easy to see the reasons for such concerns. First, the bulk of the activities of the MNCs takes place among the developed countries, and only a small proportion relates to the LDCs (see earlier). Second, there has been a shift away from manufacturing towards services in the composition of FDI, which would not help the cause of LDCs wishing to industrialise. Third, even in manufacturing, the main determinants of FDI activities seem to be technology, skills and managerial capability, which are the very factors lacking in LDCs (Kozul-Wright and Rowthorn 1998). Fourth, despite the sharp recovery of FDI flows going into LDCs, they are heavily concentrated on a handful of countries. Finally, imitating some of the more successful NICs will mean too many LDCs trying to export manufactured goods with the help of FDI, which might result in the reduction in the price of these goods and hence the deterioration in the terms of trade for these countries.

Moreover, DCs are also criticised for their attitude towards LDCs and FDI. The IMF and the World Bank advocate that LDCs liberalise and deregulate their policies regarding foreign investment. Bernal and colleagues (2004) heavily criticise the *World Development Report 2005* (World Bank 2005) as well as the new rules on investment liberalisation discussed in the WTO recently, arguing that they favour the interests of DCs to the detriment of the developmental efforts of LDCs. Lal Das (2003) is also highly critical of the attitude of the European Union in the discussion of the new rules on investment liberalisation in the WTO. (See Chapter 3 as these are part of the Singapore Issues discussed there, but also note that these 'new' rules have subsequently been dropped from the Doha Development Agenda discussions by the WTO.)

Thus, despite tremendous competition among all the countries, DCs and LDCs alike, to attract FDI to solve their economic problems, the subject remains as controversial as ever.

MOTIVES AND PROSPECTS FOR GERMAN FDI IN CHINA

Following on from our previous case study, there are certain characteristics of the Chinese market that seem to appeal to German companies:

Market potential

There were an estimated 76 million prosperous consumers in China in 2001 (people who do not have to spend the lion's share of their incomes on food and housing). This figure is larger than Germany's entire population. Up to 2015, it could increase almost tenfold.

Low-cost 'assembly line'

As a second, equally important argument companies cite the use of China as an 'extended low-cost assembly line'. Without doubt, cost pressures are a driving factor behind investment in China.

New opportunities arising from WTO membership

China's membership of the WTO has proved to be a major driver behind German FDI, as firms are now hoping for better and easier access to the Chinese market. In addition, rapid economic growth despite the Asia crisis, and not least the 2008 Olympics (estimated investment volume €24–35 billion) are raising hopes of German participation in large-scale infrastructure projects, which would be particularly attractive to the large industries.

On the other hand, there are also factors that seem to discourage German companies considering investing in China:

Lack of information and planning certainty

The main impediments that argue against involvement in China are persistent legal uncertainties, reflected not only in a lack of intellectual property rights protection but also in quickly changing framework conditions and regulatory obstacles. Another problem is limited market **transparency.** There is insufficient data on customer structures and preferences as well as potential supplier networks. Moreover, the problem of defining individual market segments and the sheer size of the country are making the search for relevant market information even more difficult. By no means can China be considered to be 'one country – one market'. China is about as large as both western and eastern Europe together, and in many respects it is just as diverse as the various countries of Europe. A balanced investment strategy should therefore be designed to either service different regions or concentrate on a smaller and relatively homogeneous main market.

High input prices

Apart from the high cost of legal and other professional services, or arising from regional protectionism or logistic and bureaucratic inefficiencies, companies are now also facing high prices for electricity and raw materials. This makes it increasingly difficult to achieve profit margins. Demand for electricity rose by 15 per cent in 2003, while capacity increased by only 8 per cent. This led to a shortage of approx. 40 gigawatts (roughly equivalent to the electricity needs of Australia).

Fierce competition

With the increasing attractiveness of the Chinese market, competition is rising. Many competitors have been active in China longer than the German firms, as EU companies have so far lagged behind their Asian peers and behind the dollar block (the United States, Canada, Australia, New Zealand) in getting involved in this vast market. Competition is particularly tough in manufacturing, which received two-thirds of foreign investments.

What about future prospects for German investment in China?

Positive trends

On the one hand, there is no doubt that more and more German companies are investing in China: annual new investment flows reached a record volume in 2002. In addition, China's share in total FDI flows rose to an estimated 6 per cent in 2003, compared with approx. 1.5 per cent in the mid-1990s (see Figure 7.4).

But also growing scepticism

According to a survey by the Shanghai office of the German Chamber of Commerce, about half of all German firms represented in China are not satisfied with the implementation to date of the WTO agreements.

There is also growing concern about excess capacities in the real estate, automotive and mobile telecommunications sectors. Especially in the automotive industry, it is feared that the massive build-up of capacities in China will result in a situation of overcapacities similar to the one in Brazil several years ago.

Given these overcapacities in some sectors but also the emergence of bottlenecks as a result of extremely high demand, the question has arisen repeatedly how much investment China can actually digest each year. Analysts estimate that direct investment of US$10 billion will create an increase in Chinese GDP of 0.9–1.6 per cent. So if annual

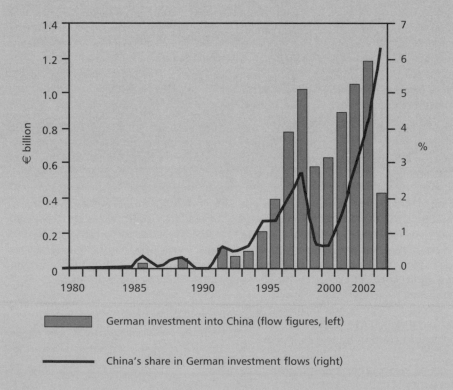

German investment into China (flow figures, left)

China's share in German investment flows (right)

Figure 7.4 German investment flows into China (1980–2003)
2003 January to September figures only

Sources: Chinese Embassy in Germany, Deutsche Bundesbank.

investment flows were to fall by half from the currently over US$50 billion per year, GDP growth would be considerably lower than the 7–8 per cent target. It cannot come as a surprise that China is keen to keep up the flow. In view of the danger of overheating, which results from over-investment, a more even sequencing of investment flows could benefit China by preventing boom–bust cycles.

Profitability has yet to materialise

It is perfectly normal that new investment needs an initial 'warm-up' phase before profits can be reaped. However, in light of these excess capacities and bottlenecks, persistent legal uncertainty and ever fiercer competition, many a foreign investor is wondering whether investment in China can actually yield adequate profits that reflect the risks taken.

Besides, the incremental capital output ratio (ICOR), the relation between capital input and economic output, has increased in China: more money must be invested in order to produce one more unit of output. So the efficiency of investments has fallen since the mid-1990s, while the ratio is more favourable today in India. China's ICOR could soon approach that of the United States (Germany lags markedly behind). Compared with the Asian tigers, though, China is still doing quite well.

Fewer large-scale investment projects

Most large international companies such as the ones listed in the DAX30 or Fortune 500 have made considerable investments recently, or launched major projects. Fewer such projects than in past years are expected to be embarked on in the coming years, especially if the existing investments fail to yield profits. In light of declining investment efficiency and looming excess capacities, profits could take longer to materialise than initially expected.

Investors will only be prepared to expand further when the current investments have proved profitable; in most cases profits from existing projects will be reinvested, so investment flows will gradually shift from foreign to domestic investment. Additional projects will have to be self-financing. Further economic development could then mean a trend away from greenfield invest-ment toward M&A investment: that is, mergers with local firms.

Source: Deutsche Bank (2004).

Questions

1 What seems to motivate German companies in China?
2 To what extent can these motives fall in within the OLI paradigm?
3 What are the main obstacles to German investment in China?

FDI in the European Union

FDI in the European Union is part of a complex worldwide network of FDI, involving investments originating outside the European Union, for example the United States, Japan and South Korea (referred to as **extra-EU FDI**), western European investment outflows, and flows of investment within the European Union (referred to as **intra-EU FDI**).

Inflows

We have seen that the share of DCs in world inflows of FDI has declined in the last ten years or so in favour of LDCs and the CEECs, and that most of this decline had to be borne by the European Union. The European Union lost further ground recently, with its share of world FDI inflows being reduced from 69.8 per cent in 2001 to 27 per cent in 2004 (UNCTAD 2005).

Within the EU15 itself, historically the most popular destination for FDI inflows has been the United Kingdom. However, that country has steadily been losing its prominent position since the end of the 1990s in parallel with the end of the M&A boom. The United Kingdom's share of EU FDI inflows went down from 20.4 per cent in the 1992–7 period to 4.9 per cent in 2003, which was just outside the top five destinations in that year (see Table 7.4).

Some people argue that staying outside the euro-zone might cost the United Kingdom dearly in terms of FDI inflows. Belgium and Luxemburg, on the other hand, have been gaining ground since the beginning of the 1990s, when they only managed 11.7 per cent, and shot to the top with a staggering 39.7 per cent in 2003 despite the decline in the absolute level of FDI they received in that year. Germany is another country that has been losing ground over the period, falling out of the top five altogether in both 2002 and 2003. FDI inflows into France and the Netherlands have also declined but they managed to keep their positions in the top five. As for Spain, after a shaky start to the decade it managed to reassert itself in 2002 and 2003 and has acquired a position in the top three of the favourite destinations for incoming FDI.

Historically, the first main source of FDI in western Europe was the United States. US investment started to be significant in the inter-war period (for example Ford's factory at Dagenham in the United Kingdom) but really grew in the 1950s and 1960s, partly as a result of the formation of the European Community.

In the 1980s and early 1990s, the role of the United States in foreign direct investment in the European Community/European Union was taken over to some extent by other countries, most notably Japan, but also increasingly other east Asian countries such as South Korea and Taiwan. The stock of Japanese FDI in the European Union grew from US$712 million in 1971 to US$26,957 million in 1993 (Dunning and Cantwell 1991; Dunning 1997a, 1997b).

Traditionally, US investment in western Europe has been in the form of takeovers whereas Japanese investment has favoured joint ventures creating greenfield investment. There was concern that these joint ventures benefited Japan more than Europe in terms of technology transfer. However, with the Japanese economy having severe problems by the mid-1990s, attention was diverted to intra-EU investment and also to FDI outflows from the European Union, as well as from the United States (El-Agraa 2004).

Outflows

In the 1990s and the first half of the present decade, with the exception of 2002, the European Union has been a net investor abroad. Net outflows were €138 billion and €41 billion in 2001 and 2003 respectively while net inflows in 2001 were €26 billion.

Outflows peaked at the end of the 1990s and assumed a downward trend in the first half of the present decade. As we have seen, world outflows of FDI were on an upward trend until 2000, then took a dip in 2001 and 2002, but

Table 7.4 EU inflows of FDI: value, share and growth

Country	1992–7 Value (US$ million)	% share	1998 Value (US$ million)	% share	% growth	2000 Value (US$ million)	% share	% growth	2002 Value (US$ million)	% share	% growth	2003 Value (US$ million)	% share	% growth
Austria	2,276	2.4	4,533	1.8	99.2	8,840	1.3	95.0	952	0.3	–89.2	6,855	2.3	620.1
Belg/Lux	11,217	11.7	22,691	9.1	102.3	88,739	13.2	291.1	131,743	35.2	48.5	117,041	39.7	–11.2
Denmark	2,582	2.7	7,730	3.1	199.4	33,818	5.0	337.5	6,637	1.8	–80.4	2,608	0.9	–60.7
Finland	1,190	1.2	2,040	0.8	71.4	8,015	1.2	292.9	7,920	2.1	–1.2	2,765	0.9	–65.1
France	19,779	20.6	30,984	12.4	56.7	43,250	6.4	39.6	48,906	13.1	13.1	46,981	15.9	–3.9
Germany	6,042	6.3	24,593	9.8	307.0	198,276	29.5	706.2	36,014	9.6	–81.8	12,866	4.4	–64.3
Greece	1,033	1.1	85	0.0	–91.8	1,089	0.2	1,181.2	51	0.0	–95.3	47	0.0	–7.8
Ireland	1,694	1.8	8,579	3.4	406.4	25,843	3.8	201.2	24,486	6.5	–5.3	25,497	8.6	4.1
Italy	3,523	3.7	2,635	1.1	–25.2	13,375	2.0	407.6	14,545	3.9	8.7	16,421	5.6	12.9
Netherlands	9,978	10.4	36,964	14.8	270.5	63,854	9.5	72.7	25,571	6.8	–60.0	19,674	6.7	–23.1
Portugal	1,554	1.6	3,144	1.3	102.3	6,787	1.0	115.9	1,844	0.5	–72.8	962	0.3	–47.8
Spain	8,615	9.0	11,797	4.7	36.9	37,523	5.6	218.1	35,908	9.6	–4.3	25,625	8.7	–28.6
Sweden	6,835	7.1	19,835	7.9	190.2	23,242	3.5	17.2	11,647	3.1	–49.9	3,296	1.1	–71.7
UK	19,527	20.4	74,321	29.7	280.6	118,764	17.7	59.8	27,776	7.4	–76.6	14,515	4.9	–47.7
The EU 15	95,845	100.0	249,931	100.0	160.8	671,415	100.0	168.6	374,000	100.0	–44.3	295,153	100.0	–21.1

Source: Adapted from UNCTAD (2004b), Ch 1, Annex table B1, p 367

Note: (1) 1992–97 figures are annual averages; (2) growth figures are based on the previous column, e.g (2000–1998)/2000

recovered in 2003, except for western Europe and Japan. We have also seen that there was unevenness in the performance of EU countries.

According to Table 7.5, outflows from the European Union declined by 56.4 per cent between 2000 and 2002 and a further 4.1 per cent in 2003. However, the individual performances vary greatly from country to country. UK outflows of FDI sustained tremendous momentum in the 1990s, growing by more than 300 per cent and maintaining the United Kingdom's leading position until 2000, but they declined by 56.4 per cent between 2000 and 2002, then recovered again to grow by 56.6 per cent in 2003. However, despite this recovery the United Kingdom lost its leading position, falling behind France and Luxemburg in recent years. France's performance followed a similar path to that of the United Kingdom except that unlike the United Kingdom, it improved its relative position, moving from third place in 1999 to second place in recent years. Germany was on an upward trend until 1999 and in fact was in second position until then; however, German FDI outflows have suffered terribly in recent years, declining by 84.8 per cent and 70.3 per cent in 2002 and 2003 respectively, causing it to lose its place in the top five. The Netherlands maintained a more or less stable relative position, never losing its place in the top five despite suffering a fall in the absolute level of its outflows in 2001 and 2002. Perhaps a more remarkable story relates to the performances of Belgium and Luxemburg, in particular Luxemburg, which has been a continuous success story culminating in it being the top investor abroad in the world, beating the United States to the second place in 2002.

Distribution of FDI in the European Union

The question of whether FDI inflows are concentrated in a relatively small number of favoured EU countries is not easy to answer. since Germany, Spain and Ireland have changed positions over the years. However, the United Kingdom, France, Belgium/Luxemburg and the Netherlands have not only maintained their positions in the top five countries receiving FDI in the last two decades, but also their shares are somewhat higher than the shares of the rest (see Table 7.4). It can be seen that the top five countries (but not necessarily the same ones) accounted for 72.1 per cent of total FDI coming into the European Union in the 1992–7 period, 76.3 per cent in 2000, and 79.6 per cent in 2003. This would indicate a fair degree of concentration.

A similar picture can be observed with respect of FDI outflows, except that concentration appears to be stronger. The top five country concentration ratio was 81.6 per cent in the 1992–7 period, 78.0 per cent in 2000 and 90.3 per cent in 2003 (see Table 7.5).

Intra-EU FDI

Since ten extra countries joined the European Union in May 2004, the European Union now means the EU25. However, the most recent FDI data currently end in 2003, therefore both the EU15 and EU25 will be considered in the context of **intra-EU FDI**. To avoid confusion we restate that intra-EU in this context means FDI flows between EU countries (either EU15 or EU25)

Table 7.5 Outflows of FDI from the European Union: value, share and growth

Country	1992–7 Value (US$ million)	% share	1998 Value (US$ million)	% share	% growth	2000 Value (US$ million)	% share	% growth	2002 Value (US$ million)	% share	% growth	2003 Value (US$ million)	% share	% growth
Austria	1,533	1.0	2,745	0.7	79.1	5,740	0.7	109.1	5,252	1.5	−8.5	7,083	2.1	34.9
Belg/Lux	7,427	5.1	28,845	6.9	288.4	86,362	10.7	199.4	138,471	39.4	60.3	132,637	39.4	−4.2
Denmark	2,928	2.0	4,477	1.1	52.9	26,558	3.3	493.2	5,686	1.6	−78.6	1,158	0.3	−79.6
Finland	2,554	1.7	18,647	4.5	630.1	22,572	2.8	21.0	7,622	2.2	−66.2	−7,370	−2.2	−196.7
France	26,045	17.7	48,611	11.7	86.6	177,449	22.0	265.0	49,434	14.1	−72.1	57,279	17.0	15.9
Germany	31,051	21.1	88,823	21.4	186.1	56,557	7.0	−36.3	8,622	2.5	−84.8	2,560	0.8	−70.3
Greece	35	0.0	262	0.1	648.6	2,102	0.3	702.3	655	0.2	−68.8	586	0.2	−10.5
Ireland	573	0.4	3,906	0.9	581.7	4,640	0.6	18.8	3,099	0.9	−33.2	1,911	0.6	−38.3
Italy	7,142	4.9	12,407	3.0	73.7	12,316	1.5	−0.7	17,123	4.9	39.0	9,121	2.7	−46.7
Netherlands	19,518	13.3	36,669	8.8	87.9	75,635	9.4	106.3	34,554	9.8	−54.3	36,092	10.7	4.5
Portugal	753	0.5	3,847	0.9	410.9	7,512	0.9	95.3	3,289	0.9	−56.2	95	0.0	−97.1
Spain	5,235	3.6	18,936	4.6	261.7	54,674	6.8	188.7	31,512	9.0	−42.4	23,373	6.9	−25.8
Sweden	6,226	4.2	24,370	5.9	291.4	40,662	5.0	66.9	10,863	3.1	−73.3	17,375	5.2	59.9
UK	35,861	24.4	122,816	29.6	242.5	233,371	28.9	90.0	35,180	10.0	−84.9	55,093	16.3	56.6
The EU 15	146,881	100.0	415,361	100.0	182.8	806,150	100.0	94.1	351,362	100.0	−56.4	336,993	100.0	−4.1

Source: Adapted from UNCTAD (2004b), Ch 1, Annex table B2, p 372

Note: (1) 1992–97 figures are annual averages; (2) growth figures are based on the previous column, e.g (2000−1998)/2000

and is based on the average between inflows and outflows. Extra-EU inflow implies FDI coming from a country outside the European Union into a country that is a member of the EU. Conversely, extra-EU outflow means an EU country investing in a non-EU country.

Intra-EU FDI flows have been increasing since the mid-1980s as a result of a dramatic increase in cross-border M&As. The number of cross-border intra-EU M&As increased from less than 100 in 1986 to well over 800 in 1991, and there was a similar rise in the number of extra-EU M&As targeting EU companies (see Chapter 6). However, the number of extra-EU bids, that is, EU companies bidding for firms outside the European Union, fell in the late 1980s. The main cause for these developments was the planned completion of the Single European Market (SEM) in late 1992 (Chesnais *et al.* 2000). There was a clearly observable impact of the SEM on M&A activity in the European Union in that period. On the one hand European firms were refocusing their activities on the European market, and on the other hand, firms outside the European Union were trying to get a foothold in this market. However, both intra-EU cross-border and extra-EU targeting levelled off after 1992 until the late 1990s, when there was another surge in the total number of M&As involving EU firms. However, in this later boom European firms appear to be favouring firms outside the European Union.

The consequences of all this were that there was a significant increase not only in the absolute level of intra-EU FDI flows, but also in their relation to GDP and trade. For example the intensity ratio, which is obtained by dividing FDI by GDP, increased steadily for most EU countries throughout the 1990s. For the EU15 it rose from 0.3 in 1992 to 3.6 in 2000, and somewhat declined afterwards to 2.4, 1.5 and 1.3 in 2001, 2002 and 2003 respectively. In comparison, the same ratio for the euro-zone was 6.7, 3.7, 2.5 and 1.8 in 2000, 2001, 2002 and 2003 respectively (Eurostat 2004a).

Table 7.6 indicates that in 2003 the total FDI received by the EU15 was €264,332 million. Out of this, €188,989 million (71.5 per cent) came from EU25 countries and the remaining €75,343 million from countries outside the EU25; just under 23 per cent of this came from the United States. The top 10 EU countries receiving FDI from the EU25, in descending order, were Luxemburg, France, Belgium, Ireland, Spain, the Netherlands, Italy, Germany, the United Kingdom and Austria.

Similarly, there was €300,517 million in total invested by the countries of the EU15. Out of this, €178,404 million (59.4 per cent) went to the other European (EU25) countries, and the remaining €122,113 million (40.6 per cent) went to countries outside the EU25. More than 40 per cent of this extra-EU25 investment went to the United States! Canada's share in the EU15's outward investment was 3.5 per cent, while the EU15 divested in Japan to the tune of €234 million in 2003. The leading European countries in extra-EU outflows of FDI, in descending order, were Luxemburg, France, Belgium, the Netherlands, the United Kingdom, Spain, Sweden and Italy.

There are different arguments regarding the reasons for changes in the levels of inward and outward FDI. Studies indicate that there is a direct relationship between FDI activity and the trade cycle: FDI tends to increase in periods of expansion and boom. Another argument is that because both

Table 7.6 Intra- and extra-EU FDI in 2003, in € million

| | Outward flows to: | | | | | Inward flows from: | | | | |
| | Extra-EU25 | of which: | | | Intra-EU25 | Extra-EU25 | of which: | | | Intra-EU25 |
		USA	Japan	Canada			USA	Japan	Canada	
EU25	11,8055	49,320	−234	4,326	185,175	77,183	18007	3,234	7,972	198,208
EU15	12,2113	49,261	−234	4,329	178,404	75,343	17157	2,937	7,919	188,989
Belgium	7,195	2,662	440	2,037	27,080	−229	537	−40	−77	26,465
Czech Rep	14	12	0	−1	192	1,129	180	224	14	1,160
Denmark	102	103	−66	−30	925	1,068	661	23	−9	1,244
Germany	7,304	4,830	1,092	−191	−5,036	2,076	4951	638	−188	9,323
Spain	7,318	1,776	12	59	13,391	6,337	3856	−3	811	16,368
France	13,218	6,258	200	1,093	37,533	11,416	3489	−437	4,580	30,211
Ireland	427	−617		1	2,712	5,222	−4034	197	169	18,601
Italy	2,031	606	63	32	6,051	1,273	720	138	17	13,276
Luxemburg	31,134	2,706	52	105	53,917	37,596	5,415	97	153	39,982
Hungary	909	3	0	0	489	−373	238	49	17	2,558
Holland	9,945	5,292	−289	583	21,031	1,821	−4828	1,086	−58	16,036
Austria	1,175	92	2	−4	5,101	1,936	816	9	2	4,137
Finland	−1,334	−900	−100	50	−5,200	1,100	850	−150	0	1,350
Sweden	−295	−1,724	−106	−170	8,604	−2,836	−605	0	478	3,492
UK	32,392	26,262	−2,082	504	16,370	7,581	4,971	1,363	1,004	5,266

Source: Adapted from Finfacts (2004).

international trade and FDI activity are dominated by MNCs, these two tend to be complements rather than substitutes for each other. It has also been stated that as international competition increases, firms find it difficult to maintain their market position in several sectors at the same time, and this has the effect of increasing factor mobility and hence FDI flows. Finally, post-Fordist type of production also encourages FDI. In recent times globalisation has changed the Fordist production model, resulting in the rationalisation and refocusing of firms' activities into such things as horizontal disintegration. This has been made possible by the integration of commodity and factor markets and technological changes. Even small (technology-oriented) firms are now able to form strategic alliances with MNCs and thus gain competitive advantage via internationalisation (El-Agraa 2004).

The sectoral distribution of FDI in the European Union

The sectoral distribution of intra-EU FDI has changed considerably in recent years. Finance, office and computing equipment and to some extent household appliances were growing fast in the early and mid-1980s, while beverages, business services and electronic components were growing strongly in the late 1980s and early 1990s. By the end of the 1990s the manufacturing sector was still maintaining its dominant position with a share of 49 per cent in all intra-EU FDI flows. However, the following year its share collapsed to a mere 5 per cent, while the transport and communication sector sprang to the dominant position with a 40 per cent share.

If we consider the number of FDI projects in Europe, there was a 2 per cent increase in 2003, reversing the trend in 2001 and 2002. This meant good news for the European Union, since it was the main beneficiary from this development. The total project numbers received by the EU countries were up by 7 per cent, driven by intra-European investment, rather than the United States or any other extra-European country, led by Belgium, Norway and Finland (EIM 2004). The main activities were manufacturing, contact centres and headquarters, while main destinations were France and the United Kingdom (followed by Denmark, Sweden, Finland and Norway), which received expansions of FDI rather than greenfield investment. The favourite destination for greenfield projects was the CEECs, particularly Russia, Hungary, Poland, the Czech Republic, Romania, Slovakia and Bulgaria. Of these projects 58 per cent originated from western Europe. Among the EU countries, France, Spain, the Czech Republic, Sweden and Denmark increased their share of incoming FDI projects compared with 1998, while the United Kingdom, Germany, the Netherlands and Ireland experienced a decline in their shares over the same period.

As for specific sectors, increasing both the absolute number and the share of projects received are business services, food, plastics, rubber and wood, while automotive, software electronics, telecoms, computers and insurance lost market share in 2003. Table 7.7 provides information on the sectoral shares in the total number of projects received in 2003.

As can be seen, the automotive sector was top of the list with 231 projects, which is 12 per cent of all the FDI projects in 2003, but it lost market share from the previous year. Germany leads the way in the auto assembly and

Table 7.7 Sectoral distribution of M&A projects in the European Union in 2003

Sector	Number of projects	Share of total (%)	Percentage change in market share
Automotive	231	12	−1
Software	180	9	−7
Business services	155	8	–
Pharmaceuticals	129	7	+14
Electronics	121	6	−1
Machinery and equipment	116	6	–
Chemicals	103	5	0
Plastic and rubber	77	4	–
Financial services	62	3	0
Telecommunications	46	2	0
Other	713	37	–
Total	1,933	100	

Source: adapted from EIM (2004).

engine sub-sector (23 per cent), followed by Japan (21 per cent) and the United States (11 per cent). However, in automotive components, Japan leads with 25 per cent, followed by the United States and Germany with 21 and 17 per cent respectively. Software is the second largest sector in terms of the number of FDI projects in 2003, with 9 per cent. However this sector also lost some of its market power from the previous year. Pharmaceuticals, on the other hand, received 129 projects (7 per cent of the total), which means an increase of 14 per cent over 2002. Other important sectors in 2003 were business services with 155 projects received (8 per cent), electronics with 121 projects (6 per cent), machinery and equipment with 116 projects (6 per cent), and chemicals with 103 projects (5 per cent).

The impact of FDI

Many countries trying to attract FDI hope that the inflow of capital will have some positive impact on the economy. The impact of FDI is very hard to measure since we do not know what would have happened if the investment had not taken place. The orthodox and most widespread view is that FDI will, in general, have a positive impact through economic integration and consequent specialisation according to comparative advantage (see Chapter 2). The ability to exploit increasing returns to scale and the benefits to the consumer of increased competition are also cited (Julius 1990). However, more particular issues are also often discussed and are more controversial. These include the impact of FDI on the labour market, the capital market, technological change, management techniques and the balance of payments.

The effect on the labour market

Some argue that FDI will have a positive effect on the employment of the host country. Such positive effects can be direct – that is, new jobs are created – or they can be indirect, through new posts created along the value chain. Furthermore, MNCs may create spillovers and increase the overall knowledge of local workers in an indirect fashion, and thus raise labour productivity.

Buckley and Artisen (1988) examined the employment effects of intra-EU investment in Greece, Portugal and Spain. They studied 19 particular cases using a questionnaire survey, and found that FDI almost always had a positive effect in the host country. The impacts on the source country were smaller, and the overall effect of the two taken together was generally positive. FDI donors did, however, experience job losses in several cases.

Although FDI is often advocated as a way of providing jobs, obviously it will fail to do this if it simply displaces domestic production, thus making workers redundant in domestic firms. Additionally, in sectors where there is a shortage of labour, the MNC will be in a position to offer better pay to workers and thus 'crowd out' local firms. Moreover, it is possible that foreign-owned firms can influence the distribution of incomes because they demand different types of labour and pay higher wages to skilled workers. As foreign firms engage in business on an international scale, they require more workers with managerial skills to run their day-to-day operations as efficiently as possible.

Furthermore, as MNCs possess technologies and R&D facilities of the highest standards, they require skilled workers who can operate such technologies and are fast learners. All these factors compel MNCs to pay higher wages to more skilled workers as they are left with little choice because of the relative lack of skilled labour in most developing countries. As a result they arguably increase wage inequality between skilled and unskilled workers.

Technology transfer

FDI has been seen as a way of encouraging technological change. MNCs are more likely to bring their technologies with them when they set up their production facilities in developing countries, since they are very unlikely to acquire them locally. The technological effect could be direct, through the transfer of technologies to a local affiliate, or indirect through technology spillovers. Technologies may spread to new users through both formal and informal means. Local firms may learn about the technology of a MNC in a formal way by being directly associated with it, for example in a **joint venture** or under a licence, or informally by being connected with the MNC through a 'linkage'. Linkages may either be backward, which arise from the MNC's relationship with local suppliers, or forward, which stem from contact with local customers. Moreover, technological know-how may spread through employees switching employment from MNCs to local firms (Bende-Nabende 2002).

However, the European reality might be more complex. In innovative and competitive industries foreign investors have tended to establish local R&D facilities to gain access to local expertise, and by doing this have further increased the rate of innovation. In declining sectors investment has been in assembly production with R&D located abroad. FDI production in such cases has competed with domestic producers who have had to cut back their R&D even further as a cost-saving measure and thus entered a vicious circle of decline (Cantwell 1988).

The effect on the capital market

An important characteristic of developing countries is that there is a relative lack of capital. This is one of the reasons that policy makers in the developing countries have eased restrictions on inward FDI, and in many instances provided special incentives for inward investment. As they are aware of the fact that MNCs do not suffer from credit constraint in the way the local firms do, they hope MNCs will bring in capital which will be available for local firms to borrow and realise their investment projects, and that this will lead to strong and sustained growth.

If, however, MNCs entering developing countries choose to finance their investment from local financial markets and therefore compete with domestic firms for the capital available, they could end up driving the local firms out of business. It is a fact that MNCs are more profitable and possess more assets than domestic firms in developing countries, and they may therefore be regarded as a more secure borrower compared with domestic firms and thereby absorb the available capital. This is the so-called 'crowding out' effect. It is further argued that the crowding-out impact of inward FDI on domestic capital accumulation is sector-specific. In particular, foreign investment in the high-wage manufacturing sector may have a far greater impact on capital available to domestic firms than in the primary sector. There is also a controversy regarding the role of FDI in creating growth. Some studies indicate that although growth often attracts FDI, there does not seem to be enough evidence to suggest that FDI contributes to growth (Calderon *et al.* 2004).

Some argue that the effect of FDI on the capital market is not clear-cut, and that it depends on the characteristics of the investment, the recipient country, and the timing of the investment. Even if the firms facing credit constraints had savings put aside for investment purposes, they might not be able to channel these funds into productive investments because of poorly developed financial markets, which exacerbate the credit deficiency in the market. Therefore, the foreign capital channelled through FDI serves as new capital and also bypasses the undeveloped domestic institutions in channelling the funds into productive investment. In this it partially replaces domestic banks or venture capitalists in the process of financial intermediation (Moosa 2002).

The effect on the balance of payments

FDI has also been seen as a way of improving the balance of payments for host countries. Inward investment can have three positive direct impacts on the host country's balance of payments. First, the initial inflow of capital is recorded as a credit in the host country's capital account, as it brings in foreign exchange. Second, if the FDI inflows replace imports, for example where an MNC decides to undertake FDI in a country to which it exported previously, this benefits the host country's current account. Third, the FDI might be motivated by a lower cost of production in the host country ('export-oriented affiliates'), which will also improve the host country's current account.

However, there are also indirect effects of FDI or spillovers from the MNCs that developing host countries, and especially their domestic firms, might benefit from and which could encourage them to export more. One such spillover effect is where local firms can learn how to succeed in foreign markets simply by imitating the activities of local MNC affiliates. Moreover, local firms may also benefit indirectly from the pressures exercised by local MNC affiliates on the liberalisation of trade. The local firms may therefore enjoy reduced trade barriers between their country and the developing world. There is also likely to be a diffusion of skills by ex-MNC employees. Employees who have been trained in export management by MNCs might decide to move to local companies and automatically take their acquired skills with them. Other channels for the diffusion of export know-how are contacts through trade associations and other industry organisations, of which MNCs and local firms are often prominent members.

However, the FDI literature also contains theories relating to the adverse balance of payments effects (Kozul-Wright and Rowthorn 1998). For example one study argues that liberalisation policies introduced by LDCs to attract FDI might have a detrimental effect on the balance of payments of the country (see Razmi 2005). It is also possible that MNCs can cause substantial current account deficits by importing more than exporting, and that since most developing countries already run such deficits, inward FDI can further worsen the host country's balance of trade. There are three factors that contribute to foreign firms' trade deficits. First, MNCs import a large amount of their machinery and technology, especially in the developing countries where these are quite scarce. Second, foreign-owned firms import the majority of their raw materials, spare parts and components. This is particularly true of MNCs that move their production facilities to developing countries in order to cut production costs and then export most of their products back to the developed world. Third, transfer prices (see Chapter 6) manipulated by MNCs for their foreign affiliates' exports and imports are a major reason for the constant increase in trade deficits of foreign firms.

The effect on management styles

Another impact of FDI is on management styles. In particular Japanese investment is often seen as bringing new innovations in management techniques, and practices such as the just-in-time (JIT) production method. The link between such changes and foreign investment is not always clear. In addition these new techniques might not be an unalloyed benefit for workers in the companies concerned. They could increase stress and the pace of work, and decrease effective union representation. A particularly notorious case occurred where in December 1984 Hitachi invited all workers over 35 years old at its factory in Hirwaun in South Wales to take voluntary retirement. The argument was that older workers are more prone to sickness, slower, have poorer eyesight and are more resistant to change (Pearson 1989).

Policy issues

Despite a somewhat timid approach to FDI by some LDCs in the past, the recent trend since the mid-1980s has been that almost all countries, including China, compete to attract as much FDI as possible. In doing so some of them, encouraged by, and some would say pressurised by, institutions such as the IMF, the World Bank and the WTO as well as some economists, followed rather dubious liberalisation policies which have caused controversy (Bernal *et al.* 2004). Both 2001 and 2002 saw a record amount of legislation in the world that favoured liberalisation and deregulation towards FDI (UNCTAD 2004b). In particular, DCs have been putting pressure on LDCs in recent years to liberalise their trade, abolish capital controls, and open up their economies to FDI inflows (Chang 2003).

There is a growing body of literature arguing that unlimited liberalisation and deregulation and uncontrolled capital inflows are actually likely to harm the development efforts of LDCs rather than help them. DCs argue that they became rich by following free trade and liberal FDI policies, and therefore LDCs should do the same. Chang (2003), on the other hand, argues that that proposition is fundamentally misguided, and that historically speaking the United States, the United Kingdom, France, Germany, Japan, Korea and Taiwan did not use liberal FDI policies before they became rich. In fact, the policies followed by a number of east Asian economies were 'strategic' rather than liberal. This means that they followed liberal policies for some sectors but highly protective ones for others. Bernal *et al.* (2004), on the other hand, are rather critical of the World Bank and the WTO approach which advises LDCs to liberalise their trade and FDI policies. They argue that such policies simply promote DCs' own narrow economic interests, that they are against historical experiences, and that they would definitely be detrimental to the interests of LDCs. Kozul-Wright and Rowthorn (1998) argue along similar lines, and suggest a cautious approach to the topic of FDI by LDCs. They recognise that globalisation, in the sense of integrating with the world commodity and capital markets, in general, and FDI in particular, could be useful to LDCs in their effort to develop, and advise them to adopt a strategic approach in formulating policies regarding international trade and FDI (also see Mallampally and Sauvant 1999).

Conclusion

Controversies surrounding FDI have lost some of their ideological dimension since the 1960s as a result of the ending of the Cold War and the advent of globalisation. Presently, both LDCs and DCs compete to attract FDI. Therefore, it is not surprising that world FDI flows have been increasing in recent times, both in absolute value and relative to world GDP. This increase is comparable to the rise of FDI flows in late 19th and early 20th centuries in terms of growth rates. However, there is a qualitative difference in FDI flows between these two periods. FDI in the earlier period mainly went from DCs to LDCs, and was concentrated on agricultural and extractive industries. However, DCs dominate the more recent FDI inflows and outflows, although some newly industrialised countries, especially east Asian ones, have also been making inroads into investing abroad. Moreover, there seems to be a discernible shift in FDI flows in recent times from the manufacturing sector to services.

European FDI has also evolved over time both quantitatively and qualitatively. While FDI inflows into the European Union increased almost threefold between the early 1990s and the early years of the present decade, outflows more than doubled during the same period. However, in more recent times the relative importance of the CEECs and LDCs with respect to FDI inflows has been increasing at the expense of the European Union. To counter this, intra-EU FDI has been increasing both in absolute value and relative to GDP and international trade. Moreover, intra-EU FDI activity is now more widely spread across borders within the European Union than ever.

Questions

1 Using the information in Table 7.3, calculate the growth rate of FDI inflows for LDCs between 1992 and 2003, and discuss the technological impact of this on local firms.

2 Explain what the 'O' stands for in 'OLI paradigm'. Give examples of firms that have used this specific advantage in determining their direct investment.

3 To what extent are radical explanations of FDI valid?

4 Table 7.2 indicates that FDI grew by almost 1000 per cent during the period 1982–2003 while exports grew by only 400 per cent in the same period. What is the implication of this difference in the two growth rates for business firms? (Hint: refer also to Chapter 2.)

5 Tables 7.3 and 7.6 indicate that recently intra-EU FDI has increased in relation to extra-EU FDI. Can you give explanations for this?

6 The automotive, pharmaceuticals and software sectors are among the ones attracting most FDI in recent times in the European Union. Can you explain this?

7 Should LDCs try to attract FDI? What are the implications of FDI inflows for the labour and capital markets of LDCs?

References

Baker, S. (1990) *An Introduction to International Economics*, Harcourt Brace Jovanovich, San Diego, Calif.

Bende-Nabende, A. (2002) *Globalisation, FDI, Regional Integration and Sustainable Development Theory, Evidence and Policy*, Ashgate, Aldershot.

Bernal, L. E., Kaukab, R. S. and Yu III, V. B. P. (2004) *The World Development Report 2005: An unbalanced message on investment liberalization*, WTO, Geneva, August.

Bevan, A., Estrin, S. and Grabbe, H. (2001) 'The impact of EU accession prospects on FDI inflows to central and eastern Europe', ESRC Policy Papers 06/01, ESRC 'One Europe or Several' Programme.

Big Picture Small World (2005) 'The flow of money: foreign direct investment', http://www.bigpicturesmallworld.com/Global%20Inc%202/pgs/fndts/fdi.html, accessed 9 March 2005.

Buckley, P. and Artisen, P. (1988) 'Policy issues of intra-EC direct investment: British, French and German multinationals in Greece, Portugal and Spain, with special reference to employment effects', in J. Dunning and P. Robson (eds), *Multinationals and the European Community*, Blackwell, Oxford.

Buckley, P. and Casson, M. (1985) *The Economic Theory of Multinational Enterprise*, Macmillan, London.

Calderon, C., Loayza, N. and Serven, L. (2004) 'Greenfield foreign direct investment and mergers and acquisitions: feedback and macroeconomic effects', World Bank Policy Research Working Paper 3192, January.

Cantwell, J. (1988) 'The reorganization of European industries after integration: selected evidence of the role of multinational enterprise activities', in J. Dunning and P. Robson (eds), *Multinationals and the European Community*, Blackwell, Oxford.

Chang, H. J. (2003) 'Foreign direct investment in historical perspective: lessons for the proposed WTO Investment Agreement', Third World Network. *Global Policy*, March, http://www.globalpolicy.org/socecon/ffd/2003/03historical.htm, accessed February 2005.

Chesnais, F., Ietto-Gillies, C. and Simonetti, R. (eds) (2000) *European Integration and Global Corporate Strategies*, Routledge, London.

Deutsche Bank (2004) Research, 'Foreign direct investment in China: good prospects for German companies?' Deutsche Bank AG, Frankfurt, 24 August.

Dunning, J. (1981) *International Production and the MNE*, George Allen and Unwin, London.

Dunning, J. (1983) 'Changes in the level and structure of international production: the last one hundred years', in M. Casson, *The Growth of International Business*, George Allen and Unwin, London.

Dunning, J. (1993) *The Globalization of Business*, Routledge, London.

Dunning, J. (1997a) 'The European internal market programme and inbound foreign direct investment: Part 1', *Journal of Common Market Studies*, vol. 35, no. 1, pp. 1–30.

Dunning, J. (1997b) 'The European internal market programme and inbound foreign direct investment: Part 2', *Journal of Common Market Studies*, vol. 35, no. 2, June, pp. 189–229.

Dunning, J. (2001) 'The eclectic (OLI) paradigm of international production: past, present and future', *International Journal of the Economics of Business*, vol. 8, no. 2, pp. 173–90.

Dunning, J. H. (2002) 'Theories and paradigms of international business activity', in *The Selected Essays of John H. Dunning, Vol. 1*, Edward Elgar, Cheltenham.

Dunning, J. and Cantwell, J. (1991) 'Japanese direct investment in Europe', in B. Burgenmeier and J. L. Mucchielli (eds), *Multinationals and Europe 1992*, Routledge, London.

Economist Intelligence Unit (EIU) (2004) *World Investment Prospects: The revival of globalisation*, 2004 edn, Economist Intelligence Unit, London.

El-Agraa, A. M. (2004) *The European Union: Economics and policies*, 7th edn, FT/Prentice Hall, Harlow.

European Investment Monitor (EIM) (2004) *2004 Report*, Ernst and Young, London.

Eurostat (2004a) *Eurostat: Intensity ratios*, European Commission, Brussels.

Eurostat (2004b) 'EU25 FDI: 2001–2003 data' *Statistics in Focus*, European Commission, Brussels.

Finfacts (2004) 'Foreign direct investment – European Union', http://www.finfacts.com/biz10/foreigndirectinvestmenteu.htm, accessed 21 March 2005.

Fischer, P. (2000) *Foreign Direct Investment in Russia: A strategy for industrial recovery*, Macmillan, Basingstoke.

Hill, C. W. L. (2005) *International Business: Competing in the Global Market Place*, 5th edn, McGraw Hill, Boston/London.

Hood, N. and Young, S. (1979) *The Economics of MNE*, Longman, London.

Hunt, E. Y. and Sherman, H. J. (1990) *Economics*, Harper and Row, New York.

Hymer, S. (1976) *The International Operations of National Firms: A study in DFI*, MIT Press, Boston, Mass.

Ietto-Gillies, G. (2005) *Transnational Corporations and International Production*, Edward Elgar, Cheltenham.

Julius, D. (1990) *Global Companies and Public Policy*, Pinter/RIIA, London.

Julius, D. (1993) 'Foreign direct investment: Is the boom bust?', paper presented at the South Bank University, Centre for International Business Studies, London, 4 March.

Kozul-Wright, R. and Rowthorn, R. (1998) 'Spoilt for choice? Multinational corporations and the geography of international production', *Oxford Review of Economic Policy*, vol. 14, no. 2.

Lal Das, B. (2003) 'A critical analysis of the proposed investment treaty in WTO', *SUNS*, July.

Lawler, K. and Seddighi, H. (2001) *International Economics*, FT/Prentice Hall, Harlow.

Mallampally, P. and Sauvant, K. P. (1999) 'Foreign direct investment in developing countries', *Finance and Development*, vol. 36, no. 1, March.

Moosa, I. (2002) *Foreign Direct Investment: Theory, evidence, and practice*, Palgrave, Basingstoke.

O'Rourke, K. (2002) 'Europe and the causes of globalisation, 1790 to 2000', CEG Working Papers no. 20021, Trinity College, Dublin.

OECD (2004) *Trends and Recent Developments in Foreign Direct Investment*, OECD Directorate for Financial and Enterprise Affairs, Paris, June.

Pearson, R. (1989) 'Women's employment and multinationals in the UK: restructuring and flexibility', in D. Elson and R. Pearson (eds), *Women's Employment and Multinationals in Europe*, Macmillan, London.

Piggott, J. and Cook, M. (1999) *International Business Economics*, 2nd edn, Longman, Harlow.

Razmi, A. (2005) 'FDI, external accounts, and income distribution in developing economies: a structuralist investigation', Working Paper 2005-03, University of Massachusetts at Amherst.

UNCTAD (2004a) *World Investment Report 2004: The shift towards services*, UN, Geneva.

UNCTAD (2004b) *Development and Globalisation: Facts and figures*, UN, Geneva.

UNCTAD (2005) Press release, UNCTAD/PRESS/PR/2005/002, 11 January.

Vernon, R. (1966) 'International investment and international trade in the product cycle', *Quarterly Journal of Economics*, vol. 80 (May), pp. 190–207.

World Bank (2005) *World Development Report 2005*, World Bank, Washington, DC.

8 International and European capital markets

Andy Kilmister

Objectives This chapter will:

- outline the differences between the main kinds of capital markets and explain the main factors affecting them, especially in Europe
- critically examine the process of European financial integration and its impact on providers and users of funds
- explain the advantages and disadvantages of different kinds of regulation for the financial sector and relate this explanation to the European case
- set developments in Europe within the broader context of global financial change.

Introduction

Financial systems exist to channel funds from the providers of capital, usually households who wish to invest their savings, to the users of capital, normally governments and companies. Such flows of capital take place both within and between individual countries. When capital flows become international we see both particular sectors within countries obtaining their financing from abroad, or providing funds to foreign users, and also countries becoming either creditors or debtors and accumulating or drawing down their stocks of foreign assets. This chapter will examine the way in which this is done, but will not consider one particular kind of capital flow, the long-term investments associated with controlling shares in enterprises. This comes under the heading of **foreign direct investment (FDI)**, which has been considered separately in Chapter 7.

Flows of capital can take place in two main ways, either through markets or through institutions. In the former case, providers and users of funds trade financial instruments with one another in the marketplace. The most important such markets are the various stock, bond and money markets and also the foreign currency markets. However, in recent years so-called 'derivatives' markets have assumed increased significance, notably the markets for **options, futures** contracts, forward contracts and swaps. In the latter case providers of funds invest their money in a financial institution, thereby pooling their resources. These resources are then channelled through the institution to the eventual users. The most important financial institutions are banks, but many other institutions are significant, for example pension funds, insurance companies and investment funds of various kinds (in the United Kingdom these are chiefly unit trusts and investment trusts).

The balance between market-based and institution-based transactions in the financial system varies both across different countries and over time. Many analysts have tended to see Continental Europe as having an institution-based system, with banks playing a central role, and have contrasted this with market-based systems in the United States and the United Kingdom (Allen and Gale 2000). However, this is rather too simple a view, since while Europe is characterised by significant bank involvement in the provision of funds and relatively small stock markets, it also has large bond markets (Freixas, Hartmann and Mayer 2004). Further, banks are becoming less important in 'traditional' lending within Europe than other financial institutions such as investment funds, pension funds and insurance companies. It may be more appropriate to place continental Europe as somewhere midway between the institution-based system of Japan and the Anglo-American system with its emphasis on markets (Hartmann, Maddaloni and Manganelli 2003).

A long tradition in financial analysis has also argued, following the pioneering work of Gerschenkron (1962), that institution-based systems will tend to evolve historically towards becoming market-based systems. Recent trends in financial deregulation and innovation have often been taken to support this hypothesis, in particular the development of 'securitisation' and 'disintermediation', whereby contracts which were previously agreed between institutions and users of funds, such as loan contracts, have been packaged up as marketable securities and traded actively on the financial markets. Such developments have put financial institutions such as banks under considerable competitive pressure.

Historical developments

In order to understand current changes in the financial system it is necessary to look how that system has changed over time. Eichengreen and Fishlow (1998) distinguish between three main periods of rapid growth in international capital flows: the 'era of bond finance' in the 1920s, the 'era of bank finance' in the 1970s and the 'era of equity finance', which began in the 1990s and continues today.

The era of bond finance was particularly centred on lending from the United States to Europe, Latin America, Canada and Australia. Bonds issued by these countries were underwritten by US banks (at the time the United States still had a system of 'universal banking' where banks were permitted both to lend money and to trade in securities) and were actively traded in a secondary market based in New York. The bonds were largely purchased by investment trusts which pooled the funds of household 'retail' investors:

> In the 1920s investment trusts played much the same role as emerging-market mutual funds in the 1990s. They pooled the subscriptions of their clients, placed their management in the hands of specialists and issued

claims entitling holders to a share of their earnings. They facilitated position-taking in foreign securities by investors who would have been otherwise deterred by transaction and information costs. Commercial banks established bond departments and securities affiliates, much in the manner that commercial banks in the 1990s created their own mutual funds.

(Eichengreen and Fishlow 1998: 28)

In 1897 more than 90 per cent of US foreign investment was direct, but by 1930 the share of **portfolio investment** had risen to 50 per cent.

The growth of international bond finance was brought to an end by interest rate rises in the United States, which shifted providers of funds towards domestic lending. Subsequently, increased US protectionism in the wake of the Great Depression of the 1930s and a decline in primary commodity prices further discouraged foreign borrowers. There was a wave of defaults among sovereign country borrowers, most notably Germany in 1933. The result was a move among both industrial and developing economies towards strategies of import substitution based on tariff protection, and a sharp decline in international capital flows. This decline was coupled with an increase in financial regulation, especially in the United States with the Glass–Steagall Act, which separated retail and investment banking.

When capital flows began to restart again in earnest in the late 1960s they did so through the medium of bank loans rather than bond issues. An important catalyst here was the growth of what is known as the '**Eurocurrency market**'. Eurocurrency deposits are bank deposits held in a currency other than the 'local' currency, for example dollar deposits held in London. (It should be noted that such deposits are not necessarily held in Europe despite the name.) The initial stimulus for the growth of these markets was in part the regulatory structure existing in the United States, especially 'Regulation Q', which was introduced in 1958, limiting the rate of interest that banks could offer depositors. During the 1960s they developed further because of the flow of dollars into foreign exchange markets resulting from the US balance of payments deficits, which arose from the financing of the Vietnam War.

Following the collapse of the Bretton-Woods system of fixed exchange rates in 1973, the market expanded to take in a wider range of currencies, with the Euro-Deutschmark being particularly important. It then grew dramatically after 1973 when oil prices quadrupled. Oil exporters were unable to use all their revenues productively at home and invested them in the Euro markets where they were lent on to borrowers who were running deficits on the current account of the balance of payments. Heavy borrowers included some of the Latin American and Eastern European economies and those countries that were especially dependent on imported oil.

The growth of international bank lending was halted in the early 1980s when US and British interest rates rose sharply with the adoption of monetarist anti-inflationary policies. As the economies of industrialised countries slowed down, reducing their imports from those countries that had borrowed, while at the same time the interest rates on any loans that were rolled over rose, it became increasingly difficult for borrowers to service their loan repayments. The crucial episode was the default of Mexico in August 1982, which brought this era of bank finance to an end and inaugurated the international debt crisis. This crisis, centred particularly in Latin America, lasted the rest of the decade.

While the debt crisis slowed the rate of new bank lending dramatically, the overall amount of international bank liabilities continued to increase as unpaid interest was consolidated into loans. However, throughout the 1980s growth in the Eurocurrency markets slowed as the trends in **disintermediation** and securitisation referred to above shifted the emphasis of the system towards asset markets, especially equity markets, rather than bank finance. In addition, financial deregulation meant that the proportion of Eurocurrency deposits in international banking markets fell to 59.6 per cent by the end of 2003 from a level of 84.8 per cent at the end of 1980 and 75.2 per cent at the end of 1990, according to Bank for International Settlements figures. Table 8.1 shows the growth of the Eurocurrency market.

Table 8.1 Eurocurrency deposits (totals taken at the end of each year)

Year	Bank liabilities in foreign currencies (US$ million)
1977	421.7
1980	838.8
1985	1,886.9
1990	4,738.2
1995	5,933.2
2000	6,990.6
2001	7,464.2
2002	8,317.2
2003	9,540.7

Source: Bank for International Settlements.

During the 1990s and since 2000, equity flows of international capital have become more important. According to Eichengreen and Fishlow (1998), this has largely been encouraged by financial **deregulation**, which has encouraged international diversification by US pension funds and insurance companies, and has opened up financial markets to a new wave of mutual funds and investment trusts. Given the crises which brought the eras of bond and bank finance to an end, an important question is, does similar turbulence lie in store for the coming period?

Eichengreen and Fishlow (1998) point out that, while the era of equity capital was accompanied by a series of financial and currency crises, for example Mexico in 1994, east and south-east Asia in 1997 and 1998, Russia in 1998 and Brazil in 1999, the impact of these has been confined to particular countries or regions, and has not had the global scope of the crisis of the 1930s, or even of the debt crisis of the 1980s. The same has been true of the financial turbulence in Turkey and Argentina that has occurred more recently. However, it cannot be guaranteed that this will continue in the future. In order to assess the possibility of more widespread disruption it is necessary to look at the question of how the financial system is regulated, both nationally and internationally.

Financial regulation

There are two main reasons that financial markets and institutions have traditionally been subject to extensive regulation by governments and central banks, in a way that participants in other markets have not. The first of these is 'systemic risk', which particularly applies in the case of banks and other deposit-taking institutions (Davis 1995). Given the large amount of inter-bank lending, the collapse of one bank can rebound through the system, threatening the solvency of other banks that have lent to it, and raising the possibility of further failures. In economic terms what we have here is a significant negative externality, in which the **social cost** of an individual bank failure exceeds the private cost to shareholders and depositors, because of the impact on the financial standing of other banks. Such externalities are generally seen as a form of market failure, which can justify government intervention.

The second reason for regulation is investor protection, which especially relates to institutions like unit trusts, investment trusts and mutual funds. The problem here is one of imperfect information. Those providing funds to such institutions have very limited means to assess the quality of the product they are buying, since given the uncertainty of the financial world past results may arise from a variety of factors other than management expertise and may not be a good guide to future performance. Not only is information imperfect here, it is also 'asymmetric' in that those managing the funds know more about their investment plans than do those investors depositing money with them. Again, asymmetric information represents a potential form of market failure, since depositors may not make the choices that they would have done in a perfect market, and so it is a reason for regulation.

In addition to these long-standing reasons for regulation of financial institutions there has more recently been a concern with the operation of financial markets. A number of writers have emphasised the way in which the behaviour of market participants can prove destabilising and result in financial turmoil. An important early analysis here was the paper by Diamond and Dybvig (1983) on bank runs, which showed how these might arise as rational self-fulfilling prophecies. This kind of approach has been strengthened by so-called 'second generation' models of currency crises, which stress the way in which such crises can arise not because of inherent economic weaknesses or policy mistakes in the countries concerned, but through the expectations of investors about how other investors will behave and about how the country's authorities will respond to such behaviour (Sachs 1998). Such models became especially popular following the 'Asian crisis' of 1997–8, where economies that had seemed to be performing well such as Thailand and South Korea suddenly became victims of what appeared to be speculative attacks.

Financial regulation has traditionally taken three main forms: regulation of price, scope of activity and geographical scope. An example of the first is the controls of interest rates offered in the United States, referred to above. The purpose of this was to avoid destabilising competition, leading to banks offering higher rates than they could afford and so putting themselves in jeopardy. Such controls have featured in a number of other industrialised economies.

Regulation of activities has been common in the financial sector, and has applied to both institutions and markets. In the case of markets an example was the separation in the London Stock Exchange between brokers who took orders on behalf of customers, and jobbers who traded on their own account on the floor of the exchange. The purpose of this regulation was to avoid a possible conflict of interest whereby traders might encourage customers to commit to those trades that would generate the maximum profit for the traders in their own buying and selling activity. With regard to institutions, the separation of retail and investment banking in the United States, referred to above, is an example of regulation of activities. A similar separation obtained for many years in Japan, giving rise to the growth of securities dealers such as Nomura. One example of regulation of activities that affected households for many years in Britain and the United States was the separation of banking and mortgage finance, with the latter being handled not by banks but by building societies in the United Kingdom and savings and loans associations in the United States. The reasons for regulating activities in these ways were predominantly fear that risks incurred in one kind of activity might spill over and affect those households who had contracted with the institutions in other areas.

Finally, regulation of geographical scope was prevalent in the financial sector for many years. This applied both to restrictions on banks and other financial institutions moving across national borders in Europe, and to movement across state boundaries in the United States. The legacy of this persists in the United States today: for example Rosengren (2002) points out that no US bank has major retail operations in all regions of the country and only 6 per cent of banks operate in more than one state. With regard to markets, geographical movement of funds was limited for most European and Asian countries during much of the post-Second World War period by capital and exchange controls. Generally, the financial sector was seen as sufficiently important and risky for governments and central banks to wish to maintain regulatory control on activities taking place within their territorial domain.

Over the last three decades nearly all of this structure of regulation has been dismantled. There are a number of reasons for this. Probably, the most important is technological change. The ability of institutions and traders to move funds electronically has made it very difficult to enforce regulations on prices and geographical scope, as shown by the growth of the **Eurocurrency market**, discussed above. In addition, technology has made some kinds of regulation appear less necessary. For example, the introduction of electronic trading schemes in stock exchanges, which opened up the possibility of tracking past transactions and uncovering fraud, made the separation between brokers and jobbers less important in protecting investor interests. In addition to technology, competitive pressure within the financial sector has been an important spur to deregulation. A case of this was the deregulation of stock exchanges in North America in the early 1980s, which then led to pressure for similar deregulation in Britain and the 'Big Bang' in the London Stock Exchange in October 1986.

The internationalisation of non-financial companies has also played a part in encouraging deregulation. This has operated through two channels. First, major multinational customers of financial institutions have demanded global services from their banks. Second, the behaviour of companies has increased the competitive pressure favouring deregulation. For example, in the 1950s and 1960s when Japanese companies largely operated at home and were linked to international markets mainly by exports, it was relatively easy for the Japanese government to maintain a highly regulated financial system. In later years, however, now that such companies have invested abroad and can obtain finance from North American and European sources more easily, tight regulations at home put Japanese institutions at a competitive disadvantage.

Further factors leading to deregulation include financial innovation and polit ical encouragement. The growth of securitisation mentioned in the introduction to this chapter has provided financial markets with a new flexibility, making the framing of regulations increasingly difficult. For example, one possible response to interest rate controls on loans might be to 'repackage' those loans as tradable securities which are not subject to control. These structural factors have been strengthened by broader political developments, especially in North America and Europe in recent years, notably increased scepticism about state interven- tion and a general view that the interests of households and companies are best served by encouraging competition, and that this applies to the financial sector as much as to other sectors.

The removal in large part of previous forms of regulation does not, however, mean that the financial sector has been completely deregulated. Rather, what has happened has been the replacement of these approaches to regulation by a new approach, which might be termed 'prudential regu- lation'. Prudential regulation concentrates not on what institutions or market participants do (the prices they charge and which markets or coun- tries they operate in) but on who is entitled to participate in the financial sector in the first place. The aim is to ensure that those who operate in the sector meet particular criteria, designed to protect providers of funds, but once those criteria have been met to allow as much freedom to them as possible in their operations.

The most important example of prudential regulation is the case of capital adequacy ratios for banks, as originally embodied in the 'Proposals for International Convergence of Capital Measurement and Capital Standards' put forward by the Bank for International Settlements (BIS) in July 1988 and imple- mented in 1993. The main element of these regulations is the requirement that 8 per cent of risk-weighted assets should be covered by bank capital. The rationale for this is that such a requirement will mean that bank shareholders have put a sufficiently large stake into the bank to ensure that they exert adequate oversight over management decisions, thus minimising the risk of insolvency. (In other words the rules ensure that shareholders have so much to lose in the case of bankruptcy, that they will make sure it does not happen.) In addition, the ratios are designed to give banks a sufficient cushion of capital to ensure that they can weather any adverse circumstances resulting from default by borrowers. As outlined below, this approach to bank regulation has largely been adopted by the European Union.

The use of capital adequacy ratios has been criticised on a number of grounds, which also have implications for prudential regulation in general. Two of these are especially important. First, it has been argued that this kind of approach is potentially destabilising in itself. If an economy runs into trouble and the stock market declines, then bank capital will fall. If this pushes the capital ratio of the bank below 8 per cent then it will have to reduce its asset base, probably by calling in, or not renewing, loans. This will then worsen the economic difficulties that sparked off the initial problem. It could be argued that this played a role in the Scandinavian financial crisis of the early 1990s. (Although the capital adequacy rules were not fully operational at this time, banks were trying to work towards them and using them as a guideline in loan decisions.) Second, the ratios have been criticised for being too undiscriminating in their assessment of risk, for example treating all loans to corporations with a particular credit rating as equivalent, even if this means that lending is concentrated in a particular sector.

The response of the BIS, followed by the European Union, to such criticisms has been to move further in the direction of self-regulation by institutions, beginning with the Amendment to the Basle Capital Accord to Incorporate Market Risk reached in 1995, which allows banks to use internal risk measurement models (so-called value-at-risk or VAR models) to determine their capital requirements. This trend has been strengthened in recent years, as Vives observes:

> This represents a movement from a rigid to a more flexible view of capital requirements. The proposal for a New Basel Capital Accord advances three pillars – minimum capital requirement, supervision, and market discipline – allowing banks to choose from a menu of approaches (for example, standardised and internal rating) to measure risk (credit, market and operational). The whole idea is to provide more risk sensitivity to capital requirements.
>
> (Vives 2001: 537)

As of April 2005 the Basle Committee on Banking Supervision planned to complete the final amendments to the Accord in spring 2006 with a view to phasing it in during 2007 and implementing it fully in 2008 (Norman 2005).

Another kind of criticism of recent approaches to financial regulation has focused on the lack of international regulatory structures which match those operating at a domestic level. Two particular instances have been highlighted. First, there is no formal legal provision for countries to declare bankruptcy or for sovereign debt workouts in the way that there is for companies (Sachs 1998). Second, there is no international 'lender of last resort' with an obligation to provide liquidity in the event of an international crisis in the way that domestic banks see themselves as required to do in order to protect the stability of national financial systems.

The problem that has been raised with introducing either of these reforms, apart from the general difficulty of international coordination, is that of 'moral hazard'. If either bankruptcy or the emergency provision of funds were to be seen as a guaranteed outcome for countries that encountered problems through excessive borrowing, then it could be argued that this would encourage reckless behaviour.

Proposals for a single European financial market

EU policies towards the financial sector, in particular the proposals put forward for a single European financial market, have closely followed the general approach to financial regulation set out above. The removal of restrictions on geographical scope has been coupled with the encouragement of competition, while the whole structure is backed by prudential regulation. There are two main aspects to the analytical framework that has governed this approach.

First, there is the view that the European financial sector has been insufficiently competitive, and this has raised the price of financial services to households and the cost of capital for companies. In the Cecchini Report of 1988 the European Commission attempted to estimate the gains resulting from the extra competition arising from creating an integrated financial market, by comparing current prices with the average of the lowest four observations across member states. The estimated falls in price, and associated gains for consumers, were significant, as shown in the case of banking, by Table 8.2.

Table 8.2 Potential falls in the price of financial products in percentage terms as estimated by the 1988 Cecchini Report

	Germany	France	Italy	UK
Commercial loans	6.0	−7.3	8.6	45.7
Consumer credit	135.9	105.1	121.0	121.5
Credit card	60.0	−29.5	88.6	16.2
Mortgages	57.3	78.5	−4.3	−20.7
Letters of credit	−10.0	−7.2	9.1	8.1
Foreign exchange draft	30.9	55.6	23.5	16.1
Travellers cheques	−7.4	38.9	22.2	−7.4

Source: Dermine (2002: 43).

Second, an influential view in modern writing on finance stresses the importance of the size of the financial sector in encouraging economic development (Levine 1997). According to this view the European financial sector is simply too small and fragmented to provide the resources necessary to encourage growth. Two recent reports using this kind of analysis estimate the effect of substantial further financial integration in Europe as an increase in the rate of GDP growth of up to 1 per cent (Giannetti et al. 2002, London Economics 2002).

Financial integration has also been seen as important for other reasons, for example because the free flow of capital is supposed to encourage countries to follow more disciplined macroeconomic policies, and because greater access to world capital markets allows more flexibility for countries to spread risk by borrowing in bad times and lending in good times. It is not clear, however, to what extent such benefits actually require regional financial integration as opposed to individual countries simply opening up their economies to global forces. The benefits of increased competition and greater size have been seen as sufficient, though, to ensure that the project of European financial integration has been regarded as central to European integration as a whole by policy makers and businesses.

The attempt to integrate the European financial markets has involved a number of stages. The First Banking Directive in 1977 established the general principle of home country control for banks operating in two or more member countries. It was a general programme which did not itself embody more specific regulations but called for further directives. The real starting point was a European Commission White Paper on *Financial Integration* in April 1983, which called for further work to achieve a better allocation of savings and investment in the European Community, as it then was (Dermine 2002). In 1985 a further White Paper on *The Completion of the Internal Market*, which led to the Single European Act, called for a single banking licence, home country control and mutual recognition. The principles were included in the Second Banking Directive, adopted in December 1989, according to which all credit institutions authorised in one EU country would be able to establish branches or supply cross-border financial services in other EU countries without further authorisation. Host countries are only able to regulate the activities of banks from other EU countries to the extent that such regulation is necessary for protection of the public interest or in certain specific areas such as liquidity, monetary policy and advertising. The Second Banking Directive also adopted capital adequacy rules modelled on the Basle Accord discussed above.

Similar directives concerning the insurance industry and financial services, which provided for mutual recognition of institutions, with regard to both the setting up of branches in other member states and cross-border trade, were passed at around this time. Notable examples in insurance were the June 1992 Third Life Insurance Directive and the November 1992 Third Non-Life Insurance Directive, both of which were modelled on the Second Banking Directive (Story and Walter 1997). In financial services the key directives were the December 1985 directive on collective investment instruments (mutual funds, unit trusts and so on) and the December 1992 Investment Services Directive.

These various directives were backed up by a number of pieces of subsidiary legislation, for example the 1994 directive on deposit guarantee schemes, which provided for mandatory insurance for all EU financial institutions.

In addition to these legislative initiatives a major stimulus to the integration of European financial markets was provided by the progressive removal of exchange controls across the European Union. Such controls had been suspended in the United Kingdom since 1979, but for continental Europe the process really began with the 1988 Directive on Liberalisation of Capital Flows and was intensified following the Treaty of Maastricht, which made the removal of such controls by 31 December 1993 a prerequisite for participation in monetary union. In turn, the creation of the euro was widely seen as likely to lead to a more unified financial market, while an integrated market has also been regarded as important for the success of monetary union. This is because if there are significant structural differences between financial markets in different countries participating in European Monetary Union (EMU), the impact of monetary policy decisions by the European Central Bank (ECB) is likely to differ between such countries, creating tensions in the operation of a common monetary policy.

It is generally agreed, however, that the gains resulting from the Single Market in the financial area have not been as large as was hoped. For example, the Single Market Review study on credit institutions and banking, commissioned by the European Commission, observed little convergence in prices (European Commission 1997). Dermine (2002) presents three other pieces of evidence to show a seeming lack of competition in various aspects of retail banking. First are the results of a Commission study at the end of 1999 concerning the cost of a cross-border transfer of €100. Total charges ranged from €8.91 in Luxemburg and €10 in the Netherlands to €29.68 in Portugal. Over the years 1993 to 2000 there had been a 50 per cent price reduction in some countries but virtually no change in price in others. Second, even within a country, price variations persist. In the case of French money market funds in 2001, the range of management fees varied from 8 basis points (bps) to 200 bps, with an average of 68 bps. The range of management fees had not decreased from 1989 to 2001, and the average had risen from the 1989 level of 50 bps (a basis point is a value of 0.01 per cent). Finally, Dermine calculated interest margins on savings deposits for six countries in 2000. While these had converged somewhat since 1980, possibly as a result of the general fall in interest rates across the euro-zone during this period, the margins still ranged from 0.75 per cent in Belgium to 2.37 per cent in Spain.

A number of reasons can be put forward for the failure to achieve the projections put forward in the Cecchini Report. Two arguments have been especially influential. First, the various special characteristics of financial markets, discussed above in the context of regulation, also make competition based on price difficult in this sector. Most important here are the informational asymmetries in the sector which lead to long-term customer relationships, reliance on reputation and very high switching costs. Second, the historical legacy of different kinds of financial development in different European countries is still powerful. Freixas, Hartmann and Mayer (2004) point out that, for example:

> In countries such as Germany, where asset management is closely associated with banks, capital requirements are regarded as an appropriate form in which to provide investor protection. In other countries, such as the UK, where there are a large number of small, independent, asset-management firms, capital requirements are viewed as unnecessary, and investor protection is regarded as possible with lighter regulation. As a consequence, it is difficult for German banks to compete for investment management services with UK firms, and for UK firms to enter German asset-management markets.
>
> (Freixas, Hartmann and Mayer 2004: 477)

The response of the European Commission to this situation has been to embark on a new set of initiatives in order to encourage financial integration across the European Union and to strengthen the single market.

Recent developments in European financial policy

The Cardiff European Council of June 1998 singled out financial services as an area where further progress was needed in completing the single market, and in response to this the Commission established a high-level Financial Services Policy Group (FSPG), chaired by Competition Commissioner Mario Monti. This group published a Financial Services Action Plan (FSAP) in May 1999 (Hartmann, Maddaloni and Manganelli 2003), which was endorsed at the EU Lisbon Summit in March 2000. The timetable laid down for the FSAP required full implementation of the plan by 2005. The FSAP proposed 42 legislative measures grouped around three policy objectives; ensuring a single EU market for wholesale financial services: creating open and secure retail markets, and improving prudential rules and supervision.

The FSAP has had rather mixed reactions. Key directives such as those on investment services and on rules for cross-border takeovers generated considerable controversy, and an adverse vote in the European Parliament in the case of the latter. A number of market participants and regulators in the City of London voiced concern about the rigidity of the plan and its emphasis on harmonisation, compared with the stress on mutual recognition in the Single European Act (Norman 2002). However, Freixas and colleagues point to the fact that 38 of the 42 measures had been agreed by June 2004, including 27 directives and two regulations, and argue that 'the first stage of the FSAP has been a political success. Few other European policy programmes have been completed so comprehensively and in such timely fashion' (Freixas, Hartmann and Mayer 2004: 479). They argue that, since the FSAP is divided into two stages with implementation at the national level following agreement at the European level, it is the question of national implementation and enforcement that is crucial.

In July 2000 the EU economics and finance ministers appointed an independent 'Committee of Wise Men' chaired by Alexandre Lamfalussy to examine the practical arrangements for implementing the FSAP and to make recommendations concerning EU financial regulation. (It should be noted that the prudential supervision of banks was excluded from the mandate of the committee.) Their report identified the slowness, complexity and rigidity of the EU legislative process as a major obstacle to European financial integration. As a result they proposed a new regulatory approach based on distinguishing between four 'levels'.

- Level 1 concerns broad regulatory 'framework principles' which would be developed through the current system of joint decisions by the Council and the Parliament based on a recommendation by the Commission.
- Level 2 relates to development of the technical details of the directives and regulations emerging from the level 1 process. Responsibility for this would be delegated to two new committees, the European Securities Committee (ESC), composed of Finance Ministry officials and chaired by a commissioner, and the Committee of European Securities Regulators (CESR), composed of the heads of national securities market regulators. These committees were approved at the Stockholm European Council in March 2001, created in June 2001 and began to operate in 2002. The proposed

structure envisages regulatory proposals being put forward by the Commission to the ESC, based on the advice of the CESR.

- The CESR will coordinate the operation of level 3 of the process which consists of the homogeneous implementation of level 1 and level 2 legislation at a national level.
- Finally, level 4 involves the enforcement of such legislation nationally and for the Commission to take the lead here.

The Lamfalussy framework was approved at the Stockholm Council with some amendments. In particular the split between level 1 principles and level 2 measures is to be decided on a case-by-case basis by the European Parliament and the Council, following proposals by the Commission. In addition, in 2002 the Econfin Council extended this framework to other financial sectors than securities markets, creating three similar level 2 committees to cover banking, insurance and financial conglomerates. It also kept the FSPG in existence as a body dealing with general strategic questions concerning financial integration, monitoring progress with the FSAP and dealing with specific short-term issues of particular concern.

The final element in the set of new initiatives designed to further the integration process is the work of the Giovannini Group. This is a group of financial market participants and experts that was established by the Commission in 1996. Their initial task was to advise the Commission on how to prepare the capital markets for stage 3 of monetary union. Since then they have produced further reports on the EU **'repo' (repurchase agreements)** market in 1999, on public debt issuance in 2000 and on cross-border clearing and settlement arrangements in 2001 and 2003.

These initiatives raise two main questions. First, it could be argued that the hoped-for increase in speed and flexibility in the area of financial regulation arising from the Lamfalussy framework will come at the expense of a decrease in the amount of democratic control over financial decision making within the European Union. Issues that were previously decided either by nationally elected politicians in the Council of Ministers or by members of the European Parliament are now the province of officials within the various level 2 and 3 committees. Second, some have put forward the view that the increasingly complex regulatory structure that is emerging should be replaced by a single regulator operating at a pan-European level (*Economist* 2001). This view has arisen in part because the current regime involves home-country control for branches set up overseas within the European Union, but host-country control for foreign subsidiaries, and this can create costs for financial groups operating across borders as they have to comply with various regulatory systems. Dermine (2002) stresses this point, and also argues that in the case of a crisis concerning a particular bank the current system may prove inadequate. Both he and Freixas and colleagues (2004) suggest that a European supervisor may be needed in the future, at least for larger institutions. Set against this, an alternative view is that such a development would be premature, since we do not yet know the optimum approach towards financial regulation, and a process of comparing the results of differing policies in different European countries may be beneficial.

With these background regulatory developments in mind, we can now move on to look at recent developments in the European capital markets themselves, with a particular focus on the level of financial integration achieved. These markets are normally divided into four groups: the money markets, the bond markets, the markets for credit and loans, and the equity markets. We shall look at each of these in turn, but in order to do this it is important to examine a bit more closely how financial integration can be measured.

Measuring financial integration

There are three main ways of measuring financial integration: price-based approaches, news-based approaches and quantity-based approaches (Cabral, Dierick and Vesala 2002, Baele *et al.* 2004a, 2004b). Baele and colleagues look at three main price-based measures of integration for the money, government bond and credit markets. First, they examine the **spread** between the yield on a particular asset and that on a benchmark asset, chosen so that the yield on the benchmark asset corresponds to the yield that could be expected to prevail in a perfectly integrated market. Second, they use what is known as the beta-convergence measure, which looks at whether yields on assets that are relatively high, compared with the yield on the benchmark asset, tend to decline more quickly than yields on assets that are relatively low. Third, they examine what is known as sigma-convergence. This is the cross-sectional dispersion in yields, as measured at a single point in time by the standard deviation.[1]

For corporate bonds no easily obtainable benchmark asset exists, so the procedure here is to run a regression equation relating yield spreads between each bond and a German government bond with identical time to maturity (chosen as a relatively riskless asset) to risk factors such as credit rating and company sector. The test for integration is to see whether the part of the yield not explained by the risk factors contains a systematic country component. A similar approach was used for equities.

The news-based integration measures involve looking at the proportion of asset price changes that is explained by news common to assets across all countries. In order to measure such common news, Baele and colleagues look at the price of an asset that they consider to be highly integrated with the particular market being studied. They then examine whether changes in the yield of this benchmark asset can predict changes in the yield of other assets.

Two kinds of quantity-based measures are used; first, the level of cross-border activities, and second, the extent of 'home bias' in asset choices. Such home bias is defined as the fact that agents tend to invest more in domestic assets than is warranted by an optimal degree of risk-sharing through diversification.

Most other recent studies of financial integration use similar measures to Baele and colleagues, and on the basis of these attempt to assess the degree to which the European Union now comprises a single financial market. It should, however, be noted that the majority of these studies are particularly concerned with the impact of the euro on financial integration, and tend to emphasise developments within the euro-zone rather than necessarily looking at changes in the European Union as a whole. Such an emphasis will be maintained in what follows.

The European money markets

The money market is normally defined as the market for short-term debt, with a maturity of up to one year (Baele *et al.* 2004b). The two main areas of this market that have been analysed are the market for unsecured debt and the repo market. **Repurchase agreements** are essentially a form of borrowing with collateral, in which the borrower sells a security to the lender, thus obtaining ready cash, then buys it back again (in other words repurchases it) for a higher price at the end of a specified time period. The difference between the two prices represents the interest payment on what is effectively a loan. Other segments of the money market, for example commercial paper and short-term derivatives, have not been analysed in detail for reasons such as shortage of data.

Unsurprisingly, all three kinds of measures of integration indicate that the unsecured debt market has become highly integrated in the euro-zone following the introduction of the euro. Hartmann and colleagues (2003) plot three-month deposit rates from January 1995 to January 2003, and show these gradually converging until January 1999, when the differences collapse to zero. A similar picture emerges from the beta and sigma convergence measures calculated by Adam and colleagues (2002). Quantity-based measures are presented by Gaspar, Hartmann and Sleijpen (2002) who show that the share of euro area cross-border interbank claims in the global total of such claims rose after 1998 by around a third before stabilising at a level of around 50 per cent in 2000.

The repo market, however, remains less integrated than the market for unsecured debt, although the level of unity here is still quite high. In terms of price-based measures Hartmann and colleagues (2003) quote studies showing differences of around 5 to 7 bps in repo rates between countries, while Baele and colleagues (2004b) quote an average cross-country dispersion of 1.6 bps compared with the dispersion within countries of 1.1 bps. With regard to quantity-based trading, in 2001 the share of trading with national counterparties was higher in the repo market, at 40 per cent, than in the unsecured debt market where the figure was about 30 per cent. In addition more than half of euro repo trading at that point was still in instruments secured by home country collateral. Cross-border trading has been increasing, however, and overall the money markets present a picture of considerable financial integration.

The European bond markets

It has been argued that the bond markets represent the most important example of the impact of the euro on European financial markets. Again, there are two areas to examine, the market for government bonds and the market for corporate bonds.

In the government bond market an important problem has been lack of liquidity, caused by the general fall in the amount of government debt issued in the years around the launch of the euro while countries attempted to meet the criteria of the Maastricht Treaty and the Stability and Growth Pact. This led to specialisation in the market, with particular governments concentrating on certain kinds of bonds in order to build up issues of a large enough size to ensure a liquid market. Examples here are German bonds representing the benchmark for a ten-year maturity, while French bonds are dominant in the five to seven-year maturity segment of the market and Italian bonds in the area of floating-rate issues. Hartmann and colleagues argue that 'these developments lead to the absence of a single homogeneous sovereign-based yield curve in Europe, which constitutes an obstacle to full financial integration, as it hinders arbitrage activity and the pricing of derivatives' (Hartmann, Maddaloni and Manganelli 2003: 194).

They present evidence showing that, while yields have converged in the ten-year bond market, spreads are still significantly different from zero, ranging between 10 and 30 bps. Adjaouté and Danthine (2003) estimate the cost of this kind of market segmentation to euro-area treasuries as at least €5 billion. On the other hand, Baele and colleagues (2004b) show that dispersions in monthly yields in the ten-year segment fell from an average of 1.98 in 1993 to 0.06 in 2002, and similar falls appear to have occurred in other segments of the market. They also estimate that before 1998 common news in the ten-year segment explained less than 50 per cent of total yield variance in Finland, Greece, Italy, Portugal and Spain, whereas from 2000 onwards less than 5 per cent of total yield variance was explained by local factors, with the exception of Greece.

Pagano and von Thadden (2004) point out that the share of euro-area government securities held by non-residents increased from 16 per cent in 1991 to 26.8 per cent in 1998 and 33.5 per cent in 2000. Much of this results from institutional investment, in particular Austrian, Finnish, French and German funds, with the biggest changes occurring at the time of the introduction of the euro. Baele and colleagues (2004a) look at the percentage of assets invested in bond market funds with a European-wide investment strategy for eight euro-area countries, and find this rising from 17 per cent in 1998 to over 60 per cent in 2002. They also investigate whether this simply resulted from globalisation rather than European integration, and find that it did not; the share of funds with a global investment strategy remained constant during this period, at about 20 per cent.

An important development in the European government bond market has been the creation for the first time of Europe-wide trading platforms. The most important of these is MTS (Mercato Telematico dei titoli di Stato). MTS is an electronic quote-driven market, with dealers continuously quoting prices for agreed securities. It has a two-tiered structure, with a central market for European government bond benchmarks and large private issues (EuroMTS) plus a set of domestic markets for national issuers. The reduction in transaction costs associated with the development of this kind of trading platform seems to have been most beneficial for the smaller issuers of bonds. Galati and Tsatsaronis (2001) report that at the beginning of 2000 about 40 per cent of European bond transactions took place through EuroMTS. It is notable, however, that MTS has a low share of the German bond market, where most trading takes place in the futures market managed by EUREX.

The MTS trading platform has however been vulnerable to market manipulation by large participants. In August 2004 Citigroup sold more than €12 billion across more than 200 bonds within seconds, pushing prices down and then buying some of the bonds back at a lower price. They were able to do this because market makers had initially committed themselves to quoting agreed prices and could not react in time to the amount of selling going on. Pagano and von Thadden (2004) suggest that this behaviour may have resulted from a conflict of interest, in that Citigroup is at the same time a market participant and dealer in all 11 MTS sovereign bond markets, a shareholder of MTS and a competitor of MTS through both its own in-house trading operations and its participation in rival trading platforms. On the other hand, Gapper (2005) is more critical of the influence of European governments over MTS. His argument is that smaller governments have forced MTS to operate in an artificial way because they are worried about not being able to sell their bonds now that they are euro-denominated and so in direct competition with the larger euro-zone governments. The result of this has been a market which discourages innovation and risk-taking, while official backing for MTS disadvantages rival trading platforms (Gapper 2005, van Duyn and Munter 2004).

Currently, 55 per cent of MTS is owned by non-Italian banks and 45 per cent by Italian banks, but it is in the process of being sold and is understood to have drawn up a shortlist of four potential purchasers: Reuters, eSpeed (the electronic bond trading arm of Cantor Fitzgerald), Euronext and Borsa Italiana (the Italian stock exchange), with the last two working together (Batchelor and Munter 2005).

Despite the advantages that trading systems like MTS have brought to the European bond markets, a final obstacle to integration comes from the fragmented system for the settlement of securities transactions. Hartmann and colleagues (2003) point out that Europe still has 14 such systems, compared with two in the United States, and cite estimates that this has resulted in costs for settling transactions in cross-border debt securities which are 10 to 20 times higher than for transactions within countries.

While developments in the government bond markets have been significant in recent years, changes in the corporate bond sector following the introduction of the euro have been even more dramatic. This is partly because this market has developed from such a low base. The majority of private bonds in the euro area continue to be issued by financial corporations, though within this there has been a significant growth in the proportion originating from non-monetary financial companies, compared with those issued by banks. Bond issuance by non-financial corporations has risen, though, to levels comparable with the United States, as shown by Table 8.3.

Table 8.3 Net issues of international debt securities
by non-financial corporations (US$ billion)

	1994	1995	1996	1997	1998	1999	2000	2001	2002	2003
US corporate issues	18.9	24.4	32.0	64.7	61.6	155.6	47.3	72.4	28.6	27.8
Euro-area corporate issues	7.2	8.1	4.4	17.1	32.0	120.5	96.1	82.7	10.6	56.8

Source: Pagano and von Thadden (2004: 538).

Pagano and von Thadden (2004) argue that the shift in European finance away from bank loans towards bond issuance has partly been driven by the reluctance of the banks to provide loans, since these inflate the asset side of the balance sheet and so lower earnings ratios and require extra capital (as discussed above). However, they also claim that the growth in the market is driven in part by enthusiasm among borrowers for a new source of finance. Not only has the market grown, the range of companies able to gain access to the market has expanded, so that while bond issuance was previously restricted to companies with AAA and AA credit ratings, almost 50 per cent of corporate bonds issued in 1999 had a single A credit rating. In addition Hartmann and colleagues (2003) quote evidence from Santos and Tsatsaronis showing that the introduction of the euro significantly lowered underwriting fees for euro-denominated corporate bonds, pushing them down to the levels seen in the US market, whereas in 1994 the average fee for such bonds in Europe was twice that in the United States.

Rajan and Zingales (2002) conducted econometric tests to compare bond market growth in the euro area with those European countries outside the euro-zone, and found that issues were significantly greater for those countries that had adopted the euro, implying that the euro has contributed to the growth of a European corporate bond market.

The size and international nature of issues has increased sharply. Pagano and von Thadden (2004) give two telling examples. In 1998 there were just three bond issues in euro legacy currencies (meaning currencies of countries that later participated in EMU) which were above the equivalent of €1 billion. However, the three issues in 1999 by Tecnost, the financing vehicle for Olivetti's takeover of Telecom Italia, raised €15.65 billion alone. Until 1998 nearly all bond distribution in the euro area was domestic. However, of the €1 billion issue by Alcatel in February 1999, 28 per cent was placed with Italian and more than 20 per cent with German investors.

While the corporate bond market grew particularly fast at the time of the introduction of the euro, the level of issuance of bonds did decrease in 2001 and 2002 (as shown above). Consequently, some have argued that the growth in the market was a temporary phenomenon, reflecting corporate restructuring, merger and acquisition activity and the liberalisation of the telecommunications industry, rather than a permanent development arising from monetary union (Carnegie-Brown and King 2002). This issue will ultimately only be settled by observing changes in the market over a longer time period.

With regard to price-based measures of the integration of the corporate bond market, Baele and colleagues (2004b) found quite small country premia compared with benchmark bonds. These premia were only slightly higher than those observed for government bonds. They also found that country effects generally explained no more than 2 per cent of corporate bond yield spreads. They conclude, on the basis of these results, that the corporate bond market is reasonably well integrated.

The European credit market

While the money and bond markets in Europe appear to be well on the road towards full integration, there are still important barriers to a unified market in the area of credit and bank loans. It is difficult to obtain summary figures relating to this market, as the products involved are heterogeneous; however, the evidence presented by Dermine and referred to above gives some indication of the price differentials that remain. Cabral and colleagues (2002) found that differences between household and corporate lending and deposit rates across euro-area countries decreased quite sharply between 1998–9 and 2001–02 (for example the standard deviation of retail deposit interest rates fell from 1.92 per cent to 0.34 per cent). However, the fall in the variability of bank margins was much less than this, especially for corporate lending, raising the possibility that the convergence of rates was mainly due to macroeconomic conditions rather than progress in financial integration. Baele and colleagues (2004b) calculated the cross-sectional dispersion of interest rates, and found significant convergence in the run-up to EMU. However, from 1999 onwards, while dispersion decreased for medium and long-term loans to enterprises and for mortgage loans, it either stayed the same or increased for short-term corporate loans and consumer credit.

Baele and colleagues (2004b) also carried out a news-based test for integration in the credit market by examining the extent to which interest rates changed as a result of common factors across the euro area, as measured by yield changes in government bonds. While there was some increase in integration, the overall level of integration was still not that high. In the case of short-term enterprise lending, the average proportion of variance in rates explained by common factors rose from 9 per cent in 1994–6 to 32 per cent in 2001–03. For medium and long-term lending to companies, the equivalent rise was from 15 per cent to 38 per cent, while for consumer credit and mortgage loans only about 8–10 per cent of variance appeared to be explained by common factors and there was no upward trend. Even in the most integrated segments of the market, then, over 60 per cent of rate changes appear to be determined by local factors.

With regard to quantity-based indicators, while there was an upward trend in euro-area cross-border loans from 1997 to 2002, the total amount of loans to non-banks remains small compared to inter-bank loans, comprising about 10 per cent of the total (Hartmann, Maddaloni and Manganelli 2003). The increase in euro-area inter-bank loans is however quite significant, as the opposite trend appears to have occurred in non-EU countries. In addition, the proportion of cross-border holdings in the total bank holdings of cross-border securities issued by banks rose from 15 per cent to 35 per cent, while the equivalent rise for securities issued by non-banks was from 20 per cent to 60 per cent. Hartmann and colleagues (2003) also argue that anecdotal evidence appears to indicate that those banks operating across the euro area tend mainly to serve corporate customers and there is limited cross-border retail activity. This view was confirmed by a Centre for Economic Policy Research (CEPR) study in March 2005 (*Economist* 2005a).

A number of reasons have been put forward for the continuing lack of integration in the credit markets. It has been argued that, especially in the small-business sector, so-called 'relationship' lending, where banks have a long-term relationship with relatively local companies, is likely to persist as the most appropriate way of coping with the informational problems involved in assessing borrowers. In addition, foreign affiliates of multinational corporations may prefer to use host-nation banks as they have superior information about local markets, culture, regulation and suppliers (Petersen and Rajan 2002, Berger *et al.* 2003). In these circumstances one of the main ways in which integration might be achieved in this market is through cross-border merger activity. However, the amount of such activity in the euro area has been rather limited. As a percentage of merger and acquisition activity involving euro-area credit institutions as a whole, cross-border deals within the area peaked at 18 per cent of the total in 1999 and fell back to 11 per cent by 2001 (Hartman, Maddaloni and Manganelli 2003). The remainder of the activity was roughly equally split between domestic deals and deals with banks outside the euro area, with the share of the latter category increasing over time at the expense of the former.

The relatively limited number of cross-border banking mergers within Europe has been attributed to 'efficiency barriers' based on differences in language, culture and regulations, and to the influence of home country supervisory authorities in approving such mergers, rather than just competition authorities. This has led to proposals for a Europe-wide banking supervisory body in order to avoid undue reluctance to approve entry into home country markets through merger (Hartmann, Maddaloni and Manganelli 2003). Case study 8.1 further examines cross-border merger activity in European banking.

Dermine (2002) points to another reason that integration in European banking has progressed somewhat slowly. In cases where there have been significant cross-border mergers the resulting institutions have tended to adopt a structure based on subsidiaries rather than on branches, so that the 'European passport' provided for in the Second Banking Directive has not actually operated in practice. As of 1999, figures for branches and subsidiaries established in European Economic Area (EEA) countries by foreign banks indicate there were 450 branches and 363 subsidiaries for banks from EEA countries, while from non-EEA countries there were 312 branches and 372 subsidiaries. Dermine goes on to say that:

> More significant for the purpose of this study, is the fact that cross-border mergers involving banks of significant size have all resulted in holding company structures with subsidiaries. This is, at first glance, a very surprising outcome of the single banking market, as it would have seemed that a single corporate bank structure would have reduced the regulatory costs significantly. Is the single banking licence an illusion?
>
> (Dermine 2002: 50)

Dermine reinforces his point by looking at three of the main cross-border banking groups to have emerged in Europe in recent years. Nordea AB, which is the outcome of the merger of Merita (Finland), Nordbanken (Sweden), Unidanmark (Denmark) and Christiana Bank (Norway), is based on a listed holding company based in Sweden with subsidiaries through Scandinavia. The ING Group from the Netherlands, which acquired the British Barings in 1995, the Belgian Bank Brussels Lambert in 1998, the German BHF-Bank in 1999 and the Polish Bank Slaski in 2001, as well as owning a number of foreign insurance companies, listed no fewer than 56 subsidiaries in a report to the US Securities and Exchange Commission (SEC) in 2001. Hypo Vereinsbank (HVB) has

CROSS-BORDER BANKING BIDS IN ITALY

In March 2005 the Italian financial system was rocked by two foreign bids for Italian banks. Both were strongly resisted. The Spanish bank BBVA launched a bid for Banca Nazionale del Lavoro (BNL), in which it already held a 14.7 per cent stake, in the face of an investor pact by a group of property developers who were shareholders in the Italian bank. The Dutch bank ABN Amro made a cash offer for Banca Antonveneta, in which again it was already a shareholder. However, Banca Popolare di Lodi quickly obtained a large rival shareholding and publicly talked about defending the autonomy of Antonveneta.

While both of these bids were relatively small in size at around €8 billion, their significance lay in the widespread belief that successful bids would be followed by further acquisitions from outside Italy, and that this would significantly change the relationship between Italian companies and their banks. From 1993 onwards Antonio Fazio, the governor of the Bank of Italy, had used his veto to stop such acquisitions while overseeing the privatisation of much of the Italian banking system. However, this use by Fazio of a veto on foreign takeovers has been criticised by the European Commission. Banca Popolare di Lodi was in regular consultation with Fazio over Antonveneta, and had received approval from him for 13 acquisitions in the preceding seven years.

The underlying motivation for foreign takeovers of Italian banks was the opportunity for growth in the future. Total loans to households in Italy in 2003 were 23 per cent of GDP, well below the euro-zone average of 47 per cent and the UK figure of more than 80 per cent. The same was true for home mortgages and consumer credit: home mortgages were 12 per cent of GDP compared with a UK figure of 70 per cent. Growth in business was expected to raise the profitability of Italian banks. Projections for 2006 saw the return on equity for such banks at just 15 per cent compared with 24 per cent in the rest of continental Europe and 28 per cent in Britain. However, these low levels of profitability meant low levels of market capitalisation for the banks and consequent vulnerability to takeover. Fazio was keen to see consolidation in the sector before opening the doors to foreign takeovers.

Consumer groups in Italy welcomed the prospect of outsiders entering the system, but fears focused on the business sector. A large part of the Italian economy consists of small and medium-sized family companies, which in 2005 were having difficulties competing with emerging economies in Eastern Europe and Asia. In these circumstances maintenance of a credit line and strong relationship with a local bank assumed great importance. Local political organisations were wary of the effect of takeovers on their area. In the 3–4 April regional elections in Veneto, where Antonveneta has its headquarters, both government and opposition candidates declared themselves against ABN Amro's bid. Nationally, the government maintained a neutral stance, but a number of politicians questioned whether the bids would be a good idea. Against this background Antonio Fazio had just a few weeks to decide whether to allow the bids to proceed.

Source: Michaels and Barber (2005).

Questions

1 Why do you think that Antonio Fazio wanted to see Italian banking consolidate before allowing foreign takeovers to take place?
2 Do you think that the European Commission was right to criticise the Italian central bank for its attitude towards such takeovers?
3 What advice would you have given Mr. Fazio in April 2005 about whether to allow the bids to take place or not?

subsidiaries in Austria (Bank Austria Creditanstalt AG, which results from the former Bank of Austria and Creditanstalt) and in central and eastern Europe.

Various reasons have been set out for the maintenance of subsidiary structures despite the provisions of the single market. Home-country shareholders may feel more reassured that foreign operations are not going to absorb resources through getting into difficulties, as a subsidiary is more likely than a branch to have a 'stand alone' financial structure. Dermine does point out, however, that it is easy to imagine situations where the parent bank would regard it as too harmful to its reputation to allow a subsidiary to default. In the case of the initial period following merger or takeover it may be that becoming a subsidiary is more acceptable to local management than becoming a branch. It may also be that a subsidiary structure is useful in protecting the brand image built up before the merger. A subsidiary structure may reduce deposit insurance premia by allowing these to be paid in the countries where they are lowest. Finally, if the merger goes wrong, a subsidiary may be easier to sell off. Overall though, the continued popularity of subsidiary-based banking structures is likely to slow down the pace of financial integration in the credit markets.

The European equity markets

As with the credit markets, the degree of integration in the European equity markets is still not complete. Baele and colleagues (2004b) conducted a regression analysis to look at the sensitivity of share returns to changes in the US equity market (a proxy for world news) and to changes in the European equity market (a proxy for regional European news). To the extent that returns cannot be explained by these two factors and so reflect individual country influences, we can conclude that markets are not fully integrated. From 1973–86 only about 8 per cent of local return variance was explained by common European shocks, but this proportion increased gradually to about 23 per cent from 1999–2003. The contribution of world news increased gradually to around 20 per cent over this period, having been greater than European news during the 1970s and 1980s, but the faster increase in the impact of European news leads Baele and colleagues to conclude that euro-area integration has proceeded more quickly than global market integration.

Even in the event of financial markets being fully integrated one would not expect to see all returns explained by external news, since the changing expected fortunes of domestic companies will also have an influence. Baele and colleagues compared the 43 per cent of stock return variance in euro-area countries explained by common European and US shocks with the equivalent figures of about 28.5 per cent for Argentina and Brazil and 30 per cent for Hungary and Poland, and concluded that the euro-area markets are relatively highly integrated.

Baele and colleagues (2004b) also looked at quantity-based measures of integration. They examined the share of euro-area investment funds, as measured by assets, within domestic, European and global investment strategies, concentrating on changes from 1995 to 2002. During this period the share of domestic funds fell from about 60 per cent to less than 35 per cent. Global funds were the main beneficiaries, with their share rising from about 40 per cent to close on 70 per cent. European funds saw their share increase only modestly.

An important question here is whether such movements towards integration have actually lowered the cost of capital for European companies. To the extent that integration allows for greater possibilities of diversification, companies can benefit from decreased risk. However, it can also be argued that since stock markets across Europe (and indeed globally) have tended to move more closely together in recent years, the benefits from international diversification have become less. This issue was discussed by Adjaouté and Danthine (2004). They analysed the dispersion of euro-area share price returns across both countries and sectors, in order to measure the benefits of diversification. They concluded that during the 1980s and 1990s, up until the autumn of 1996, there was a general downward trend in both country and sector dispersion, with country dispersion generally being greater than sector dispersion. From 1996 to 1999 this situation changed in two ways: dispersion of both kinds increased and sector dispersion rose above country dispersion. However, from 1999 onwards the previous trends reasserted themselves, with both measures falling and converging by 2004 at roughly the same level. The conclusion drawn by Adjaouté and Danthine was that those wishing to diversify should adopt a strategy targeting both countries and sectors simultaneously. (They identify 77 such 'country-sectors' within the euro area.)

Cross-border activity in equity markets has greatly affected the consolidation of stock exchanges across Europe. The most notable event here has been the merger of the Amsterdam, Brussels and Paris exchanges in September 2000 to form Euronext. Euronext is subject to Dutch legislation and has a subsidiary in each of the participating countries (Hartmann, Maddaloni and Manganelli 2003). Each subsidiary holds a local licence giving access to trading in all the countries involved. The market integrates some, but not all, of the features of the preceding national exchanges. There is single quotation of share prices as well as a common order book, price dissemination systems, a unified trading platform and a single clearing and settlement system, Euroclear. However, the regulatory body in each of the participating countries retains its prerogatives. In 2001 Euronext acquired LIFFE (the London futures exchange), and the Portuguese exchanges of Lisbon and Porto were integrated into the Euronext structure, although they do not settle transactions through Euroclear.

In 1998, as a response to increasing competition from other European exchanges, the London Stock Exchange (LSE) and Deutsche Börse planned a merger, the details of which were announced on May 2000. However, while the negotiations around this merger were still in progress the OM Gruppen, owners of the Stockholm exchange, made a public offer for the LSE. This adversely affected the projected merger, which was rejected by the LSE Board. Among the reasons for rejection of the merger were doubts about economies of scale, given that the projected new exchange would have seen 'blue chip' companies being traded in London and technology stocks in Frankfurt. Furthermore the difficulties of dealing with changes in regulations and supervisory authorities for those companies that would have had to move the location of their listing, and the fact that the merger proposals did not provide for the creation of a common clearing and settlement system and so would not have lowered costs in this area, were also noted.

Recent developments in the projected consolidation of European stock exchanges are covered in the case study below.

THE FUTURE OF THE LONDON STOCK EXCHANGE (LSE)

In December 2004 Deutsche Börse once more made a preliminary bid for the LSE, valuing it at £1.3 billion. The LSE rejected the offer but invited further talks, and on 20 December Euronext announced its intention to launch a rival bid. On 27 January 2005 Deutsche Börse revealed more details of its merger proposal but was again rebuffed by the LSE. On 9 February Euronext announced details of its proposal but not an offer price. However, on 7 March Deutsche Börse had to withdraw its offer following a shareholder's revolt led by Anglo-American hedge fund investors representing some 40 per cent of the group's share capital, who regarded the LSE as over-valued and wanted the bid money to be used to increase dividends. On 14 March Deutsche Börse signalled that it could renew its bid on a debt-funded basis, and on 29 March the Office of Fair Trading referred Euronext's bid to the Competition Commission.

The background to this battle was greatly increased competition between exchanges in the wake of the bursting of the dotcom bubble and subsequent falls in equity markets. This led fund managers to try to trade more cheaply and to pressurise their intermediaries, banks and brokerages, to cut costs. The intermediaries in turn put pressure on the exchanges. At the same time analysts pointed to the fact that other assets such as bonds could be traded much more cheaply than equities. A number of US stock and derivatives exchanges at this time were looking with interest at the various bids for the LSE. In 2000 the Nasdaq stock market spent a year working on a possible merger with the LSE, while in 2004 the Chicago Mercantile Exchange studied the exchange as a possible acquisition.

The LSE at this time had a number of advantages. Its trading volume was growing fast. It was located in Europe's largest financial centre. There was increased demand for the pricing data that the LSE sold. However, its biggest single problem was that it was almost entirely a cash market with a tiny derivatives business, and derivatives were predicted to deliver better volume growth than equities over the long term. This was especially true since over-the-counter derivatives business was moving to the exchanges, attracted by their falling trading costs and safe systems of counterparty clearing. Both Deutsche Börse, through part-ownership of Eurex, and Euronext, through ownership of LIFFE, had strong derivatives businesses. However, the LSE had taken the lead in developing the capability for derivatives trading, with a platform allowing such trading scheduled to open in early 2007. Euronext, in its bid, suggested some of the possibilities opened up by this, such as the packaging of LSE-traded equities with index derivatives trade on LIFFE, or linking up cash bonds traded on the LSE with Euronext's gilts futures market. The possibilities for such developments, however, depended on the attitude of the UK competition policy authorities.

Sources: Cohen, Grant and Postelnicu (2005), Cohen (2005), Jenkins and Milne (2005), *Economist* (2005b).

Questions

1 Do you think the shareholders in Deutsche Börse were sensible in forcing the exchange to abandon its bid for the LSE in favour of higher dividend payments?

2 What attitude do you think the European Commission should take in the event of a US exchange launching a bid for one of the major European exchanges?

3 What advice would you have given the Competition Commission in April 2005 with regard to the proposed merger between the LSE and Euronext?

Conclusion

European financial integration has in many ways been a success. While there has been a growing recognition that some of the more optimistic targets and predictions of the Cecchini Report will be more difficult to achieve than was thought likely two decades ago, the pace of change has been rapid and has brought about significant results for both the providers and users of funds. In both the creation of a more open, competitive marketplace and the emphasis on prudential regulation, the process of change in the European financial markets has exhibited important similarities to that taking place in the financial sector globally. However, the introduction of the euro has been a further spur to integration which is specific to those countries participating in the euro-zone, and the evidence indicates that it has had a distinct effect on the financial markets, in addition to broader international trends. In turn, financial market developments are likely to be crucial for the future success of monetary union.

It is worth concluding by mentioning briefly some of the key challenges that remain for European countries in building a single financial market. First, the regulatory system which has evolved has not yet been tested in a period of deep financial turbulence within Europe. It has been argued that the New Basle Accord, by making asset risk management more accurate, may actually worsen the destabilising effect of capital adequacy ratios in difficult times, and that this effect may be accentuated by the amount of lending that banks have made to hedge funds and other largely unregulated parties (Plender 2005). Second, key elements of the financial markets remain less integrated than others. This is especially true for retail banking and also to a lesser extent for wholesale banking, the repo market and equities. To the extent that further developments in the banking sector are led by mergers and acquisitions, there will be important issues for competition policy authorities in ensuring that market power is not used to exploit customers. Third, the development of cross-border trading platforms is still an issue of concern, over both the future of MTS after the problems of 1994 and the question of future consolidation among stock exchanges. Fourth, the question of the extent to which financial regulation can remain at the national level, or whether a pan-European regulator is required, remains an open one. Finally, it remains to be seen whether the Lamfalussy framework can balance the competing claims of democratic accountability and legislative flexibility in an adequate way.

The ability of market participants and regulators to address these key issues is likely to determine the level of success in integrating the European financial sector in the coming period.

Questions

1   What do you think are the main advantages and disadvantages involved in organising the financial system around either markets or institutions? Can

you think of any reasons that the United Kingdom has tended to use markets more than continental Europe? Why do you think Gerschenkron argued that markets would become more important than institutions over time?

2 Which of the three eras in the international financial system, as identified by Eichengreen and Fishlow, namely the eras of bond finance, bank finance and equity finance, was most desirable from the point of view of (a) the availability of funds for individual countries and firms, and (b) the stability of the overall system?

3 Why do you think the Eurocurrency market grew so fast? Which kinds of businesses do you think particularly benefited from the growth of this market? Were any problems associated with this growth?

4 Many people have argued that asymmetric information and systemic risk justify government regulation of financial institutions and markets. Can you think of any ways in which such institutions and markets have been able to limit these problems on their own account, without having to rely on outside regulators? Are such alternative approaches to dealing with these problems preferable to regulation from the point of view of the businesses who are customers of these institutions and who deal in these markets?

5 The proposals for an international lender of last resort and an international bankruptcy court, which are outlined in the chapter, have been criticised because it is thought they might lead to moral hazard. Can you think of any ways in which these proposals might be modified in order to avoid this happening?

6 What are the main problems involved in relying on capital adequacy ratios as a means of regulating the financial system? Can you think of any ways in which the use of these ratios might be altered in order to avoid such problems? What changes do you think the introduction of such ratios might make to the strategies adopted by banks to obtain competitive advantage?

7 What are the main arguments for and against having a single European financial regulator? Do you think it would be a good idea to introduce such a regulator?

8 What are the main advantages and disadvantages of the approach to financial regulation proposed by the Lamfalussy Commission? Do you think that companies in the financial and non-financial sectors might differ regarding the desirability of this approach, and if so, why?

9 What do you think are the main obstacles remaining to the creation of a single European financial market? Would such a single market provide significant benefits for European businesses?

Note

1 The cross-sectional dispersion of returns or prices simply measures how widely the various returns and prices are spread at a particular point in time around their average value. The statistical concept of a standard deviation represents

one, but not the only, way of measuring the dispersion. In an integrated market we would expect the returns and prices in different countries to be similar and so the dispersion would be small. Other things being equal, then, a large dispersion can be taken as evidence that the market is not fully integrated.

 ## References

Adam, K., Japelli, T., Menichini, A., Padula, M. and Pagano, M. (2002) *Study to Analyse, Compare and Apply Alternative Indicators and Monitoring Methodologies to Measure the Evolution of Capital Market Integration in the European Union*, prepared by the Centre for Studies in Economics and Finance for the European Commission.

Adjaouté, K. and Danthine, J. (2003) 'European financial integration and equity returns: a theory-based assessment', in V. Gaspar, P. Hartmann and O. Sleijpen (eds), *The Transformation of the European Financial System*, European Central Bank, Frankfurt.

Adjaouté, K. and Danthine, J. (2004) 'Equity returns and integration: is Europe changing?', *Oxford Review of Economic Policy*, December.

Allen, F. and Gale, D. (2000) *Comparing Financial Systems*, MIT Press, Boston, Mass.

Baele, L., Ferrando, A., Hördahl, P., Krylova, E. and Monnet, C. (2004a) *Measuring Financial Integration in the Euro Area*, ECB Occasional Paper no. 14, European Central Bank, Frankfurt.

Baele, L., Ferrando, A., Hördahl, P., Krylova, E. and Monnet, C. (2004b) 'Measuring European financial integration', *Oxford Review of Economic Policy*, Winter.

Bank for International Settlements (no date) 'International banking statistics', http://www.bis.org, accessed on 20 May 2005.

Batchelor, C. and Munter, P. (2005) 'Four on shortlist to buy MTS platform', *Financial Times*, 28 March, p. 17.

Berger, A., Dai, Q., Ongena, S. and Smith, D. (2003) 'To what extent will the banking industry be globalized? A study of bank nationality and reach in 20 European nations', *Journal of Banking and Finance*, March.

Cabral, I., Dierick, F. and Vesala, J. (2002) *Banking Integration in the Euro Area*, ECB Occasional Paper no. 6 European Central Bank, Frankfurt.

Carnegie-Brown, B. and King, M. (2002) 'Development of European bond markets', in V. Gaspar, P. Hartmann and O. Sleijpen (eds), *The Transformation of the European Financial System*, European Central Bank, Frankfurt.

Cohen, N. (2005) 'Big banks and listed companies welcome referral of LSE bids', *Financial Times*, 30 March, p. 21.

Cohen, N., Grant, J. and Postelnicu, A. (2005) 'Leading exchanges consider their moves in the race to compete and consolidate', *Financial Times*, 11 March, p. 15.

Davis, E. P. (1995) *Debt, Financial Fragility and Systemic Risk*, revised edition, Oxford University Press, Oxford.

Dermine, J. (2002) 'Banking in Europe: past, present and future', in V. Gaspar, P. Hartmann and O. Sleijpen (eds), *The Transformation of the European Financial System*, European Central Bank, Frankfurt.

Diamond, D. and Dybvig, P. (1983) 'Bank runs, deposit insurance and liquidity', *Journal of Political Economy*, June.

Economist (2001) 'EU financial regulation: a ragbag of reform', 3 March, p. 93.

Economist (2005a) 'European banks: divided we fall', 19 March, p. 96.

Economist (2005b) 'Stock and derivatives exchanges: the wedding's off', 12 March, pp. 87–8.

Eichengreen, B. and Fishlow, A. (1998) 'Contending with capital flows: what is different about the 1990s?', in M. Kahler (ed.), *Capital Flows and Financial Crises*, Manchester University Press, Manchester.

European Commission (1997) *The Single Market Review: Credit institutions and banking*, Kogan Page, London.

Freixas, X., Hartmann, P. and Mayer, C. (2004) 'The assessment: European financial integration', *Oxford Review of Economic Policy*, Winter.

Galati, G. and Tsatsaronis, K. (2001) *The Impact of the Euro on Europe's Financial Markets*, Bank for International Settlements Working paper no. 100, BIS, Basle.

Gapper, J. (2005) 'The market's true manipulators', *Financial Times,* 10 February, p. 17.

Gaspar, V., Hartmann, P. and Sleijpen, O. (2002) 'Introduction' in V. Gaspar, O, Hartmann and O. Sleijpen (eds), *The Transformation of the European Financial System*, European Central Bank, Frankfurt.

Gerschenkron, A. (1962) *Economic Backwardness in Historical Perspective*, Harvard University Press, Boston, Mass.

Giannetti, M., Guiso, L., Japelli, T., Pauda, M. and Pagano, M. (2002) *Financial Integration, Corporate Financing and Economic Growth*, Centre for Economic Policy Research Report for the European Commission.

Hartmann, P., Maddaloni, A. and Manganelli, S. (2003) 'The euro-area financial system: structure, integration and policy initiatives', *Oxford Review of Economic Policy*, Spring.

Jenkins, P. and Milne, R. (2005) 'The coming powers : how German companies are being bound to the interest of foreign investors', *Financial Times,*1 April, p. 17.

Levine, R. (1997) 'Financial development and economic growth: views and agenda', *Journal of Economic Literature*, June.

London Economics (2002) *Quantification of the Macroeconomic Impact of Integration of EU Financial Markets*, Report by London Economics in association with PricewaterhouseCoopers and Oxford Economic Forecasting for the European Commission.

Michaels, A. and Barber, T. (2005) 'New allure: why foreign banks are battling for Italian assets', *Financial Times*, 12 April, p. 17.

Norman, P. (2002) 'London resists a "retrograde" plan', *Financial Times*, 4 December, p. 17.

Norman, P. (2005) 'Basel II chairman says rules will be hard to implement', *Financial Times*, 11 April, p. 23.

Pagano, M. and von Thadden, E-L. (2004) 'The European bond markets under EMU', *Oxford Review of Economic Policy*, December.

Petersen, M. and Rajan, R. (2002) 'Does distance still matter? The information revolution and small business lending', *Journal of Finance*, December.

Plender, J. (2005) 'Shock of the new: a changed financial landscape may be eroding resistance to systemic risk', *Financial Times,* 16 February, p. 17.

Rajan, R. and Zingales, L. (2002) 'Banks and markets: the changing character of European finance', in V. Gaspar, P. Hartmann and O. Sleijpen (eds), *The Transformation of the European Financial System*, European Central Bank, Frankfurt.

Rosengren, E. (2002) 'Comment on Dermine', in V. Gaspar, P. Hartmann and O. Sleijpen (eds), *The Transformation of the European Financial System*, European Central Bank, Frankfurt.

Sachs, J. (1998) 'Alternative approaches to financial crises in emerging markets', in M. Kahler (ed.), *Capital Flows and Financial Crises*, Manchester University Press, Manchester.

Story, J. and Walter, I. (1997) *Political Economy of Financial Integration in Europe: The battle of the systems*, Manchester University Press, Manchester.

Van Duyn, A. and Munter, P. (2004) 'How Citigroup shook Europe's bond markets with two minutes of trading', *Financial Times*, 10 September, p. 17.

Vives, X. (2001) 'Competition in the changing world of banking', *Oxford Review of Economic Policy*, December.

9 Labour markets

Mark Cook

Objectives

This chapter will:

- outline the changes that have taken place in EU and international labour markets
- develop and analyse the move towards flexible labour markets
- investigate the impact of demographic change on EU labour markets
- outline the skills needs and skills deficiencies of European labour markets
- discuss the changes in productivity levels in Europe and their impact upon European employment.

EU and international/global labour markets

Employment matters. Within the European Union the Lisbon European Council of March 2000 put employment at the heart of the EU agenda, recognising the importance of employment and its effect on economic growth, social exclusion, an ageing population, the sustainability of pensions and public services. In doing this the Lisbon conference strengthened measures that had been put forward at the Luxemburg Jobs Summit in 1997, which was the first European Council meeting to be devoted to employment. It based its employment strategy around four pillars: measures to improve employability, support for entrepreneurship, increased adaptability and strengthened equal opportunities. The Lisbon Summit then set forward some far-reaching and ambitious objectives to make Europe the most competitive and dynamic knowledge-based economy in the world, capable of sustaining economic growth with more and better jobs and greater social cohesion (European Commission 2001a). A pivotal aspiration was the setting of targets for the increase in both total and female employment within a ten-year period of 70 and 60 per cent respectively, with a further target of 50 per cent for older workers (55–64 years of age). However, meeting the aspirations of the Lisbon Agenda has not always been easy, and as Case study 9.1 suggests, there is still a long way to go.

The European Union has tried to address its problem of poor employment growth by looking at the workings of its own labour market. Nonetheless, changes have been taking place in the global economy that have begun to impact on EU labour markets. The OECD (2003) has argued that globalisation

BACK TO BREAD AND BUTTER FOR EUROPE

Back in March 2000, the European Union's heads of governments grandly announced in their own inimitable fashion at a summit in Lisbon that the union would by 2010 become 'the most competitive and dynamic knowledge-based economy in the world, capable of sustainable economic growth with more and better jobs and greater social cohesion'. The Lisbon goals include reaching an overall employment rate of 67 per cent by 2005 and 70 per cent by 2010; a female employment rate of 57 per cent in 2005 and more than 60 per cent in 2010; and an employment rate for workers aged 55–64 of 50 per cent in 2010. Needless to say, almost four years later, there has been virtually no progress in achieving any of the Lisbon objectives. The few improvements have had more to do with luck than with good policies; in fact, as Mary Harney, the Irish deputy prime minister, rightly acknowledged the gulf between the United States and the European Union, which Lisbon was supposed to tackle, has instead continued to grow. After increasing from 60.7 per cent in 1997 to 64.3 per cent in 2002, partly because of the one-off boost to growth from the US-led dotcom bubble, the overall employment rate across the European Union subsequently fell slightly last year to an estimated 64.2 per cent.

Assuming a moderate economic recovery in 2004, employment will probably nudge up a little and could reach 65 per cent in 2005, still a full two percentage points below the target set out in Lisbon and a vivid illustration that Europe is still crying out for reform. Since 2001, unemployment has risen across the European Union and probably reached 8.1 per cent of the workforce in 2003. At least 14 million people are officially on the dole and millions more are on job creation schemes, in early retirement or claiming incapacity or other benefits.

The average employment rate is only around 56 per cent in the ten new member states; the situation is particularly bad in Slovakia, which suffers from 17.7 per cent unemployment, and Poland, where 20.6 per cent of the population is out of work.

Since 1997 total employment in the European Union has increased by about 11 million, according to the European Commission (an improvement on the 1980s and 1990s when disastrous economic policies prevented employment growth). But the average annual rate of employment growth was no more than 1.3 per cent, a rate which the European Union will find difficult to sustain, especially if the euro strengthens and stabilises over US$1.40.

To reach an employment rate of 70 per cent by 2010, the Lisbon goal, 15 million jobs would need to be created in current member states. An average annual increase in employment of about 1.5 per cent is required, greater than seen between 1997 and 2002. The average masks huge national differences: only Denmark, the Netherlands, Sweden and the United Kingdom have achieved employment rates of above 70 per cent. Employment rates in Belgium, Greece, Spain and Italy are all below 60 per cent. In January 2004, Ms Harney pledged that regulatory reform to reduce the burden of red tape and restrictions on business would be one of her main priorities over the next six months. 'We need fewer, not more, prescriptive proposals from Europe,' she said. While such sentiments are music to some people's ears, in practice the likelihood of even a few European regulations being repealed is nil. Barring a miracle or a sudden conversion of the European elites to market liberalism, the Lisbon goals remain as unreachable as ever. There is some chance of progress being made on the margins, however, and that is where the Irish presidency could truly make a difference. This is especially true of the proposed services trade liberalisation, which the Irish are planning to push during the next few months. By contrast, it would be a distraction for the Irish presidency to spend too much time on the proposed European Research Area, as it appears to want to do.

The biggest problem in Europe is that the economy is not sufficiently competitive and flexible to ensure that research that does take place is converted into faster productivity growth. Reducing taxes and cutting regulation, together with increased competition, would do more to boost productivity growth than any number of European-backed research initiatives. As the latest figures reveal, productivity is now almost stagnant in Europe. The collapse of productivity growth in the European Union can only partly be explained by the drop in the average number of hours worked per person. Worryingly, the level of output per hour was also 15 per cent lower in the European Union than in the United States in 2002; given the current accelerating productivity miracle across the Atlantic, this gap will already be significantly larger and closer to 20 per cent.

Source: Adapted from *Sunday Business* (2004).

Questions

1 Why is the European Union worried about its employment growth?
2 Is making EU labour markets more flexible the way to improve employment growth prospects?

is increasing the need to have labour market flexibility (see later in this chapter). However, a study by the International Labour Organization (ILO) (2000) into labour market flexibility and stability of industrialised countries found that there had been a marginal increase in flexibility in these countries while at the same time their labour markets were characterised by employment stability. Core stability is strong, and flexibility where it occurs is at the margins. Similarly for small developed economies such as Ireland, the Netherlands, Austria and Denmark which have been very successful in the globalisation process, their strength lay in social dialogue, stability-oriented macroeconomic policies and both active and passive labour market policies helping labour markets to adjust within a framework of security. Therefore, the ILO has concluded that what developing countries need in an increasingly globalised market for improvement in employment is not flexibility of their labour markets but ways in which they can establish more stability in such markets. Therefore if change can be well managed through appropriate investment in education and skills development, active labour market policies and innovative and affordable social protection, a country is in a better position to get the best from the major forces of change such as trade, **foreign direct investment (FDI)**, technology (especially information technology), entrepreneurship and private investment (ILO 2000).

As international markets become more and more globalised, not only are organisations seeking ways to reduce costs as a result of increased competition through the growth of FDI and increased trade, but governments, both at a national level and in partnership with other members of their trading blocs, need to consider ways that they can both create jobs internally and create the conditions to attract investment from overseas. At the same time labour also needs protecting from the behaviour of some producers who may seek to take advantage of lower levels of social protection for employees. One way that the European Union sought to protect its workers in its labour market was through the development of the Social Charter.

The Social Charter

For those that believed in the free workings of the market mechanism the Social Charter, developed in 1989, which guaranteed a whole range of minimum rights to workers, was seen as a means to reduce labour market flexibility and make industry less competitive. The Social Charter – more precisely, the Community Charter of Fundamental Social Rights – was developed as a parallel set of actions to safeguard social rights for EU citizens that might be threatened by the increased competition that followed from the development of the Single European Market (SEM). The Social Charter therefore established a list of minimum conditions under which all countries should operate so that social dumping did not occur. Social dumping occurs where employers in a competitive market exploit employees through reduced social protection. The Charter was approved by 11 of the 12 member states at the Strasbourg summit in December 1989, though at the time the United Kingdom was unable to accept a number of conditions and opted out from signing it (it subsequently signed up to the Social Charter in 1997). As a result of the Social Charter three new objectives were added to Article 117 of the Treaty of Rome (now Article 136 of the Treaty of Amsterdam in 1997, which renumbered the original Treaty of Rome Articles): 'proper social protection', 'social dialogue' and 'the development of human resources to achieve lasting employment'.

The Charter outlined basic employment rights concerning the free movement of labour within the EU; 'fair' remuneration in employment; improvement and approximation of conditions of employment EU-wide; collective bargaining and freedom of association; the right to training; equal opportunities for women, people with disabilities and racial minorities; information, consultation and participation arrangements for workers; health and safety provisions and protection of young people at work; minimum wage provision; and the right to transfer pensions and social security provisions (European Commission 1990).

Although the original Social Charter was controversial, when the final draft was approved it was a much watered-down version of the original. Of the 47 proposals only 28 involved binding directives or regulations – ten covering occupational health and safety, three improvements in living and working conditions, and two on equal opportunities. For all its controversy the Social Charter was purely a declaration and had no legal force. Many of the specific principles were already enshrined in other articles of the European Union, such as the case of the equal treatment of women at work. Moreover, many of the directives or regulations were far less stringent than existing national laws. For example the Working Time Directive provides for a maximum working week of 48 hours on average (including overtime), for minimum rest breaks during working hours, and for four weeks' annual paid holiday. In many countries employees already receive above the minimum. The directive also allowed for a range of occupational exemptions, therefore its impact on the labour market was limited.

Nonetheless, the Social Charter has introduced some important changes. The 'atypical' workers' directive has extended to part-time and fixed-term workers the same rights as are enjoyed by full-time workers, such as employment conditions, written contracts of employment, maximum working hours and the like. There have been other successes too in the areas of parental leave and maternity benefits, and the regulation of the employment of young people. However, in other areas such rights as freedom of association, collective bargaining and the right to strike have been compromised by non-binding agreements and recommendations and often made subject to national 'traditions'. Similarly the idea of EU-wide minimum wages has been changed to 'fair wages', that is, a wage set at a level to maintain a satisfactory standard of living. Therefore, on the one hand the Social Charter has not led to some of the major costs and rigidities that employers, particularly in the United Kingdom, were expecting, but it did bring to the forefront once again that the labour market is not like other markets.

Flexible labour markets

What do we mean by labour mobility or flexibility? Usually it has been used to encompass a number of themes.

- **Wage or earning flexibility:** this is the responsiveness of wages to market pressures. At the micro level it is about matching pay with productivity, for example performance-related pay. At the macro level it is the degree to which wages respond to changes in the demand for and supply of labour.
- **Labour mobility:** this concerns the ability of individuals to move between jobs, occupations, regions and countries, and includes the level of movement within a company.
- **Functional flexibility:** this refers to reducing the demarcation lines between occupations. It has been linked with core–periphery models of the flexible organisation, where core workers (full-time permanent members of staff) may receive different levels of training from those in the periphery (part-time staff), with the view that they adopt working practices based upon greater task flexibility.
- **Flexibility in the pattern and organisation of work:** in this category is included flexibility in the place of work and numerical flexibility, where organisations change the number of staff or hours in response to change in market conditions. In other words such flexibility is related to the use of part-time, temporary, self-employed and short-contract workers. Working-time flexibility is also placed in this category: that is, being able to offer different amounts of time per week/month/quarter to coincide with peak demand pressures (Cook and Farquharson 1998).

So how does the European Union fare in terms of labour market flexibility? In terms of geographic mobility, the incentive to move for employment purposes depends on the discounted difference in real disposable income, minus the transaction cost and other costs of moving. Therefore, things like the size of the home ownership sector compared with the rental sector may have an effect on geographical mobility. Gardner, Pierre and Oswald (2001) suggest that there is a positive link between the level of private rental housing and the mobility of the workforce. This is supported by the example of Spain, with one of the highest home ownership records in the OECD and also one of the highest levels of unemployment. However, home ownership is only one factor behind lower mobility. In fact although home owners may not be very mobile during the downturn phase of an economy, they are more likely to move in a rising housing market (Gardner, Pierre and Oswald 2001).

There are a number of common factors that can inhibit labour mobility within a country. These include:

● the inability to sell or purchase a house or to leave or enter the rental sector
● difficulties in obtaining a mortgage
● the availability, and quality, of schooling
● a partner's career
● lack of information about job opportunities in other regions
● overly protective employment legislation
● a benefits system that does not encourage mobility
● regional differences in the cost of living not compensated for by regional wage differences.

Restrictions between countries include:

● restrictions on the portability of qualifications
● lack of information about job opportunities in other countries
● career progression by partner
● language constraints
● differential healthcare systems (Mayes and Kilponen 2004).

In addition to the above, income, education, age and gender limit geographic mobility (Cook and Jones 2003). Those with higher incomes and better levels of education have greater geographic mobility within the European Union (European Commission 2002a). Moreover those aged 35 and over tend to have lower geographical mobility, which over the longer term in Europe suggests that mobility will fall as the population ages. Within Europe more mobility occurs at a younger age in the north, and family ties appear stronger in the southern EU states. Further compared with the United States, the European Union's younger age mobility tends to be focused on the 16–30 age group, whereas in the United States younger age mobility appears to continue until the mid-thirties (European Commission 2002a).

Within Europe, cross-border mobility can be created by either temporary or long-term migration; there may be cross-border commuting too. Intra-country mobility in the European Union has reduced since the 1960s as a result of the catch-up of the Southern European states and the growth in Ireland, though there is some evidence that it is beginning to rise again. The European Commission (2001a) suggested that around 5 per cent of the resident population are non-nationals of the member state in which they live, and two-thirds of these are non-EU nationals. However, geographical mobility with the United

States appears to be larger. Although the numbers who have moved to another member state to work are low, the proportion of EU citizens who commute to another country is also low. Moreover, not only is inter-country migration low along with inter-country commuting, but inter-regional mobility is also low. For the whole of the European Union inter-regional mobility is around 1.2 per cent while in the United States the inter-regional flows may be at least three times this figure (European Commission 2001a).

What are the reasons for this mobility in both the both United States and the European Union? For both areas, the main impetus for mobility is not job-related but for family reasons. In fact in a European study about a third of respondents would prefer to remain in a region as unemployed than move to a region where there is employment (Eurobarometer 2001).

Variations in regional unemployment are a good indicator of lack of mobility, inappropriate skills of the workforce and lack of occupational mobility. Improved regional mobility would help to improve the mismatch between jobs and workers. However, this may have **social costs** and perhaps a better approach is to address deficiencies in the education, training and wage flexibility of the working population. Mayes and Kilponen (2004) argue that there is little evidence inside the European Union that there are large labour movements purely as a result of the existence of the European Union. There is some evidence of adjacent movements, especially where countries are small, and some evidence of an income effect until recently, with movements from the south of the European Union to the richer northern EU members. The major movement has been the inflow of workers from outside the European Union, primarily into Germany and France.

Given the low level of labour mobility within the European Union, to what extent can it be blamed on a lack of occupational mobility or failure to possess the appropriate skills?

Occupational mobility

While the proportion of people in the European Union who had worked for their current employer for less than one year (used as an indicator of increased occupational mobility) had increased between 1995 and 2000, so had the proportion of people who had been with their current employer for more than ten years. In fact what may be witnessed within the European Union is a polarisation of tenure. The overall picture for the European Union also hides important differences by country. Average tenure has been growing in Luxemburg, the Netherlands, Belgium and Sweden, but has been declining in Denmark and Ireland. Japan matches the former set of countries while the United States matches the latter. For other countries there is a high degree of stability in the tenure of the workforce – more so for men, while tenure has been lengthening for women. Moreover, tenure tends to be shorter in economic upswings. A larger number of new entrants commence employment during an upswing in the economy, and this pushes down average tenure. At the same time tenure increases for those in employment but is further reduced by those who quit one job and move to another during favourable economic upswings. Finally, a further factor that affects tenure is the ageing population, in that average tenure tends to increase with age. But there may also be political, legal and other economic reasons that affect tenure and turnover.

High job turnover does not necessarily signify a flexible labour market. For example, in Spain companies have made increasing use of fixed-term contracts to circumvent increased labour costs which come into operation when they employ labour over the longer term. However, low turnover can have an impact on the unemployed, who now find it more difficult to find employment. This can tend to raise the equilibrium unemployment rate, as those who stay out of the labour market longer find it increasingly difficult to re-enter it.

Skills level and mobility

Different levels of skill may permit a move not only between organisations within the same sector but also between sectors. Those with low levels of skills and low specific job knowledge can move between sectors since there is little to be lost by staying in the same sector and little 'lost experience' from switching. Individuals with intermediate skill levels probably have more to gain by switching within sectors. Intermediate skills tend to be more transferable between firms within the same sector rather than between sectors. On the other hand highly skilled workers with their greater transferable skills may have high mobility between and within sectors. Those highly trained people with very specialised skills may however be extremely mobile but within a finely divided occupation level. Even for highly skilled people, the ability to shift between sectors may be constrained through the lack of recognition of professional qualifications, status and reputation, differing wage rates, and lack of knowledge of opportunities elsewhere (European Commission 2002b).

Regional impact of skills

Particular geographical areas may be associated with high skill levels. People in other regions see little reason to train for these skills if employers or potential employers are not going to offer those types of jobs or be attracted to their region. Often these higher-skilled jobs are associated with metropolitan areas. Therefore some regions become associated with good jobs and high skills, and other become associated with low skills and bad jobs. Such a situation may not exist over the long term, as externalities build up in highly favoured areas, thereby raising the costs of moving or employing there. But even before externalities build up, skilled, often younger, people with their greater mobility may begin moving from low-skill, low-pay regions. One factor that affects mobility between areas and regions is a worker's level of education or skill. In 2000, more than half the working-age population in low-employment regions had less than upper-secondary education, compared with less than 25 per cent of those in high-employment areas (European Commission 2001b).

The type of sector too may influence employment opportunities. However, while the sectoral and occupational composition of employment is a factor in regional employment differences, it matters less than differences in education, mobility and innovative capacity. Not surprisingly, within the European Union the European Commission (2001a) has found that the areas that had the lowest levels of unemployment were those that saw both their service sectors growing more rapidly, and employment opportunities rising in the knowledge-intensive sectors.

For the European Union the biggest problem may not be that employees will not move between countries, but that there is reluctance by EU citizens to move between immediate neighbouring areas or regions.

Demographic change and its impact on labour markets

During the next 30 years labour markets throughout the global community are going to be seriously challenged by demographic change. The European labour market has stopped growing in size, and in some countries such as Italy, Germany, Denmark and Austria the decrease in working population has already begun (see Figure 9.1).

During the period 1997–2005, the 15–29 age group from which entrants into the labour markets are drawn declined in size while at the same time older age cohorts grew. At an EU level the impact of these changes varied due to their intensity and timing. In general employment in the European Union has grown at 0.6 per cent on average since 1985, and if this rate is to be maintained then the European economies need to draw more upon the inactive human resources in each age group. In other words participation rates need to increase (OECD 1998). So how do the participation rates vary between member states?

Taking the differences in participation rates between men and women and also between three age groups (15–29, 30–49 and 50–64), both between genders and within them, the main distinguishing factor between member

Figure 9.1 First calendar year of the decrease in the working-age population for selected EU countries

Source: European Commission, 'Towards a Europe for all ages: promoting prosperity and intergenerational solidarity', COM(1999)221.

states with the highest employment rates and those with the lowest, is the level of female employment. The participation of males among the 30–49 age group is fairly similar across all countries. The participation by younger and older age groups in the labour market is also important. The Netherlands, the United Kingdom, Austria and Portugal have fairly high participation rates while the Mediterranean countries of Greece, Italy and Spain have the lowest level of employment because of lower female participation and the delayed entry into the labour market by younger people. For the Mediterranean countries their culture and the role of the family have affected women's participation rates. For younger people in this area, higher education courses may be longer and there is also a lack of employment opportunities.

Part-time employment is also important, playing a major role for older and younger age groups as well as for women. It can allow young people to continue their studies, and act as the transition into and out of full-time work. The countries with the highest amount of part-time employment are Denmark, the Netherlands and the United Kingdom. For example in the Netherlands just over two-thirds of employed females between the ages of 15 and 64 are in part-time work.

During the next 20 years what should be seen is an improvement in the employment rate for those in the 15–29 age group, since the slowdown in population growth makes this group relatively scarce. The take-up from this group will prove problematic for countries where its employment rate is already high, such as Denmark, the Netherlands, Austria and to a lesser extent the United Kingdom and Luxemburg. The reverse is probably true for Spain, Italy and Greece. However, the decline in fertility rates generally within Europe could lead to this latter group of countries also experiencing labour shortage problems within the 15–29 age group in the medium rather than long term (OECD 1998).

In the intermediate age group (30–49), male employment rates are already high and there will be an increased demand for female employment. For those countries that already have relatively high employment rates for female workers, the pool of inactive women is relatively low. The 'baby-boomers' (those born in the period of above-average birth rate from 1945 to 1960) will soon enter the 50–64 age group (OECD 1998). Therefore the population over 50 years of age will continue to be a large reserve of labour supply, especially women, because of their currently low participation in the labour market. Sweden, Denmark, Portugal, the United Kingdom, Greece (only for men) and Finland (only for women) are the countries with the highest employment rates among the oldest population. The situation is reversed in Belgium, Luxemburg and the Mediterranean countries, with low female employment rates, and in France and Finland with low male employment rates for the older age groups as a consequence of early retirement policies. However, these demographic changes caused by ageing are not unique to Europe. In Japan the working age population will decline by over 37 per cent by 2050 (Helgerson 2002), but it will take until 2022 in both Canada and the United States for the proportion of their population over 65 years of age to reach the level currently being experienced by Italy.

What these changes mean for Europe and Europe's businesses is that the European Union and the governments of the member states need to consider more closely human resource management and the need for better-skilled and more employable workers, together with more adaptable workplaces. If skill training and education have been aimed at the younger cohorts, the shift in the demographic profile of the population in Europe may require attention to be given to skills and training at the older age levels. If measures are not undertaken, older workers who are going to be an increasing part of the pool of the working population will find themselves available for work but without the correct skills for employability.

It is not just that the older population will make up a bigger proportion of the workforce, they will also become a bigger proportion of consumers. As this occurs, they will influence overall consumer tastes (in addition they are the first generation who will inherit houses, and thus wealth, on a large scale) and may demand services from other older employers who understand their shopping needs. There also may be a need to further develop temporary work and part-time work to fit with the lifestyles of the older working population. Many of the jobs that have been created throughout the last ten years have come through the small and medium-sized enterprise (SME) sector (see Chapter 12), and here too, SMEs may need to develop systems and practices that are adaptable to the hours that may be required by older workers (OECD 1998).

It has been shown earlier that there is scope to increase the workforce through the growth in female participation; therefore the gender balance of many workforces will change. In this respect policies may have to reconsider the difficulties some women have in balancing work and family obligations. In a Europe accustomed to generous social safety nets via pensions and health care, unless there are policy changes over the next two decades many economies could face increased debt and/or higher taxes, both of which could lead to a slowdown in economic growth. In the global economy Japan is of particular concern. Its debt has climbed to 12 per cent of the world's GDP, and a continuation to this trend could see a recession in east Asia and weakened growth in both Europe and the United States (ILO 2002).

Within Europe the regions likely to experience the greatest difficulties in the future are southern Scandinavia, northern Italy, England, central Portugal and southern Germany. All these regions currently have high participation rates and are more likely to experience a greater impact from the demographic changes in the labour market. If these regions are not to suffer from slowdowns in economic growth then a raft of social, educational and employment policies may be needed. This brings to the fore the issues that surround the mobility of labour. Increased labour mobility is one way to deal with the issues these regions face – that is, improvement in mobility between jobs, regions, and industries together with increased training and retraining of the workforce.

If it proves difficult to find the appropriate labour within Europe, will there be a drift of employment to other areas of the global economy? For example, there could be a more pronounced shift of jobs to Asia where the population will be fairly young and fertility rates are still high. For governments there is the increased costs of providing pensions for an ever-increasing ageing population, and this might result in the equalisation of retirement ages between men and women in the first instance, and an increase in the retirement age in the medium to long term. Further, organisations may have to examine the training that they have been giving to their older workforces. Some older employees may have made the decision not to seek further training because they consider themselves too old and feel there are not enough different job opportunities open to them. Employers for their part may not encourage older workers to take on extra training since they consider the increased marginal returns do not exceed the marginal costs of training over the remaining lifetime of the older worker. All this could change in the future as the decline in the younger age cohorts comes to bear on the labour market.

Conversely, some organisations may decide to replace declining younger cohorts not with increased demand for older workers but with more and better technology (OECD 1998). For example, the introduction of greater quantities of technology in the banking sector has resulted in a large shake-out of employment from this sector. There may also be a link between older workers and levels of productivity. They are often seen as less productive workers and lacking flexibility. In this respect they are often linked with simple and repetitive tasks with low levels of leadership and responsibility. On the other hand older workers may be more productive since they tend to have more work experience (Disney 1996). An ageing workforce may be more costly through the process of incremental drift (that is, staff are paid more each year they remain in post).

For some employers a less productive workforce that is becoming more expensive is not a scenario they wish to face. For their part, employed older workers who do receive high wages may feel that there is no point in quitting their current employment since age might be a factor that caused employers to discriminate against them if they were to apply for other employment. Moreover they are more likely to have found a good job match (Groot and Verberne 1997). This factor may restrict their mobility (Gregg, Knight and Wadsworth 1999). If older workers are less mobile, employers may need to make greater use of redundancy to adjust the size of their workforces (OECD 1998).

All these factors together suggest that both organisations and governments have a great deal of work to do to address the issues faced by the demographic changes in their workforce. Organisations may have to address some of their prejudices about older workers, and governments and organisations may have to consider various forms of migration to fill the working population gaps that exist within their economies.

Skills needs and skill deficiencies of industry

A dynamic economy is built on the skills, not just of employees, but also of employers, financiers and policy makers. Skill shortages reflect insufficient, inappropriate or obsolete skills across the existing workforce. It may be possible to overcome these problems through a process of immigration in the short to medium term, but tackling the issue at a more fundamental level requires governments to review their current education and training policies. A survey by PricewaterhouseCoopers (2002) indicated that many European firms considered not that there were skill shortages at the Europe-wide level but that the problem lay with 'the right people being in the wrong places'. Nonetheless other studies by the *Daily Telegraph* (2002) and European Observatory (2001) in the United Kingdom and the Netherlands found that many candidates for employment lack suitable skills. Furthermore, existing employees and organisations were having to respond in a variety of ways, through higher pay, flexible working and the like to attract appropriate applicants, and in some case needed to reduce entry-level job requirements.

Skills mismatches too are a problem, and require an emphasis on policies for education, training and lifelong learning. These mismatches, unlike skill shortages, may be reduced through measures to improve occupational and regional mobility as highlighted earlier in this chapter. Where mismatches occur there can be a high level of vacancies arising in the domestic economy coexisting with high levels of unemployment elsewhere in the economy; a feature noted by European Observatory (2001). This relationship between the growth in vacancies and unemployment is shown by the Beveridge curve (see Figure 9.2). The more efficient is the job-matching process between the unemployed and job vacancies, the closer to the origin is the Beveridge curve.

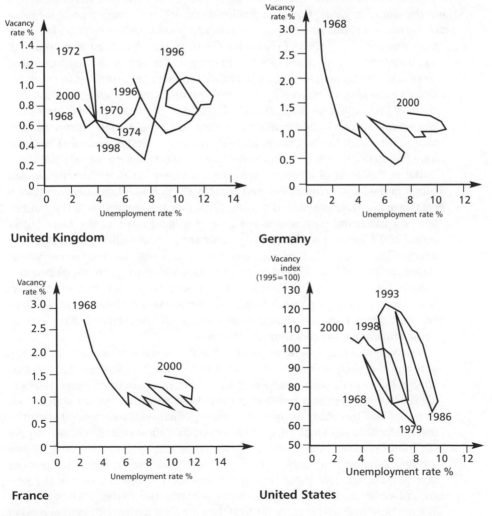

Figure 9.2 The Beveridge curve

In the United Kingdom the Beveridge curve has clearly started to shift to the left, having shown shifts to the right during the 1980s and early 1990s. In the United States there appears to a consistent shift to the left of the curve, and in France and Germany (until recently) the curve has been shifting to the right. The European Central Bank (ECB) (2002) suggest that this can be explained by the difficulties labour supply has in adjusting to the changes in demand placed upon it by globalisation and technological change. But skills mismatches are only one factor behind the shifts in the Beveridge curve: the growth in the numbers of long-term unemployed may also be to blame. Employers are less likely to hire these type of workers because of their inappropriate skills, and the long-term unemployed may become disheartened about applying for jobs the longer they stay out of the labour market (Layard, Nickell and Jackman, 1994)

So how severe are skill constraints in the European Union? One way of attempting to measure these is through comparable educational qualifications in the member states. However qualifications are not always a good measure of the level of skills, since a person with, say, good problem-solving skills may have relatively low levels of educational attainment. An alternative approach has been through the level of adult literacy. If literacy is divided into three groups, low, intermediate and high, Muhlau and Horgan (2001) noted that the United States, the United Kingdom and Ireland have a higher than average share of low-skilled workers, though the United States combines this with a large share of high-skilled workers. Sweden has a much higher proportion of people with high literacy rates, and Germany, the Netherlands and Belgium have populations with a greater proportion of intermediate literacy skills.

But is this level of literacy a mismatch between what the population can supply and what employers demand? Employers in Ireland and Belgium have a greater demand for low-skilled workers. This may be a reflection of their industrial or agricultural past, and in the case of Ireland many of the more highly skilled and educated workers left the country to find employment elsewhere where the job opportunities matched their skill levels, leaving behind lower-skilled workers. In the United States, the demand is for both low-skilled and high-skilled workers, while Germany and Sweden have a low demand for low-skilled workers with a more even demand for workers with intermediate skills and high skills. Both the United Kingdom and the Netherlands have a more equal demand for workers from all skill levels.

This suggests that Ireland in particular and to some extent the United Kingdom and the United States have too many lower-skilled workers for the jobs offered, but in most countries there is a good balance between intermediate and high-skilled workers and the demand for these people. It would appear that Germany has too many people with intermediate skills compared with the demand for these by employers, and Sweden has a surplus of high-skilled people (ECB 2002). Some of the mismatch between the skill levels of the workforce and the jobs being made available is related to poor basic literacy skills that prevent skills acquisition. This problem may become more acute as many of the jobs created within the European Union during the latter part of the 1990s were more likely to be in high-skill sectors. If this is the case then it may require intervention at both national and supra-national level if the growth targets set by the European

Union are to be attained. If skills are so important, unemployment rates should be higher for those with lower levels of education and skills.

Table 9.1 indicates the percentage of people in the EU15 who have at least upper secondary education. The three countries at the top of the list owe their positions to the fact that a greater proportion of their population in the 45+ age groups have at least upper-secondary level education. Other countries like the United Kingdom and Finland have greatly improved their educational attainments of their 25–44 age groups. The table also reveals that as the workforce gradually ages, the educational attainments of the 45+ age groups will improve as better-educated younger people feed through into these age groups. However, the reaching of a particular level of education does not necessarily tell us whether the skills of such people are increasing. Crafts (2002) reports that British 16–25 year olds performed less well in measures of numeracy and literacy than did 26–35 year olds, which suggests a decline in basic education. Interestingly, a number of the new member states of the EU25, the Czech Republic, Hungary and Poland, perform better than Greece, Spain, Italy and Portugal in areas of reading literacy, scientific literacy and numeracy (European Commission 2002a). Therefore, part of the problem that the original EU15 envisaged with a mismatch between labour skills and job opportunities may be solved by the entry of the new member states. However, this does rest on the mobility of labour between the new entrants and the EU15.

Not only does education have an impact upon the world of work at the commencement of employment, but skills and qualifications need continual updating. This process of lifelong learning is important for the continued

Table 9.1 Percentage of people with at least secondary education (2000)

Country	25–34	35–44	45–54	55–64	25–64
Denmark	84.8	78.7	78.0	68.2	78.0
Sweden	86.8	81.8	73.7	62.2	76.8
Germany	81.4	81.3	76.7	67.0	76.7
Austria	83.8	81.2	71.9	62.9	76.1
Finland	85.6	82.8	67.8	49.3	72.5
UK	82.7	77.4	66.4	45.7	70.0
Netherlands	72.0	66.8	58.7	50.4	63.2
France	76.3	65.3	56.9	43.6	62.6
Luxemburg	66.7	63.2	55.9	47.4	59.6
Belgium	75.4	62.4	51.5	37.2	58.3
Greece	72.5	59.2	43.4	26.6	51.2
Italy	58.6	50.8	38.4	21.8	43.9
Spain	56.2	43.1	27.0	15.4	37.1
Portugal	31.0	19.3	14.1	7.7	19.2
EU15	71.5	65.8	56.1	43.5	60.3

Source: European Commission (2002a).

Data on Ireland not available.

dynamism of the EU economy. The ILO (2002) cites the United Kingdom as being at the forefront of lifelong learning. In the European Union in 2000, 8 per cent of the working age population participated in training, but this was more likely to have been undertaken by those with higher levels of education. This may not be a reflection solely of ability or discrimination, since higher-skilled workers are more likely to be employed in organisations that offer training for their employees. Indeed training is also more likely in organisations that lie in the more dynamic sectors of the economy. To address this market failure, governments may need to operate in the market, and there may need also to be encouragement through subsidies and through the process of collective bargaining. In relation to the latter, lifelong learning has become increasingly important on the agendas of trade unions, since without continuous training and learning their members will possess redundant skills and find it increasingly difficult to find or remain in employment (ILO 2002).

Although training rates for men and women are approximately the same (8.4 per cent for women and 7.6 per cent for men in 2000), training appears to decline by age (an issue that is discussed elsewhere in this chapter). This may have to change as the working population ages, although some employers argue that training older workers is not worthwhile since there is not a sufficient time horizon to get the returns back from training such people. There is some evidence to suggest that the returns from training happen over relatively short time horizons and that such a view is false. Across Europe, the Nordic countries, the United Kingdom and the Netherlands undertake more training than the other EU member countries, though care must be taken with the statistics. First, training can be of different duration, and the data used by the European Commission takes no account of this. Second, countries that have higher levels of training may be compensating for lower levels of educational attainment. Finally, some jobs, such as those requiring apprenticeships, have traditionally incorporated 'on-the-job' training and this might not be registered as separate training.

The skills of the workforce therefore prove an important factor in retaining employers and attracting new employers, but other factors such as labour costs also play their part.

Labour costs and business location

Labour costs and in particular wages can play an important role in the location of industry (European Industrial Relations Observatory, 1998). This can be at both a regional and national level. For example, Invest UK (2005) markets the United Kingdom as having low-cost flexible labour markets amongst other factors, as a means of attracting FDI.

However, labour costs are all relative. Labour costs may be cheaper in the United Kingdom than in Denmark, and until recently Germany, but they are much lower still in the new accession countries of the European Union such as Poland, Hungary and Slovakia (see Table 9.2). Moreover, low wage costs can be offset by non-wage labour costs such as payments to pension funds and insurance payments. Furthermore, low wage costs need to be considered alongside levels of productivity. A high-wage/high-productivity economy may be preferred

Table 9.2 Labour costs in selected European countries

Average gross annual earnings in industry and services, for full-time employees in enterprises with 10 or more employees (in ECU/euros)

Country	1998	2000	2002
EU15	22,142	25,527	–
Euro-zone	20,970	22,413	–
Belgium	29,616	31,644	34,330
Denmark	37,209	40,962	43,577
Germany	36,033	37,862	39,440
Greece	13,209	14,721	16,278
Spain	16,528	17,432	18,462
France	25,519	26,521	–
Cyprus	14,709	16,335	17,740
Luxemburg	33,462	35,910	38,551
Hungary	3,686	4,172	5,871
Malta	10,713	12,553	13,460
Netherlands	29,189	31,901	35,200
Poland	4,156	–	7,172
Slovakia	3,292	3,583	4,582
Finland	24,944	27,398	–
Sweden	–	31,621	31,164
UK	29,370	37,677	40,553

Source: Eurostat Yearbook 2004.

by a producer to a low-wage/low-productivity economy since it all comes down to the cost of output per unit of labour.

If wage costs were important determinants of business location, this should explain FDI flow. For the United Kingdom, however, the great majority of UK FDI goes to countries where labour costs are higher than the United Kingdom, such as the United States, France, Germany and the Netherlands. Less than 20 per cent goes to countries where labour costs are lower than the United Kingdom's. So maybe the cost of unit of output argument stated above is not true. Perhaps something else has changed to affect location decisions? Labour costs are becoming an increasingly small proportion of total costs (Ferner 1997). This reflects the greater productivity of the workforce and the greater use of, and expenditure on, capital and technology as a means to improve a company's competitiveness.

Even though the United Kingdom appears to be a competitive labour cost economy in Europe and has benefited from improved levels of productivity, Baunton (cited in Caulkin 2004) suggests that increased labour costs in the United Kingdom are driving manufacturers and service operators offshore. These increased costs include pensions and national insurance. Initially jobs that were exported abroad were low-skill, relatively mechanised and repetitive manufacturing jobs. (Part of this process resulted in the de-industrialisation of many of the developed countries' economies.) However, as these economies moved into service-sector employment it has now resulted in a number of service-sector jobs being outsourced, such as call centres, booking companies and even basic legal services, particularly to India.

The movement of jobs to low-cost labour areas and away from the developed economies has prompted both governments and trade unions in the developed economies to consider the social dimension of globalisation within the labour market, and led to the ILO Declaration on Fundamental Principles and Rights at Work in 1998. This covered areas such as:

- freedom of association and the right to collective bargaining
- the elimination of child labour
- the elimination of forced or compulsory labour
- the elimination of discrimination in occupation and employment.

Although these proposals might improve the social rights of workers, particularly in developing countries, it will also increase these countries' labour costs, and could be seen as a means of slowing down the transfer of jobs from the developed world to the developing world. In the meantime does this mean that low labour cost countries will continue to benefit from the flow of jobs from high wage cost countries?

Low labour costs can be a competitive disadvantage. This is because labour can be easily substituted and cheap labour provides little stimulus for company innovation. Conversely, high labour costs can lead to company innovation, as in Japan and in the Dutch horticultural industry, where the Dutch use of greenhouses, propagation methods and marketing has enabled them to compete successfully with lower labour cost producers. If jobs are continuously lost by high-cost producers to low-cost producers it forces an economy to consider education and the skill levels of its workforce. If the jobs that are being lost are low-skilled jobs, this releases productive employment in the developed economy. This can then be used with more education and training to develop higher value-added products and services. As incomes grow in those developing economies to which jobs are transferred, this may also improve the exports from developed economies to these economies.

From the organisation's perspective, outsourcing may be a means to lower the company's cost base. Moreover, these new jobs may attract a different and 'better' employee in the developing economy than in the developed economy, and this would improve overall company performance. For example, many call centre jobs in the United Kingdom are filled by students who undertake these on a temporary basis, but such jobs in India may attract highly committed graduate applicants.

Wages and other labour costs

Within Europe most countries operate minimum wage schemes. These may be set nationally, may come via negotiations between government and the trade unions, be paid as part of a fixed formula related to other wages, or be set differently at an industry level or state/region authority level. For its part the United Kingdom, particularly during the period 1979–97, viewed the minimum wage as reducing labour market flexibility, and no such system existed. However follow-ing the election of the Labour Party in 1997, the United Kingdom introduced its own minimum wage. The argument had been put forward that it would raise unemployment and that part of the United Kingdom's strong performance on employment during the late 1980s and early 1990s was due to the lack of a minimum wage. Why this was thought to be the case can be seen in Figure 9.3.

The minimum wage W_{min} is set above the equilibrium wage, W_0. The result is a reduction in the demand for labour from L_0 to L_d and an increase in the supply of labour to L_s. There is now excess supply of workers, which includes some of those previously employed before the introduction of a minimum wage $(L_0 - L_d)$.

There is, however, research work in the United States (Card 1992, Card and Kreuger 1994) and in the United Kingdom (Machin and Manning 1994) that indicates when the minimum wage increased, employment actually increased. Similarly, in the United Kingdom the introduction of the minimum wage occurred at a time when employment was increasing and unemployment falling. One reason for this is that when the wages of the lowest-paid workers increase to the minimum wage level, total expenditure increases, thereby creating new jobs to replace those destroyed. Second, the minimum wage in the United Kingdom has been set relatively low, so that the impact on the organisation is small. Third, labour costs as a proportion of total production costs may be rela-tively low, so that for some employers at least, the impact of the minimum wage is only slight. Furthermore, many people already earn above the minimum wage and therefore are not affected.

However, although total unemployment may not be affected greatly by the introduction of a minimum wage, paradoxically it can have an important impact on youth employment. If the minimum wage for young people is a relatively high proportion of adult minimum wages, organisations may substitute adult

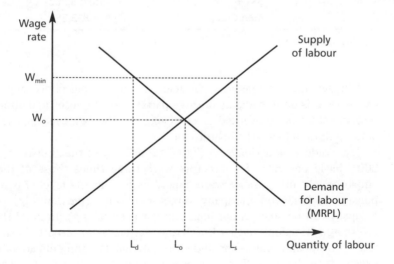

Figure 9.3 Effect of a minimum wage on the labour market

workers for young people. This might help to explain why there is higher youth unemployment in France, where at 16 years of age the youth minimum wage is 80 per cent of adult minimum, whereas for 16 year olds in the United States the minimum wage is under 40 per cent of the adult wage. It is also generally the case that minimum wages as a proportion of average earnings are greater in the European Union than in the United States, and this might go some way in explaining why the US unemployment rate is around half of that in the European Union (Muhlau and Horgan 2001).

Corporate pay

Whereas many employees have been asked to embrace flexibility in their pay packages, linking payment to productivity, pay at the corporate level does not appear to follow this process. Table 9.3 shows the top ten earners in the United Kingdom in 2003.

Table 9.3 The top ten earners in the United Kingdom, 2003

Director	Company	Total package (£)
Tony Ball	BSkyB	11,456,210
Ken Hydon	Vodafone	9,894,223
Michael Green	Carlton	9,445,280
David Reid	Tesco	8,619,000
Bart Brecht	Reckitt Benckiser	7,747,000
Stanley Fink	Man Group	6,951,345
Crispin Davis	Reed Elsevier	6,678,529
Jean-Pierre Garnier	GlaxoSmithKline	5,884,260
Martin Stewart	BSkyB	5,496,262
Peter Clarke	Man Group	4,813,550

Source: French and Treanor (2004).

Although the remuneration for many of the people above appears to be excessive, it is often made up of three parts: salary, bonuses and options. Often how directors are rewarded is complex, but the rewards appear to vastly outstrip those outside the boardroom.

The Trade Union Congress (TUC) (2002) noted that between 1994 and 2001, basic pay rises for directors were three times those of the average employee, but other issues were important such as the level of pensions and pension rights, and company director payoffs (particularly where the company can be seen as not improving or even failing). In 2003 the TUC in the United Kingdom and its Dutch and German counterparts both appealed to the European Commission and their national governments about excessive executive settlements. The issue was that company boards appear to award themselves large pay increases without a clear link to performance. A number of the unions felt this indicated a failure of corporate governance, when a company focused too heavily on rewarding its directors rather than improving profitability or market share. Currently fund managers, who control the power of the institutional investors, are not publicly required to disclose how they vote, so it is not possible to tell which of them are trying to address the issues of corporate governance failure and which of them are not.

Another issue of concern for the unions is how the level of remuneration is decided. If the remuneration committees are composed of company executives, the executives are deciding on their own pay, and this may lead to excessive pay rewards and unchallenging targets. In this respect European trade unions would like more employee representatives involved on remuneration committees, a transparent set of information concerning the rewards for each director of a company in the company accounts, and a limitation on stock options.

To address some of the concerns of trade unions, employees and shareholders, the UK government from April 2005 has introduced a maximum level that a pension fund can reach over the lifetime of the employee (£1.5 million). Many FTSE executives currently have a pension fund in excess of this. Connon (2004) argues that capping UK executives' and directors' pension funds could lead to a 'brain drain' of senior executives unless other types of incentives are used instead. At present pension funds can be used as a retention mechanism for executives, and it is possible that once the maximum pension fund is established, some senior executives will leave their current employment for jobs with enhanced salaries, not necessarily in the United Kingdom. In addition, some senior executives began to receive higher salary settlements in the run-up to April 2005 so that they could get as much money as possible into their pension fund before the pensions cap came into play. For example Sir Roy Gardner's salary grew by 13 per cent in 2003, improving his pension fund from £2,883,000 to £3,885,000, giving a £50,000 rise in annual pension entitlement to £233,400 (Connon 2004).

Part of the argument for the high rewards paid to senior executives comes from the link between pay, ability and performance. If a company does not reward its executives it may find it difficult to keep or attract high-quality executives. However, what can a company do when its chief executive appears to be managing the company into decline? For example, Sir Peter Davis of Sainsbury saw the company fall from its position as number one in the supermarket sector to third place behind Tesco and Asda, profits dropped to a 15 per cent low by 2004 and he received a £2.1 million pay-off in recognition of his work (Cohen 2004). As Cohen (2004) notes further, many conventional economists can find no link between executive pay and performance. Importantly, other parts of executive rewards such as options, pensions, bonuses and the like are linked to salary, and the faster this increases, the faster the other parts of the pay package increase. At present it seems that executives and company managers are getting richer because they can, but not because they deserve to, and there are not sufficient safeguards from remuneration committees, pension funds and government to stop this.

As can be seen, salary is only one of the labour costs incurred for executives, but even for lower-grade employees the 'other' labour costs can be fairly high.

Other labour costs

The cost of labour to businesses is substantially greater than the take-home pay of employees in many EU member states. A distinguishing feature of most EU economies is the high level of social protection provided by the state. To fund this social protection, charges are made on businesses, and as international competitiveness has grown, there has been concern that the effects on labour costs are putting European organisations at a competitive disadvantage and discouraging them from employing people. In addition because these charges differ between countries, they can put some countries at a competitive disadvantage. It would be expected that the impact of these labour charges will depend on the organisation and its willingness to accept and absorb them. It also depends on the market in which the organisation finds itself. However it could also lead to the organisation looking for ways to substitute capital for labour and search for opportunities in low-cost areas of production.

Of course direct and indirect labour costs are only some of the factors that lead to business location choices. In a recent survey by KPMG (2004), Canada was seen as the cheapest location, followed by Australia. The United States was seventh, with Germany and Japan as the most costly business locations. These costs include such things as labour costs, taxes, transport and utilities, with labour costs typically representing 56–72 per cent of location-sensitive costs for manufacturing and 75–85 per cent for non-manufacturing operations. Therefore it may not be actual labour costs that are an issue, but all the other types of costs, some of which are outside the control of the organisation.

Wages and productivity play a part in the output of employees, and organisations can affect the productivity of their workforce through appropriate reward schemes. Nonetheless, labour productivity is also determined by a whole range of other factors, for example, government policy on R&D and the level of competition within markets.

Productivity in European and international labour markets

Labour productivity is defined as a country's gross domestic product (GDP) per capita of employed population. Its growth can be affected by the quality of physical capital, improvements in the skill levels of the work force, technological advances and new ways of organising production. Productivity growth is seen as an important source of economic growth. The Lisbon Council declaration of 2000 aimed to make Europe the most competitive and dynamic knowledge-based economy in the world, capable of sustained economic growth, with more and better jobs and greater social cohesion. This goal was set for 2010, but currently the level and trends of economic growth are not sufficient to reach this target.

During the latter part of the 1990s growth in labour productivity in the European Union slowed from an average 1.9 per cent between the period 1990–5 to 1.2 per cent between 1996–2001, while at the same time employment growth grew. Since 1990 some EU countries have done better than others in productivity performance. For example, Austria, Ireland and Greece have recorded constant productivity growth at a level matching the United States. So why haven't all EU countries done as well?

Europa (2003) stresses the link between information and communication technologies (ICT) and productivity performance. ICT is a core element of the knowledge society and an important complement to research and development, and those countries where ICT is pervasive have higher levels of productivity growth. The productivity gap between the European Union and the United States is in part, therefore, a reflection of the lower levels of ICT spending in the European Union compared with the United States.

This is productivity performance at a national level, so how does the European Union compare with the United States if different industrial sectors are considered? Within the different sectors, the 1990s saw lower productivity growth in manufacturing in the European Union than in the United States. However the picture for capital-intensive industries such as textile fibres, pulp and paper, and iron and steel has been positive, and in technology-driven industries such as pharmaceuticals, chemical products, office machinery and computers, and electronics production, the growth in productivity compared with the United States has been notable. However, it is still the case that in comparison with the US technology-driven industries the value added of EU technology industries is only 24 per cent compared with the United States's 35 per cent. This could be a reflection of the lower level of ICT in these industries in the European Union.

In the service sector productivity is notoriously difficult to measure, but the levels of productivity in this sector again compare unfavourably with those of the United States. Once again this can be related back to ICT, where the European Union has made slower progress than the United States in incorporating it into the service sector. Within the European Union there are also noticeable differences in productivity performance between countries, with those such as the United Kingdom and Finland, which deregulated their markets earlier, having higher productivity growth in this sector during the 1990s than other countries (Europa 2003). Productivity differences between the United States and the European Union may also be more complex than those described above. For example, should we consider comparisons in terms of output per employee or output per hour worked, and what about occupations where output is difficult to measure, particularly those in the service sector? These and other issues are discussed in Case study 9.2.

Both enterprise policy and competition policy within the European Union can improve enterprise growth and productivity. The former can do this by correcting market failure and enabling more firms to engage in market transactions while increasing their innovative potential. The latter encourages firms to search for efficiency-enhancing solutions that lead to product and market innovation. Such policies have different emphases, and the European Union needs to take a balanced approach which reduces the use of state aid (or at least assesses better the legitimacy of state aid), helps with inter-firm cooperation particularly in the area of innovation, considers better the nature of products, and the sector and market in which organisations sell their products, and helps with restructuring through merger and acquisition.

PRODUCTIVITY IN EUROPEAN AND INTERNATIONAL LABOUR MARKETS

One of the most striking statistics about European productivity is the gap between output per employee and output per hour worked. Output per employee in the European Union was only 70 per cent of US levels in 2000, up by only 1 percentage point since 1970. However, output per hour worked was 91 per cent of US levels, compared with 65 per cent in 1970. In France, which now has the second shortest average working hours in the European Union, productivity per hour worked was 105 per cent of US levels. If the gap between European and US productivity is accounted for mainly by working hours rather than efficiency, the best way for the European Union to close the productivity gap might be simply to work longer hours. In an employment outlook published in July 2004, the OECD writes that recent research has clearly established:

> that the sizeable US advantage in real gross domestic product per capita, particularly as compared with the most advanced European economies, is largely due to differences in total hours worked per capita, rather than to higher output per hour worked. ... It had not been appreciated that this divergence was becoming a major factor in determining relative growth performance.

Productivity statistics, however, must be treated with caution. There are still unresolved problems of measuring productivity, especially measuring output per worker in the services sector. The numbers are also notoriously difficult to interpret. For example, the high productivity levels in the French and German manufacturing sector are a sign of weakness because many unproductive companies have gone bust, and as a result average measured

productivity has risen. In its July monthly report, the European Central Bank observed that while growth in labour productivity is 'the single most important determinant of longer term improvements in potential output and living standards', working hours cannot be the sole explanation for the gap in productivity growth rates. 'The finding that in the period since the mid-1990s productivity growth continued to decline in the euro area while it increased in the United States is independent of the concept (the specific measure of productivity) used'.

Another factor putting downward pressure on productivity growth has been what the ECB says is the 'relatively subdued' impact of ICT in Europe – in other words, Europe failed to improve productivity during the high-technology revolution of the late 1990s. Daniel Gros, director at the Centre for European Policy Studies in Brussels, argues that the European economy was doing relatively well until 2000, but because European companies and governments placed a greater emphasis on stability over flexibility they were unprepared for the technology explosion. Professor Gros said:

> You had a drop in demand and structural change – think of the internet – and that situation is exactly what the European economy is not designed for. You can't fire people and send them somewhere else. You have young people, they have big ideas and they run with them – that is not exactly the German model, in which you have years of schooling, apprenticeships and so on, and then when you finally arrive after 20 years the world is completely different.

The European economy also suffers from selective skills shortages. For instance, Infineon, the semiconductor manufacturer, opened a development centre in China late in 2003 – and not just because of the lower costs and the higher sales potential there. An Infineon spokesperson said that 'certainly the availability of well trained engineers' was a deciding factor in the move, as was the ability to work around the clock across three continents. Moreover, the chief executive of one of the world's largest US-based information technology companies recently told a gathering of European ministers in a private meeting that his company invested in China not for cost reasons but because the skills needed were more readily available there than in the European Union.

Information technology also plays a significant role in explaining the productivity gap between the European Union and the United States, according to Bart van Ark, professor of economics at the University of Groningen in the Netherlands and an expert on productivity. He says that the key element is not IT production but IT consumption. Professor van Ark found that a large part of the productivity gap between the European Union and the United States is accounted for by only a few sectors, most notably retailers, wholesalers and the financial services industry. By contrast, Europe has some of the most outstanding manufacturers of IT products and services. In IT services, such as telecommunications, the European Union has not only a higher level of productivity than the United States, but also a higher rate of productivity growth. A rough calculation suggests that if the European Union had the same rate of productivity growth in these three sectors – and all other things being equal – the EU economy would actually have a higher rate of productivity growth than the United States.

Source: Munchau and Atkins (2004).

Questions

1 What explanations have been put forward to explain the European Union's poor productivity performance?
2 What policies can be used to improve the European Union's level of productivity?

Apart from comparing itself with the United States, how do some of the bigger EU countries measure up in their productivity performance against each other, Japan and the G7 countries?

On an inter-country level, Table 9.4 shows that the United Kingdom appears to have been catching up with some of its main competitors. In 2002 the United Kingdom's productivity performance was almost the same as Germany's and better than Japan's. However the United States still appears to have the highest GDP per worker, though even here the United Kingdom is catching it up. The United Kingdom's productivity record has improved significantly over the last ten years compared with other countries. For example it has improved dramatically against France, while the French themselves have fallen further behind the United States. Still, however, the United Kingdom lies approximately 12 percentage points behind the other G7 countries. This does not mean that other countries have become less productive, but that the United Kingdom's productivity level has been growing at a faster rate. The picture for GDP per hour worked shows a similar picture, though the comparison against other countries except Japan has been consistently weaker on a per-hour basis than per worker.

Table 9.4 GDP per worker

Year	France	Germany	Japan	UK	USA	G7
1990	129.7	–	105.2	100	137.0	–
1991	129.6	111.5	105.9	100	136.9	122.1
1992	129.7	112.7	103.2	100	137.0	121.6
1993	124.8	108.8	99.5	100	133.8	118.8
1994	123.2	108.1	96.9	100	131.3	117.1
1995	121.3	108.0	97.0	100	130.2	116.7
1996	120.3	107.4	97.6	100	130.1	116.5
1997	119.6	105.1	95.2	100	128.5	114.8
1998	119.1	103.3	92.8	100	129.0	114.4
1999	118.8	104.2	92.9	100	131.7	115.8
2000	116.5	103.0	93.7	100	130.5	115.2
2001	115.1	100.5	92.5	100	128.0	113.1
2002	112.9	98.8	90.6	100	127.4	111.7

Source: Office for National Statistics.

In Europe there are some particular national productivity success stories, the United Kingdom and Ireland for example, but if the targets specified at the Lisbon Conference are to be realised then greater emphasis needs to be placed on research and development (R&D) as indicated at the Barcelona Summit of 2002. The knowledge-based industries have been successful in creating employment over the last decade, but overall productivity has been disappointing compared with the United States. Therefore EU policy needs to be directed more at business R&D to further stimulate productivity and provide competitive jobs for the future (Barnes and Asogbon 2004).

Conclusion

The demands made upon the labour market are ever-increasing. Today labour is required to be flexible, highly motivated, highly skilled and willing to adapt to change. Part of the force behind these changes in labour markets has been the globalisation of production and increased level of FDI and international trade (see Chapters 2, 6 and 7). The European Union has sought to make its economy one of the most competitive in the world, improving job opportunities and employment for the total workforce and in particular women and the young. At the same time competition has grown globally. One result of this is the great fear of social dumping. EU governments have sought ways to protect their labour forces from this. However, large amounts of social protection have resulted in the EU labour market being less flexible and more costly than some of its major competitors, the result of which has been a higher proportion of unemployment. EU labour markets are also characterised as being less flexible and lacking the mobility of those in the United

States. Partly this is a problem of language and culture, although issues about pensions and social security rights play their part too.

On the horizon for Europe as well as other parts of the world are also the demographic changes in the workforce, and the impact these changes will have on organisations and consumer demand. An ageing workforce requires both national and EU policies to deal with pensions, training, future labour shortages and issues about migration. It may well require a complete shift by some organisations in the way they consider the older workforce. However, for others the response may be to substitute capital for labour or to shift production outside the European Union altogether. Outsourcing/offshoring is not only a response to demographic change, but also a means by which organisations can achieve reductions in their cost base as well as improvements in technology. It appears that this is not going to disappear, and that other sectors and activities within the economy will go along the same route. This raises a number of important policy decisions, which some governments in Europe have been putting off for too long. They need to move on to higher valued-added products and services, and to do so they will need a flexible and well-educated and skilled workforce. Over the last decade there have been massive changes in the labour force and the demands placed upon it, and the future is likely to see even more change.

Questions

1   Currently more women and more part-time workers are employed in European labour markets but the level of unionisation has fallen. Alongside these facts, the European Union has introduced policies on maternity and paternity leave. Do all these features suggest that labour markets are becoming more flexible in Europe?

2   The managing directors of the Rover Group earned high rewards whilst the company incurred high levels of debt before going into receivership in 2005. Do you consider that Rover executives' pay should have been more of a reflection of the company performance?

3   Ignomenti, a dynamic Italian clothing firm, has always employed young designers and a young workforce while selling its products throughout Europe mainly to the 18–25 age group. What might be the implications for Ignomenti as the European population ages?

4   In the United Kingdom the introduction of a minimum wage in 1997 and its subsequent upward revisions have been associated with a period of growing male and female employment. Reconcile this with the theoretical view that the introduction of minimum wages should lead to a fall in employment.

5   In Europe there are skill shortages in many of its craft industries of workers such as electricians, plumbers and builders. What could be the impact on the European Union if it does not deal with the skill deficiencies in these areas?

6   What is the importance of labour productivity to an economy? Using Table 9.5, explain why the United Kingdom has begun to catch up other European countries.

Table 9.5 GDP per worker

Year	France	Germany	UK
1998	119.1	103.3	100
1999	118.8	104.2	100
2000	116.5	103.0	100
2001	115.1	100.5	100
2002	112.9	98.8	100

Source: Office for National Statistics.

References

Barnes, M. and Asogbon, G. (2004) *International Comparisons of Productivity: Better data improve UK productivity position*, Office for National Statistics, London.

Card, C. (1992) 'Do minimum wages reduce unemployment? A case study of California, 1987–89', *Industrial and Labour Relations Review*, vol. 46, no.1, pp. 38–54.

Card, C. and Kreuger, A. (1994) 'Minimum wages and unemployment: a case study of the fast food industry in New Jersey and Pennsylvania', *American Economic Review*, vol. 84, no. 4, pp. 772–93.

Caulkin, S. (2004) 'Why brain still beats brawn', *Observer Business*, 22 February, p. 9.

Cohen, N. (2004) 'When you fail, fail big', *Observer*, 4 July.

Connon, H. (2004) 'Executives eye pay rises to beat pensions cap', *Observer*, 3 October.

Cook, M. and Farquharson, C. (1998) *Business Economics*, Pitman, London.

Cook, M. and Jones, J. (2003) *Labour Market Information to Support Wellingborough East Masterplanning*, Report produced for Wellingborough District council, Matters of Fact.

Crafts, N. (2002) *Britain's Relative Economic Performance, 1870–1999*, Institute of Economic Affairs, London.

Daily Telegraph (2002) 'Daily Telegraph Recruitment Confidence Index', 11 April.

Disney, R. (1996) 'Why have older men stopped working?' in P. Gregg and J. Wadsworth (eds), *The State of Working Britain*, Manchester University Press, Manchester, pp. 58–74.

Eurobarometer (2001) 54.2, February.

Europa (2003) *Productivity: The Key to Competitiveness of European Economies and Enterprise*, European Commission, Brussels

European Central Bank (2002) *Labour Market Mismatches in Euro Area Countries*, March.

European Commission (1990) *1990–1991 The Social Dimension, Periodical 2*, Brussels.

European Commission (2001a) *Employment in Europe 2001*, Brussels.

European Commission (2001b) *New Labour Markets, Open for All with Access to All*, Brussels.

European Commission (2002a) *Action Plan for Skills and Mobility*, Brussels.

European Commission (2002b) *The Social Situation in the European Union 2002 – In brief*, Brussels.

European Industrial Relations Observatory (1998) *The UK and the International Division of Labour,* Brussels.

European Observatory (2001), *European Employment,* Spring, Brussels.

Ferner, A. (1997) 'Multinationals, relocation and employment in Europe', in J. Gual (ed.), *Job Creation: The role of labour market institutions,* Edward Elgar, Cheltenham.

French, J. and Treanor, J. (2004) 'Boardroom pay bonanza goes on', *Guardian,* 27 August.

Gardner, J., Pierre, G. and Oswald, A. (2001) *Moving for Job Reasons,* University of Warwick, September.

Gregg, P., Knight, G. and Wadsworth, J. (1999), 'The cost of job loss', in P. Gregg and J. Wadsworth (eds), *The State of Working Britain,* Manchester University Press, Manchester, pp. 249–58.

Groot, W. and Verberne, M. (1997) 'Ageing, job mobility and compensation', *Oxford Economic Papers,* 49, pp. 380–403.

Helgerson, J. L. (2002) 'The national security implications of global demographic change', *Better World Campaign,* 30 April, Denver, Colo.

Horvath, F. (2001) *An Overview of Labour Mobility in the United States,* US Bureau of Labour Statistics, Washington.

International Labour Organization (ILO) (2000) 'Conclusions concerning human resources development', International Labour Conference, 88th Session.

ILO (2002) 'An inclusive society for an ageing population: the employment and social protection challenge', April, Geneva.

Invest UK (2005) www.UK.gov.investUK, accessed 18 March 2005.

KPMG (2004) 'Australia ranks as one of the lowest cost business locations in the world', Sydney.

Layard, R., Nickell, S. and Jackman, R. (1994) *The Unemployment Crisis,* Oxford University Press, Oxford.

Machin, S. and Manning, A. (1994) 'The effects of minimum wages on wage dispersion and employment: evidence from the UK wages councils', *Industrial and Labour Relations Review,* vol. 47, no.2, pp. 319–29.

Mayes, D. and Kilponen, J. (2004) 'Factor mobility', in A. M. El-Agraa (ed.), *The European Union: Economics and policies,* 7th edn, Prentice Hall, Harlow.

Muhlau, P. and Horgan, J. (2001) 'Labour market status and the wage position of the lower skilled: the role of institutions and of demand and supply', European Low-Wage Employment Research Working Paper, July.

Munchau, W. and Atkins, R. (2004) 'EU productivity performance', *Financial Times,* 23 July , p. 17.

O'Mahoney, M. (1999) *Britain's Productivity Performance 1950–96: An international perspective,* NIESR, London.

OECD (1998) 'Work-force ageing', *OECD Employment Outlook,* pp. 123–51.

OECD (2003) *Economic Outlook* no. 73, report produced by J-P. Cotis, Paris.

PricewaterhouseCoopers (2002) *Managing Mobility Matters: A European Perspective,* London.

Sunday Business (2004) 'Back to bread and butter for Europe', 11 January.

TUC (2002) '"Fat cat" pay gap continues to rise: TUC calls for disclosure and restraint', press release, 21 March, London.

10 Industry policy and competition policy

Alan Jarman

Objectives

This chapter will consider:

■ the concept of competitiveness and the Lisbon strategy
■ **industry policy** (IP) and **competition policy** (CP) and their importance for EU competitiveness
■ definitions of and the rationale for IP and CP
■ the development of IP and CP in the European Union in the last 50 years
■ public procurement and state aid as aspects of IP
■ cartels, dominant firms, mergers and **joint ventures** as part of EU CP.

Introduction

This chapter considers two policy areas which are of great significance for the success of the new enlarged European Union: **industry policy** (IP) and **competition policy** (CP). The distinction between IP and CP is to some extent arbitrary and artificial, and there is considerable overlap between them; they are closely connected ideas. The key conceptual link for these two policy areas is the notion of 'competitiveness', a matter much referred to and discussed at all levels of the European Union.

The chapter first considers some possible definitions of and discussions of IP and its significance as indicated by the European Commission and others. It examines the rationale for, and the possible scope of, IP and the recent history of the concept in the EU context. Two important aspects of IP in particular will then be discussed, public procurement and state aid. The discussion of IP leads into our treatment of CP, as CP is usually considered as a part, or subset, of IP.

Aspects of IP are debated and commented on very frequently in the European Union by reporters, individual commissioners and EU MEPs as well as by politicians, academics, journalists, and business people in the individual states. For example the French Finance Minister Nicolas Sarkozy said (in the spring of 2004) that it was his intention to set up 'an interventionist industry policy to support French companies ... [and to] support economic activity despite all the budget constraints, and face world competition head-on with a pro-active industry policy' (*Guardian* 2004a). More recently he has argued that 'the question of an industry policy for Europe is a fundamental issue. ... The state has a role to provide for the future' (*Guardian* 2004b). Similarly French President Jacques Chirac has called on the European Union to help create industry champions in the new 25-state EU bloc: 'Let's strongly support the creation of European industrial champions. We have all the assets and all the talents that we need to succeed' (*European Business* 2004: 1). But what does IP mean in the EU context, and how can the development of the concept be traced?

IP in the EU context

The first elements of pan-European IP precede even the Treaty of Rome which set up the original European Economic Community of 'the six'. The Treaty of Paris of 1951 set up the European Coal and Steel Community (ECSC), with detailed plans for government investment in, and subsidy for, these two then vitally important industries. Interestingly this treaty, which was apparently occupied with specific economic affairs, has been seen by many commentators then and since as a key symbol of the real purpose of European integration: the creation of a stable and peaceful new western Europe.

The Rome treaty had little to say specifically about IP though individual member countries' governments were all, to some extent, involved in key industries like transport, shipbuilding and of course coal and steel. For example the French have a reputation for, and history of, direct government involvement in industrial affairs, the so-called 'dirigisme' and the 'indicative planning' they have used since the 1960s. In the United Kingdom too there has been much debate on the proper role of governments in industry; basically to intervene or to remain 'hands-off'. In the 1960s UK IP was based in the National Economic Development Office ('Neddy' as it came to be called) and the National Plan of the Wilson government. These are well-known exercises in interventionist government policies, an approach turned on its head by the privatisation and deregulation spirit of the Thatcher years in the 1980s and beyond. The Single Market initiatives and the Maastricht Treaty of the 1980s sought to tidy up and regularise the EU situation relating to member states' IPs, though it is still felt by some that 'a framework for an integrated Industry Policy is really yet to emerge' (Mercado, Welford and Prescott 2001: 193).

The evidence of recent years, and since 2000 in particular, shows considerable determination to press ahead with the process of creating such a framework for economic prosperity throughout the European Union, and this chapter reviews some important statements and opinions relating to IP in the European Union since 2000.

The year 2000 is significant as the year of the European Council meeting, in March at Lisbon. The Lisbon Agenda or the Lisbon Strategy which arose from this meeting laid great stress on the need for mutually agreed targets, processes and procedures to encourage and stimulate the economies of the members to become more productive, innovative and competitive. Specifically the meeting was to agree 'a new strategic goal for the next decade: to become the most competitive economy in the world by 2010' (Presidency Conclusions 2000: 1). Clearly these are very bold ideas and targets, and there was widespread agreement amongst the participants at the Lisbon meeting that 'something must be done'. All this does not seem very new, and it is not. The SEM initiatives in the 1980s were largely about **Eurosclerosis** and the need for a reinvigorated European Union, better to compete with the United States and Japan. The year after Lisbon, the Goteborg (Gothenburg) European Council had amongst its conclusions: 'The modernization of the European Economy must be vigorously pursued to achieve the Union's strategic goal ... competition in markets for goods, services and capital is vital' (Presidency Conclusions 2001: 3).

In September 2004 the individual commissioners of the new European Commission designate were asked to answer various questions set to them by relevant committees, prior to the new commission being ratified by the European Parliament. The committee on Industry, Research and Energy put some questions to the commissioner designate for Industry and Enterprise, Günter Verheugen. The first question they asked was the following:

> The 2004 Spring European Council ... asked the Commission to propose 'concrete steps aimed at increasing the competitiveness of European industry' implying the need for economic reforms. How should such reforms be financed, and what effects would a policy of national or even EU champions have on competition policy, innovative sectors and optimum market conditions for industry?
>
> (European Parliament 2004: 1)

In response Verheugen argued that there were few financial implications, and that the approach would be to increase competitiveness by 'the completion of the internal market' (still recognised as unfinished business after more than 15 years), and all that entails such that 'it will be necessary to improve the contri-bution of all Community policies to the fulfilment of the objective of industrial competitiveness' (European Parliament 2004: 2). Some commentators felt obliged to point out the irony of having Verheugen, a German Social Democrat, 'in charge of competitiveness' as the new commissioner for Enterprise and Industry, given that Germany has the third worst record for implementing inter-nal market legislation, only France and Greece having worse records (*Economist* 2004a). It should be noted here that there is a specific commis-sioner for CP as well as the commissioner for Enterprise and Industry. At pres-ent the CP head is Neelie Kroes, the Dutch nominee, with a reputation for hard work and integrity, and experience on the boards of several multinationals (*Economist* 2004b).

What is IP?

'Industry Policy means the initiation and co-ordination of governmental activi-ties to leverage up the productivity and competitiveness of the whole economy and particular industries within. Above all it means the infusion of goal-oriented strategic thinking into economic policy' (Van Zon 1996: 119). Van Zon's approach could include most micro and macroeconomic government activities that influence industry and business. The focus of EU IP is indeed about trying to coordinate policies, the policies of the member states, as well as initiating some of them. The role of the European Union is primarily that of trying to set a framework in which private economic activity can flourish, and especially one in which international competitiveness can be encouraged and enhanced.

The sorts of framework policy areas that can be viewed as coming within the range of EU IP could be regional policy, enterprise policy, research and development (R&D), transport, tourism, implementation of the Maastricht Treaty and the Single European Market (SEM), public procurement, state aid, mergers and alliances, and CP in general. The relevant commissioners therefore could include those for Regional Policy, Enterprise and Industry, Science and Research, Transport, Internal Market and Services, Competition, and also Employment, Social Affairs and Equal Opportunities, Trade, Energy, and Taxation and Customs.

From this list of some of the main relevant commissioners' areas of responsibility, it can be seen that the objective of promoting cohesion and coordination in member states' business and economic activities may need to start with efforts to coordinate policy making among these overlapping commissioners and their activities; something perhaps easier said than done.

Whatever may be argued about the nature of IP and how it works in practice, it must be recognised that this is a very political arena. A detailed study of IP in the United Kingdom which examined the special case of policy towards the shipbuilding industry in the 1980s and 1990s concluded that the 'policy' seemed to be no more than pragmatic politics, with little or no theoretical consistency of approach (Kean 1996). Barberis and May (1993) similarly argue that IP is fundamentally and inevitably a mixture of ideology, technical realities, pragmatism and politics, and indeed that IP is in fact really 'just politics'. Whilst this may appear to be an extreme position it is by no means a lone view, as Ward argues: 'The economic rationale has always been subservient to the demands of the various nation states, and not vice versa. Ideology always gives place to political expedience and accommodation' (Ward 1996: 101).

The theory behind, and the rationale for, IP

Whatever the theory or ideology behind any particular policy might be, two general observations may be made. First, there is widespread agreement that no interventionist policies should be pursued unless there is a clear expectation that the benefits will exceed the costs significantly. Second, as a corollary, it is agreed that any policy involving resource allocation decisions involves opportunity costs: in other words resources used in accordance with policy directives are not available for other uses. Here we encounter elements of the 'crowding out' argument. Government expenditure has to come from somewhere, and it may well deprive private sector enterprises of these resources. At the same time it may lead to higher interest rates, adding further costs to the private sector at large.

If, as has been suggested above, IP is about politics, defending national interests and governments seeking the approval of their electorates, it will be difficult to discern much theoretical support for these policies. Although it may be argued that it is difficult to unscramble the political and economic aspects of most policies nominally described as 'economic policies', it is possible to identify some different approaches to IP (Drazen 2000). Lynch (2003) discusses some types of IP and their possible business effects. He argues that it is possible to identify two distinct approaches to IP, an 'Anglo-Saxon', largely hands-off model and the 'dirigiste' model. The United States, the United Kingdom and Germany would be found in the Anglo-Saxon group, and typical dirigistes would be France, Italy and Greece. Lynch gives the information in Table 10.1.

Table 10.1 Government and industry policy

Laissez faire: free-market approach	*Dirigiste: centrally directed approach*
Competition encouraged	National companies/champions supported
Little/no support for industry	State ownership of some key industries
Self-interest leads to wealth creation	Profit motive benefits the few not the many
Belief in efficient markets	Market failure may adversely affect the poor, and lead to monopolies: state intervention may be required

Source: Lynch (2003).

He goes on to point out that most countries worldwide have a mix of these two; even the predominantly 'hands-off' regime in Singapore has strong government initiatives in education and certain favoured industries. The significance of understanding the different perspectives for businesses is that:

> Corporate strategy should therefore anticipate that politics will continue to be a part of the equation. Companies may benefit from policies such as state subsidies … but may be hindered by measures such as new laws restricting competition, [and] new taxes on profits. Hence corporate strategy needs to be acutely aware of the benefits and problems associated with government policies. It will certainly wish to press for policies that it regards as beneficial. … [L]obbying of governments by companies is a legitimate part of corporate strategy.
>
> (Lynch 2003: 150)

An example of a policy change, to be introduced in the European Union at least in part as a result of business lobbying, is the Bolkestein Directive due to come into force in 2006 at the earliest (Rowland 2005). This directive will make life easier for big firms operating in the European Union, specifically by prohibiting national rules or standards that make it difficult for European companies to enter the markets of other member states, and allow European companies to operate their businesses anywhere in the European Union according to the rules of their country of origin (Rowland 2005).

Another way of categorising IP approaches is suggested in Ferguson and Ferguson (1994): see Table 10.2.

The **laissez faire** approach according to Milton Friedman (1962) would involve the government in establishing a legal system, anti-trust agencies and control of the money supply, and very little else. Thus this policy approach is about setting up a framework in which private enterprise free markets can flourish, with the minimum of regulation and intervention by governments. The supportive approach is broadly similar to laissez faire but admits more instances

Table 10.2 Possible forms of industry policy

Policy approach	Policy form
Laissez faire	Very limited intervention through neutral policies
Supportive	Neutral policies
Active	Accelerative and or decelerative policies
Planning	Accelerative and or decelerative policies

Source: Ferguson and Ferguson (1994).

when some government involvement may be desirable, for example 'to improve the allocation and enforcement of property rights, to encourage education and entrepreneurship in order to foster the process of economic change [and] to adopt (retaliatory) protectionist measures (when appropriate)' (Ferguson and Ferguson 1994: 149). The active approach sees a much more involved role for government and government agencies, and supports for selected industries and possible protectionist measures, which are not necessarily retaliatory. The planning approach 'is a more extreme version of the active approach. Its rationale is that welfare can be improved through centralised planning' (Ferguson and Ferguson 1994: 149).

In terms of the policy form that may be taken, accelerative policies aim to promote economic growth by providing financial support to the most promising firms, markets or technologies. Perhaps the best known example of these sorts of initiatives are those of the Japanese MITI (the Ministry of International Trade and Industry). Decelerative policies are aimed either at temporary support for firms in trouble, or to help a dying firm to phase out with a minimum of disruption to the local and national economies.

IP in the United Kingdom

UK IP may be regarded as broadly falling in the supportive category of the Ferguson taxonomy. There is an emphasis on skills, enterprise, and research and development (R&D), rather than on subsidies and active planning interventions. The government wants to encourage competitiveness with horizontal approaches, rather than targeting specific firms (DTI 2002a). CP (see below) is a vital part of the government's stated strategy for competitiveness along with two other main components: technology policy, and education and training policy. Clearly education, particularly higher education, may contribute significantly to raising productivity and international competitiveness; however this is too broad a topic to discuss here. R&D policy is even more closely linked with IP, and we outline the UK government's position on R&D.

The scientific and engineering R&D done in UK universities is regarded as of special importance, and this is supported by the UK government, mainly through funding of research councils (Beath 2002). For R&D in the private sector the key incentive is the R&D tax credit which was made available to all UK firms in the 2002 budget. There is some evidence from the US that the elasticity of research spending with respect to tax credits (which have existed since 1981) is above unity. This means that every dollar of tax credit allowed (revenue lost to the government) generates more than a dollar of R&D spending (Beath 2002). Even if the UK R&D elasticities are similar, the introduction of such tax credits here may not be enough to achieve the improvements in R&D performance that the government hopes for, but it seems to be a step in the right direction. Furthermore, in December 1999 the UK government published the first-ever set of Competitiveness Indicators for the United Kingdom, designed to compare UK economic performance with that of other advanced economies. The indicators cover five key areas: investment, innovation, skills, enterprise and competitive markets. Many of these are highly relevant to our discussion here of IP and CP. The second (and latest) set of figures came out in February 2001 (DTI 2002b). The publication of this data is an interesting development, and is perhaps further evidence of the UK government's commitment to improving UK competitiveness and productivity.

IP in the European Union

In general, the European Union may also be considered to have a broadly supportive approach to IP, which means that the policy is generally non-interventionist but is used when deemed necessary to foster change and competitiveness, and perhaps may contain a retaliatory aspect if that is thought to be required. Using this theoretical framework two very important areas of EU IP can be examined: public procurement and state aid.

Public procurement

Public procurement is the purchase of goods and services by governments, national and local, and state-owned companies, usually by contract or tender. This includes, for example, purchases of cars for the police, IT equipment for state schools and public hospitals, and road building contracts. This public expenditure on supplies to the public sector is a very significant, and rising, proportion of the total GDP of the European Union. In the late 1990s official EU estimates of public procurement were at approximately 11 per cent of EU GDP. The estimate for 2002 (that is pre-enlargement to 25 member states) was 16 per cent or €1,500 billion, varying between member states from 11 to 20 per cent (SIMAP 2004).[1] €1,500 billion is, to state the somewhat obvious, very big business indeed, accounting for about one-sixth of all EU GDP.

The big issue in relation to public procurement is that nearly all governments tend to be highly nationalistic in the conduct of their public procurement and buy predominantly from domestic firms. Some estimates suggest that public authorities could save up to 30 per cent on the prices they pay to private suppliers and contractors if procurement operations were conducted in more open and competitive markets (*Financial Times* 2004). Moreover there is a long and murky history of collusive tendering for public contracts in the United Kingdom and the European Union, and indeed in North America too. Collusive tendering is much easier if the colluding companies know each other and operate in the same language. National governments, in their tendency to favour domestic firms, may actually be facilitating collusion among the tendering companies. So not only are governments who procure at home excluding the possibility of better, more competitive contracts with 'foreign' firms, they also may also be inadvertently encouraging deception as well. Such collusive tendering is notoriously difficult for CP authorities to detect.

European Commission directives urging more **transparency** in public procurement and more openness to bids from non-national firms have been issued periodically since they first appeared at the time of the Treaty of Rome in 1957 (Piggott and Cook 1999). These directives are supported by international agreements too. In 1979 the EC countries plus EFTA members and the United States, Canada, Japan and others, all agreed to, and signed, the Government Procurement Agreement (GPA). This proposed opening public procurement to full international competition. In 2004 the GPA, organised under the auspices of the World Trade Organization (WTO), was enlarged to include the ten new member states of the European Union, and it has now extended to Hong Kong, China and Switzerland. The GPA is the first WTO agreement to be adapted to the enlarged European Union. The commissioner for the Internal Market, Frits Bolkestein, argued that this was good news for the old as well as the new member states and should lead to significantly lower supply prices for public authorities (Europa 2004a). Thus there seems to be some progress towards greater openness and competition in public procurement. However it could be argued that the need for such 'progress' is evidence that things are not yet satisfactory in the public procurement sphere. It does seem that the Commission is willing to endorse change in its systems, if changes appear necessary to promote competition, in accordance with Ferguson's 'supportive' hypothesis.

So far, so good. However a very damning report on the state of EU public procurement was published in November 2004. The Wood Report (2004), a UK Treasury-commissioned report from the Chief Executive of Siemens UK, Alan Wood, argued that across the European Union, public procurement was still largely conducted in opaque ways. UK firms were losing out, argued Wood, because of the predominantly nationalistic purchasing policies of most EU states. As a result both Gordon Brown, the UK chancellor of the Exchequer, and John Cridland, of the UK Confederation of British Industry (CBI), called for more rigorous enforcement of the existing EU procurement directives (*Guardian* 2004c).

Apart from these sorts of problems there are also language difficulties. The Commission has urged all public authorities and others to use a Common Procurement Vocabulary (CPV) when drafting public procurement notices, in an attempt to make them easier for potential suppliers to understand. To appreciate the complexities we can note that the CPV lists 6,000 terms used in the procurement process in all EU official languages; and since the enlargement of the CBI to 25 the number of official languages has risen from 11 to 20! Simultaneous translation is supposed to happen between all 20 languages in all important meetings and for all significant documents. Attempts to do all the necessary translating are hardly working: only half of the required translators and interpreters have so far been recruited. The European Union of 25 states may well find itself lost for words (*Observer* 2004).

To conclude, it seems that between linguistic confusion and the negative remarks of the Wood Report, there is still much work for the Commission to do in terms of procurement policy before this aspect of IP in the European Union can be properly considered open and competitive.

State aid

State aid refers to the support that member states' governments give to individual companies or to specific sectors of the economy. It may also include so-called horizontal aid. Horizontal aid refers to the creation of frameworks or institutional arrangements which are designed to assist all industries, for example research and development initiatives. Current EU attitudes are strongly in favour of horizontal industry policy rather than aid to specific firms or industries.

The sort of things that are referred to as state aid include the following:

> *The obvious*: grants to firms for investment, research and development, training and cash injections to public enterprises. *The not-so obvious*: loans and guarantees, consultancy advice, creation of enterprise zones, aid to help environmental projects, tax deferrals, tax exemptions, aid to help public enterprises preparation for privatisation, [and so on]. *The surprising*: free advertising on State owned television, infrastructural projects benefiting identifiable end users.
>
> (DTI 2005, original italics)

The monitoring and reporting on state aid in the European Union is under the auspices of the Competition Commissioner. This reflects the fact that in the European Union state aid is seen, in theory at least, as an undesirable threat to or restriction of competition, and in general is subject to prohibition. It may be undesirable in theory perhaps, but it is still clearly much in favour with some EU governments wishing to support their own domestic firms or economies. Again the political dimension arises, with public procurement. A recent report on state aid, the *State Aid Scoreboard* (European Commission 2004) indicates the extent of state aid within the European Union. Total EU state aid for manufacturing, services, coal, agriculture, fisheries and transport was US$49 billion in 2002. This sort of spending is in decline. In 1997 it was €67 billion, in 1999 €52 billion and in 2001 €50 billion.

Clearly these are still absolutely large sums of money, but they are relatively small in comparison with the spending on public procurement. In absolute terms Germany granted the most aid with €13 billion, then France with €10 billion and Italy €6 billion. As a percentage of GDP, Denmark gave most aid at 0.72 per cent of GDP. Germany, Spain and Portugal made grants worth 0.55 per cent, and the United Kingdom, Finland, Sweden and the Netherlands spent about 0.2 per cent (European Commission 2004). The figures for 2002 confirm that member states are, for the most part, reducing aid levels in GDP percentage terms, and in absolute euros spent. They are also successfully redirecting aid towards horizontal objectives of common interest such as the strengthening of economic and social cohesion, environmental protection, promotion of R&D, and small and medium-sized enterprises (SMEs). In several member states nearly all the aid awarded in 2002 was for horizontal objectives, and in seven member states virtually all aid awarded in 2002 was for horizontal objectives. The Commission will often exempt aid from the general prohibition if market failures are being addressed, especially with respect to schemes to facilitate job creation for the recruitment of disadvantaged or disabled workers.

What forms do state aid typically take? Grants are by far the most common form of aid, being almost 60 per cent of the total, and tax exemptions make up 24 per cent. Of the cases it examines the Commission approves the vast majority: 95 per cent in 2003 (European Commission 2004).

However the Commission is still vigilant in monitoring state aid. 'This is because state aid that is not a part of a coherent EU-wide policy will frustrate free competition and prevent the most efficient allocation of resources', as Mario Monti, the then Commissioner for Competition, stated in April 2004. (*Guardian* 2004d). The EU 'official line' on state aid is fairly clear:

> Aids are prohibited in principle as they distort competition in the free market. Exceptions may be allowed by the Commission. If an exception is granted by the Commission it is done so to pursue the general objectives of the European Union, such as economic integration and cohesion, social welfare and environmental protection.
>
> The aim of these regulations is to create a level playing field for all industries in the Union and to stop companies gaining unfair competitive advantage due to government assistance. Regulations are essential as aid can strain national budgets and impede economic convergence. Aid to inefficient firms, which should restructure or disappear, prejudices the functioning of viable enterprises.
>
> (European Commission 1995: 3)

State aid: the legal framework

State aid is dealt with in EC Treaty Articles 87 and 88. The basic prohibition is set out in Article 87(1):

> Save as otherwise provided in this Treaty, any aid granted by a Member State or through State resources in any form whatsoever which distorts or threatens to distort competition by favouring certain undertakings or the production of certain goods shall, in so far as it affects trade between Member States, be incompatible with the common market.

There are however some clear and important exceptions to this blanket prohibition. The main discretionary exceptions are in Article 87(3) and cover:

a. regional aid to areas with abnormally low standards of living
b. projects of common European interest
c. the development of certain economic activities [sic]
d. the promotion of culture and heritage conservation.

Among the most commonly granted discretionary aids are those called 'rescue aids' and 'restructuring aids'. The guidelines for these aids were set out in a 1979 directive. Rescue aid must:

- consist of guarantees or loans bearing normal commercial interest rates
- be restricted to the amount needed to keep the firm in business
- be paid as part of a feasible recovery plan
- have no adverse effects on the industrial situation
- be a one-off operation.

Restructuring aid must meet five conditions:

- The *sine qua non* is that a restructuring plan must be capable of restoring long-term viability of the enterprise within a reasonable time scale.
- Measures must be instituted to offset as far as possible adverse effects on competitors. If there is overcapacity the aid recipient must cut capacity on a proportionate basis. If there is no overcapacity the aid recipient may not increase capacity.
- The amount of aid must be the minimum needed to enable restructuring to be undertaken; specific conditions and obligations are laid down.
- Detailed reports are required.

Procedures for supervision of state aid

Article 88 states the main procedures by which state aid is supervised. Article 88 states that the Commission shall keep under constant review all systems of aid existing in member states, and that if the Commission finds that aid is not compatible with the common market, or that such aid is being misused, it shall decide that the aid shall be abolished or altered. It also requires that the Commission shall be informed of any plans to grant or alter aid.

Thus from Articles 87 and 88 and the relevant directives, it would appear that the definition of state aid is open and transparent, with clear formal procedures for monitoring and control. As with many other aspects of business and economic life in the European Union, the reality is not quite so straightforward.

Another of the rules of Commission aid policy is the 'one-time, last-time' principle. This states that aid may be allowed (as above) for 'rescue' and or 'restructuring', but not as ongoing support. This one-time, last-time rule seems particularly feeble in the aviation context, as shown in two cases. In 1992 the Commission approved nearly £700 million of state aid to Iberia, on certain conditions: that the one-time last-time rule would have to apply, and that restructuring would take place. However in January 1996 the commissioner for Transport decided that Iberia could receive a further government hand-out of £460 million. The Commissioner's decision was unanimously adopted on the rather dubious grounds that the cash for the struggling airline was not aid in the traditional sense, and should be treated as an investment, justifiable on commercial grounds. Not surprisingly this decision caused some strong responses. The British Transport Secretary commented that the decision taken in the case of Iberia would 'undermine all our efforts to establish fair competition in the community aviation market' (*Guardian* 1996: 5). Almost ten years later the Iberia case has an almost exact parallel. Alitalia, the Italian national carrier airline was given €495 million in January 2005. Both the Italian government and Alitalia denied that the money was state aid; they claimed it was part of a vital restructuring plan. Alitalia had already enjoyed a very considerable amount of state aid in 1997. Having lost €330 million in 2003, the airline struggled to deal with high costs, higher oil prices, budget carrier competition and falling demand. Rival carriers Lufthansa, British Airways and interestingly also Iberia, complained to the Commission concerning the Italian government's aid to Alitalia, arguing that the one-time last-time rule should apply. The investigation into the Alitalia situation is expected to take up to 18 months, during which time of course it will keep the €495 million handout (BBC 2005).

The recent dispute between Ryanair and the European Commission in the case study on the following page illustrates the many points of debate concerning state aid in Europe.

A particular problem with state aid as a part of IP is the tendency for some governments to gamble on projects that may appear to be interesting, but are unable to obtain commercial funding in the marketplace. Specifically the question is, can governments 'pick winners'? The history of governments' attempts to do so is mixed, to say the least. In the United Kingdom the aid to the car company De Lorean in the late 1970s was an extreme example of active policy failure. John de Lorean, once a top US auto industry executive, received many millions of pounds from the UK government to build a totally new factory near Belfast, for a totally new car. The scheme failed, costing the UK taxpayer millions, though a few 'de Loreans' were in fact made, and one can be seen as the time machine in the *Back to the Future* films. Obituaries for de Lorean in the British press, in March 2005, described him as a con man, but one who was able to persuade the UK government to part with millions of pounds.

The European Union and the relevant commissioners pour out directives, statements of intent and exhortations to member states, in respect of making the European Union a more competitive environment for business. The ambitious Lisbon Agenda, with its objective, or dream, of Europe becoming the most competitive economy in the world by 2010, still seems a very long way off. It appears that the 'integrated' European Union can still be described as a loose grouping of nation states whose governments are likely to pursue their own national and political interests first, and that the objectives of cooperation, cohesion and integration are still to be achieved.

Does EU competition policy (CP) work in a more coherent and consistent way to contribute to the achievement of the aims and objectives of the European Union?

What is meant by CP?

CP is open to several interpretations. It can be interpreted as any activities or rules designed either to promote competitive economic or business behaviour, or to inhibit the restriction of competitive forces. By this interpretation economic policies, directives and initiatives of individual governments and the European Union could be included. However this is too wide, thus the focus here will be to consider the laws and regulations directly relating to monopoly, merger, acquisition, restrictive practices and the like. In the European Union this stems mainly from Article 81 (formerly Article 85) and Article 82 (formerly Article 86) of the Treaty of Rome, and is the responsibility of the commissioner

RYANAIR AND CHARLEROI AIRPORT

Charleroi is a town in a region of high unemployment in the Walloon region of Belgium south of Brussels. The regional authorities had been subsidising Ryanair flights into and out of the publicly owned Charleroi airport to about 12 destinations. Some were near major cities like Glasgow, Rome, Dublin, Milan, Venice and Stockholm, but others were smaller places like Shannon, in the west of Ireland, Valladolid in north-west Spain, and Carcassonne in south-west France. All of these flights were to relatively under-used airports, like Skavsta (60 miles from Stockholm) and Treviso (30 miles from Venice). The authorities in Charleroi were more than happy to give some financial support to Ryanair's venture. To them, in an area of economic downturn, the opportunity to encourage visitors from these cities was very welcome. Ryanair was given rebates in landing taxes, grants towards the cost of accommodation for crews between flights, and cash to help pay for its pilot training programme.

In the spring of 2004 the European Commission ordered Ryanair to pay back €4 million that Ryanair had received as 'illegal subsidies'. As the airport was state-owned, the grants given to Ryanair amounted to state aid, the Transport commissioner argued. In October Ryanair agreed to put the €4 million into an escrow (holding) account until its appeal had been heard. It also announced that it had lodged an appeal at the Court of First Instance, challenging the decision that the subsidies were illegal.

Ryanair argued that the partnership with the Walloon authorities had enabled ordinary consumers to fly at Europe's lowest fares, encouraging development of unused, empty secondary regional airports. Ian Hudghton, a Scottish MEP, argued that it was not just the Charleroi region that gained:

The route from Glasgow-Prestwick to Charleroi is the only air link from the west of Scotland, a very populous area, to the capital of Europe area. I hope that the Commission will not be over-enthusiastic and end up disadvantaging consumers, including many who wish, and need, to visit the EU's headquarters and the other European institutions.

(Hudghton 2004)

Two of Ryanair's low-cost flight competitors, BMIbaby and Easyjet, argued otherwise. They said that the Charleroi decision would increase competition, and declared themselves to be against state aid in the aviation industry. Though the decision relates specifically to Ryanair and Charleroi, Easyjet chief executive Ray Webster said:

we understand the Commission will use this ruling as the basis for bringing forward guidelines on the commercial relationship between airlines and publicly-owned airports. We look forward to working with the Commission to produce guidelines that will benefit the EU consumer.

(*Derby Evening Telegraph* 2004: 14)

Sources: *Derby Evening Telegraph* (2004), Hudghton (2004), BBC (2004b).

Questions

1　Would you support or condemn the subsidies paid to Ryanair? Explain carefully why.
2　Do you think these subsidies are in fact state aid, or might they be classified as regional assistance, or be entitled to exemption under Article 87 on other grounds?

for Competition. There is a distinct overlap between areas designated as 'industry policy' and 'competition policy', and their effects on companies may also overlap and intertwine. Similarly the areas of influence of the commissioners for Enterprise and Industry, Competition and the Internal Market could overlap.

The objectives of CP

There is considerable debate about the objectives and the efficacy of CP, both in the United Kingdom and in the European Union. The United States has the oldest system of CP rules in the world, dating back to 1890, apart from the Romans who had a law that punished price-fixing by death, or banishment to Britain (Beath 2002). In the European Union the SEM has a very strong presumption that competition is a 'good thing', and that the 'restructuring' of industry anticipated as a result of the SEM and the enforcement of EU CP will give rise to substantial efficiency gains (see Chapter 4).

Neo-classical theory tells us that welfare is optimised, or achieves Pareto optimum, when perfect competition prevails in all markets. The welfare gains from competition may paradoxically be easier to illustrate in reverse, by consideration of the situation where welfare is forfeited because elements of monopoly are present.

Figure 10.1 shows an industry operating both under perfectly competitive conditions and where an element of monopoly is present. In perfect conditions the competitive price is set equal to marginal cost, at P_c, and output is Q_c. If the industry becomes a monopoly overnight, price will be set above P_c at P_m, and output will fall to Q_m. This is the 'classic case' against monopoly: so long as cost conditions stay the same, the price is higher, and output lower, under monopoly than under competitive conditions.

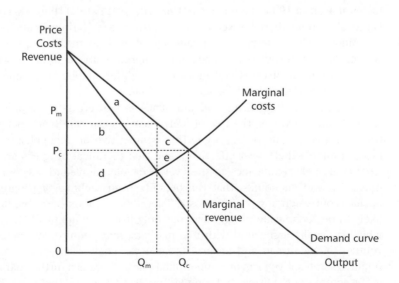

Figure 10.1 The deadweight loss of welfare as a result of monopoly

Under competitive conditions the triangle a+b+c is consumers' surplus, and the area d+e is producers' surplus. Under monopoly conditions consumers' surplus is reduced to triangle a and producers' surplus is now b+d. There is a possible value judgement that transferring area b from consumers to producers generates a loss to society, but this argument involves the idea that producers' surplus is somehow worth less to society than is consumers' surplus. This value judgement does not need to be made, however, to identify the absolute loss of triangles c+e. They are simply gone; this is the so-called 'deadweight loss' to society as a result of monopoly pricing and output, in contrast with what would happen under competitive conditions. Monopoly, therefore leads to social welfare losses, and is a 'bad thing'. This in essence is the rationale behind most forms of CP. Competition is said to have other desirable effects too. Carlin calls these the 'incentive effect' and the 'selection effect'. The incentives are to increase market share, reduce average costs and make more profit. The selection effect is the process whereby inefficient firms get driven out by the efficient and innovative (Carlin, Haskel and Seabright 2001).

Attempts have been made to estimate the extent of the loss of GNP attributable to the output-restricting effects of monopoly. The seminal work on this question was undertaken by Harberger (1954), who suggested that for the United States the loss, depending on the nature of the various elasticities and other estimates, would only be about 0.1 per cent of GNP per year. If Harberger's estimate is reliable this would suggest that monopoly power is a fairly trivial matter as far as society's welfare is concerned, and that CP would hardly be necessary. If the losses due to monopoly are trivial it might also be argued that the potential gains from an increase in competition may have been overstated hitherto.

Many other analysts have considered this question of the costs of monopoly. Cowling and Mueller (1978) reworked the figures and assumed a high degree of monopoly control over prices; on their various assumptions they estimated the losses at around 10 per cent of GNP. The 'true' estimate, if there exists a figure, is probably somewhere between the two extremes of Harberger and of Cowling and Mueller. Critics argue that in this line of analysis the attempt to measure welfare loss or resource misallocation is merely static analysis based on the price and output of firms and industries at different points in time, without consideration of their 'performance' over time.

If the behaviour of firms and industries is viewed as a dynamic process through time, however, the role of R&D becomes critical. Schumpeter (1954), Galbraith (1963) and others argue that competitive or oligopolistic 'big business' promotes R&D most effectively, and that technical progress arising from R&D is of such significance in the overall development and success of firms, industries and economies that the benefits from technically progressive big business outweigh any possible costs. There is a paradox here: big business is likely to be technically progressive, but only if it is competitive. Competition, which is usually associated with free markets, may require government intervention to encourage and ensure its success. That is, effective competition requires some active form of competition policy. There is a further paradox, too, in the context of EU firms, and competition. It is often said that many European firms are too large relative to the size of their domestic and European markets, leading to dominant or monopoly behaviour and a lack of competitive pressures; while at the same time these very firms that are 'too large' may be too small to effectively compete with US and Japanese firms for global markets.

The purpose of EU CP

The main elements of the law relating to CP in the European Union are stated in Articles 81 and 82 of the Treaty of Rome. However, even before the drawing up and signing of the Treaty of Rome, in March 1957, the concept of competition had figured prominently in the deliberations of the original six member states. The foreign ministers of the Six met at Messina in Sicily in 1955 to produce a declaration, a key phrase of which referred to the vital role to be played by the forces of unfettered competition in the Community. Following on from this declaration came the Spaak Report (1957), which declared that:

> The object of the European Common Market should be to create a vast zone of common economic policy, constituting a powerful unit of production permitting continuous expansion and increased stability and accelerated raising of the standard of living ... [in] Member States. ... These advantages of a Common Market cannot be obtained unless ... practices whereby competition between producers is distorted are put to an end.
>
> (Spaak 1957: 10)

The report went on to give clear and detailed requirements of the CP to be incorporated in the Treaty.

> It will be necessary to prevent
> - a division of markets by agreement between enterprises, since this would be tantamount to re-establishing the compartmentalisation of the market;
> - agreements to limit production or curb technical progress because they would run counter to progress and productivity;
> - the absorption or domination of the market for a product by a single enterprise, since this would eliminate one of the essential advantages of a vast market, namely that it reconciles the use of mass production techniques with the maintenance of competition.
>
> (Spaak 1957: 13)

Following in the tradition of the very pro-competition statements made in the Messina Declaration and the Spaak Report, the Commission has continued to make its feelings well known on the importance of competition and CP. Each year since 1972 the Commission has published a report on CP. The first report (1972) contains a very clear statement of the benefits of competition:

> Competition is the best stimulant of economic activity since it guarantees the widest possible freedom of action to all. An active competition policy pursued in accordance with the provisions of the Treaties establishing the Communities makes it easier for the supply and demand structures

continually to adjust to technological development. Through the interplay of decentralised decision-making machinery, competition enables enterprises continuously to improve their efficiency, which is the *sine qua non* for a steady improvement in living standards and employment prospects within the countries of the Community. From this point of view, competition policy is an essential means for satisfying to a great extent the individual and collective needs of our society.

(European Commission 1972: 12)

In the ninth report on Competition Policy (1980) the Commission took the argument a step further:

It is an established fact that competition carries within it the seeds of its own destruction. An excessive concentration of economic, financial and commercial power can produce such far-reaching structural changes that free competition is no longer able to fulfil its role as an effective regulator of economic activity.

(European Commission 1980: 3)

The Commission argued, here, that any genuine competition by its very nature must have winners and losers. The winners may be expected to go from strength to strength, ultimately achieving a position of some dominance. It is in this sense that 'competition carries within it the seeds of its own destruction', and competition policy has a vital role to play in ensuring and maintaining competitive market structures.

This view of the importance of competitive market structures, to be maintained by competition policy, is at odds with the Chicago School view. These theorists assume that if barriers to market entry are typically low, any excess or monopoly profit will quickly attract new entrants, thus driving down profit rates to something approaching 'normal' profit levels. Competition policy administrators should intervene only therefore in those cases where price/cost margins are abnormally high (as the result of cartels or other collusive behaviour). The Commission in reality is clearly unwilling to accept this reliance on market forces.

The Commission further developed its position on competition policy and market structure (abuse of dominant firm position), as well as in the policing of restrictive practices, in the seventeenth report (1988):

As the completion of the internal market by 1992 gathers pace, competition policy is coming more to the fore. ... There is an increasing awareness amongst the general public that the absence of an effective competition policy entails substantial costs since it is always the taxpayer who pays for unjustified State subsidies and the consumer who pays through higher prices and lower efficiency due to cartels, price fixing, abuses by dominant firms and other restrictive practices. ... The overall economic policy of the Community has the threefold aim of promoting a co-operative strategy for the creation of employment, of strengthening economic and social cohesion and of achieving an internal market.

(European Commission 1988: 7)

Thus the task of Community CP, according to the Commission, is to determine how best to contribute to the achievement of these major economic objectives.

The Commission continues to state its commitment to a vigorous and effective CP. The newly appointed commissioner for Competition made a powerful statement of the values and purposes of CP in February 2005 (Kroes 2005). Thus CP is seen as vital and has a key role to play in ensuring that the gains from the SEM are realised. But how do these very clear and strong 'mission' statements fit with the practice of competition policy within the European Union?

The practice of EU CP

The two main pillars of Community competition law applying to private firms or 'undertakings' are Articles 81 and 82. Article 81 prohibits agreements and concerted practices with an anticompetitive object or effect on the market, and agreements that may restrict competition in inter-state trade. Article 82 prohibits abuse of a dominant position. This paragraph and what follows are heavily dependent on an official EU website for CP (Europa 2004b, *Competition Introduction*).

Article 81

We have a very clear statement of the law in Article 81, which 'prohibits agreements and concerted practices between firms which may affect trade between member states and which have as their object or effect the prevention, restriction or distortion of competition within the common market' (Europa 2004b). More specifically we are told that 'a restrictive agreement is an agreement between undertakings whose objective is to limit or eliminate competition between them in order to increase the prices and profits of the undertakings concerned without producing any counterbalancing advantages'. Examples of restrictive agreements are 'price fixing; production quotas; sharing markets, customers or geographical areas; bid-rigging; or a combination of these practices'. Article 81 also considers 'concerted practices', and states:

> a concerted practice is a step below a restrictive agreement. It involves coordination among firms which falls short of an agreement proper. A concerted practice may take the form of direct or indirect contact between undertakings whose object or effect is either to influence market behaviour or to let each other know what conduct they intend to adopt in the future.
>
> (Europa 2004b)

The concept of a concerted practice has been taken to include something less than a formal agreement or contract, but which nonetheless is designed to replace competition by cooperation. The phrase 'which may affect trade between member states' is also an important part of Article 81. If there is no effect, actual or potential, on inter-member trade then Article 81 does not apply; but individual national CP rules could still operate. 'Affect' has been interpreted by the European Court of Justice (ECJ) to mean activities that undermine the unity of the market, irrespective of whether the activity actually increases or decreases trade. Thus it is the distortion of the conditions of, and for, competition and not the consequences which are vital. Furthermore, agreements may be caught by Article 81 if they 'may' affect competition. That is, potential restrictions on competition may be enough for an agreement to be prohibited, as illustrated in the well-known *Pronuptia* case [1986 ECR 353], where a potential limitation on the franchisee's areas of operation was enough for the ECJ to condemn the agreement (Korah 2003). Indeed even:

> the term competition has been interpreted as referring not only to actual but also to potential competition. ... [in one case] the Court ruled that a commitment not to manufacture a product, undertaken by a firm not presently capable of manufacturing such product, constituted a restriction of competition.
>
> (Van Bael and Bellis 1989: 33)

Since it is not easy to distinguish between restrictive agreements, and concerted practices a broad overall policy has been established.

> Certain types of agreement are prohibited almost without exception. These are
> - horizontal or vertical agreements that fix prices directly
> - agreements on conditions of sale
> - agreements that partition or share markets
> - agreements on production or delivery quotas
> - agreements on investments
> - agreements conferring exclusive rights to public service contracts
> - agreements leading to discrimination against other trading parties
> - collective boycotts
> - agreements not to engage in certain types of competitive behaviour.
>
> (Europa 2004b)

These Article 81 prohibitions cover horizontal and vertical agreements (see Chapter 1). Horizontal agreements refer to firms at the same stage of a productive process, for example two maltsters both sourcing beer brewers. A vertical agreement could be one between a maltster and a brewer, that is, firms at different stages of a production or distribution process. (These firms could also be described as being at different stages in the supply chain.)

Certain types of agreement may be exempted from the general prohibition of Article 81; there may be block exemptions and individual exemptions. Block exemptions exist for certain categories of vertical agreement, such as supply or distribution agreements, and also for some horizontal agreements such as R&D agreements. Furthermore agreements that do not formally qualify for block exemption may still be granted individual exemption status if the agreement's restrictive effect is counterbalanced by contributions it makes to general welfare, again emphasising possibilities for research or technical progress benefits. A classic example of the block exemption scheme and its problems can be seen in Case study 10.2

However before considering the case study, it must be noted that another possible exemption route exists too. The *de mimimis* principle can apply to agreements deemed to be of minor importance, and which would not affect competition in the common market, and may encourage cooperation between SMEs. Such exemptions can only be granted by the Commission, thus inevitably slowing the whole process down. Thus a whole range of restrictive practices are outlawed by Article 81.

UK legislation in Chapter 1 of the Competition Act of 2000 has provisions against restrictive agreements in language and purpose that are very similar to Article 81. The previous legislation under the Restrictive Practices Acts was different from the EU rules in various ways, and this added to business uncertainties over what the different competition authorities might seek to permit or to condemn. The new UK regime, and the Competition Commission it has established, go some way to removing these differences and uncertainties. However the UK CP authorities still seem some way behind the new Competition Commissioner, Neelie Kroes, in her enthusiasm to invigorate the operation of EU CP:

> I want to get out there and actively promote good competitive practice in the internal market. It is not enough to try to correct anticompetitive behaviour once the damage has been done. ... the regulatory framework may [itself] unnecessarily and as an unintended by-product, hold back competition. We need to look again at how we can improve the effective enforcement of the competition rules.
>
> (Kroes 2005: 4)

Historically the Commission has sometimes taken a rather 'softly softly' approach in Article 81 cases. In the Interbrew case of 1994, the Belgian brewer had negotiated rights to be the sole distributor in Belgium of two luxury lagers, the Danish brands Tuborg and Carlsberg. The Commission first said that this sole distributorship was against the public interest. Tuborg and Carlsberg then entered into a joint venture for the distribution of its products with a second Belgian distributor. The Commission was satisfied with this result, as it increased competition in this market. The Commission also approved an agreement in the Dutch brickmaking industry designed to reduce capacity by 30 per cent. This could be considered as collusive practice; however the Commission allowed the proposal to go ahead, seeing it as a constructive reorganisation of the industry which was expected to reduce costs and hopefully lead to lower prices to the end consumer.

By contrast, in 1996 the Commission announced substantial fines on five cross-Channel ferry companies, deemed to have violated Article 81. The five companies had been operating a cartel inasmuch as they raised prices in an agreed and collective manner. The companies argued in their own defence that the price rises (a surcharge on cross-Channel freight shipments) were necessary to maintain a reasonable level of profits and to compensate for the effects of the depreciation of the pound (at that time). The Commission dismissed this 'defence', and declared against the cartel: it was a 'concerted practice' coming

CAR PRICES IN THE EUROPEAN UNION

For many years there has been discussion and debate about the different levels of prices for cars in the various countries of the European Union. Why was it the case for example that prices for cars made in one country might actually be higher than in other European countries? There were issues about exclusive dealerships, after-sales service and so on, and the motor trade tried hard to justify the prices charged with reference to different market conditions in different countries. In 2002 the European Commission adopted new rules covering the way cars are sold and repaired across the European Union.

The car industry had been exempt from normal EU competition legislation under the so-called block exemptions. Both consumer groups and non-traditional car dealers, such as car supermarkets and online showrooms, have long argued that the block exemption rules robbed consumers of choice. The key elements in the exemption were these:

● The requirement that dealers of new cars must also provide after-sales services (including regular servicing). This is called 'tying' in competition policy jargon, and is not usually permitted.
● The requirement to use brand specialists 'for the repairs of complex modern cars'.
● Manufacturers were allowed to limit the number of authorised dealers and to decide on the location of authorised repairers.
● Independent garages were not able to get access to technical information, training, tools, repair shop equipment and original spare parts on the same terms as authorised dealers.

All of these conditions were to be removed. The removal of the first was welcomed by the authorised dealers, but the other changes were all objected to either by them and/or the manufacturers. However the (then) Competition Commissioner, Mario Monti, said that 'rather than being a freely competitive market, the European auto sector has for years been dominated by a handful of firms in an oligopoly situation' (BBC 2002: 5). The car makers said they wanted to avoid supermarket-style car showrooms run by independent car distributors, arguing that consumers would lose out if specialist after-sales care was put at risk, that small dealers could be driven out, and that brand integrity might be 'diluted'.

Christopher Macgowan of the UK Society of Motor Manufacturers and Traders said there was 'no evidence of a shortage of consumer choice, and that prices were not influenced by the block exemption' (BBC 2002: 7). Further the German chancellor, Gerhard Schroeder, warned that destruction of the block exemption could prompt job losses in Germany's auto industry and might bring serious competitive disadvantage to the German car industry (BBC 2002: 6). The restrictions on 'car supermarkets' are due to be phased out in late 2005.

By contrast the British Consumers Association had lobbied for these sorts of changes, the UK Office of Fair Trading pointed out that cars cost more in the United Kingdom than elsewhere in the European Union, and between 2001 and 2002 UK car prices fell by about 10 per cent after the government ordered the industry to stop 'ripping off' customers.

Since the rules were changed prices have started to converge across the member states. In 2005 the Competition Commissioner, Neelie Kroes, said 'the new legal framework for car distribution and strict enforcement of EU competition rules will contribute to further price convergence throughout the EU' (*EU Business* 2005: 2). Estonia is now the cheapest place in the European Union to buy cars, though the cheapest car on sale was the Fiat Panda in Poland. Finland is the least expensive market among the European Union's old 15 members, with prices on average 10 per cent less than in Germany, which is the most expensive. The Opel Astra costs 50 per cent more in Germany than in Denmark, a saving for a German consumer of €3,700 for simply crossing the border to make the purchase.

Sources: BBC (2002), EU Business (2005).

Questions

1 Put forward arguments in favour of, and against, the block exemption regime that existed before 2002.

2 What would you expect to happen to car prices, and the quality of after-sales service, in the UK and EU car markets in the next two to three years? Explain your answers carefully.

within the scope of Article 81. More recently the EU CP authorities have shown more determination. In January 2005 three chemical firms were fined a total of €220 million for fixing the market in monochloroacetic acid, a widely used household and industrial chemical. The three firms, Hoechst, Atofina and AkzoNobel, along with the Swiss firm Clariant controlled over 90 per cent of the €125 million European market for the chemical. The companies had allocated volumes and customers and agreed prices. Clariant were given immunity as a reward for 'whistleblowing' on the others and cooperating with the investigating authorities, whereas Hoechst and Atofina had their fines increased as repeat offenders (*Guardian* 2005a).

The whistleblower immunity is an interesting part of EU CP which has only recently been introduced in the United Kingdom. One 2003 case which has received some publicity involved a fee-fixing cartel involving many of England's most famous and prestigious private schools. One of the schools cooperated with the CP authorities and informed on the other cartel members, and thus escaped penalty. This variant of the **prisoner's dilemma** has been a part of EU CP for some time, but is new to the United Kingdom.

Article 82

Article 82 provides that:

> Any abuse by one or more undertakings of a dominant position within the common market or in a substantial part of it shall be prohibited as incompatible with the common market in so far as it may affect trade between Member States.

> (Europa 2004b)

Again we rely on this official EU CP source for the next paragraph. There is abuse of a dominant position when the conduct of the firm in question is such that it may influence the structure of its market and/or the extent of competition therein. This prohibition shall operate even if the activity in question is permitted by the company's national law. As usual where there is a conflict of laws, the EU law takes precedence. A dominant position, to come within Article 82, must prevail in at least a substantial part of the common market.

Such abuse may, in particular, consist in:

- directly or indirectly imposing unfair purchase or selling prices or other unfair trading conditions
- limiting production, markets or technical development to the prejudice of consumers
- applying dissimilar conditions to equivalent transactions with other trading parties
- making the conclusion of contracts subject to acceptance by the other parties of supplementary obligations which, by their nature or according to commercial usage, have no connection with the subject of such contracts.

Thus the first paragraph of the Article sets out the prohibition of any abuse of a dominant position within the common market and its possible effects on trade between member states. The second paragraph gives some illustrative examples of abuse of a dominant position. It is worth noting here that Article 82, unlike Article 81, does not provide for block or individual exemptions.

In the *Continental Can* case [1973, ECR 215] the ECJ made it clear that Article 82 would cover not only practices that cause damage to consumers directly, but also those that are detrimental to consumers' interests through their impact on effective competitive structures, as in the last three points above. In any action under Article 82 two elements must be present, the existence of a 'dominant position' and 'abuse' of the dominant position.

The 'dominant position argument'

In the *Sirena* case [1971, CMLR 260] dominance was stated to be a position that could prevent effective competition within an important part of the market. In the case of *United Brands* [1978, ECR 207] it was stated that a dominant position is 'a position of economic strength enjoyed by an undertaking which enables it to prevent competition being maintained in the relevant market by giving it the power to behave to an appreciable extent independently of its competitors, customers and ultimately of its consumers' (Van Bael and Bellis, 1989: 49).

But how is the 'relevant market' defined? Over the years many aspects of the relevant market have been considered in various test cases. The degree of interchangeability, or substitutability has been used as an attempt to define the relevant market. Thus in the *United Brands* case the banana was considered to be sufficiently different from other fruits as to constitute a market on its own; in *Hoffman-La Roche* [1979, 3 CMLR 211] it was held that vitamins for industrial and bio-nutritive uses were in different product markets, while in *Michelin* [1983, ECR 3461], it was held that the markets for replacement tyres for trucks and buses were different from the market for the supply of tyres to original vehicles. The relevant geographic market also needs to be defined. Article 82 refers to dominance 'within the common market or in a substantial part of it'. On the whole the court is willing to define relevant geographic markets quite narrowly, even going as far as the smallest of member states.

Having determined the relevant market, the court then has to consider whether a company is indeed dominant within it; the concept of market power. In *Hoffman-La Roche* the court referred to a number of elements comprising market power: market share, and the share of competitors, the company's technical lead, its highly developed sales network and the absence of potential competition. Barriers to entry and vertical integration have also been considered in the market power context. Thus it can be said that the court typically tries to define relevance quite narrowly, making it easier for the court to establish dominance.

'Abuse' of a dominant position

In contrast to the narrow definitions of the market, abuse of a dominant position has been construed rather widely. In *Hoffman-La Roche* (see above) an objective test was used in which the court considered whether firms' operating methods were different from those which exist under conditions of normal competition. The sorts of behaviour which may be considered different are such things as excessive prices, discriminatory prices, predatory pricing and refusal to supply. Thus it seems that the court is willing to try to extend the scope of Article 82, and that the abuse of monopoly power will frequently be condemned by the court. But as Ward notes, 'this area of law is riddled by the inconsistencies which beset any jurisprudence which is decided on an essentially ad hoc basis' (1996: 130). It is not always easy to predict what the court or Commission's view is likely to be in any given case, adding uncertainty and increased transaction costs to the firm's wish to find out where it stands in relation to the CP rules, and this is far from satisfactory.

Overall, Articles 81 and 82 of the Treaty of Rome appear to give the Commission wide powers of enforcement and prohibition in CP. The way in which CP has been used, and applied, has not always been consistent and has been surrounded by a certain degree of complexity. For example, from 1962 onward the Commission had exclusive powers to authorise restrictive agreements under Article 81; this led companies to notify large numbers of agreements to the Commission (Europa 2004b). The Commission then had to consider centrally all these thousands of notified agreements, which was not surprisingly a cumbersome and slow process. However new rules were introduced in May 2004 (at last!), which replaced the previous centralised control system with a directly applicable exception system based on decentralised application of the CP rules. It is hoped that these reforms will greatly shorten the time taken for agreements to be notified and adjudicated upon. Certainly it has long been felt that many aspects of the administration of the CP rules need simplifying and speeding up. If not, they may similarly exhibit the economic problem of market failure that the rules are designed to remedy.

Each of the 25 commissioners (one from each member state) has an area of responsibility rather similar to a ministry within the UK government. The Commission develops policy proposals, which must then go through a process of deliberation and discussion involving the Council of Ministers and the European Parliament. When policies have been decided upon the Commission then implements them as directives, decisions and regulations. All three have the force of law. Directives act through national legislatures, requiring legislation to be developed appropriate to each country. Decisions normally affect a specific company, person or country. Regulations have general applicability throughout the European Union. The ECJ has a wide jurisdiction, including the interpretation of, and adjudication on, disputes arising from EU legislation, and the court has taken a number of decisions which have altered or extended some EU laws. In addition to the ECJ, another court, the Court of First Instance, was established in 1989. This court has a more limited jurisdiction but can deal with actions initiated by Commission officials, damages cases and competition cases.

Both the ECJ and the Court of First Instance have a considerable volume of work to handle. The ECJ has a backlog that increases each year, and even the new Court of First Instance began with a deficit. Competition rules become part of the law of all member states, and in the spirit of the *aquis communautaire* it is assumed that all member states will comply. Any agreements or arrangements that infringe these rules are prohibited, and national courts will not enforce contracts that infringe the rules. The interaction between national courts and the EU courts can and does give rise to considerable complexities, and it may be very important for companies to consider the implications of CP when planning marketing and production activities. Fines can be levied on companies that are deemed to have violated Article 81 or 82 (as high as 10 per cent of the previous year's turnover), and contracts that violate the rules are void and unenforceable. Thus we can see that the implications of CP for business can be very significant. The CP rules have wide application and can carry severe penalties. Firms need to be aware of these rules and to behave accordingly.

Some heavy fines have been imposed (see the 2005 chemicals case, above) and the existence of the rules and the threat of substantial fines seem to have a deterrent effect on the behaviour of organisations. On the other hand, there is no doubt that the Competition Commissioner's department is under-resourced in its budget and its staffing. It is a familiar part of the critique of CP in the United Kingdom, United States and Canada as well as the European Union, that the strong words of the legislation and regulations do not always tally with the power of the bureaucrats to 'make things happen'.

Sampson (1983, 2004) has written extensively on the interconnections between government, civil service and business in the United Kingdom. In the 21st century he argues, 'the elite looks [even] more unified, as a small number of familiar names keep reappearing in different disguises' (2004: 355). In Europe too there is a close socio-economic class linkage between governments, civil servants (that is to say, European commissioners and their staffs) and business executives. From this point of view it should not really be surprising if CP is not vigorously enforced, or adequately resourced, as those who are expected to police the business world and its behaviour are from precisely the same group of people as those who run the businesses. Put a little more technically, this is the theory of regulatory 'capture'. The regulators and the businesses they are supposed to regulate are bound to be closely connected by the very nature of their activities; therefore there is a distinct possibility that the regulators simply become the 'puppets' of their industrial charges. The comparisons with IP are plain. There is a very strong argument that IP, both of the European Union and of member states, is primarily driven by political considerations both formal and informal. To the extent that this is true of IP, it is surely likely to be similarly so in the CP arena.

Mergers, acquisitions and joint ventures

A **merger** is usually taken to mean the situation where two or more independent businesses come together to form one new organisation, usually a new legal entity. This may be done by mutual consent, or it could be an aggressive act by one firm as a 'takeover' without the agreement of the 'victim'. Such an aggressive or unwelcome takeover is referred to as an **acquisition**. The word 'merger' from now on will be used to mean mergers and acquisitions, while recognising that they may have very different objectives. The CP authorities do not typically give much importance to the merger and acquisition distinction.

Both mergers and acquisitions can be differentiated from a **joint venture,** which is an agreement between two or more companies to cooperate in some way(s). This cooperation may be fairly trivial, or it may be fundamental to the operation of either or both or all of the parties involved, but the important point is that each company will maintain its own separate legal identity. Joint ventures could also involve the creation of a new company jointly owned by the cooperating parties. Both mergers and joint ventures could be seen as methods of integration and or diversification (see Chapter 1).

The rationale for mergers and joint ventures

This can be judged from two very different perspectives, that of the companies involved and their commercial objectives, and that of 'the public interest'. Such growth may sometimes be undertaken by management as a matter of fashion or fancy, whether the expansion be at home or abroad. Porter (1987) has argued that too many mergers are undertaken on a whim, or at least not properly thought through (see Kane below, also). Under these circumstances the performance of the diversified operation may be largely determined by luck. If however an 'expansion decision' (whether at home or abroad) has been undertaken after some serious consideration, success is a good deal more likely.

> Whilst market entry is not, by itself, a source of competitive advantage, it can unlock the value of the competitive advantages that either of the firms may have, by enabling the advantages to be extended to new markets. In this respect, mergers motivated by the desire to enter new markets appear to be directed more toward the exploitation of potential synergies than their domestic counterparts.
>
> (Davis, Shore and Thompson 1991: 67)

From companies' perspectives it can be argued that either mergers or joint ventures could be attractive strategies, under suitable conditions. But from whose perspectives should mergers and joint ventures be judged?

Public policy and mergers

The joint venture as a route to growth appears to have a number of specific advantages, and it also appears that both UK and EU authorities may be reasonably well disposed to this form of company expansion. How does this compare with the alternative of a merger, and how does public policy treat the merger approach to corporate growth and development?

Much of the early empirical work done in the United Kingdom on post-merger performance has been highly critical. From Meeks' (1977) investigation to Newbould and Luffman (1978), and Cowling and colleagues (1986), the conclusions have been broadly similar: mergers do not seem to give rise to obvious or clear efficiency or performance gains. More recently similar doubts have been expressed as to the efficacy of merger as a strategy. Bruton, Oviatt and White (1994) identified the importance of firms having some prior experience of the merger process, and the general observation that any financial advantages to acquiring firms may take some time to show up was made by Loderer and Martin (1992). Heather has recently argued that:

> the weight of evidence appears to be that in whatever field, horizontal or diversified or vertically integrated, on average merger activity does not seem to enhance the well-being of the company that engages in that activity. This seems to be true in many countries over a substantial time period. It also seems to be true however 'success' is measured.
>
> (Heather 2002: 139)

A recent paper confirmed the problems associated with mergers from a business insider's perspective. Archie Kane, a senior strategist at LloydsTSB, has argued that most mergers do not lead to improved corporate performance, for a variety of reasons. Not least amongst the reasons is the probability that the major upheaval that a merger represents is simply too often not properly thought through (Kane 2003). Thus regardless of the synergy and related arguments in favour of mergers, the impact of mergers is all too often to the detriment of both firms, their shareholders, their employees and their customers. When the added complexities and transaction costs associated with cross-border mergers are taken into account, further doubts creep in about the post-merger performance of international acquisitions. Only in the case of the genuinely 'failing firm', rescued by the optimistic acquiring purchaser, may the public interest be expected to be served in the majority of cases. Given this very pessimistic appraisal of the likely results of mergers, what has been the attitude of EU legislators towards mergers?

Mergers and EU CP

The Treaty of Rome did not deal specifically with mergers and takeovers, but this did not mean that there was no interest in mergers from the EU CP authorities. In the early years of the European Economic Community the treatment of mergers was by case law in the ECJ. The *Continental Can* case of 1973 established that Article 82 could apply to mergers, as the Court ruled that there is an abuse of a dominant position if an undertaking already holding such a position strengthens it by acquiring a competitor. In 1987 in the *BAT/PhillipMorris* case the ECJ went further and declared that in the absence of a dominant position, a horizontal acquisition could be penalised as forming an anti-competitive agreement under Article 81. But even with these judicial interventions, it was felt by some commentators that the approach to mergers was inadequate. In particular this was argued because the case law system allowed only for *ex post* interventions.

However mergers are a very sensitive area in EU political and economic circles. Concentration levels and attitudes to mergers and big business vary from country to country. Denmark, for example, has a very high standard of living coupled with a low level of business concentration; this, the Danes argue, is not coincidental. The Danes have no affection for mergers and the increase in market and/or aggregate concentration levels that follows. On the other hand some countries such as Greece and Portugal, which like Denmark, also have relatively small-sized business units, have resisted moves to restrict mergers. These countries argue that the 'restructuring' advantages expected to flow from the SEM should not be inhibited by unnecessarily stringent anti-merger rules.

In 1990, a new Merger Regulation was introduced in the European Union, and this came into force as the Merger Control Regulation in September 1990. A merger was deemed to have a EU dimension, and so to be subject to the regulation, if it leads to concentration and passes three tests:

- The aggregate world-wide turnover exceeds €5 billion.
- The aggregate EU turnover of each of at least two firms involved exceeds €250 million.
- None of the firms has two-thirds of its EU-wide turnover in one member state.

Subsequent criticism of these regulations related to the magnitude of the thresholds, to issues of 'subsidiarity' (allowing national authorities where possible to determine national cases), and to questions of 'dominance' and 'substantial lessening of competition'. The criterion for judging mergers in the United States, Canada and Australia is the 'lessening of competition' test, and not the emphasis on dominance which prevailed in EU CP. After considerable debate and discussion a new Merger Regulation (EC No 139/2004) came into effect on 1 May 2004, the same day as the European Union was enlarged from 15 to 25 member states. This date was no coincidence, as the new rules encourage participation by national competition authorities. By following the interpretation of the courts in which the European Union has extended the scope of coverage of merger cases to include duopolies (*Kali* case, and *Genco/Lonrho* case) and 'collective dominant positions' or oligopolies (*Airtours/FirstChoice* case), the new Merger Regulation now covers all anti-competitive effects on oligopolistic markets where the firm resulting from the merger is not, strictly speaking, a dominant firm (Europa 2004b: 5). Announcing the 'new merger review package' an official EU CP source declared:

This far-reaching package of reforms is composed of four main elements:
- a revised merger regulation
- guidelines on the assessment of horizontal mergers
- a set of best practice guidelines for merger investigations
- reforms designed to strengthen the objectivity and soundness of decisions in merger cases.

(Europa 2004c: 1)

The source continues:

> all post-merger scenarios posing a threat to competition, including oligopolies, are covered by the test. ... [This] enables the Commission to intervene against all anti-competitive mergers. This is a very welcome development, which brings to an end a long-running debate about the scope of the old 'dominance' test.
>
> (Europa 2004c: 1)

Thus the new situation in the enlarged European Union of 25 member states with regards to mergers is that 'A concentration which would significantly impede effective competition, in the common market or a substantial part of it, in particular by the creation of or strengthening of a dominant position, shall be declared incompatible with the common market' (Europa 2004c: 1). It is of course too early yet to say how the new regulations will take effect. What can be said, though, is that up to now the EU CP authorities have not been very vigorous in denying potential mergers the right to proceed. Since the new regulations first appeared in 1990, over 2,000 merger proposals have been considered and only about 20 were prohibited. In the year 2003 there were 222 decisions made by the EU CP authorities and all were given 'clearance', though a small number involved some remedies, such as guaranteeing supplies to some competitors (Europa 2004c).

In 2002 the UK Enterprise Act was passed, which uses the same sort of criteria to judge UK mergers as those in the new EU 2004 regulations. So at least the UK and EU rules are coming closer together, and the possibility of conflicts arising appears to be reducing. This must be a good thing, not least for businesses for whom uncertainty in respect of rules of operation is so undesirable. We have seen the very strong arguments put forward to suggest that post-merger performance is likely to be poor. However it seems that the merger authorities are not significantly influenced by these arguments into preventing mergers to any significant extent.

Joint ventures

Chapter 1 included some discussion of why joint ventures may be of interest to firms, including 'to strengthen a firm's market position', but it is the potential for joint ventures to have anti-competitive effects that may be relevant in the CP context. In both UK and EU CP rules, joint ventures could come within the scope of the merger regulations or laws relating to restrictive or concerted practices, or to the possibility of abuse of market dominance. Thus in EU terms specifically joint ventures could be dealt with under any of Articles 81 and 82 or the Merger Regulations.

There is some EU case law on joint ventures, but the position is not entirely clear or straightforward. Goyder (2003) points out that Article 82 (abuse of a dominant position) could be applicable to joint ventures, but has been little used. The court makes a distinction between 'concentrative' joint ventures and 'cooperative' joint ventures. It might be expected that 'concentrative' ventures would be treated more harshly than 'cooperative' activities; however the opposite is the case. If a joint venture is of the type where the parties set up a jointly owned new company to fulfil the joint purpose, then the merger regulations apply, with their very high thresholds, and so very few, if any, concentrative joint ventures would be stopped (by the merger regulation). However, 'cooperative' joint ventures arise where the parties simply collaborate, in order to test the situation and to see if the joint endeavour works. These are likely to fall under Article 81, and to be prohibited as limiting competition like any other restrictive practice or concerted action. Thus what might seem like a sensible approach to a new arrangement, try it and see ('collaborative'), is likely to be prohibited, whereas the full-blown intervention of a new 'concentration' is likely to be permitted because it is too small to be of concern to the merger authorities (Goyder 2003).

Even when the 'parents' of a joint venture are not actually in competition, it may still be possible for a joint venture to come within the scope of Article 81(1) if it has an adverse effect on potential competition. This might seem to raise matters of 'justiciability', that is, to ask the question about the fitness or ability of the legal process to judge the possible economic consequences of business behaviour. If it is felt that the partners to the potential joint venture might reasonably be expected to enter the market separately and as competitors in the not too distant future, then the planned joint venture could be deemed to be a restriction on potential competition and be disallowed.

In *Vacuum Interrupters* [OJ 1977, L 48/32], the damage to potential competition was widely interpreted. In this case, two UK firms started to develop a new form of switch gear, the vacuum interrupter. Each abandoned the research on the grounds that the risk in the competitive nature of the research made it not worth continuing, and to reduce the competitive risk the two companies decided to collaborate. The Commission declared that this would restrict competition between the two (parent) companies, as naturally they would not wish to compete with the joint venture. It was considered that this was likely to affect trade between member states, and might discourage other firms from starting research in this area. Exemption was granted, nonetheless, as it was considered that technical and economic progress would be enhanced by the joint venture.

Regardless of how widely Article 81(1) may be interpreted, however, there is always Article 81(3) to follow. Article 81(3) allows exemption to be granted under a wide range of circumstances. In fact in nearly all cases considered by the Commission the exemption clause has been used. This section has a strongly worded presumption that joint ventures are likely to bring forth all sorts of economic benefits, such as rationalisation and innovation. Thus if joint ventures come under Article 81, they are likely to be permitted by the exemption clause, and similarly if they come under Article 82 or the merger regulations, they may also be allowed to go ahead.

Conclusion

As we have seen there is a great deal of discussion in relation to both IP and CP in the European Union and the United Kingdom. The European Union has its grand mission, outlined in the Lisbon strategy, to become the most competitive economy in the world by 2010. This seems rather fanciful at the moment. In November 2004, Wim Kok, the former prime minister of the

Netherlands, presented a report to the Commission (Kok 2004). This was an officially commissioned report to indicate the extent to which the Lisbon goals were being achieved (Europa 2004d). The report concluded that there was a great deal to be done if the European Union was to improve its competitiveness to meet the challenges of global markets. There had been 'a lack of determined political action', and for the future 'The status quo is not an option' (Europa 2004d: 1). The report called for more action on competition policy, on R&D, on removing obstacles to free markets within the internal market, and so on. Whatever the policies on IP and CP have been, more vision and vigour was still needed, Kok concluded.

Also in November 2004 the UK government called for improvements in the public procurement sphere (Wood 2004). Just a little earlier that year Frits Bolkestein, the Internal Market commissioner, had condemned both France and Germany, in very strong terms, for being too interventionist. France was criticised for its assistance to the engineering giant Alstom, and Germany was condemned for its attempts to protect Volkswagen from being taken over. Both countries were also criticised for seeking to impose higher corporate taxes on the ten new member states, at levels more similar to those in France and Germany, to help keep French and German companies competitive. 'Their agenda in my view is to restrict competition. You don't help industry by protecting it. This interventionist policy has been tried before and failed' (BBC 2004a). So on the one hand we have the Kok Report, the Wood Report and Frits Bolkestein all calling, in very forceful language, for more competition and enterprise in the European Union. On the other hand we can see very clearly that countries like France and Germany are still very committed to a more interventionist role for governments. 'The state dreams of French industrial strategy' would come to fruition in a new agency for industrial innovation designed to reinvigorate French industry policy, it was recently reported (*Liberation* 2005). We may agree with Beath and others, that UK and EU policy is mainly supportive, and less interventionist than previously. However we cannot say that this is the single, united voice of the European Union.

Questions

1   The Lisbon Agenda, or the Lisbon strategy, aims to establish the European Union as the most competitive economy in the world by 2010. What are the chances of this becoming reality? How do you think that either EU IP or CP could help in achieving these goals for the European Union?

2   Both Lynch and Ferguson have approaches to classifying IP. Describe both UK and EU IP using both of their models.

3   Argue the case that state aid is an unwarranted distortion of free markets and therefore should be totally outlawed in the European Union. How likely do you think it is that state aid will, one day, be totally banned in the European Union? Explain carefully.

4   Public procurement accounts for about 15–20 per cent of EU GDP. It is currently not conducted in very open and competitive markets. First, outline some arguments why public procurement should be more open and competitive, and show how businesses might gain. Then second, discuss what the main issues are in trying to make it more transparent.

5   It is sometimes said that business people know their own business best, and therefore there should be no interference at all by such bodies as the CP authorities. Defend and support this position.

6   Given the evidence that suggests most, or nearly all, mergers have a negative effect on business performance, do you think that all mergers should be banned? Why or why not? Explain carefully and give some recent examples of where a merger has been banned and where it has not, and why.

7   What are the theoretical grounds for expecting monopolistic market structures to lead to poor economic performance? How does this relate to reality?

8   It is sometimes argued that in modern economies, in which multinational corporations and globalisation are now the norm, the attempts to control big business behaviour by CP authorities are doomed to fail. Discuss this point of view.

9   Following on from question 8, consider the argument that CP is no more than a pretence, or an attempt to persuade the public that they are protected from the power of monopolies and cartels. Is this a sound argument? State your case carefully.

Note

1   SIMAP stands for Système d'Information pour les Marchés Publics, or Information System for Public Markets.

References

Barberis, P. and May, T. (1993) *Government, Industry and Political Economy*, Open University Press, Milton Keynes.

BBC (2002) 'European car market set for shake-up', *BBC News*, 23 July, news.bbc.co.uk/1/hi/business/1775384.stm accessed February 2005.

BBC (2004a) 'Brussels slams state interference', *BBC News*, news.bbc.co.uk/1/hi/business/3830401.stm, accessed March 2005.

BBC (2004b) 'Ryanair to repay illegal subsidy', *BBC News*, 28 October, newsvote.bbc.co.uk/mpapps/pagetools/print/news.bbc.co.uk/1/hi/business/3962, accessed March 2005

BBC (2005) 'EU to probe Alitalia "state aid"', *BBC News*, news.bbc.co.uk/2/hi/business/4189565.stm, accessed April 2005.

Beath, J. (2002) 'UK industrial policy: old tunes on new instruments?' *Oxford Review of Economic Policy*, vol. 18, no. 2, pp. 221–39.

Bruton, G., Oviatt, B. and White, M. (1994) 'Performance of acquisition of distressed firms', *Academy of Management Journal*, vol. 37, no. 4.

Carlin, W., Haskel, J. and Seabright, P. (2001) 'Understanding "the essential fact about Capitalism"', *National Institute Economic Review*, vol. 175, pp. 67–84.

Cowling, K. and Mueller, D. (1978) 'The social costs of monopoly', *Economic Journal*, vol. 88, pp. 727–48.

Cowling, K., Stoneman, P. and Cubbin, J. (1986) *Mergers and Economic Performance*, Cambridge University Press, Cambridge.

Davis, E., Shore, G. and Thompson, D. (1991) 'Continental mergers are different', *Business Strategy Review*, Spring, pp. 49–69.

Derby Evening Telegraph (2004) 'BMI Baby applauds legal blow to rival', 4 February, p. 14.

Drazen, A. (2000) *Political Economy in Macroeconomics*, Princeton University Press, New Jersey.

UK Department of Trade and Industry (DTI) (2002a) *The Government's Manufacturing Strategy*, HMSO, London.

DTI (2002b) *Competitiveness Indicators*, HMSO, London.

DTI (2005) www.dtistats.net/competitiveness/ch1/10htm accessed March 2005.

Dutton, P. (1980) *Mergers and Economic Performance*, Cambridge University Press, Cambridge.

Economist (2004a) 'The European Commission: a leap forward, or a long march', 21 August, p. 42.

Economist (2004b) 'The EU and competition: a real Monti?', 21 August, p. 42.

Europa (2004a) 'Public procurement: WTO GPA extended to the enlarged EU', 15 June, europa.eu.int/rapid/pressRelease.../04/744&format=HTML&aged=0&language=EN &guiLanguage=en, accessed July 2004.

Europa (2004b) *Competition Introduction*, 1 September, europa.eu.int/scadplus/leg/en/ lvb/126055.htm, accessed October 2004

Europa (2004c) *Merger Control: Merger review package in a nutshell*, 1 May, europa.eu.int/comm./competition/publications/special/3_merger.pdf, accessed January 2005.

Europa (2004e) *Kok Report Calls for More Determined Political Action to Revitalize Lisbon Strategy*, 3 November, Europa.eu.int/comm./Lisbon_strategy/index_en.html, accessed November 2004.

European Business (2004) 'Chirac calls on EU to create industrial champions', 27 August, pp. 1–3.

EU Business (2005) 'Estonia is Europe's car bargain basement', 11 March, www.eu business.com/afp/050308144701.ll6a6v5a, accessed March 2005

European Commission (1972) *First Report on Competition Policy*, Brussels.

European Commission (1980) *Ninth Report on Competition Policy*, Brussels.

European Commission (1988) *Seventeenth Report on Competition Policy*, Brussels.

European Commission (1994) *Growth, Competitiveness, Employment, the Challenges and the Way Forward into the 21st Century*, Brussels.

European Commission (1995) *Background Report: State aid*, March, Brussels.

European Commission (2004) *State Aid Scoreboard: Spring 2004 update*, 20 April, COM (2004) 256 final.

European Parliament (2004) 'Specific questionnaire for Mr Günter Verheugen', PE347.095 DV\541019EN.doc.

Ferguson, P. R. and Ferguson, G. J. (1994) *Industrial Economics, Issues and Perspectives*, 2nd edn, Macmillan, Basingstoke.

Financial Times (2004) 'Brussels deals double blow to Paris government contracts', 5 February, p. 6.

Friedman, M. (1962) *Capitalism and Freedom*, University of Chicago Press, Chicago.

Galbraith, J. K. (1963) *American Capitalism*, rev. edn, Penguin, London.

Goyder, D. G. (2003) *EC Competition Law*, 4th edn, Oxford University Press, Oxford.

Guardian (1996) 'Unfair aviators', 1 February, p. 5.

Guardian (2004a) 'Sarkovy applies stick and carrot to rouse France', 5 May, p. 17.

Guardian (2004b) 'Sarkozy defends French backing for Alstom', 10 November, p. 25.

Guardian (2004c) 'Campaign for fair competition in European tenders', 16 November, p. 20.

Guardian (2004d) 'Germany leads the state aid table', 20 April, p. 18.

Guardian (2005a) 'Price-fixing firms fined', 20 January, p. 20.

Guardian (2005b) 'Controversial new European Directive', 20 January, p. 25.

Harberger, A. (1954) 'Monopoly and resource allocation', *American Economic Review*, vol. 44, pp.77–87.

Heather, K. (2002) *Economics of Industries and Firms*, FT Prentice Hall, Harlow.

Hudghton, I. (2004) Speeches: Charleroi Airport and Ryanair, 9 February, www.hudghtonmep.com/speeches/040209.htm accessed March 2005.

Kane, A. (2003) 'Managing acquisitions and mergers', Conference paper given at Oxford Brookes University, 19 February.

Kean, A. R. (1996) 'An analysis of UK industry policy with particular reference to ship-building', unpublished dissertation, Oxford Brookes University.

Kok, W. (2004) *Facing the Challenge: the Lisbon strategy for growth and employment*, November, Office for the Publications of the European Community, Luxemburg.

Korah, V. (2003) *An Introductory Guide to EC Competition Law and Practice*, 8th edn, Hart, Oxford.

Kroes, N. (2005) 'Competition policy and the relaunch of the Lisbon Strategy', speech delivered at a conference at Bocconi University, Milan, 7 February, Europa.eu.int/ rapid/ pressReleasesAction.do?reference+SPEECH/05/78&format, accessed February 2005.

Liberation (2005) 'L'Etat se rêve en stratège de l'industrie française', 6 January, p. 19.

Loderer, C. and Martin, K. (1992) 'Postacquisition performance of acquiring firms', *Financial Management*, vol. 21, no. 3.

Lynch, R. L. (2003) *Corporate Strategy*, 3rd edn, FT-Prentice Hall, Harlow.

Meeks, G. (1977) *Disappointing Marriage: A study of the gains from merger*, Cambridge University Press, Cambridge.

Mercado, S., Welford, R. and Prescott, K. (2001) *European Business*, FT Prentice Hall, Harlow.

Newbould, G. D. and Luffman, G. A. (1978) *Successful Business Policies*, Gower Press, Farnborough.

Observer (2004) 'Europe finds itself lost for words', 19 September, p. 24.

Piggott, J. and Cook, M. (1999) *International Business Economics: A European perspective*, 2nd edn, Longman, Harlow.

Porter, M. E. (1987) 'The state of strategic thinking', *Economist*, 23 May, pp. 21–8.

Presidency Conclusions (2000) Lisbon Economic Council 23/24 March, www.ue.Eu.int/ ueDocs/cms_Data/docs/pressData/en/ec/00100-rl.en0.htm, accessed February 2005.

Presidency Conclusions (2001) Goteborg Economic Council 15/16 June, SN 200/1/01/REV 1.

Rowland, J. (2005) 'In the health trade',*Guardian*, 20 January.

Sampson, A. (1983) *The Changing Anatomy of Britain*, Coronet, Philadelphia.

Sampson, A. (2004) *Who RunsThis Place? The anatomy of Britain in the 21st century*, John Murray, London.

Schumpeter, J. A. (1954) *Capitalism, Socialism and Democracy*, 4th edn, Allen and Unwin, London.

SIMAP (2004) *Procurement Rules and Guidelines*, simap.eu.int/EN/pub/src/main2.htm accessed July 2004.

Spaak, P. H. (1957) *The Spaak Report*, Intergovernmental Committee on European Integration. The Brussels Report on the General Common Market, Brussels.

Van Bael, I. and Bellis, J. F. (1989) *Competition Law of the EEC*, CCH Editions, Oxford.

Van Zon, H. (1996) T*he Future of Industry in Central and Eastern Europe*, Avebury, Aldershot.

Ward, I. (1996) *A Critical Introduction to European Law*, Butterworths, London.

Wood, A. (2004) *Investigating the Business Experiences of Competing for Public Contracts in Other EU Countries*. Office of Government Commerce, London, November.

11 EU policy and its impact on business: regional, transport and environmental policy

Mark Cook

Objectives   This chapter will:

- outline the case for, and development of, EU regional policy
- consider its effectiveness
- investigate the development and effectiveness of EU transport policy
- provide an overview of EU environmental policy and its impact on business.

Introduction

This chapter considers a number of salient areas of EU policy. In particular it focuses on three of the areas of EU policy that have had, and will continue to have, an important effect on European business. The areas of regional, environmental and transport policy also show important inter-linkages, and indicate that the separate policy areas cannot be discussed in isolation.

Regional policy

Theories behind the need for regional policy

Neo-classical theory suggests the free movement of capital will tend to equalise factor earnings between participating countries or regions, leading to convergence. A critique of neo-classical theory, however, suggests that no such convergence will take place, but instead the free movement of capital will exacerbate national and regional differences in real income and welfare, with the well-off regions gaining at the expense of the poorer ones. Myrdal (1957) held the view that this free movement of capital would lead to 'polarisation' effects through a process of 'cumulative causation', that is, the inflow of capital goes to where its marginal productivity is greatest and sets in motion dynamic processes that reinforce the attractiveness of these host areas. These then grow in prosperity, attracting even more capital. Similarly less prosperous areas may be attractive because of lower labour costs, less congestion, less pollution and so on, but this is insufficient to offset the polarisation effect described above (Baldwin and Wyplosz 2004). If Myrdal's view is to be believed and capital and labour are not completely mobile, persistent discrepancies among regions may exist and may in fact grow. In addition, the movement of labour and capital in response to market forces will be determined by private rather than social costs, and organisations will seek the most highly profitable locations, which if regions differ appreciably can lead to a serious misallocation of resources. Finally there may be a lack of knowledge of other regions and constraints on wages, such as minimum wage legislation, which may prevent the flexibility required in the labour market.

Thus some regions may always have advantages over others. In this case new industry and trade will be attracted to where similar industries already exist, and where the infrastructure is already in place. This 'honeypot' principle can lead to large discrepancies in regional performance, and this may force governments to act not only on economic grounds but also on political ones. Regional inequalities are felt to be a political problem chiefly because large sections of the population feel that unequal access to wealth and opportunity is morally unjust as well as socially unacceptable. This call for 'equity' is supported from an economic standpoint, in that regional disparities prevent optimum use of resources and thus keep total wealth below its maximum potential.

But why is there the need for a European regional policy? The European Union is seen as facing a number of regional challenges, which may be more extreme versions of the issues outlined above.

Disparity of income

Levi Sandri (1965) showed that the per capita income of the most favoured region in the Community (Hamburg, in Germany) was about seven times that of the least well-off area (Calabria, in Italy). In 2004 inner London (289.1; EU25 GDP per head average was 100) was around nine times better off in terms of GDP per head than Lubelskie (Poland) (31.4). In addition, as the Community has grown over time from six to 25 members, income disparities have been further highlighted. Measured by country, Luxemburg (212.9) has the highest GDP average per country using the same index, followed by Ireland (129.1), Denmark (126.5) and the Netherlands (124.3). Countries such as Spain, Portugal and Greece together with all the ten new member states are below the EU25 average, with Latvia the lowest (36.6) and Romania as a potential new entrant in 2007 with a GDP per head index of 26.8.

These poor regions tend to fall into one of two categories. They are either areas with a traditional dependence on small-scale agriculture which have never developed the infrastructure for industrial development, or they are regions that have been heavily dependent on traditional industries, such as steel, textiles or shipbuilding. The latter's decline could have been the result of a loss in comparative advantage, a decrease in demand for a region's output or shifts in technology (see Table 11.1). Their difficulty is in attracting investment in modern, productive industrial activities. For the first group, their lack of infrastructure is the major problem, whereas for the second group, infrastructure is in place, but it is often in a poor condition and/or the workforce has inappropriate skills.

Table 11.1 Main regional indicators

Member state	GDP growth, annual average percentage change, 1995 2001			GDP per head, EU 25 = 100			Unemployment rate per cent, 2002		
	National average	Regional maximum	Regional minimum	National average	Regional maximum	Regional minimum	National average	Regional maximum	Regional minimum
Belgium	2.4	4.3	1.4	117.3	238.5	75.9	7.5	14.5	3.8
Denmark	2.5	2.5	2.5	126.5	126.5	126.5	4.6	4.6	4.6
Germany	1.6	−1.0	3.6	110.2	187.3	66.0	9.4	27.1	3.8
Greece	3.5	5.0	2.1	73.7	104.2	57.8	10.0	14.7	7.3
Spain	3.7	5.3	2.4	92.4	123.3	58.7	11.4	19.6	5.3
France	2.6	4.4	−0.4	115.0	180.7	52.9	8.7	29.3	6.4
Ireland	9.2	9.5	8.1	129.1	141.8	93.7	4.3	5.5	3.8
Italy	1.9	2.7	0.6	109.9	146.0	68.1	9.0	24.6	2.6
Luxemburg	6.1	6.1	6.1	212.9	212.9	212.9	2.6	2.6	2.6
Netherlands	3.3	5.8	0.8	124.3	156.7	90.4	2.8	3.7	2.2
Austria	2.4	3.1	1.7	122.8	135.7	83.6	4.0	7.2	2.0
Portugal	3.5	5.4	2.1	77.6	115.4	61.2	5.1	6.6	2.5
Finland	4.1	5.9	2.0	114.1	153.9	83.0	9.1	14.1	2.9
Sweden	2.9	4.7	0.4	116.5	159.0	98.0	5.1	6.3	3.9
UK	3.0	5.2	−0.9	115.7	289.1	65.3	5.1	9.0	3.4
Bulgaria	0.0	1.0	−0.7	28.6	39.9	23.8	18.2	26.9	13.3
Cyprus	3.8	3.8	3.8	85.4	85.4	85.4	3.3	3.3	3.3
Czech Republic	1.5	4.4	−1.2	66.5	148.7	52.6	7.3	13.4	3.6
Estonia	5.2	5.2	5.2	42.3	42.3	42.3	10.3	10.3	10.3
Hungary	4.0	5.2	1.6	56.5	89.2	37.0	5.9	8.9	4.0
Lithuania	5.1	5.1	5.1	40.8	40.8	40.8	13.7	13.7	13.7
Latvia	5.7	5.7	5.7	36.6	36.6	36.6	12.1	12.1	12.1
Malta	4.8	4.8	4.8	76.2	76.2	76.2	5.2	5.2	5.2
Poland	6.3	10.4	2.7	44.9	69.9	31.4	19.9	26.3	16.2
Romania	−0.1	7.4	−2.3	26.8	57.3	18.9	8.4	10.6	6.7
Slovenia	5.1	5.1	5.1	74.4	74.4	74.4	6.3	6.3	6.3
Slovak Republic	3.9	5.7	3.2	49.0	111.7	37.3	18.7	22.2	8.7

Source: Eurostat (2004a).

Community membership

If a country, on joining of the European Union, has to adopt less strict restrictions on imports from non-EU countries, and so forth, then there may be structural changes in the country's economy leading to regional difficulties. Non-tariff protection against other members of the Community may also be dropped over time, and this can further exacerbate these problems. These regional impediments may manifest themselves in a decline in the balance of payments, which historically could have been addressed by a depreciation in the country's currency under a flexible exchange rate regime. However for the 12 EU countries that are part of the European single currency such a procedure is not an option, and regional disparities may continue to exist in the longer term.

External/internal borders

Armstrong and Taylor (1985) suggest that countries may lose out after a union is in place because the internal border will not profit from border activities. The same applies to an external border. Thus, a country that was previously outside the union and obtained finance from external trading activities with another non-union country will lose these once it becomes a member of the union, as trade gets redirected within the union. For example, Poland could have had external tariffs on imports from EU countries. After its entry into the European Union in 2004, such tariffs would have been removed and the tax revenue from trade lost.

Gravitation principle

Attention has been drawn to the possible tendency for industrial activity to gravitate towards the centre of the community – what is sometimes called the 'Golden triangle' or 'Blue banana' (London, Frankfurt and Turin) – to the exclusion of the other regions. Reasons for this are potential economies of scale, closeness to markets, and agglomeration economies that occur through concentration in one area, such as transport and telecommunication facilities. However, diseconomies may also emerge from pollution, for example, leading to companies moving out of this area. An example of a 'congested region' would be the area around Paris, which consists of 2 per cent of French territory, and contains almost 20 per cent of the population and 25 per cent of the total employment, producing 30 per cent of the national output (European Commission 2004). Similar congested areas are Berlin and the Rhine–Ruhr area of Germany, London and greater Athens. The regional problem here is how to divert activity away from these regions to the peripheral areas. During the 1990s there has also been the emergence of a 'Latin arc' or 'Mediterranean arc' stretching from Barcelona to Genoa. Hospers (2002) suggests that in the future the 'Blue banana' will change to a 'Yellow banana' stretching from Paris to Warsaw.

Changes in other EU policies

Alterations in the Common Agricultural Policy (CAP) mechanism or attempts at an overall energy policy may cause regional problems as a by-product. For example, reducing milk subsidies may hit some countries harder than others, and some regions in these countries will suffer more.

Other factors

An EU regional policy can also be justified on the grounds that it may make national policies more effective: for example, it can prevent competition between member states in the giving of state aids. An EU problem may also cut across national boundaries, requiring EU action rather than individual action. One source of the regional disparities that have occurred in the European Union has been the Single European Market (SEM) process and monetary union. If the full benefits of the SEM and European monetary union are to be felt, then a strong regional policy is required. There are also issues that affect a number of member states, for example transportation issues, where a common regional policy could cut across country discrepancies and enable the whole European Union to benefit from a particular element of regional policy. Coordination of policy is also needed as a way of getting different decision-making bodies to integrate better, and to make sure that domestic regional policies are not used as a means to improve one country's competitiveness in comparison with another.

The regional disparities depicted in Table 11.1 are large, and in some countries at least, do not appear to be diminishing. The knock-on effects from this are social unrest, moves towards devolution and other social and political issues. Moreover, regional imbalances in unemployment can lead to a mismatch between labour supply and labour demand, in both the quantity of labour and labour skills. Conversely regions that are successful in attracting investment may suffer from a growth in regional inflation which can be transmitted to less prosperous regions, resulting in a further reduction in regional competitiveness.

Thus regional policy both at an EU level and at a national level seeks to reduce disparities between regions, reduce the loss that might occur in social capital (such as having the wrong type of skills for the types of jobs that are on offer), improve overall growth performance and achieve a more equitable distribution of income.

The EU states' approach to regional policy

Regional policy in the individual European countries existed in its many guises long before the setting-up of regional policy at EU level. It could operate to induce inward investment via some form of carrot and stick policy, a practice that was seen in the United Kingdom and Germany. During the 1980s this policy was to change, focusing on stimulating indigenous growth rather than encouraging inward investment. Part of the explanation for this change was the growth of interest in small and medium-sized enterprises (SMEs) as job creators (see Chapter 12), and the notion of entrepreneurship and the 'rolling back' of the state. Nonetheless, the individual member states still continued to try to attract large overseas companies. Regional policy in the individual states, however, has also been used to counteract social issues in their deprived areas by improving infrastructure and educational facilities. For example, one of the reasons for the

European Union's policy for the development of a high-speed rail network was to link often peripheral areas of the European Union to the more prosperous core regions.

Within the broad policy areas of regional policy there have been a number of common features in the way regional policy has been pursued by the member states, but at the same time also important differences. Germany's approach to regional policy was somewhat similar to that adopted by the Netherlands. Regional policy was used as a means to diffuse inflationary pressures and to maximise national economic growth as well as to deal with comparatively poor regions. On the other hand the United Kingdom's regional policy was influenced by the its worse economic performance than its main northern European competitors. In the post Second World War period through to the mid-1970s UK regional policy concentrated on inward investment into declining areas. From the mid-1970s regional policy was formulated alongside policies to deal with ever-increasing economic crises. The financial constraints faced by governments at that time also led to cuts in regional policy. The 1980s saw government relying more on market forces. The regional policy that was pursued was more related to encouraging indigenous firms to develop rather than encouraging inward investment, though FDI was still courted.

In France regional policy was set against more distinctive regional problems than in other EU countries. There were major discrepancies between the region around Paris and rural areas, and regional policy was used in the period up to the 1960s as a means to reduce social inequalities. In the 1960s regional policy switched to maximising economy growth from all the regions, but by the 1970s global economic crises meant that regional policy appeared to become less effective. On the whole French regional policy appeared to be of a very ad hoc nature.

In Italy regional policy was dominated by the problems of the south, a strongly based but rural economy with comparatively low GDP per capita. The emphasis on helping the south was to some extent clouded by the need to improve overall economic growth, the major generator of which was the north of Italy. Given the economic pressures that built up in the north during the latter part of the 1960s, Italy's strategy for the regions shifted more towards a set of balanced economic policies similar to those adopted in other countries (El-Agraa 2004).

Comparing the EU regional approaches

As noted above, regional policy in the different EU countries shows both similarities and differences. The instruments used can be grouped into those aimed at influencing the labour market, those aimed at industry and those concerned with improving infrastructure. Labour policy has rarely been to encourage labour mobility. In general, regional policies concerning labour have focused more on general training programmes.

The focus of regional policy to help industry has been to encourage new industries into deprived regions as well as to make it more difficult for industries to set up in prosperous regions. This was an approach adopted by the UK's Industrial Development Certificate Scheme, France's Agreements Mechanism and the Selective Investment Levy of the Netherlands. Governments have also used the public sector as a means to locate industry in deprived areas. For example Italy used its state corporations to direct 60 per cent of new investment to the south of the country. The main approach to industry, however, has been to use financial incentives to encourage private-sector companies to move towards depressed areas. Italy, France, the United Kingdom and the Netherlands have used this approach. Financial incentives can be discretionary and/or automatic. The 1980s saw the United Kingdom switch from automatic to discretionary incentives. Other countries such as the Netherlands continued with a combination package of the two, although the trend generally for most countries has been towards discretionary financial regional support and away from automatic incentives. This switch was a result of reducing the financial burden to the nation's government, as some organisations that would have moved to a depressed region without the incentives began to receive a range of financial incentives which governments believed would not have influenced their choice of region.

These financial incentives discussed above could also be capital or labour related, with the former taking precedence. In addition, they could be available nationally, as in Italy, or regionally as in the Netherlands. Moreover, the financial incentives could be targeted at particular sectors. Manufacturing has been well supported in many countries, but in both Germany and the Netherlands the service sector has also been well favoured. Increasingly the service sector in all EU states has become encompassed in regional support programmes, and at the same time 'special' sectors have also been targeted, such as small firms and high-technology companies.

Infrastructure development has also been a means for regional development and support. This began with the development of trading estates but has since moved on to the development of office and science parks. In this respect the development of growth centres has played a part in regional development in Germany, France, Italy and the Netherlands. Such centres constitute a concentration of state investment in particular locations, with the aim that the linkages between the investment should improve the growth potential effect from the region and lead to spillover effects into surrounding areas (Artis and Nixson 2001).

Assessing regional policy at the member state level

A question often asked about regional policy is: without such a policy would organisations have gone to a less-prosperous region anyway? When organisations in declining or lagging regions were asked about regional policy as a 'push factor' it did not feature highly compared with other competitive factors (Mason and Harrison 1990). It has also been said that restricting development in one area will not necessarily mean that organisations will set up in declining or lagging areas. Instead they may just move to areas near the prosperous area.

When organisations do move to poorer areas it may be through a branch plant of the main organisation, and as such this does not develop any major inter-regional linkages with other existing firms. These branch plants may be more akin to 'screwdriver' plants using a small proportion of localised production and parts. The French regional policy to develop growth centres in under-performing regions faced similar problems, as some of them developed by attracting companies to a region in which they had little connection to other industries in the locality; therefore the spill-over effects were minimal (Mason and Harrison 1990).

EU regional policy has been developed alongside that of the member states, and since 1989 has been strengthened appreciably. The reasons that a Europe-wide approach might be needed to regional policy are centred on social cohesion (see earlier), the means by which regional disparities between and within countries can be reduced.

Historically EU regional policy followed two main objectives: to assist areas within the community that were/are lagging behind, and to reduce the regional imbalances in the member states. The emphasis of EU regional policy has been on the latter rather than the former, and in this respect EU policy has been focused on the so-called cohesion problem. In other words it has emphasised getting the lagging community areas such as Spain, Portugal, Ireland, Greece, the Italian south and east Germany into a position where they can narrow the gap with the northern and western parts of the European Union (prior to entry of the poorer central and eastern European countries (CEECs) in May 2004).

Changes in EU regional policy over the past 20 years

Before 1989 the funding for regional policy could come from a variety of sources, but in 1989 the three major sources of structural funds, the European Research and Development Fund (ERDF), European Social Fund (ESF) and the Guidance section of the European Agriculture Guidance and Guarantee Fund (EAGGF), were combined and joined by two other sources of funding, the European Investment Bank (EIB) and the European Coal and Steel Community (ECSC), to provide a larger source of money for regional funding. This was seen as imperative to stop the SEM leading to wider economic disparities between member states. As a result of this process and a further reworking of regional funding in 1993, a number of common objectives for structural funding were developed, some of which operate today.

Objective 1 regions

These were regions whose development was lagging behind other regions. Such regions have GDPs less than 75 per cent of the EU average. They included a large section of the Mediterranean south, east Germany, Ireland and parts of the United Kingdom. The European Union also designated some countries as cohesion countries. These were defined as countries whose national GDP per capita was less than 90 per cent of the EU average. For many of these countries the majority, if not all, of their regions were of Objective 1 status.

Objective 2 regions

These were regions suffering from declining industrial areas. Certain parts of the United Kingdom, France, Germany, Spain, Sweden, Finland and Italy fitted into this category.

Objective 5 regions

Objective 5 regional funding was split into two parts. Objective 5a was concerned with structural or regional problems that occur through changes in the CAP. Objective 5b was concerned with rural areas that required development and structural adjustment. Parts of the United Kingdom, Sweden, France, Germany, Austria, Spain and Finland qualified for this type of funding.

Objective 6 regions

These were regions where the population density was low and there was a need to make sure that they obtained an equitable distribution of the wealth of the European Union. These regions included the sub-arctic regions of both Sweden and Finland.

Of total EU regional funding two-thirds went to objective 1 regions. As a proportion of GDP, regional funding went more to the cohesion countries, and any transfers to the richer countries, even where some of their regions had objective 1 status, were relatively small.

By the end of the 20th century peripheral regions of the European Union had achieved some progress in their drive to catch up the richest regions/countries. For example Ireland, which was one of the cohesion countries, had attained a GDP per head greater than the EU average, and the transport infrastructure in Spain had been modernised. In fact without tackling the cohesion issues faced by the existing EU15 countries the European Union might not have been in any position to face the problems that arose with the absorption of the new central and eastern European economies in May 2004.

Although EU regional policy had begun to reduce some of the regional disparities within the European Union, the problem during the new millennium was how to deal with the bigger problem of very poor regions within the CEECs while at the same time tightly controlling the regional budget.

Following on from the policy guidelines of Agenda 2000, the level of regional support was fixed for the period 2000–06 at 0.46 per cent of EU GDP, representing a figure of €213 billion. In addition there was €22 billion in pre-accession aid and a further €22 billion for interventions for the new member states, giving a total of €257 billion. This figure represents about 37 per cent of the EU budget.

Tables 11.2a, and 11.2b set out the distribution of regional funding to the EU15 and the new member countries through to 2006. Along with the structural funds, regional support can also come from a number of other areas. One is the cohesion fund (discussed earlier), the second is the 'fisheries instrument' and the third is 'community initiatives'. The latter includes support for cross-border and transnational cooperation (INTERREG), URBAN which provides support for innovative projects in cities and urban neighbourhoods, EQUAL, a fund to combat discrimination in the labour market, and LEADER which provides assistance in rural areas (Europa 2004). The new spending round for the period 2000–06 also saw a reformation of the objective areas of regional funding outlined above. Objective 6 funding was absorbed into

Table 11.2a Structural funds and instruments for EU15, 2000–06, (€ million)

Member state	Objective 1	Objective 2	Objective 3	FIFG (Fisheries guidance)	Cohesion fund	Community initiatives*	Total
Austria	288	740	585	0	0	395	2,008
Belgium	690	486	817	33	0	231	2,257
Denmark	0	199	397	221	0	92	909
Finland	1,008	541	442	33	0	280	2,304
France	4,201	6,569	5,013	254	0	1,155	17,192
Germany	22,035	3,776	5,057	121	0	1,775	32,765
Greece	23,143	0	0	0	3,388	952	27,483
Ireland	3,409	0	0	0	584	183	4,177
Italy	24,424	2,749	4,129	110	0	1,294	32,707
Luxemburg	0	44	44	0	0	14	103
Netherlands	136	861	1,866	33	0	719	3,615
Portugal	21,010	0	0	0	3,388	741	25,139
Spain	42,061	2,904	2,363	221	12,357	2,162	62,067
Sweden	797	431	795	66	0	307	2,396
UK	6,902	5,068	5,046	132	0	1,061	18,209
EU15	150,104	24,367	26,553	1,226	19,717	11,361	233,328

* Community Initiatives include INTERREG, EQUAL and LEADER

Source: Eurostat (2004b).

Table 11.2b New member states and structural funds and instruments, 2004–06, (€ million)

Member state	Objective 1	Objective 2	Objective 3	Interreg	EQUAL	Cohesion fund	Total
Cyprus*	0	28.02	21.95	4.30	1.81	53.94	113.44
Czech Republic	1,454.27	71.30	58.79	68.68	32.10	936.05	2,621.19
Estonia	371.36	0	0	10.60	4.07	309.03	695.06
Hungary	1,995.72	0	0	68.68	30.29	1,112.67	3,207.36
Latvia	625.57	0	0	15.26	8.03	515.43	1,164.29
Lithuania	895.17	0	0	22.49	11.87	608.17	1,537.70
Malta	63.19	0	0	2.37	1.24	21.94	88.74
Poland	8,275.81	0	0	221.36	133.93	4,178.60	12,809.70
Slovakia	1,041.04	37.17	44.94	41.47	22.27	570.50	1,757.39
Slovenia	237.51	0	0	23.65	6.44	188.71	456.31
Total	14,959.64	136.49	125.68	478.86	252.05	8,495.04	24,451.18

* Including Fisheries Fund

Source: Eurostat (2004b).

objective 1 funding but the definition of objective 1 funding remained the same. Objective 1 funding is still associated with regions whose GDP is less than 75 per cent of the EU average, and 75 per cent of structural funding is targeted at these regions. Regions that had previously received objective 1 funding but had achieved the threshold level, either through the growth in their region or because the average EU GDP level had fallen after the entry of the new member states, would get reduced funding based upon a sliding scale up until 2005. It was generally the case that most member states lost one of their objective 1 regions under the 2000–06 policy guidelines, and the overall result was a fall in objective 1 territory from 27 per cent of the EU population in 1994–9 to 22 per cent for the 2000–06 period (Europa 2004).

The cohesion fund still exists under the structural fund guidelines of 2000–06, though this has come under increasing scrutiny by the major paying members (Germany, the Netherlands, the United Kingdom, Austria and Sweden). Ireland's pre-eminence in cohesion funding has changed, as Table 11.2a shows, because of its high growth and low unemployment performance during the latter part of the 1990s. Although its GDP is above the EU average it still receives some cohesion funding (due to be reconsidered), and although Spain now receives the greatest amount of funding, it is Greece followed by Portugal that receives the largest amount of cohesion funding per capita (Europa 2004).

Objective 2 regions under regional policy for the period 2000–06 include the old objective 2 regions together with objective 5b regions. Again because of the financial constraints applied to the regional policy budget being applied to 25 countries rather than 15, the percentage of the population covered by new objective 2 funding fell from 25 per cent of the EU population to 18 per cent. It was also agreed that no member state would lose more than a third of its objective 2 funding. Overall objective 2 funding was expected to be around 11 per cent of overall structural funding (Europa 2004). New objective 3 funding encompasses the old objective 3 and 4 areas, and is around 12 per cent of total EU regional funding.

Regional policy as a proportion of total expenditure by the European Union has grown immeasurably over the past 25 years, because of the reforms of the policy itself and the need to expand the European Union's role through the SEM, the single European currency, and further enlargement. From constituting only around 5 per cent of the annual EU budget in the early 1980s it now accounts for approximately 35 per cent. In addition the funding is biased towards the most disadvantaged regions; those designated as objective 1 regions (cohesion regions) (El-Agraa 2004).

Although regional funding has grown, the funds that make up the total have slightly different objectives, and the European Commission has sought ways to reduce the time taken in making decisions and assessing the outcome of funding. Of the five funds involved with regional funding, the three designated as structural funds, the ERDF, ESF and EAGGF, supply grants, while the EIB and ECSC supply loans. Before the 1989 reforms of regional policy, the assistance required to gain ERDF funding and the type of funding given required extensive work by the European Commission to ascertain detailed knowledge of plans and to gain expertise on projects.

Such information gathering was particularly time-consuming, and since 1989 the approach has been to streamline regional funding through a process of planning, partnership, subsidiarity and additionality.

Assessing the performance of regional policy

Under the regional policy guidelines of 1989–93 and 1994–9 the absorption of allocated funding was slow and often delayed. Part of this could be a reflection of the difficulties some governments had with the additionality principle (matched funding that had to be provided by a nation's government); partly it was down to poor financial management, and there were also issues with the documentation of funding.

The European Union has established a system of stronger financial management, where problems with projects are detected earlier. Each member state was required to undertake and submit an annual report into its regional funding activities where the European Union supported them. Member states were encouraged to use joint computer facilities and share information. This, together with more detailed analysis of the projects themselves, was expected to improve transparency and policy evaluation (Artis and Nixson 2001).

The way payments are made has also changed in the regional policy proposals of 2000–06. Agreed projects for which there are no actual payments in the first two years will be automatically decommitted. Advanced funding of projects is to be vastly reduced, and for projects that have not started within 18 months, any advance payments will have to be repaid. Therefore the monitoring of structural funding has been improved greatly, and this, together with an assessment ex-ante, mid-term and ex-post, should improve the effectiveness of regional policy support (El-Agraa 2004).

Assessing cohesion policies

There are large differences between the performance of the member states and the performances of regions within the member states. For example Table 11.3 shows the differences between the regions of Greece, Greece as a whole and the EU average for a range of economic indicators. Greece as a whole is below the EU25 average GDP per head, yet within Greece the region Sterea Ellada has almost twice the GDP of Dytiki Ellada. This latter region is far more agricultural, whilst the former is more industrial. Differences between the regions in other countries are even larger: see Italy, the United Kingdom and Germany.

So have the regional disparities declined over time? Dunford (2000) among others has shown that income disparities have shown a modest fall, while the European Commission (2000) has shown only a weak convergence in growth performance. However there have been some outstanding regional successes within the overall picture, such as the case of Ireland, whose southern and eastern region now records a GDP per capita of 141 compared with an EU25 average of 100. Its annual average growth performance between 1995 and 2001 was 9.5 per cent compared with an EU15 position of 2.5 per cent over the same period, and the level of unemployment in the region has fallen from 15.4 per cent in 1992 to 3.8 per cent in 2002. For other countries the picture is less rosy. For example

Table 11.3 Regional disparities in Greece

Region/sub-region	GDP growth, annual average percentage change 1995–2001	GDP per head 2001, EU25=100	Unemployment 2002, per cent
Voreia Ellada	3.5	73.7	11.3
Anatolki Makedonia, Thraki	2.9	58.6	10.4
Kentiki Makedonia	4.2	73.6	11.5
Dyitki Makedonia	3.5	75.4	14.7
Thessalia	3.4	66.1	10.6
Kentriki Ellada	3.2	72.4	9.3
Iperios	5.0	59.3	10.6
Ionia Nisia	4.6	65.8	9.0
Dytiki Ellada	2.3	57.8	10.5
Strea Ellada	2.1	104.2	9.8
Peleponnisos	4.3	70.2	7.3
Attiki	3.4	78.1	9.2
Nisia Aigaiou, Kriti	4.1	73.8	9.7
Voreio Aigaio	4.8	68.2	9.2
Notio Aigaio	4.9	83.9	14.2
Kriti	3.4	70.7	7.7
Greece	3.5	73.7	10.0
EU15	2.5	109.7	7.8

Source: Eurostat (2004a).

in Germany unemployment rates in most regions have grown between 1992 and 2002. A similar feature can be seen in Belgium (Eurostat 2004a).

In their third report on economic and social cohesion, the Commission argued that since 1994 the disparities between member states and between regions have been decreasing, and that GDP and productivity have increased more quickly in the four countries eligible for cohesion funding. However, for those countries outside the cohesion group the catch-up process is more variable, and differs from one region to another. The poor growth performances of some of these economies have slowed the catch-up of some objective 1 regions, while some older industrial regions that do not have objective 1 status, such as north-east England, the regions of northern Germany and the sparsely populated areas of Sweden, have had growth performances below the EU average since 1994.

There are still wide regional disparities in employment levels. The cohesion countries have performed well, particularly Spain and Ireland, but only 43 per cent of those in working age were in work in the regions of southern Italy. In the new member states, one problem is that a high proportion of the workforce is associated with agriculture, and rising unemployment is likely to follow, which will exacerbate the problem that in 2003 only 56 per cent of those of working age are in employment compared with an EU average of 64 per cent (European Commission 2004).

Proposals for a regional policy after 2006

In February 2004 the Commission adopted a budget proposal for the EU27 covering the period 2007–13. It has proposed a budget of 0.41 per cent of EU GDP, equivalent to €336.3 billion, for that period. This extra funding over the budget for the period 2000–06 is required for the existing poor regions of the EU15 and the very poor regions of the new member states.

For the period between 2000 and 2004 when they were in the pre-entry phase, €3 billion in structural assistance was provided under the pre-accession financial instruments, ISPA (transport and the environment) and SAPARD (agriculture and rural development) and the Phare projects (improving administrative capacity). The new accession countries along with Bulgaria and Romania will receive a further €1.6 billion per year through Phare until 2006. During the period 2004–06, the new member states were in a period of transition, and until they became accustomed to managing the structural funds, the total amount paid to these countries was to be capped. Nonetheless the total support for the CEEC countries was still €21.8 billion, concentrated on infrastructure, human resources and productive investment (European Commission 2004). Changes to regional funding are needed if the European Union is to deal with a growing number of poorer new accession countries, yet the approach suggested of targeting poorer regions leaves those deprived enclaves situated in rather prosperous areas with a lack of funding in the future, as the case study below argues.

The revised cohesion policy for 2006–13

Given the expansion of the European Union in 2004 and the future expansion to include a number of poorer central and eastern European economies, and set against a regional budget that is fairly fixed, the European Union has decided to focus its regional funding within the cohesion countries on a limited number of key topics:

● innovation and the knowledge economy
● the environment and risk prevention
● access and public services.

These three topics will be pursued under the umbrella of three priority themes: convergence, regional competitiveness and employment, and territorial cooperation. These three EU priorities replace the current breakdown between objective regions 1, 2 and 3.

The convergence programmes are to be used as a means to support growth and job creation in the least-developed member states and regions. The focus on convergence is a result of the enlargement process which has brought about an unprecedented increase in the disparities within the European Union, the reduction of which will require long-term sustained efforts. Of the different funding mechanisms within the European Union, regional funding (ERDF) will part-finance the modernisation of basic infrastructure (transport, telecommunications and energy), the economic diversification of territories and the protection of the

POORER EU AREAS LOSE FUNDING

Older industrial areas face the loss of state funding for private-sector projects worth billions of pounds a year under European Commission proposals, the government has warned. Plans by the EC's Competition Directorate would prevent national governments in the better-off, longer-standing EU countries from giving financial support to developments in some of their poorer areas. In the United Kingdom, that would deprive the government of the right to spend £300–500 million a year, unlocking investments potentially worth billions, according to a regional affairs expert.

A consultation paper issued in 2004 by the Department of Trade and Industry estimated the Commission proposals would see the proportion of the UK population eligible for state aid fall from 30.9 per cent to 9.1 per cent. Other countries badly affected include France, Ireland, Germany, Austria and Finland, according to the DTI. Patricia Hewitt, Trade and Industry Secretary, said the consequence for the United Kingdom would be regional selective assistance (RSA) – the government's long-established grants for businesses planning to invest in assisted areas – becoming 'very, very severely limited'. She told a conference in Newcastle on Monday, 'The Commission's proposals do not adequately meet the needs of disadvantaged areas of the north-east and other parts of the country.'

An insider said the government was concerned the proposals did not give enough flexibility for aid to areas that needed it most. He claimed the proposed formula failed to take into account the fact that some of the poorest areas in the United Kingdom were in the richest regions. Steve Fothergill, Professor of Regional Development at Sheffield Hallam University and co-ordinator of the Alliance for Regional Aid, told a conference in Newcastle, 'The commission's proposals do not adequately meet the needs of disadvantaged areas of the north-east and other parts of the country.'

RSA has been the main regional aid tool of the government for 40 years and was instrumental in bringing Nissan to Sunderland, but has been criticised in the past few years over high-profile failures such as LG, the South Korean electronics group, in south Wales. The proposals, warned Professor Fothergill, would deliver a 'double whammy' to struggling regional economies that already face losing EU structural funds due to the shift of resources following EU enlargement.

The European Commission's plans to change EU state aid rules would affect areas designated as tier two. In the United Kingdom, this includes north-east England, central Scotland and parts of the Midlands, Yorkshire and Hull – the constituency of John Prescott, the deputy prime minister. The European Commission is keen to tackle economic disparities, with many new entrants among the poorest of the countries in the enlarged Europe.

Projects in tier-two areas of the United Kingdom which are furthering regional economic development may qualify for state aid of about 15 per cent. This applies to RSA as well as schemes that encourage property development and provide regional venture capital funds. But under the Commission proposals this potential 15 per cent funding would vanish.

Professor Fothergill said the implications for the government of the loss of £300–500 million a year of regional aid were huge. 'We have to ask if Nissan would ever have come to Sunderland if it hadn't been able to access state funding,' he said. 'Assistance to industry has been a cornerstone of regional policy since the early 1960s.' Ms Hewitt said while the government did not want to get into a 'subsidy race' with other developed countries, 'we have to be able to meet the needs of our most disadvantaged communities for economic development and business growth'. A spokesman for the Commission argued that the proposals were a reflection of the Union's enlargement into the poorer states of central and southern Europe. 'The Commission has to redraw the regional aid map and recalculate the maximum aid intensity. Should a region in the old member states lose out in the process, the proposals provide for a generous transition period,' he said.

Source: Blitz, Eaglesham and Tighe (2004).

Questions

1 What reasons are given for the decline in UK regional funding from the European Union?
2 What might be the implications of this reduced funding for the United Kingdom?

environment. The ESF will be used to develop the European Union's employment strategy to help member states reform their labour markets. The relative weight of the cohesion fund will increase because of the new member states.

In the second priority theme, 'regional competitiveness and employment', regional policy seeks to improve the economic framework, making the economies of the cohesion countries/regions more dynamic in line with the Lisbon and Nice objectives. Regional programmes are to be used to help anticipate economic change, while national programmes will improve implementation of the European Employment Strategy. ESF will provide the funding under the three headings of adjusting the working population to changes in work, promoting employment, and reducing early departure from the labour market.

Territorial cooperation will seek to promote the balanced development of the territory. The Commission is proposing a new objective for cross-border, transnational and inter-regional cooperation which will receive approximately 4 per cent of regional funding, expanding the role of INTERREG funding. In addition, because some old EU15 regions have lost out on objective 1 funding through the fall in average EU GDP after enlargement, transitional funding will also be provided for those regions.

In the future regional policy faces a range of new challenges, and it begs the question whether any of the new accession states can make the move from a below-EU-average GDP to one above the average, as has been the case with Ireland and parts of Spain.

EU environmental policy

On the whole the pressure to develop an environmental policy within the European Union began with the growth of the Green movement in the 1970s. By 1972 the European Commission forced the pace, and the heads of government called for the development of an environmental programme. In 1973 this led to the first Environmental Action Programme (EAP). The European Union is currently in its sixth EAP, agreed in July 2002, which runs from the period 2000–12. This sixth programme has identified four environmental areas for improvement:

- climate change
- nature and diversity
- environment and health and the quality of life
- natural resources and waste.

There are seven thematic strategies within the sixth EAP:

- clean air for Europe (CAFE)
- soil protection
- sustainable use of pesticides
- protection and conservation of the marine environment
- waste prevention and recycling
- sustainable use of natural resources
- the urban environment.

There were periods at the beginning of the development of environmental policy where there was a lack of commitment to joint policies and doubt over the legal basis for issuing directives in this area. On one level joint action could be argued to be appropriate. This was in areas where EU harmonisation was needed because different national standards could give one country a competitive advantage, such as those for noise, exhaust emissions, packaging and labelling of solvents, and biodegradable detergents. Other areas such as some types of pollution and environmental standards, for example the quality of bathing water, could not be considered as hindering inter-state trade and therefore could be addressed locally rather than at an EU level.

Nonetheless, the Treaty of Rome was concerned that measures to protect the environment were important, and could be considered as a means to provide a further balanced expansion of the European Union and to raise living standards and well-being. On these grounds an EU-wide policy could be considered appropriate.

Later on the development of the Single European Act (SEA) had a specific requirement that actions to complete the internal market should take into account a high level of environmental protection, and therefore specific articles were included in the SEA. Policies on the environment were also strengthened further through the Treaty on European Union and the Amsterdam treaties, as the role of the European Parliament was developed. This latter body, with its membership of 'green' MEPs, was able to push the Council further on environmental matters. Even so, where environmental protection occurred in areas where products and services were not traded, it still could be argued that national rather than EU-wide legislation might be appropriate. However, if each government were allowed to have its own policies, those with higher standards than others might face unfair competition. An EU-wide Uniform Emission Standards (UES) would reduce this threat of unfair competition. Hence governments had a greater desire for EU-wide policies which would affect all countries equally.

In 2001, the European Council in Gothenburg added the environment as the third strand to the Lisbon Strategy for Economic and Social Development, thereby confirming their commitment to sustainability. EU policy is now therefore aimed at creating a virtuous circle within which regional development both reduces economic and social disparities and leads to an improvement in the environment.

Nonetheless, there are substantial differences between member states and regions as regards the present state of the environment, the nature and scale of problems that threaten it, and the local capacity to combat them. In fact there tends to be a positive correlation between the state of the environment and economic and social performance. The areas in which EU environmental policy has operated are manifold. This chapter focuses on a number of the more important: water, waste, climate change and environmental standards.

Water

Access to clean water and the preservation of fresh water supplies are factors of regional competitiveness. Water is a scare resource and in a number of regions the amount abstracted annually is at, or above, critical levels (20 per cent or more of the total resources) (European Commission 2001a). This can threaten ecosystems. Consumption of water is very high in the south of Europe, in the cohesion countries and in objective 1 regions in Italy. Conversely in the new accession countries of the European Union consumption is generally below the EU average.

The Water Framework Directive suggests limiting abstraction in line with availability, ensuring reasonable prices and involving people in tackling problems. Until the Urban Waste Water directive of 1991 the recycling of waste water was poor in the European Union. Since then it has improved substantially, though the proportion of the population in objective 1 regions and cohesion countries who are connected to waste water treatment plants is only around 50 per cent, compared with 80–90 per cent in Nordic countries. The proportion connected to recycling plants is also relatively small in accession countries (European Commission 2001a).

Waste

Annually, 1.3 billion tonnes of waste are generated in the European Union. This leads to a loss of resources but also to a major environmental problem, because of waste disposal via landfill and incineration rather than recycling the waste through reusing glass products, re-pulping paper and making garden waste into compost. The level of waste is approximately 480 kg of municipal waste per head. In objective 1 regions the average per head is around this level. It is higher in the cohesion countries and lower in accession countries, probably reflecting their lower real incomes.

The disposal of waste through landfill contributes to increased greenhouse gases and other emissions. The amount of landfill is much higher in cohesion and objective 1 countries. Community directives in this area have promoted prevention of waste, recycling and reuse rather then final disposal. A new directive that came into operation in 2005 required organisations to collect old fridges and washing machines on the delivery of a new machine where there are no recycling centres for the consumer. Furthermore, many local authorities have been set targets for recycling, and this has led to the development of a wide range of different coloured bins into which each household places its rubbish for recycling. The downside to this has been the growth in 'fly-tipping' as tyres, cars, asbestos and building materials need to be disposed of correctly, and to do this is often costly; therefore people dispose of them illegally.

Climate change

Greenhouse gases generated by human activity cause climate change, especially carbon dioxide from the combustion of fossil fuels. The United Nations Framework Convention on Climate Change (UNFCCC), adopted in 1992 at the Rio Earth Summit, had as its ultimate objective the stabilisation of greenhouse gas concentrations, with the emphasis on the developed economies taking the lead. Both developed and developing economies were to reduce greenhouse gas emissions at source. The Convention eventually came into force in March 1994.

The Kyoto Protocol added new commitments which were stronger and more complex than the Convention. It was adopted in December 1997 and was to come into force when 55 parties to the Convention, which accounted for 55 per cent of the total carbon dioxide emissions for 1990 from that group, had deposited their instruments of ratification, acceptance, approval or accession. The European Union ratified the Kyoto Protocol in May 2002. By January 2003, 84 parties had signed and 104 parties had ratified or acceded to the Kyoto Protocol (see also Chapter 13).

Ten of the EU15 members (prior to May 2004) are still a long way from achieving their agreed share of emissions targets to meet the Kyoto Protocol (overall, to reduce emissions by 2010 by 8 per cent of the 1990 level). These include the cohesion countries. For example in Ireland emissions in 2001 were 31 per cent higher than in 1990, as against the increase of 13 per cent allowed between 1990 and 2008–12 (see Table 12.4).

The United States has refused to sign the Kyoto Agreement, which its government sees as damaging to US industry (since its industries might become less competitive). It also considered that other countries were not doing enough, and argued the case for carbon sinks. Carbon sinks are areas of forest, for example, which are capable of absorbing carbon dioxide. The United States has argued these should be included as a contribution towards meeting the treaty goals. If this were the case it would cover half the US commitment to the Kyoto agreement. The US administration also wanted a global system for the selling of rights to pollute. This means, for example, that if less-developed countries had surplus pollution rights, perhaps through a lack of industrialisation, they could sell these to the United States and other developed economies, allowing them to overshoot their pollution quota. It was also postulated that industries in the developed world could preserve woodland in developing countries, and thereby obtain the rights to pollute in their own country.

Monitoring such a mechanism would be problematic, and the rich industrial nations could be seen as simply buying their way out of having to make any changes at home. If forests were allowed as carbon sinks, then other forms of energy production, such as nuclear plants and hydro-electric dams for example, should also be given credit, some argued.

The European Union argued heavily against carbon sinks, but perhaps it did so because it had fewer forests to use as sinks than did the United States. Other

Table 11.4 Greenhouse gas emissions 2000, EU15

Member state	Index, base year, 1990 = 100	Kyoto target
EU15	96	92
Belgium	106.2	92.5
Denmark	99	79
Germany	81	79
Greece	124	125
Spain	135	115
France	98	100
Ireland	124	113
Italy	104	93.5
Luxemburg	55	72
Netherlands	103	94
Austria	103	87
Portugal	130	127
Finland	96	100
Sweden	98	104
UK	87	87.5

Source: European Union Environment Agency (EEA) and Eurostat.

problems with this approach surround the inflation of the figures associated with the pollution being traded, the difficulty of checking the validity of the data, and the way that property rights are initially assigned, since this would favour the developed countries (if it was based on current levels of pollution). Trading pollution rights might also stifle technological breakthroughs in pollution reduction, since it would reduce the incentive to look for these.

However, it is not only the total greenhouse gas emissions that are important, but the type and source of the emissions. In fact within Europe there are important differences. In the accession countries a higher proportion of greenhouse emissions comes from energy production compared with the EU15, since there is a greater reliance on fossil fuels. In the EU15 it is the transport sector that is responsible for a higher proportion of greenhouse gases. However, this scenario is likely to change as real incomes in accession countries increase and their road networks improve. Moreover, car fleets of the accession countries are on average four to five years older than those of the EU15, so the accession countries lag several years behind in the uptake of cleaner technologies and fuels. (There is a lower use of catalytic converters – devices used to remove a high proportion of the noxious exhaust gases – in the accession countries since the take-up of catalytic converters in the European Union was a result of changes in EU environmental policy.) In addition in the accession countries urban air quality remains poor. It might be expected that without an agreement to sign up to the Kyoto Agreement, companies will give lower priority to curbing greenhouse emissions, yet even though there are often extra costs, the case study below indicates that a number of organisations are building emission targets into their company performance monitoring.

A DIVERSE APPROACH TO CURBING GREENHOUSE GASES

When President Vladimir Putin refused to commit Russia to ratifying the Kyoto Protocol in September 2003, he sent an unsettling message to business. Companies at the sharp end of the global effort to curb greenhouse gases face continuing uncertainty about the international legal regime governing climate change. Until the future of the Kyoto Protocol is resolved, many long-term decisions on tackling carbon emissions are likely to stay on the back burner. Yet in spite of the delays to the ratification of the Kyoto Protocol, businesses are starting to adapt to a carbon-constrained world in which emissions of carbon into the atmosphere will carry a cost. They are also trying to maximise the opportunities likely to be presented by a shift to low-carbon fuels and energy-efficient technologies.

More than half the world's top 500 companies have recognised climate change as a serious issue, and are developing strategies to reduce greenhouse gas emissions. Only a minority, however, are already taking action to deal with the risks of global warming, according to a survey conducted by the Carbon Disclosure Project (CDP), a joint initiative by 35 institutional investors representing US$4,500 billion in assets.

This study of the climate-related risks faced by companies concluded that some heavy industrial companies could see their value tumble by as much as 40 per cent if they ignored the threat to their business. Companies face several risks.

- First, climate change will have a direct impact on companies vulnerable to intense and frequent storms, changes in temperature and rainfall, rising sea levels, drought and other climate-related extremes. Although most enterprises will be threatened by these changes, some – such as agricultural businesses in northern regions – could become more productive.

- Second, businesses could conceivably face litigation over their greenhouse gas emissions. Already, two carbon-related legal cases have been launched in the United States against regulators and agencies.

Although it seems unlikely that a company could successfully be sued merely because of its greenhouse gas emissions, some lawyers warn that companies might be at risk if they are deemed to have acted culpably by, say, lobbying against greenhouse gas regulations. Companies that delay taking action on climate change could also be at risk of being sued by their investors. They could be accused of incurring higher costs as a result of unduly delaying emission reductions, damaging their reputation and failing to disclose investment-relevant information.

- Third, company profitability could be affected by new government regulations designed to curb greenhouse gas emissions. Emissions restrictions and trading schemes are – or soon will be – a reality in Japan, the European Union, Canada and parts of the United States. The impact of these regulations will be much wider than is generally recognised, according to the CDP.

Research by the International Energy Authority found that the use of emission trading schemes is most pronounced in Europe. Voluntary agreements are prevalent in both the Pacific countries and North America, while North America is largely championing government-backed research and development. These diverse approaches present business with very different challenges. A recent study by the Royal Institute of International Affairs (RIIA) in London argued that US businesses face 'complexity and uncertainty' in climate policy. This lack of certainty stems from the possibility of the United States re-entering the Kyoto system at some point, coupled with the contrast between the administration's 'hands-off' voluntary approach and the firmer policies being pursued by Congress and at state level.

By contrast, EU companies face a more predictable policy environment, owing to the high-level commitment to Kyoto and a strong public expectation of business responsibility on climate and other environmental issues. Nonetheless, there are extensive lobbying efforts by business associations in an effort to secure voluntary or market approaches, ostensibly to protect international competitiveness, the study says. 'The progressive business voice is growing, it but remains relatively small and fragmented within many EU countries.'

In Japan, the RIIA study reported some resentment of the Kyoto Protocol on the part of business, which is faced with considerably higher marginal abatement costs than its European or US counterparts. However, the study notes that 'a more aggressive approach to emissions reductions and technological leadership opportunities is emerging, particularly within the automobile manufacturing sector'.

The RIIA reports also highlighted growing differences between businesses on how to respond to climate change. In the United States, for example, there are increasing splits between and within sectors. 'While there remains an extensive and powerful lobby against any mandatory approach to emissions reduction, there is also a gradual acceptance that more mitigation measures are likely, and many companies now have emissions goals of widely varying types and stringency,' the report says. It expects such divergent attitudes to become increasingly apparent across the world. 'Business approaches to climate policy will diverge as markets for emission reductions and low carbon technologies develop and concerns over liabilities grow.'

Source: Houlder (2003).

Questions

1 Will business change its view about pollution without the Kyoto Agreement?
2 Why might businesses in countries that have signed up to the Kyoto Agreement consider that they are at a competitive disadvantage?

Environmental standards

Higher environmental standards can make regions more attractive to investors while improving the quality of life of people who live there. Cohesion policy within the European Union has helped the less-prosperous member states to comply with EU environmental requirements. However, the growth in transport in both cohesion countries and accession countries poses increasing concerns for the future. The future is likely to require substantial investment in the accession countries so that they can meet the environmental standards set out in the *acquis*. In addition throughout the European Union there will need to be greater support for the development of eco-industries and the use of cleaner technologies, especially in SMEs. There also needs to be emphasis on the use of brownfield sites rather than developing new **greenfield** sites. Incentives may have to be provided for the use of cleaner methods of transport and vehicles as well as for the use of renewable energy. The European Union will also have to consider ways of ensuring adequate water and waste management so that the regions are improved in their attractiveness for business expansion and inward investment.

How can the European Union achieve its policy of protecting the environment?

Figure 11.1 shows a simple model for determining the optimum level of pollution. Marginal pollution costs (MPC) increase with output beyond Q_0. Up to Q_0 the environment is seen as being able to absorb any costs of pollution. Pollution is a 'negative externality'. Firms are imposing costs on society for which they are not paying. The marginal net private benefit (MNPB) of each unit of output is assumed to decline as the level of economic activity rises. MNPB is the addition to private benefit received by firms from selling the last unit of output minus the addition to private cost incurred by producing the last unit of output.

If pollution is not taken into account then firms would produce up to the level of output Q_1, where MNPB equals zero. Here total net private benefit (total profit) would be at a maximum. The socially optimum level of output is where MNPB = MRC, shown as Q_e. Every unit of output beyond Q_e adds more pollution costs to society than it does to net private benefit. Similarly it would not be socially efficient to produce at points to the left of Q_e.

The socially optimum level does not indicate that there is no pollution, but suggest that the benefits to society are greatest at output level Q_e. But how can the socially optimum position be achieved? There are a number of approaches, which can be separated into market-based approaches and non-market-based approaches. The market-based approaches include environmental taxes, tradable permits and bargains (where property rights are assigned to either polluters or sufferers from pollution). The non-market-based incentives stress the role of regulations. Here standards might be set for air or water quality. For example in the UK, the Environmental Protection Act (1989) prescribed the

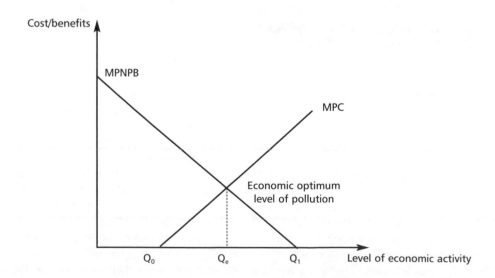

Figure 11.1 Finding the optimum level of pollution

minimum environmental standards for emissions for over 3,500 factories involved in chemical processes, waste incineration and oil refining. Regulations have also played a major part in the six Environmental Action Programmes (EAP) of the European Union, where specific standards have been set for the quality of bathing and drinking water. These non-market approaches may be an integral part of an overall environmental policy that also includes market-based approaches. For example in the United States a tradable permits system for sulphur dioxide emissions has been established which works alongside the standards set by the US Clean Air Act.

These are not the only differences between the market-based instruments used by the United States and the European Union. The United States has not often used environmental taxes at the federal level, while the European Union has often adopted this approach. The United States has preferred tradable permit schemes (similar to the quota systems that operate in the fishing industry). Permits will be bought under a market system so long as the cost is less than the marginal abatement cost. That is, if the cost of undertaking action to reduce pollution is greater than that of purchasing a permit to pollute, the permit will be purchased.

Why should tradable permits be used more in the United States than in the European Union? US citizens and businesses are more opposed to taxes than the citizens of the European Union. There is also the feeling in Europe that a tradable permit system between two countries in the European Union may harm a third party. Such spillovers are tolerated more in the United States since the spill-over is likely to be into another state, whilst in Europe it is into another country. Even where taxes have been used in Europe they are often sector-specific, may only affect part of a sector, and are not necessarily applied nationally but regionally (see Table 12.5).

The environment and trade

Environmental concerns can also be used to restrict trade (see Chapter 3). The US Marine Mammal Protection Act (MMPA) of 1972 required tuna fishers to use dolphin-friendly technology or have their products barred from US markets. A similar practice was used to protect endangered sea turtles. The World Trade Organization (WTO) ruled that in both cases the United States was illegally encroaching on the sovereignty of other governments by deciding individually what the rules were for entry into their domestic market. This contravenes the ideas of free trade.

On the international stage the World Bank has also been criticised. The reason for this is that it is a powerful force in genetic erosion. Its encouragement of borrowers to concentrate on cash crops and the use of fewer and better high-yield seeds can promote monoculture. (This can lead to dependency on a single crop or single type of seed, which may not always be the best for the local environment and can damage the export performance of an economy if this particular strain becomes subject to disease.) Further, the accompanying chemical packages can also cause environmental damage. Moreover by promoting export-led growth the Bank has encouraged natural resource exploitation which endangers local communities that depend on these resources for

Table 11.5 Environmental taxes and charges in selected EU countries

Country	Natural resources				Waste			Emissions		Selected products					Other	
	a	b	c	d	e	f	g	h	i	j	k	l	m	n	o	p
Austria			✓	✓				✓		✓	✓					
Belgium	○	○						○		✓	✓	✓				
Czech Republic	✓	✓				✓	✓	✓	✓						→	✓
Denmark	✓		✓		✓	✓		✓	✓	✓	✓	✓	✓			
France		✓						✓	✓							
Germany			○			✓		✓								
Portugal			✓													
UK	✓					✓										

Source: EEA (2003).

Key: → Aircraft only

○ At the regional (sub-national) level

a Mining, minerals, gravel, sand etc.
b Groundwater, surface water
c Hunting, fishing
d Forest use, tree cutting
e Landfilling
f Incineration
g Hazardous waste
h To air

i To water
j Chemical substances
k Packaging
l Batteries
m Pesticides
n Plastic bags
o Noise
p Land use change

survival. Other financial bodies have also affected the environment and the trading performance of some countries. The US Overseas Private Investment Corporation and the Export Bank of the United States have also been seen as climate destabilisers as they have underwritten support for financing for oil, gas and coal production, which would release even more carbon dioxide into the atmosphere.

Therefore on the one hand national governments have begun to deal with the problems of pollution and the environment, though their approaches can be very different. On the other hand a number of mainstream financial institutions can be seen to be adding to environmental problems through their lending policies.

Transport policy

Although the Treaty of Rome established the ideas of a common transport policy (CTP) under Articles 3e and 74–84, the move towards developing this within the European Union has been very slow. The basic principles of a CTP were set out in the Schaus Memorandum of 1961, and the measures suggested were incorporated into the Commission's First Action Programme of 1962 under the following headings:

- Liberalisation measures: these allowed carriers greater access to supply services across national boundaries within the European Union.
- Anti-discrimination measures: it was intended that discrimination between member states and between different modes of transport should be eliminated.
- Harmonisation measures: items such as the weights and dimensions of road vehicles and the taxation of vehicles among other items were to be standardised.

The reason that progress in developing these was slow lies in the distinctive nature of transport systems in the member states and their desire to move transport policy forward along one, not necessarily the same one, of the approaches above. Peripheral countries of the Union (such as Denmark, the United Kingdom and Ireland which are on the geographical edge), wanted a move towards the liberalisation of transport, for example, while Germany and Italy wanted more emphasis on harmonisation (Hitiris 2003). Moreover, the relative share of the different transport modes differs markedly between member states. Inland waterway traffic is more important in the Netherlands than in the United Kingdom, while in terms of freight haulage the use of roads is more important in Spain than in the Netherlands. Similarly the transport of freight by rail is more important in Germany than in the Netherlands.

Despite these differences there are some common problems to be faced within the transport sector of the European Union. First, there is increasing pressure on transport infrastructure as passenger traffic has increased, particularly on roads. This has led to lost resources, congestion, pollution and safety issues. Second, there has been increasing pressure on public provision for transport as car ownership has continued to rise.

Perhaps it was because the different member states wanted different things from EU transport policy that the European Union failed to develop a common policy up to the mid-1980s, but all this was to change. In 1985 the European Court of Justice was successful in convicting the Council of Transport Ministers for its 'failure to act' upon its duty to set up a common transport policy. Such a policy was needed if the full benefits from a single market were to be established. The Commission thereafter put forward a series of proposals for harmonisation of road haulage, civil aviation, rail, road passenger transport, sea transport, and for structural improvement in inland waterways. The following sections concentrate on the first two in particular, since these are two important areas subject to change.

Road haulage

Following the 1985 changes in transport policy, certain minimum levels of harmonisation in road haulage were developed, concentrating on technical requirements such as weight and length of vehicles, as well as social aspects such as number of driving hours. In 1988 the Council adopted its regulation on access to the market for the carriage of goods by road. The regulation required by 1993 the abolition for Community hauliers of all Community quotas, bilateral quotas between member states, and quotas for transit traffic to and from non-member countries. Access to the market for cross-border carriage of goods by road within the Community was now governed by a system of Community licences. There were still, however, a number of major sticking points in the road haulage sector, particularly in the areas of taxation, user charges and cabotage. Transport companies argued that after dropping off a load in another country they would like to use the same lorry to bring back a delivery from the destination country to their home country. UK lorries that transported goods from the United Kingdom to Italy, for example, would like to bring back a return load from Italy. However, this was resisted by Italian transport companies who would lose business.

Moreover, road use by transport companies was heavier in some countries. Those in the more central region of the European Union were more likely to have their roads used by other countries' hauliers. One way to overcome this problem was through a system of tolls. In the north-western EU countries an alternative system, the residence principle, was adopted, which meant that the individual country taxed the carrier. By allowing cabotage to take place, non-domestic freight hauliers can provide haulage services in the domestic market of a member state. If this is coupled with the better use of technology which can allow a home office to trace trucks at all times, this then allows international hauliers to compete with domestic ones.

Cabotage was fully liberalised within the European Union by July 1998. Although liberalisation of the road haulage sector has progressed fairly quickly, there still is the problem of differences between member states in their use of road user charging systems; therefore in some countries it is more expensive to transport goods. The result is that some transport companies attempt to reduce their toll fees by using minor roads or rescheduling their journeys through countries where the road usage fees are lower.

The EU transport policy for 2010 has sought to address the issue of congestion and the way it is spreading to major trunk routes. The estimate is that much of this increased congestion will be caused by international road haulage, which is expected to increase by 50 per cent by 2010. While transport over short distances may be unavoidable, since there may be no other mode of transport, for medium to long distances the question is what other factors are sustaining or even encouraging the growth of transport.

One of the factors is unfair competition. On the one hand the haulage sector is very competitive, and in order to survive in this highly competitive environment some haulage companies have sought to circumvent the rules on working hours and road safety. The risks of this happening in the future are likely to become greater after the accession of the new member countries in May 2004, because there will be increased cost competition from hauliers in the CEECs with lower overheads. On the other hand, although road haulage may be considered to be at a cost disadvantage when compared with the more state-subsidised rail companies, the hauliers do not face the true costs of motoring. In fact the hauliers do receive public benefits since the cost of motorway maintenance would be six times less if only cars were to use the motorway system. Furthermore the precarious nature of many small haulage companies means that when diesel costs are increased they could receive tax relief, and some see this as a hidden subsidy.

Despite these facts no real plan to restructure the sector has yet been produced in the European Union. The European Union envisages a situation where transport contracts should include clauses where revisions of tariffs faced by haulage companies vary, as say the price of fuel varies. However, as haulage may be the only mode of transport in some areas, this approach may deter any other modes from entry and thereby suppress the growth performance of some economies.

The European Union has, however, addressed the issue of low-cost competition from the CEECs which could result in some higher-wage countries requiring their drivers to work longer hours to compete. The 48-hour average working time per week (with a maximum of 60 hours) has been introduced for drivers, though there are still exemptions for self-employed drivers. Furthermore, there are moves to harmonise weekend bans on lorries, and plans to introduce a 'driver's certificate' and to develop vocational training for drivers (European Commission 2001b). In addition by the end of 2003 the digital tachograph had been introduced, which is better at monitoring driving than its mechanical relative, and the Galileo programme (a satellite tracking system) for tracking goods and vehicles is to be developed further.

The controls have been not only on drivers but also on hauliers. The European Union is attempting to tighten up controls and penalties on licensing. It seeks to harmonise penalties and the conditions for immobilising vehicles, to increase the number of checks made on vehicles, and to encourage the systematic exchange of information between hauliers.

Although hauliers dominate the transport of goods, air transport also plays a significant part, and it is to this sector that the chapter now turns.

The air transport and passenger industry

Air transport in the European Union has grown at an average annual rate of 7 per cent for the past 20 years, while in the passenger market, between 85 and 90 per cent of EU air passengers travel on reduced or discounted tickets (Hitiris 2003). This growth in passenger numbers has pushed some airlines to saturation point and overloaded the traffic control systems. Costly delays result, flights leave and arrive late, and pollution increases as aircraft burn additional fuel during waiting time on the ground and queuing in the skies. These delays cost EU airlines somewhere between €1.3 and 1.9 billion per year (European Commission 2001b).

Initially air transport remained outside the influence of EU regulation. In 1974, however, an ECJ ruling brought it under the general rules of the Treaty of Rome with regard to the free movement of services and competition rules.

The market for air transport can be broken down into three parts: charter, cargo and scheduled passenger traffic. Both cargo and charter traffic are subject to light regulatory regimes and are on the whole competitive. However, it is in the passenger aircraft market that complications can be found.

Until the 1990s the lack of competition in this market arose from the Chicago Convention of 1944. This convention permitted each state to have its own flag-carrying airline, and these were usually in public ownership. Thus they could receive state aid (see Chapter 10). States had bilateral agreements with each other about landing rights and flight routes between the two countries. Often the flights between two carriers were shared on a 50:50 basis. Fare levels were negotiated within the framework of the International Air Transport Association (IATA) but were subject to government approval. The result of the Chicago Convention meant that airfares were likely to be higher than true competitive airfares, cost levels were higher because of the lack of competition, and consumer choice was limited. In addition while the bilateral arrangements placed restrictions on existing carriers they virtually excluded new entrants from international markets. By the mid-1980s there were about 200 bilateral agreements providing air transport services between 22 countries in Europe (El-Agraa 2004). The rights of Community carriers to offer services between two other member states, known as 'fifth freedom' rights, were very restricted, being offered on only 44 of the 400 routes. The 1985 white paper on transport liberalisation set about altering this, expressing a need for the Community to liberalise its air transport services, particularly with respect to tariffs, capacity control and access to the market (European Commission 1985).

In December 1987 the Council adopted measures to regulate airfares, capacity sharing and the application of competition rules to civil aviation. Although the first package of proposals did little to liberalise the market they did set in train important developments. The second 'package' continued the opening-up of the market developed in the first package but also developed greater flexibility in pricing and the allocation of seat capacity. The lower fares offered to passengers were then extended to the freight industry in 1990 (European Commission 2001b).

The third package of measures was a major turning point in liberalising the air transport market. It covered scheduled, non-scheduled and cargo services, and came into force on 1 January 1993. This package made it easier to get an EU operator's licence, the great majority of intra-EU air routes were to be opened to recognised EU operators, cabotage restrictions were reduced with full cabotage rights (with some minor restrictions) established by April 1997, and airlines were free to determine their own scheduled passenger fares, subject to certain safeguards. In addition all restrictions on charter fares were removed and cargo rates continued to be unregulated.

Although the liberalisation of the air transport sector has come a long way since 1985, it still faces further difficulties. Some exemptions still apply, such as the allocation of landing and take-off slots. State aid is still given, often linked to state-run airlines and allowed through the money being used to rationalise the airline business. Although the level of state aid has been reduced in the airline industry it is resented by the privatised airlines, carriers and budget airlines which have to operate as private business enterprises. In addition, making airlines compete against one another could result in the market becoming more oligopolistic in the long term as less profitable airlines either go out of business or are purchased by more profitable airlines. Some airlines have also complained about interlining. This is where passengers can exchange tickets between one airline and another (which are often in strategic alliance) on the same route. Thus a competitor is unable to offer the customer a ticket. Other airlines have complained that computer reservation systems such as Galileo used by travel agents provide the owning airline with the ability to give priority to its own services and restrict access to competitors. This gives an airline, via its travel agent, the opportunity to offer better access and timing than competitors and thereby remove a potential competitor from a route.

One major difficulty facing the European Union's airline industry is that air traffic is expected to double by 2010 (European Commission 2001b). Part of the problem with congestion has been reduced by implementation of the hub and spoke network in Europe; nonetheless there is still congestion. This is not helped by the differences in national practices and legislation. For example the European air traffic control system is divided up into 26 subsystems consisting of 58 en route control centres, three times as many as exist in a comparable area in the United States. Therefore the European Union is handicapped by air traffic control systems that are not sufficiently integrated. In its desire to improve integration between the EU states' air traffic control centres, the European Union set itself the goal of creating a Single European Sky by 2005.

The European Union also acknowledges that the current infrastructure in the old EU15, and in particular in the new accession countries, will not be able to cope with the growth in passenger numbers, and intends to pursue changes in airport charges to deter the bunching of flights at certain times of the day. Intermodality between rail and airport will be further developed and where a high-speed rail route exists, capacity could be transferred to this mode.

As for road hauliers, the true cost of air transport is not being borne by the air passenger and air transport companies. There is no tax on aviation kerosene, and this does not encourage airlines to use the most efficient aircraft. It also provides for a situation where the competition between air and other forms of transport is unfair, since rail companies pay taxes on their use of diesel and electricity yet the airlines appear to be receiving a subsidy. The European Union is seeking ways in which air travel can be charged properly for the costs that it incurs.

Conclusion

The continued growth in the European Union has led it to examine, modify and develop new policies to cater for the changing nature of international competition and for the development of closer harmonisation of policy by the individual member states. All three areas of EU policy explored in this chapter reveal that the European Union is driven by both the need to harmonise between member states and the need to become more competitive in global markets. At the same time it also wishes to show that it is taking a leading role in global concerns.

Regional policy was set up to reduce regional inequalities. There have been some notable success stories, such as Ireland and Spain, yet some regional disparities have widened. Regional differences have also increased through the admission to the European Union of the new accession countries in May 2004. Addressing regional inequalities can have profound effects on EU growth performance, employment, unemployment, social deprivation and the environment.

EU environmental policy indicates a willingness to face up to global concerns, some of which have been created by a number of the different policy areas of the European Union itself. For example, unless regional policy is a success, there will be an increased risk of environmental degradation and pollution in some regions. The approach adopted to address environmental concerns has often been through environmental taxes. Some EU countries such as Greece come fairly high up on the list of member states that are using environmental taxes to curb pollution, yet it has been argued that the real reason for this is the revenue-raising ability of these taxes rather than care for the environment. The Kyoto Agreement is still a problem, particularly as some countries, notably the United States, have argued that they cannot accede to such an agreement unless all other countries sign up, and if they were to do so then their industries (lobbied by various pressure groups) might become less competitive.

The environment is also a factor for the airline and road haulage industries. EU transport policy had a distinct lack of focus until 1985. However, since then, the European Union's approach has been to reduce the fragmentation of the member states' transport markets, particularly road haulage and air transport, so as to improve their global competitiveness. Nonetheless, there is still a long way to go to develop a common and effective transport policy within the European Union. Problems such as addressing bottlenecks, the creation of a trans-European network, how to deal with urban transportation and how to address the needs of users who want increased mobility and high-quality transport services are still to be dealt with.

Questions

1 Choose a large organisation in a European country. To what extent can regional policy at the national and European level be seen to have influenced its location?

2 To what extent is the United States's stance toward environmental policy influenced by its energy-producing companies?

3 In the road haulage sector, how has EU transport policy increased the costs of road haulage firms? What have been the benefits experienced by hauliers from EU transport policy?

4 Consider Table 11.1. What factors suggest that regional policy should take a much higher profile in EU policy making since the admission of the new accession countries in May 2004?

5 Spain was a major beneficiary of regional funding throughout the 1990s. How might the development of those regions in receipt of funding influence transport and the environment issues there?

6 The United States has so far refused to sign up to the Kyoto Agreement,

while the European Union has done so. What impact will this have on the competitiveness of US and EU car makers?

References

Armstrong, H. and Taylor, J. (1985) *Regional Economics and Policy*, Philip Allen, Oxford.

Artis, M. and Nixson, F. (2001) T*he Economics of the European Union: Policy and analysis*, 3rd edn, Oxford University Press, Oxford.

Baldwin, R. and Wyplosz, C. (2004) *The Economics of European Integration*, McGraw-Hill, Maidenhead.

Blitz, R., Eaglesham, J. and Tighe, C. (2004) 'Poor areas face loss of billions in aid schemes regional development', *Financial Times*, 17 June, p. 4.

Dunford, M. (2000) 'Catching up or falling behind? Economic performance and regional trajectories in the new Europe', E*conomic Geography*, vol. 76, no. 2.

El-Agraa, A.M. (2004), *The European Union: Economics and politics*, 7th edn, Prentice Hall, Harlow.

Europa (2004) *Working for the Regions*, Brussels.

European Commission (1985) *Transport Policy in the European Community*, Brussels.

European Commission (2000) *The Impact of Economic and Monetary Union on Cohesion*, Regional Studies 35, Office for Official Publications, Brussels.

European Commission (2001a) *Second Report on Economic and Social Cohesion*, Office for Official Publications, Brussels.

European Commission (2001b) *European Transport Policy for 2010: Time to decide*, Luxemburg.

European Commission (2004) *Third Report on Economic and Social Cohesion*, Brussels, Office for Official Publications, Brussels.

Eurostat (2004a) *Third Report on Economic and Social Cohesion*, Brussels.

Eurostat (2004b) *Europa – Working for the Regions*, Brussels.

Hitiris, T. (2003) *European Union Economics*, 5th edn, Prentice Hall, Harlow.

Hospers, G. J. (2002) 'Beyond the blue banana? Structural change in Europe's geo-economy', paper presented at 42nd European Congress of the Regional Science Association, Dortmund, Germany.

Houlder, V. (2003) 'A diverse approach to curb greenhouse gases', *Financial Times*, 16 October, p. 2.

Levi Sandri, L. (1965) 'The contribution of regional action to the construction of Europe', Third International Congress on Regional Economics, Rome.

Mason, C. M. and Harrison, R. T. (1990) 'Small firms: phoenix from the ashes', in D. Pinter (ed.), *Western Europe: Challenges and change*, Belhaven, London, pp. 72–90.

McDonald, F. and Dearden, S. (1999) *European Economic Integration*, 3rd edn, Longman, Harlow.

Myrdal, G. (1957) *The Theory of Underdeveloped Regions*, Duckworth, London.

12 Small business and EU policy

Mark Cook

Objectives

This chapter will:

- consider the importance of the small-firm sector in Europe and the global community
- investigate the growth of the small-firm sector in Europe
- outline the development of European small firms policy
- consider the role of small firms in the internationalisation process.

Introduction

Over the last two decades entrepreneurship and small and medium-sized enterprises (SMEs) have emerged as the engines of economic and social development throughout the world. SMEs are now considered as important drivers behind the growth and creation of employment, economic growth and increased national and regional competitiveness in a globalised economy. Within the European Union the SME sector is seen as a major feature of the economy. SMEs are key to entrepreneurial spirit and innovation, and therefore crucial to ensuring EU competitiveness.

Historically it was believed that larger firms were the dynamic forces behind economic growth. Work by Caves (1982) and Teece (1993) indicated the increasing role of large-scale enterprises in both domestic and international economies. Moreover, given that knowledge is expensive and that there are fixed costs to be faced by all firms, particularly in the area of internationalisation, it is not surprising to see large firms dominant in global markets, with SMEs at a distinct disadvantage. Despite this, entrepreneurship and the small-firm sector have emerged as major engines of economic growth and social development throughout the world. World economies have moved from the model of the managed economy suggested by Audretsch and Thurik (2001) to one of the entrepreneurial economy.

The theoretical framework linking entrepreneurship and economic growth is provided by the new theories of industry evolution (Ericson and Pakes 1995, Klepper 1996). This contrasts with the traditional theories which suggest that entrepreneurship and the small-firm sector actually retard economic growth. In these theories, entrepreneurship plays no role, with the advantages attributed to large firms being associated with scale economies.

What is critical in the newer approaches to industry evolution is the role knowledge plays and the dynamic, or flux, that occurs through this. Entry, growth, survival and the way enterprises and entire industries change over time are linked to innovation. The dynamic performances of regions and even entire economies are linked to how well the potential from innovation is used and the extent of entrepreneurial activity. There is also a two-way relationship between the level of dynamism in an economy or region and innovation. Moreover, the more innovative an economy, the more likely there will be spillovers from this innovation to other firms, competitors and organisations in the supply chain. The SME sector also can be the initiator of innovation, which results in the growth of some of these companies into medium-sized or large companies, or in the innovations being purchased by large companies to improve their competitive positions.

So in what ways is the SME sector important for economic growth?

- There are spillover effects from knowledge.
- Entrepreneurship has a positive impact on economic output through increased levels of competition.
- Entrepreneurship generates a greater diversity of firms and output.

More recent studies by Birch (1981) in the United States and Gallagher and Stewart (1986), Storey and Johnson (1987), Heshmati (2001), Hohti (2000) and Klette and Mathiassen (1996) in the European framework found also that small firms were the main job creators, while it was large firms that were shedding jobs.

Given the contribution by SMEs to economic growth and global competitiveness, just how important are they?

Size and structure of European SMEs

In the Europe19 (the EU15 together with Switzerland and the European Economic Area of Norway, Liechtenstein and Iceland) there were approximately 19 million enterprises in 2003 providing work for almost 140 million people. There were only 40,000 large enterprises accounting for 0.2 percent of all enterprises. Therefore the great majority of enterprises in the Europe19 (99.8 per cent) were SMEs.

In May 2003 the European Commission adopted new definitions of micro, small and medium-sized enterprises. This updated the thresholds of the financial ceilings for turnover and balance sheet totals, and therefore will help this sector to get access to national and European support provisions. These new definitions came into operation on 1 January 2005 and can be seen in Table 12.1.

Based on these definitions the great majority of business in Europe are micro enterprises (over 90 per cent), with approximately half of these micro enterprises having no employees at all (that is, they consist of one self-employed individual).

The role of SMEs in exporting is less than large organisations (with more than 250 employees). European enterprises export an average of 17 per cent of turnover, with micro enterprises having the lowest share of turnover (9 per

Table 12.1 SME definitions in the European Union

Enterprise category	Employees	Turnover limit (€ million)	1996 turnover limit (€ million)	Balance sheet total (€ million)	1996 balance sheet total (€ million)
Micro	<10	2	not defined	2	not defined
Small	<50	10	7	10	5
Medium	<250	50	40	43	27

Source: Europa (2003).

cent) and large firms the greatest at 23 per cent. However, the area of internationalisation and the SME sector will be considered later in this chapter. It is also the case that labour productivity is lower in SMEs than in large organisations. This may be explained partly by the sectoral composition of firms. For example, a larger number of smaller organisations are to be found in the retail sector, and this sector tends to exhibit lower levels of productivity. If this sectoral difference is taken into account, the productivity differences between the small and large firm sectors almost disappear, though there is a lower level of productivity in micro firms.

Profitability also tends to be lower in the SME sector, though once again, if sectoral differences are taken into account there is little to distinguish the profitability of the small and larger organisations. Once again, however, even allowing for sectoral differences the micro-firm sector has a lower level of profitability.

The country level

Table 12.2 gives the size-class structure of organisations in the European Union, and shows that the average size for organisations differs between European countries. Large companies dominate the economies of Germany, the United Kingdom and the Netherlands (that is, they account for 50 per cent or more of employment). In Italy, France, Spain and Sweden it is micro organisations that dominate.

SMEs and industrial sectors

Within Europe the role of SMEs is not constant across different industrial sectors. Large organisations tend to dominate the manufacturing, mining and extraction, and energy sectors, which is not surprising given the use of large-scale industrial processes. Although large firms appear to dominate the transport sector and the banking and finance sectors, these three sectors can be further disaggregated, and if this is done, there are seen to be many parts of these sectors where small firms dominate. Other industry groups such as construction, trade hotels and restaurants tend to be small-scale activities.

Table 12.2 Dominant size of organisations in EU member states

Country	Number of enterprises (000)	Occupied persons per enterprise	Size-class dominance
Austria	270	11	Micro
Belgium	440	7	Micro
Denmark	210	10	SME
Finland	220	7	LSE
France	2,500	8	Micro
Germany	3,020	10	LSE
Greece	770	2	Micro
Ireland	100	10	SME
Italy	4,490	4	Micro
Luxemburg	20	9	SME
Netherlands	570	12	LSE
Portugal	690	5	SME
Spain	2,680	6	Micro
Sweden	490	7	Micro
UK	2,230	11	LSE
EU15	18,700	7	Micro

SME: small and medium-sized enterprises

LSE: large-sized enterprises.

Source: Eurostat Structural Statistics Database, 2003.

SMEs in the enlarged Europe

The movement from planned economies to market-based economies in a number of the central and eastern European countries (CEECs) has seen the development of the SME sector as an important part of economic reform policies (European Observatory 2003a). A large number of SMEs have been created through the promotion of entrepreneurship and the role of privatisation as inefficient state-owned enterprises have been sold off or broken up. The growth of the SME sector has been important in the development of a flexible and dynamic enterprise economy in these countries.

Many of the new entrants to the European Union in 2004 have an average firm size similar to those in the Mediterranean area, though those in the Baltic countries are much larger on average than those to be found in the EU15. However, in the latter part of the 1990s the Baltic states exhibited falls in their average firm size, suggesting that they are coming more into line with the EU average through the process of restructuring.

SMEs in the United States and Japan

If Europe is compared with the United States and Japan, we can see some areas of commonality and some important differences. The share of enterprises in each size class is almost the same in Europe and the United States. In terms of employment, however, there are differences. The United States has a much lower share of employment in SMEs and a higher proportion of employment in large organisations. Part of the explanation is that in the United States there are a lot more sole proprietors, which means that although there is much the same proportion of SMEs as in Europe, on average they are smaller. In addition the US market is more integrated than Europe, and this has led to the development of more very large-scale businesses. Finally, in the United States it tends to be easier to start up and close down enterprises, so more companies are in the micro start-up stage, and hence are smaller.

The employment shares of Japanese SMEs reflect the European rather than the US pattern.

The United States has often been seen as a yardstick to which EU member states compare themselves in terms of entrepreneurial activity. It is the leader among the G7 countries in this respect (Global Enterprise Monitor (GEM) 2003). However, the United States is only seventh behind Uganda, Venezuela, Argentina, Chile, New Zealand and Brazil in its level of total entrepreneurial activity (TEA) (GEM 2003). In comparison with other countries, a higher percentage of both men and women believe that good opportunities will be available to them, and that they have the skills, knowledge and experience to start new businesses. People in the United States benefit more from a 'role model' effect in that they are more likely to know someone who is an entrepreneur. The GEM report for the United States also indicates that the fear of business failure is lower in the United States.

Levels of support also appear to be different. Financing from informal investors for SMEs in the United States is around 1 per cent of GDP. This is the highest rate amongst the G7 countries. Five out of every 100 adults invested in someone else's business in the period 2000–03. Much of this was in new start-up businesses. The venture capital market appears to have bottomed out in the United States, registering a total of US$418.2 billion in 2003, only 18 per cent of the total invested in 2000 before the Internet bubble burst. Although there has been a recovery of venture capital levels, the focus has moved away from seed and start-up funding. Nonetheless, the United States still outranks the rest of the world in areas such as financial support, entrepreneurship education and training, and the social norms favouring entrepreneurship. There are also indications from the US GEM report that the US small firms sector is flexible and has the capacity to adapt quickly. Against this background the European Union has sought ways to improve the level of entrepreneurship in Europe, although as the case study opposite indicates, its approaches are not necessarily the same as those adopted in the United States.

Changes in the performance of SMEs

If the non-primary sector in Europe is considered, in the period 1998–2003 the growth rate in annual average turnover was slightly larger for large enterprises than for SMEs (2.7 per cent compared with 2.4 per cent), while employment growth was 0.1 per cent for large enterprises compared with 0.2 per cent for SMEs. What could explain the differences in turnover described above? One

EUROPEAN AND US ENTREPRENEURSHIP ACTIVITY

It is four years since EU leaders met in Lisbon and set out a strategy for economic reform that would enable Europe to outstrip the United States as the world's leading economic power. Tony Blair liked the idea of reform, and Jacques Chirac liked the idea of 'besting' the United States. So reform it was to be.

One need only dip into the new report to understand that the seeds of American entrepreneurialism cannot successfully be planted in the hostile soil of today's Europe. The tools that the European Commission would use to catch up with America, and move European GDP up from its present 72 per cent of the US level, include passing a 'framework directive on eco-design of energy-using products', devising 'social inclusion strategies' and establishing 'National Action Plans ... to set national targets' to improve social cohesion, and developing a 'new industrial policy approach'. There is more, lots more, including new regulations and taxes.

Meanwhile, in the United States the White House is trying to reduce taxation and red tape (bureaucracy). In short, the European Union aspires to US performance, and sees greater involvement of government bureaucracies as the path to that goal, while US policy is to reduce the role of government in business.

Even in Britain, which has taken the lead in fighting the worst examples of the EU tendency to prefer regulation to markets, government just cannot grasp what American entrepreneurship is all about. In a recent report, the agency charged with fostering British competitiveness bemoaned the fact that half of London's small businesses don't have business plans – and then went on to report that a great many of these benighted firms are – surprise – chalking up higher sales and rising profits. Given the opportunity, the small-business owners would tell the government planners that they are

succeeding precisely because they spend their time satisfying customers rather than producing elaborate plans of the sort that bureaucrats often use as a substitute for accomplishment.

It should come as no surprise, then, that British productivity lags behind America's, and that the European Union's productivity growth rate has been declining since the mid-1990s and is now a fraction of that in the United States. And there is an added lesson for policy makers in the fact that the countries cited by the commission as the least enthusiastic reformers – France, Germany, Belgium and Luxemburg – are the loudest cheerleaders for greater European integration.

The failure of Europe to solve its problems is becoming more than a little annoying to American policy makers. As they see it, the United States has to be the world's economic locomotive because Europe will not take the steps needed to stimulate domestic demand. Instead, like China and Japan, Europe is hoping for an export-led recovery, with Americans the consumers of last resort.

Meanwhile, the European Central Bank (ECB) refuses to follow America's Federal Reserve and lower interest rates so as to stimulate business investment and consumer spending, and European governments either raise taxes (the United Kingdom), or make tax cuts too trivial to stimulate domestic demand. The hypocrisy of relying on American consumers to bail out Europe's unreformed economies, while at the same time criticising the United States for running large trade deficits, is so self-evident as to be embarrassing to all save European politicians too timid to institute the labour-market and other policy reforms that would produce a more balanced global economy.

That harsh view, it should be noted, is not confined to Americans. Romano Prodi, former president of the European

Commission, says that Europe's dismal economic performance should serve as 'a strong wake-up call to governments'. And Otmar Lessing, a member of the ECB's Executive Board, has bemoaned the lack of structural reforms in both labour and product markets. The commission itself concedes that 'measures to increase the volume of, and improve the environment for, research investment have been fragmented and sluggish'.

In the end, the issue is whether Europe can cling to its social-market, welfare-state model and at the same time overtake the United States as the world's most productive economy. So far, Europe has avoided that hard choice, preferring instead to grope for a probably nonexistent third way.

Source: Stelzer (2004).

Questions

1 Why is the level of entrepreneurship greater in the United States?

2 What policies have been put forward to stimulate the level of entrepreneurship in the European Union?

factor is that SMEs and large organisations may operate in different markets. Large firms have a greater proportion of their sales in export markets, and these have grown at a faster rate than the domestic markets in which many SMEs operate. The European Observatory (2003a) also suggests that another reason for the slower growth in sales by SMEs is that their prices have increased more than those for large organisations. One reason for this is that their costs have also increased. Labour productivity is lower for SMEs than for large organisations, hence costs per unit of output are higher in the SME sector. If labour costs increase in the large-firm sector, this encourages enterprises to replace labour with capital (which they can generally do because of their better access to financial resources) thereby raising productivity. It is also the case that over the same period, employment growth has tended to be greater in SMEs, and particularly in micro enterprises.

Compared with Europe, employment creation in the United States was more likely to have taken place in large organisations during the periods 1993–8 and 1998–2001. Therefore in the United States there is a positive correlation between employment growth and the size of the organisation, while in Europe the reverse is true. More importantly however, in these two periods employment growth was greater for all types of organisation in the United States than for similar-sized organisations in Europe. Only in the period 1996–2001 was the employment growth of one particular size group (the micro organisation) greater in Europe than in the United States.

The accession countries since 1995 have seen an increase in SMEs and a decline in large enterprises. This can be explained partly by the breaking-up of large state-run or owned enterprises and the formation from many of these of SMEs (see earlier).

Changes in performance across European countries

As Table 12.3 indicates, labour productivity and employment differed not only by country but also by size of organisation in the EU15 during the period 1988 to 2003.

Table 12.3 Annual average change in labour productivity and employment by country and size class, 1998–2003

Country	Labour productivity			Employment		
	SME	Large	Total	SME	Large	Total
Austria	1.5	1.2	1.4	0	0.1	0.1
Belgium	1.7	2.0	1.8	–0.1	–0.1	–0.1
Denmark	2.6	2.6	2.6	–0.2	0.0	–0.2
Finland	2.2	2.4	2.3	–1.5	–1.6	–1.5
France	1.1	1.4	1.4	0.1	0.7	0.3
Germany	2.1	3.0	2.4	0	–0.4	–0.2
Greece	1.8	–4.3	0.6	1.5	0.6	1.3
Ireland	4.5	5.6	5.3	2.7	2.9	2.7
Italy	1.5	1.9	1.6	–0.1	–0.2	–0.1
Luxemburg	1.7	2.9	2.1	2.6	1.2	2.2
Netherlands	1.1	1.3	1.2	0.5	0.9	0.7
Portugal	2.7	2.8	2.8	0.2	0.4	0.3
Spain	1.3	1.3	1.3	1.2	1.2	1.2
Sweden	3.0	2.7	2.8	–1.2	–1.3	–1.2
UK	2.6	3.2	2.8	–0.2	–0.9	–0.5
EU15	1.9	2.6	2.2	0.1	–0.2	0.1

Sources: *European Economy* (2003), OECD (2003).

In some countries, such as Luxemburg and Spain, SMEs contributed to an increase in employment over the period 1988–2003, while in countries such as Belgium, Denmark and Finland, SMEs exhibited a fall in employment. Generally large organisations tend to show better productivity than do SMEs across all countries.

Internationalisation and SMEs

During the last decade we have seen enhanced international competition both for organisations with an export focus and for those that have focused more on their domestic markets. The growth in SME internationalisation can be seen in the context of political, technological and economic changes. Through the actions of the World Trade Organization (WTO), world trade has been liberalised (see Chapter 3), while in Europe markets have become more integrated, enlarged, liberalised and deregulated. Technology has improved access to information and communication, and also the management of scattered production. More efficient and low-priced transport has also aided the growth in internationalisation by SMEs.

Although exporting has been considered one of the main forms of internationalisation, there are other forms such as importing from a foreign supplier, the development of foreign partnerships, foreign investments and cross-border clustering. There is further evidence from Spigarelli (2003) that a presence in foreign outlet markets and the possibility of delocalising part of the value chain allow SMEs to achieve more solidarity and durability in production than SMEs that develop an international strategy based solely on exporting. In other words the value chain has become an increasingly important aspect of the internationalisation of SMEs. So what is the incidence of international activity amongst SMEs?

An ENSR (2003a) study indicates that 18 per cent of SMEs had a foreign supplier as their only form of internationalisation, with a further 12 per cent having imports in combination with exports, or foreign subsidiaries. Six per cent of SMEs were only involved in exporting, and just over 60 per cent had not internationalised. More firms had both import and export activities than only exported, which suggests that having a foreign supplier somehow improves export-related activities. This result is consistent with the results of Overweel (1991) in his study of Dutch SMEs. The level of export activity is also likely to have been understated since the ENSR study does not include indirect exporting, that is, where a domestic organisation contracts with another domestic organisation which then sells the product abroad.

While only 3 percent of SMEs noted that they had subsidiaries, branches or joint ventures abroad, the numbers were growing at a faster rate than for large enterprises. Almost a third of those SMEs with subsidiaries abroad had no exports. Subsidiaries were therefore used not just as sales platforms but as a means of accessing cheaper labour via sub-suppliers or accessing knowledge and technology. In other words some SMEs are using subsidiaries as a way of improving their competitiveness and enhancing their value chains.

The level of internationalisation within European countries

The level of internationalisation amongst SMEs varies substantially between countries (ENSR 2003b). SMEs in small countries are more likely to have foreign suppliers than SMEs in large ones. SMEs in central Europe are more likely to use foreign suppliers than SMEs in the Nordic countries. However, having a foreign supplier does not mean that the SMEs in that country are likely to be export-active. Germany is the only country in the European Union where more than 20 per cent of SMEs are involved with exporting. This suggests that in some sectors at least, domestic markets are not big enough to support SME activity and firms are pushed into exporting.

In terms of export intensity (the percentage of exports out of turnover), approximately half of exporting European SMEs export 10 per cent or less of their total turnover. Almost 20 per cent export more than half of their turnover and 12 per cent more than 75 per cent of their turnover.

Very few SMEs possess subsidiaries. On average between 1 and 4 per cent of SMEs in the various European countries have subsidiaries, though countries such as Switzerland (with 7 per cent), Denmark (9 per cent) and Iceland (11 per cent) lie outside this range. This suggests that in small open economies there is a greater emphasis on the establishment of subsidiaries.

When SMEs are involved in exporting, importing, the establishment of subsidiaries or joint ventures, the activity tends to be located in neighbouring countries or in the larger economies of the global community.

Size and internationalisation

As Table 12.4 indicates, micro enterprises are less likely to be involved in the various aspects of internationalisation than SMEs. The differences in size are more marked if more complex forms of internationalisation are considered, such as the establishment of subsidiaries and **joint ventures**. In addition non-exporting behaviour is higher in micro enterprises, and export intensity increases with the size of the firm. However, the difference in export intensity between micro firms and SMEs is not as marked as the difference in level of internationalisation. Therefore smaller enterprises export less than their larger contemporaries, but when they do so, their level of export intensity is closer to that of larger organisations.

A further question to be considered about SMEs and internationalisation is whether activity is related to sector.

Table 12.4 Size and internationalisation of SMEs

	Non-international %	Foreign supplier only %	Export only %	Subsidiary abroad or more than one form of internation-alisation %
Micro firms (0–9 employees)	64	18	5	10
Small enterprises (10–49 employees)	41	19	10	27
Medium-sized organisations (50–249 employees)	35	10	7	46

Source: ENSR (2003b).

Table 12.5 Internationalisation by sector

Sector	Foreign supplier only %	Export only %	Subsidiary abroad or more than one form of internation-alisation %
Retail	31	4	9
Wholesale	27	8	34
Manufacturing	17	18	28
Personal services	14	4	7
Construction	13	1.5	8
Transport/communications	12	9	16
Business services	11	7	10

Source: ENSR (2003b).

It might be expected that different sectors would have different levels of involvement in external markets, and that there would be also differences within some of the sectors. For example, would the subsectors of business services, such as legal services, accounting and software design, all have the same level of export activity, and is this changing over time?

Where relationships have been developed with a foreign supplier only, Table 12.5 indicates that the retail sector is most actively involved, with business services the sector least likely to have developed this type of activity. Other forms of internationalisation such as the development of subsidiaries are prevalent in the manufacturing and wholesale sectors. Transport and communications joins these two sectors in showing a sizeable percentage of SMEs with subsidiaries, or more than one form of internationalisation. The same three sectors – manufacturing, wholesale and transport/communications – also have a high propensity to export (whether as a sole form of internationalisation or in combination with other forms). Conversely the retail and construction sectors contain fewer SMEs that are export oriented.

In terms of export intensity, the transport and communications SME sector has the highest intensity, with around a third of the SMEs in this sector exporting in excess of 50 per cent of their turnover. SMEs in the retail sector are the least export-intensive organisations. Again, although the manufacturing sector is the most export-oriented, once exports begin, the export intensity of manufacturing SMEs is similar to SMEs in the business services and personal services sectors.

The development of alliances and networks

Networking has become an increasingly important aspect of SME behaviour. These networks can be both formal and informal. SMEs that internationalise appear to be more involved in both types of networks than SMEs that are domestically focused.

Many SMEs are also involved in alliances. These alliances with larger enterprises or even multinational enterprises (MNEs) are important ways for SMEs to internationalise (Sakai 2002). The development of alliances has become more frequent as larger organisations have concentrated on their core competencies and increasingly outsourced a number of their activities to SMEs. In addition MNEs may use SMEs in a foreign economy to gain market information and leverage into a foreign market. Concentration on core competencies leads to de-internalisation, and this leads to the development of new SMEs, and causes larger organisations to further develop their network of alliances. Sakai (2002) indicates that alliances can relate to quite diverse activities such as joint R&D activities, manufacturing, marketing and sourcing of inputs, and can be a useful way for SMEs to improve the indirect export flows.

Over the last 18 years alliances between service-sector SMEs have grown appreciably, in particular since the mid-1990s. Alliances between manufacturing SMEs have also grown since 1998 but have stabilised since the mid-1990s. The extent of alliances between SMEs and other organisations has probably been understated, since many of the data sources only include those alliances that come into the national or international framework. Since many of the alliances between SMEs do not get external exposure, they may go unregistered. Christiansen and Bertrand (2003) suggest nonetheless that the extent of external alliances may have been reduced during the early part of this century as a result of the slowdown in economic activity.

Towards a theory of SME internationalisation

One view about how SME involvement in international markets takes place is given by stage theory (Gankema, Snuif and van Dijken 1997). Here SMEs are categorised as following a range of stages to internationalisation, starting from the point of no regular internationalisation behaviour, through to production facilities abroad. The stages are shown below:

1. No regular export activity (sporadic exporting).
2. Exports via independent representatives.
3. Establishment of own sales subsidiaries abroad.
4. The setting-up of production facilities abroad.

This approach minimises the risks that arise through the development of an external strategy, and also lowers the capital investment in the early stages. This and other variations on the stages approach to internationalisation have their grounding in the behavioural theory of the firm (Cyert and March 1963, Penrose 1959). The stages approach is supported by work by Johanson and Vahlne (1978, 1990) and the Uppsala School, and suggests that SMEs target 'psychically close' countries initially before moving on to countries that are more psychically distant. The idea of psychically close countries encompasses those that are geographically close as well as those that have common languages, common cultures and common political and economic environments.

A further extension to this model was made by Wiederscheim-Paul, Olson and Welch (1978), who expanded the model to include pre-export behaviour. They argued that to move towards exporting required a number of clear conditions to be in place for any SME, relating to the individual decision maker's characteristics, the history of the firm, levels of education and the like (see Hall, Giewen and Cook 2006).

The stages approach to internationalisation can also be considered from the perspective of innovation-related models. This later approach sees export development as an innovation–adoption cycle (Reid 1981), whereas Cavusgil (1980), Czinkota and Johnston (1982) and Crick (1995) see it as a learning curve influenced by stimuli from the external environment and internal provoking factors such as managerial ambitions and excess capacity.

Although Pia Barber's (1998) work has supported the stages approach to internationalisation, over the last 15 years there have been various criticisms of it. The stage models do not necessarily have all the same stages (Anderson 1993), but the main issues are related to the lack of proper design to explain the development process, the absence of clear-cut boundaries between the stages, and issues with the tests of validity and reliability. In addition Haynes and Hauge (2002) found that over 40 percent of SMEs in their Norwegian study followed a discontinuous development pattern that is inconsistent with stage theory. At the same time, other studies do not give any evidence for the suggestion that once SMEs begin the internationalisation stages, they proceed through them in order. Some firms stagnate and do not progress; others appear to leapfrog stages. One other criticism of the stages approach is that there are organisations that adopt a global focus from their conception, the so-called 'born globals', and these go through none of the stages.

Born globals

These are defined as organisations that have products or services that are global in nature, or have little domestic demand. These companies often begin exporting within the first five years of their existence. According to Littunen (1997), one in ten new firms in the metal industry and in services is born global in the sense that its existence is dependent on export markets. Saarenketo and Sundqvist (2002) suggest that in the knowledge-intensive sector a significant number of organisations are born global. Thus born global organisations discredit many of the notions of stage theory. In other words stage theory may be appropriate for the internationalisation behaviour of some SMEs but not for all.

The holistic approach to internationalisation

So as seen above, it can be argued that some SMEs appear to follow the stage approach to internationalisation while others are born global. However, this difference may lose its distinctiveness over time. Born globals may follow the stages approach to internationalisation, except their stages are shorter or concentrated into a small time horizon. In other words some born globals follow a much more rapid stages approach to internationalisation. Other SMEs may follow the stages approach to internationalisation, and then a change in strategy propels them faster along the internationalisation route, redefining their businesses as born globals or reborn globals.

Another reason to question the distinction between born globals and SMEs following the stages approach to internationalisation is that there may be time during one of the stages of internationalisation where the organisation has to develop networks, set up subsidiaries, connect with foreign suppliers and the like. The different stages in the stage model therefore become required all at the same time, rather than being used successively.

Finally for some SMEs, particularly those in the service sector, it may be more useful to set up a strategic alliance or joint venture straight away rather than to go through the various stages of internationalisation. This could particularly be the case where the organisation is seeking know-how or access to technology. Therefore by taking a holistic view of internationalisation SMEs can use a whole variety of means or options in international markets to optimise their positions.

There is some evidence to support such a view, as ENSR (2003b) found that one-third of SMEs without exports have subsidiaries. Therefore, for some SMEs the gradualist stages approach to internationalisation is appropriate, while for others a much more multi-dimensional approach is used. Where resources are limited, a more gradualist approach to internationalisation may be the better strategy.

Psychic distance research

Styles and Ambler (1997) and Cook, Coskeran and Weatherston (2000) find some evidence to support the notion that psychic distance plays an important part in the way SMEs internationalise. Nonetheless, Czinkota and Ursic (1987) and Johanson and Mattsson (1988) have argued that the concept of psychic distance plays an ever-decreasing role in internationalisation in a global community with improved telecommunications and transportation links. These two facts at least have led to increasing market convergence and hence reduced psychic distance. Moreover, in a globalised market with increased use of telecommunications and where supply chains are important to adding value, network theory and client follower models may provide a better explanation of the internationalisation process.

Network theory

Internationalisation through network theory is based on developing relationships, and is linked to international industrial marketing. Increasing involvement in foreign markets comes about through the increasing commitment to internationalisation, and improved knowledge of these markets that arrives via the interactions with foreign markets. Increased internationalisation improves inter-market and inter-firm relationships. Network theory postulates that markets are a system of relationships amongst the main stakeholders, and that strategic international action is rarely based on a single firm's behaviour but on the nature of the relationships developed between others.

Internationalisation may also be driven by following customers or clients, or customer-driven internationalisation, particularly in the service or computer software sectors. So success in international markets is not the result of reduced psychic distance but is achieved through an SME's development of relationships with current markets, both domestically and internationally.

The drivers of internationalisation among SMEs

There are many factors that can influence internationalisation by SMEs, and these differ depending on whether the SME is an importer, exporter or has a subsidiary abroad. Access to raw materials is the most important motive for those SMEs that are purely exporters or have establishments abroad (ENSR 2003b).

Access to know-how or technology is the most important motive for pure importers, and the second most cited motive for SMEs with more complex forms of internationalisation. Even for those that just export, more than one-third of organisations are motivated by access to knowledge and technology. Therefore the decision to internationalise is not simply one of increasing sales, but also related to gaining knowledge to improve competitive advantage.

Push or pull factors

SMEs' activity in a new or larger market may be the result of two important drivers behind the process: push factors and pull factors. Push factors apply in situations where the domestic market is insufficiently large for a particular product or service, or where there is insufficient market development. It may also be the case that the level of competition in the domestic market is very intense, because of low import barriers, high concentration ratios and the like. Pull factors occur where foreign buyers make unsolicited demands for a product or service, but this may also occur where a major partner requests that the SME accompany it into an external market. SMEs may also act together in internationalisation, where one partner has the expertise and knowledge while the other has access through contacts to an external market. The push driver has been seen as more important in studies undertaken in Ireland and Finland (O'Malley and O'Gorman 2001, Kailaranta 1998) while pull factors have been in greater evidence in Belgium (Donckels and Aerts 1992, Luxembourg Centre for Promotion and Research 1992).

It should also be acknowledged that some SMEs are not involved with international markets. Some of these may have been involved in the past but such activity has ceased, others do not intend developing external markets now or in the future, while others might like to internationalise but find the barriers, both internal and external, too difficult to surmount. The type of product or service that some SMEs offer might be considered not appropriate for international markets, while others may consider that the foreign demand for their products/services currently and in the future will only ever provide a small proportion of turnover. Some entrepreneurs have little ambition to expand their business externally, and for some there may be issues of fear of external dependence or loss of control.

Barriers to exporting by SMEs

One factor that may inhibit internationalisation is the lack of strategic planning for this activity. Personal features of the entrepreneur may also provide barriers to internationalisation. These include knowledge of foreign markets, language competence, and level of experience of foreign markets and foreign culture. The European Centre for the Development of Vocational Training (CEDEFOP) (2002) also suggests that the personality and individual preferences of the owner manager, and his or her persistence and commitment, are crucial.

Compared with large companies, SMEs face proportionately higher labour costs of employing people with the correct skills for cross-border activities. So what barriers to internationalisation do SMEs consider important? Do they actually consider surmounting these barriers, and how do they deal with them?

For those that had considered or had undertaken exporting, the most cited barrier was the high costs of the internationalisation process. This included the costs of external market analysis, the translation of documents and the adaptation of products for external markets. In general almost a quarter of SMEs with a subsidiary abroad found these high costs a barrier (CEDEFOP 2002).

For those that were just importers internal barriers, such as insufficient skills or the competence of staff, were considered to be less of a problem than for those that were exporters or had subsidiaries. The more complex the external international arrangements conducted by SMEs, the more important they found internal barriers. However, almost one-third of SMEs in Europe did not consider that there were any external barriers to internationalisation. Of the barriers that exist, the least problematic were lack of support/advice or lack of information. The most cited barrier, however, was the existing laws and regulations of the target country.

This type of barrier was considered most important by almost a quarter of those SMEs with subsidiaries abroad, and by those that were involved with multiple forms of internationalisation (such as exporting and having a subsidiary abroad). In addition this type of barrier was almost as important for SMEs that had internationalised via having a foreign supplier. Therefore importers require almost the same level of support as those SMEs that export. However, it is difficult to disentangle which part of the laws and regulations forms the most important barrier. Oxford Research (2002), for example, concluded that for a number of the Nordic countries, tax regulations and company laws represented significant barriers.

The role of the Internet

The Internet has played an important part in the internationalisation of SMEs, through web-based sales, Internet marketing and communications networks. Spigarelli (2003) and Dellner and Lundgren (1999) have noted that the Internet has permitted SMEs rapid access to international markets, and helped them to collaborate in flexible and decentralised markets with a minimum level of effort. Access to the Internet is also size-dependent, with medium-sized firms more likely to have access than small and micro firms, although even among the latter in the early part of this new decade, over 70 per cent had access.

At the same time we need to consider how the Internet is used. Access is fine but if it is not used in the appropriate way it might not improve customer reach. Conversely SMEs might be able to sell more services and products in international markets because more of their potential customers have Internet access. Not surprisingly, SMEs in the ICT industry have achieved a higher degree of internationalisation than their contemporaries in other sectors (Sakai 2002).

Shortages of capital as a barrier

Research by CEDEFOP (2002) found that lack of capital was not seen as a major barrier to internationalisation by Europe's SMEs. It is interesting to note that even though capital shortages are less important than laws and regulations, this is still the second most important barrier, and one that increases once internationalisation is under way. In other words capital shortages are less likely to be considered as a barrier before internationalisation takes place, but are more likely to occur later in the internationalisation process. Considering that some SME sectors are more internationalised than others, it is these sectors that are more likely to experience capital shortage. They include the manufacturing, transportation/communication and wholesale sectors. Small companies also perceived the lack of capital to be more of a barrier, but perhaps the biggest difference lies between countries. SMEs in Norway, the Netherlands and Greece have the lowest perception of capital as a barrier to internationalisation, while SMEs in Austria, Luxemburg and Iceland cite this factor more highly (Kisslinger 2002).

Trade barriers

Following the development of the General Agreement on Tariffs and Trade (GATT)/WTO and the Single European Market (SEM) (see Chapters 3 and 4), many formal trade barriers have been reduced, but there still exists within Europe a range of non-tariff barriers that may inhibit internationalisation. A study undertaken into the internationalisation behaviour of Danish SMEs (Danish National Agency for Enterprise and Housing 2003) found that 55 percent of them experienced trade barriers in export markets, a figure similar to that five years earlier. In fact the level of trade barriers was almost the same in 2003 as it was some ten years earlier, suggesting that the internal market had not reduced technical barriers significantly. However, the type of technical barrier might have altered. Product requirements such as those for retesting or certification to meet specific national or local standards have been reduced by the internal market; however, specific marketing requirements such as labels/declaration of contents as well as language requirements have actually increased (ENSR 2003a). The use of the SEM as a means of reducing the barriers to internationalisation faced by SMEs is only one of many policy initiatives that have been used in Europe to support the SME sector.

European policy towards SMEs

Encouraging entrepreneurship is seen to be central to creating jobs and improving competitiveness and economic growth throughout Europe. Thus the European Union has sought to support the SME sector in a number of ways. One of its first priorities has been to expand its knowledge of SMEs by improving the collection of statistics, since without knowing the size and distribution of SMEs within the European Union the Commission would be unable to estimate the 'knock-on' effects of any policy changes and the cost of policy initiatives. It is also acknowledged that SMEs have been affected by both direct and indirect policy initiatives, and these can come through what was initially a number of policy areas. Therefore in January 2000 the whole range of policies relating to the SME sector became the responsibility of the Enterprise Directorate-General (DG), which combines the previous directorates of Industry, SME and Information Society. Although the policy areas that affect SMEs are numerous, they can be divided into direct and indirect measures, and the following sections give a flavour of these.

Other policy measures affecting SMEs

One aspect of the changes in competition policy, such as the use of state aid, has been to reorientate state aid from sectoral and regional issues to policy decisions that have a more horizontal objective, such as the support provided to different-sized firms, including the promotion of SMEs. This objective was first endorsed by the Lisbon European Council in 2000, and reinforced at the Stockholm European Council in March 2001 and again at the Barcelona European Council in March 2002.

There has been block exemption for SMEs in state aid provision. This allows investment aid to be given to SMEs (15 per cent of the total investment costs for small enterprises and 7.5 per cent for medium-sized enterprises). SMEs can be aided with up to 50 per cent of eligible costs for consultancy and the same figure for costs associated with the participation in fairs and exhibitions. The European Union has also allowed governments to give risk capital to SMEs, and this is differentiated from state aid. The reasoning behind these approaches can be related to the special difficulties SMEs face with raising finance, networking and affording advice.

SMEs have also been affected by employment and social policies. The employment guidelines in the European Union following from the Treaty of Amsterdam 1997 were based on four pillars: employability, entrepreneurship, adaptability and equal opportunities for men and women. The second pillar, on entrepreneurship, focused on the way jobs can be created. It concentrated on the ways businesses might be able to start up and grow. The *Joint Employment Report* (European Commission 2002b) considered member states' initiatives to improve entrepreneurship, with measures to facilitate business registration, encourage self-employment and to develop an entrepreneurial culture, particularly among women.

In the area of corporate responsibility, the changes were driven initially by large businesses, but this is increasing seen as being relevant for SMEs. A project entitled 'Responsible Entrepreneurship for SMEs' (European Commission 2002a) was begun to consider the extent to which SMEs were involved in socially and environmentally responsible practices.

In the area of environmental policy (see Chapter 11), the European Commission launched a best practice project to determine the member states' best initiatives to promote environmental management systems (EMSs) in SMEs. The tools of the sixth Environmental Action Programme 2001–10 have been specifically tailored to the needs of SMEs. SMEs have also been the main beneficiary of the Financial Instrument for the Environment (LIFE) programme. This financial support has a specific objective to contribute to the development of innovative and integrated techniques and methods, and to the further development of Community environmental policy, through the co-financing of demonstration projects (Infobase Europe Factsheet 2004).

Energy policy has impinged on SMEs in a number of ways. The most direct way has been through the improvement in the conditions for competition in the energy markets, making energy available at competitive prices. The adoption of the directive on energy performance on buildings is likely to lead to job creation in the SME sector, through the certification and installation of more energy-efficient equipment. The ALTENER programme to promote renewable energy and SAVE to develop energy efficiency both benefit some SMEs greatly, since the renewable energy industry is mainly made up of SMEs (European Commission 2003).

As of March 2005 the Working Time Directive applies to further aspects of the transport industry. This has imposed restrictions on the working time of employed drivers. Self-employed drivers, who comprise a large part of the road transport sector, are affected but for SMEs there is a delay in bringing in the directive until 2009. The development of the Trans-European Network

(TEN), whose guidelines were adopted in 1995, has seen approximately €16–20 billion invested every year. Contracts have gone to SMEs for a significant part of the programme in the area of the extension of road, rail, seaport and inland waterways. The TEN will also improve infrastructure links that will aid the performance of SMEs (European Commission 2003).

SMEs have further received support from EU structural funds. Around 11 per cent of the total structural funds have helped this sector, and this is due to rise to 20 per cent between 2000 and 2006. In member states where regions have been given objective 1 status, SMEs have also benefited from this funding. For example, in Belgium about a quarter of the funding goes to SMEs, and in a number of countries such as Italy and France funding has been used to develop advisory services (European Commission 2003).

Direct policy measures affecting SMEs

The European Union has sought to develop entrepreneurship skills among its citizens. It has attempted to benchmark a range of European entrepreneurship training curricula, particularly concerning entrepreneurship among women and ethnic minorities. This has been financed in part through the various Leonardo da Vinci and Socrates support programmes. In this way the European Union hoped to improve the rates of start-up and development of new businesses.

The European Union has also been concerned more directly with start-ups. The difficulties experienced with starting up a business can constrain entrepreneurship. Following on from the Lisbon European Council a series of best practice exercises were undertaken within member states to explore ways of reducing the delays facing start-ups.

The European Union has also sought to improve the skills and competitiveness of the SME workforce. SMEs play an important part in lifelong learning, and a key role in EU competitiveness and employment, yet they undertake less training than large firms. An ambitious set of goals for training and education systems has been agreed and should be reached by 2010 (European Commission 2003). In addition the European Union has sought to address some of the financial matters that face SMEs. A Risk Capital Action Plan has been developed, and a code of conduct for banks and SMEs is in preparation. Work on best practices in micro lending is under way and a benchmarking exercise of business angel policies in member states has been undertaken (Europa 2002). With respect to financial problems, developments in the internal market have improved the framework for cross-border payments and there have been further developments to help late payment. Furthermore a benchmarking exercise of business angel policies was undertaken in 2002, and a pan-European database of investment opportunities (Gate2growth) has been established.

A number of financial instruments managed by the European Investment Fund (EIF) have been operational since the beginning of 2002. These are the start-up scheme, the SME Guarantee Facility and the Seed Capital Action. In addition to these instruments there has been work on the financing of innovation, and the technological capacity of SMEs has been strengthened. The sixth

Framework Programme for Research and Technological Development also attaches great importance to the participation of SMEs.

To overcome the barriers that some SMEs have with ICT and e-business, the eEurope Action Plan has been developed to highlight the actions necessary in relation to legislation, e-skills, inter-operability, and trust and confidence that have constrained the SME sector. Finally, to help the SME sector to get the highest-quality business support services, a best procedure project was carried out in the early part of the millennium to study the support services for micro, small and sole-proprietor businesses. The Support Measures and Initiatives (SMIE) databases are an important reference tool on business support measures for SMEs and good practice in this area.

Therefore both directly and indirectly the European Union has sought to develop and remove the barriers faced by the SME sector, the main creator of jobs in the region (European Commission 2003b). The removal of a number of these barriers may also be apposite as the European Union's SME sector faces a new challenge and a range of opportunities from the EU enlargement process.

SMEs and EU enlargement

The impact of EU enlargement has implications for SMEs both in the EU15 and those in the new accession countries following 1 May 2004. The enlargement process has resulted in the removal of many barriers to the flow of goods, services, capital and labour, and also provided new market opportunities, increased competition in domestic markets, and permitted access to new sources of inputs, especially low-cost labour, as the case study below indicates.

The impact of the enlargement process is however felt unequally by SMEs. It is likely to be larger in the new entrant countries than in the original EU15, and also likely to vary by sector and region. For example the SMEs in the new entrant countries are likely to benefit more through increased export opportunities to the EU15 as markets are opened up. This flow will greatly exceed the flow from the SMEs in the original EU15 to the markets in the new entrant countries. The sectors that are already benefiting are those where liberalisation of trade rules have taken place, and thus SMEs in the manufacturing and wholesale sectors are expected to be the main beneficiaries from enlargement, particularly in the new entrant countries. Even in these two sectors evidence from the European Observatory (2003b) suggests that medium-sized enterprises should benefit more than small enterprises, with their increased export flows.

Over time these two sectors and others can expect to lose their relative wage cost advantages as real wages increase in the new entrant countries. However, to compensate for real wage increases, the SMEs in the new entrant counties can expect to benefit from catch-up in the areas of productivity and technology use. This may greatly favour medium and high-technology SMEs. SMEs in bordering regions may also be expected to benefit more than SMEs in other areas of the European Union (ENSR 2003b).

The growth in trade that will be experienced by SMEs and large companies in both the EU15 and the new member countries will open up new opportunities

EU ENLARGEMENT AND THE SME SECTOR

The small business sector is being urged to get ready to take advantage of the huge opportunities that the recent expansion of the European Union will provide. At the beginning of May 2004, following years of planning and negotiations, ten new member states from central and eastern Europe and the Mediterranean were welcomed into the European Union.

The economic implications are enormous, with the expansion creating a single market bigger than the United States and Japan combined, and comprising about 74 million new customers. But there is evidence that not all SMEs share the government's enthusiasm for the newly expanded European Union.

A survey conducted by accountancy firm Grant Thornton found that four in five businesses were sceptical of the business benefits of EU enlargement. Nearly four in ten businesses felt that the expansion could lead to higher taxes, while just under half predicted that more red tape would result. Adrian Chambers, Sales Director of Bibby Factors West Midlands, said: 'There are very mixed feelings about Europe within the UK business community.' This is because trading with our European counterparts has historically presented a big risk for SMEs.

> They have been faced with a myriad of local legal and customs standards, not to mention the currency and language hurdles to be climbed. But with the harmonisation of trade rules, tariffs and administrative procedures, the UK small business sector needs to gear up in order to capitalise on the significant overseas trading opportunities on offer and stay ahead of the competition.

One area that small business owners and managers and business support organisa-

tions did agree upon was that the EU expansion should alleviate the chronic lack of skilled staff in the United Kingdom. According to the Institute of Directors, around 60 per cent of IoD members felt that workers from the ten countries that had just joined the European Union would help plug the gaps in the British labour market. A lack of skills is still high on the list of concerns for UK businesses, and a survey carried out by Bibby Factors West Midlands in 2003 found that 76 per cent of small business owners and managers believed that the skills gap in their industry sector was getting worse.

This was backed by recent figures from the Learning and Skills Council, which found that there were 135,000 unfilled vacancies in the United Kingdom because employers could not find appropriately skilled people. Mr Chambers said:

> It is encouraging that small business owners and managers agree that EU expansion will help the ever-widening skills gap. It is disturbing that so many firms are sceptical about the huge opportunities that EU enlargement will bring. While UK business is distracting itself with the ever increasing red tape and higher taxes and British bosses worry about the potential perceived pitfalls, other countries' small firms are just getting on with it.

Sources: *Birmingham Post* (2004).

Questions

1 Why do some SMEs not share the government's enthusiasm for enlargement?
2 What opportunities does an enlarged European Union offer for the SME sector?

for transport companies in the newly enlarged Europe. SMEs in the new entrant countries might benefit from the cabotage liberalisation that has taken place in the EU15, but at the same time transport companies in the new entrant countries will now have to adhere to EU15 standards and therefore they might lose some of their cost advantages (Ahlo, Kaitila and Widgren 2001).

For the construction sector, SMEs in the new entrants are expected to benefit from infrastructure developments in these countries, while the SMEs in the original EU15 can be expected to benefit from access to a greater quantity of resources as well as cheaper resources (particularly labour). As integration proceeds it might be expected that cross-border construction services will be provided, and this will increase competition particularly for those SMEs in border regions and those that use low levels of technology (Ahlo, Kaitila and Widgren 2001).

The move to market-based economies and the increased requirements of data on marketing, legal advice and translation are likely to improve the demand for professional business services. Information technology services are required to develop and modernise the infrastructure in the new member countries, and there is increased demand for civil engineering services and recycling. The evidence from the European Observatory (2003b) again indicates that the SMEs rather than the micro industries in the EU15 are likely to benefit more from enlargement in this area, since size appears to be a crucial factor in gaining contracts.

One problem for SMEs in the new entrant countries is that meeting the *acquis communautaire* can be costly, and the cost burden may threaten the existence of some SMEs. The compliance burden associated with the *acquis communautaire* is also more heavily weighted on smaller firms.

Larger companies in the new member states are better prepared and informed. In the lead-up to enlargement there was a major shift in the foreign direct investment (FDI) entering the new member states (Fallon, Cook and Jones 2004). This represented a range of new clients for these countries' SMEs through the supply chain networks, and some SMEs may have benefited through improved transfer of technology and the transfer of management skills. Conversely foreign companies increase the competitive environment in the new member countries and may drive some of these countries' existing SMEs out of the market.

For their part SMEs in the EU15 were hoping that the enlargement process would lead to an improvement in the level of, and skills of, their work forces. Conversely, some SMEs in the new member countries were concerned about the loss of some of their best-skilled workers, particularly those in border regions.

Enlargement of the European Union therefore provides both opportunities and threats for SMEs in the original EU15 and the enlarged union. Their business environment has changed. The introduction of the free movement of labour and capital along with the free movement of goods and services increases market access and the availability of new resources. At the same time competition in domestic markets will increase. For some countries at least there will be more winners than losers, and various forms of SME support may have to be addressed.

Conclusion

SMEs are the most prevalent type of business unit in the developed and developing world, and their role and importance in internationalisation is increasing. It may still be that in quantity terms, large firms dominate in the field of internationalisation, yet SMEs are increasingly becoming the dynamic forces behind economic growth, by filling market niches, and being associated with supply chains and other networks. This chapter has revealed that the level of entrepreneurial activity varies between countries. The Lisbon Conference in 2002 put forward a proposal that the European Union was to be seen as one of the most dynamic areas by the year 2010, and in this context the European Union has sought to develop a range of policies which have both directly and indirectly affected the level, and development, of entrepreneurial activity within the Union.

Enlarging the Union in May 2004 also provided a number of opportunities for SMEs, though it also posed a number of threats. These opportunities and threats were not likely to be equally distributed by country or by sector.

Many see the SME sector as providing a cornerstone of EU competitiveness for the future, and the European Union faces an important balancing act between encouraging SME activity through a range of support policy, allowing some derogations, and at the same time introducing a range of regulatory provisions to protect both consumers and employees.

Questions

1 Using information from this chapter and other supporting material, consider why the SME sector is important for the economic growth, job creation and export growth of the European Union.

2 SMEs often argue that they are constrained by labour market shortages and lack of finance. To what extent has the European Union successfully addressed these problems

3 Outline the main arguments for and against the stages approach to internationalisation.

4 For large organisations entry into international markets often occurs through merger and acquisition, exporting and joint ventures. Which of the above, if any, are the approaches more likely to be taken by SMEs entering international markets?

5 To what extent do firm factors, such as the size of the organisation and the level of competition in markets, rather than personal factors such as the willingness to take risks or the entrepreneur's experience of export markets, determine SME internationalisation?

6 The Polish Linen Company employs 25 people and has traditionally undertaken

the majority of its sales in Eastern European markets. Its manager is aware of the potential that EU enlargement might bring to the organisation. Produce a report for the Polish Linen Company outlining the opportunities and threats to the organisation following from EU enlargement.

References

Ahlo, K., Kaitila, V. and Widgren, M. (2001) *The Effects of EU Eastern Enlargement on Finnish Firms*, Research Institute of the Finnish Economy (ETLA), Series B.

Anderson, O. (1993) 'On the internationalisation process of firms: a critical analysis', *Journal of International Business Studies*, Second Quarter, pp. 209–31.

Audretsch, D. B. and Thurik, A. R. (2001) 'Capitalism and democracy in the 21st century: from the managed to the entrepreneurial economy', *Journal of Evolutionary Economics*, vol. 10, pp. 17–34.

Birch, D. L. (1981) 'Who creates jobs?' *The Public Interest*, vol. 65, Autumn, pp. 3–14.

Birmingham Post (2004) 'Take advantage of opportunities the expanded EU will provide', 16 June, p. 22.

Caves, R. (1982) *Multinational Enterprise and Economic Analysis*, Cambridge University Press, Cambridge.

Cavusgil, S. T. (1980) 'On the internationalisation process of firms', *European Research*, vol. 8, November, pp. 273–81.

CEDEFOP (European Centre for the Development of Vocational Training) (2002) *Internationalisation and Changing Skills Needs in European Small Firms*, Synthesis Report no. 23, Luxemburg.

Christiansen, H. and Bertrand, A. (2003), *Trends and Developments in Foreign Direct Investment*, OECD, Paris, June.

Cook, M., Coskeran, T. and Weatherston, J. (2000) *The Northamptonshire Export Survey 2000*, research report commissioned by Northamptonshire Chamber, December,

Crick, D. (1995) 'An investigation into the targeting of UK export assistance', *European Journal of Marketing*, vol. 29, no. 8, pp. 76—94.

Cyert, R. M. and March, I. G. (1963) *A Behavioural Theory of the Firm*, Prentice Hall, Englewood Cliffs, N.J.

Czinkota, M. R. and Johnston, W. J. (1982) 'Exporting: does sales volume make a difference? A reply', *Journal of International Business Studies*, Summer, pp. 157–61.

Czinkota, M. R. and Ursic, M. L. (1987) 'A refutation of the psychic distance effect on export development', *Developments in Marketing Science*, vol. 10, pp. 157–60.

Danish National Agency for Enterprise and Housing (2003) *Trade Barriers for Danish Exporting Companies*, Copenhagen.

Dellner, E. and Lundgren, A. (1999) *Globalisation via the Internet: An Internet-based business model*, Stockholm University.

Donckels, R. and Aerts, R. (1992) *SMEs and Internationalisation*, Koning Boudewijnstichting in cooperation with the Small Business Research Institute and CERA, Brussels.

Ericson, R. and Pakes, A. (1995) 'Markov-perfect industry dynamics: a framework for empirical work', *Review of Economic Studies*, vol. 62, pp. 53–82.

Europa (2002) *Benchmarking Business Angels*, Enterprise DG, Brussels.

Europa (2003) 'Commission adopts a new definition of micro, small and medium sized enterprises in Europe', press release, Brussels, 8 May.

European Commission (2002a) *Responsible Entrepreneurship for SMEs*, COM (2002), No. 347, Luxemburg.

European Commission (2002b) *Joint Employment Report*, COM Council Decision on Guidelines for Member States' Employment Policies for the Year 2002 (2002/176/EC), Brussels

European Commission (2003) *Creating an Entrepreneurial Europe: The activities of the European Union for small and medium-sized enterprises*, Commission Staff Working Paper no. 26, Brussels.

European Economy (2003) Supplement A, May.

European Network for SME Research (ENSR) (2003a) *Internationalisation of SMEs*, Observatory of European SMEs, Office for Official Publications of the European Communities, Luxemburg.

ENSR (2003b) *Enterprise Survey*, Observatory of European SMEs, Luxemburg.

European Observatory (2003a) *SMEs in Europe 2003*, Office for Official Publications of the European Communities, Luxemburg.

European Observatory (2003b) *The Impact of EU Enlargement on European SMEs*, No. 6, Office for Official Publications of the European Communities, Luxemburg.

Fallon, G., Cook, M. and Jones, A. (2004) 'The determinants of foreign direct investment location in central and eastern Europe', paper given at 31st Annual UKAIB conference, University of Ulster, April.

Gallagher, C. C. and Stewart, H. (1986) 'Jobs and the business cycle in the UK', *Applied Economics*, vol. 18, pp. 875–900.

Gankema, H. G. J., Snuif, H. R. and Van Dijken, K. A. (1997) 'The internationalisation process of small and medium sized enterprises: an evaluation of the stage theory', in R. Donckels and A. Meittinen (eds), *Entrepreneurship and SME Research: On its way to the next millennium*, Ashgate, Aldershot, pp. 185–99.

Global Enterprise Monitor (2003) *National Entrepreneurship Assessment United States of America*, Babson College, Massachusetts.

Hall, G., Ciwen, T. and Cook, M. (2006) 'Factors influencing the export propensity of UK SMEs', *Journal of International Business Studies*.

Haynes, P. and Hauge, E. (2002) *Development of the Regional Maritime Sector: Internationalisation of suppliers*, FoU-rapport, no. 1.

Heshmati, A. (2001), 'On the growth of micro and small firms: evidence from Sweden', *Small Business Economics*, vol. 17, no. 3, November, pp. 213–28.

Hohti, S. (2000) 'Job flows and job quality by establishment size in the Finnish manufacturing sector, 1980–1994', *Small Business Economics*, vol. 15, no. 4, pp. 265–81.

Infobase Europe Factsheet (2004) *The LIFE 111 Financial Instrument*, Factsheet no. 29, August, Online European Information Service, http://www.ibeurope.com/Factfile/29life.htm, accessed on 15 March 2005.

Johanson, J. and Mattsson, L. G. (1988) 'Internationalisation in industrial systems: a network approach', in N. Hood and J. E. Vahlne (eds), *Strategies in Global Competition*, Croom-Helm, Kent.

Johanson, J. and Vahlne, J. E. (1978) 'A model for the decision making affecting the pattern and pace of internationalisation of the firm', in M. Ghertman and J. Leontiades (eds), *European Research in International Business*, Croom Helm, New York, pp. 283–305.

Johanson, J. and Vahlne, J. E. (1990) 'The mechanism of internationalisation', *International Marketing Review*, vol. 7, no. 4, pp. 11–24.

Kailaranta, J. (1998) *Strengths and Development Needs of Internationalising SMEs*, ESF Publications, 26/1998, Ministry of Labour, Helsinki.

Kisslinger, M (2002) *Success Factors of Co-operation: A potential internationalisation strategy of SMEs*, University of Linz.

Klepper, S. (1996) 'Entry, exit, growth and innovation over the product life-cycle', *American Economic Review*, vol. 86, no. 3, pp. 562–83.

Klette, T. and Mathiassen, A. (1996), 'Job creation, job destruction and plant turnover in Norwegian manufacturing', *Annales d'Economie et de Statistique*, vol. 41/42, pp. 97–125.

Littunen, H. (1997) *The Success of New Firms: Part IV Stabilisation stage*, Paper no. 140, Economic Research Centre of Central Finland.

Luxembourg Centre for Promotion and Research (1992) *Investigation of the Export Activity and the Participation in National and International Fairs of Companies Belonging to the Craft Sector*, Chamber of Commerce, Luxemburg.

OECD (2003) *Economic Outlook*, no. 71, June, Paris.

O'Malley, E. and O'Gorman, C. (2001) 'Competitive Advantage in the Irish indigenous software industry and the role of inward foreign direct investment', *European Planning Studies*, vol. 9, no. 3.

Overweel, E. J. W. (1991) *Full Speed Abroad*, ABN-AMRO Bank, Amsterdam.

Oxford Research (2002) *Crossing the Border to Gain Competitiveness*, for Nordic Industrial Fund and Nordic Council of Ministers, Copenhagen.

Penrose, E. (1959) *The Theory of the Growth of the Firm*, John Wiley, London.

Pia Barber, J. (1998) 'An empirical analysis of Spanish internationalisation: entry patterns and enterprise factors', paper for Acede National Annual Congress, Gran Canaria.

Reid, S. D. (1981) 'The decision-maker and export entry and expansion', *Journal of International Business Studies*, vol. 12, no. 2, pp. 101–12.

Saarenketo, S. and Sundqvist, S. (2002) 'Comparison of born global and traditionally internal firms: effects of industry and managerial characteristics, born globals – internationalisation of small and medium-sized knowledge-intensive firms', *Acta universitas Lappeenrantaensis*, 145.

Sakai, K. (2002) *Global Industrial Restructuring: Implications for small firms*, OECD Working paper 2002/4, February.

Spigarelli, F. (2003) 'Internationalisation processes of SMEs: an empirical analysis of the productive context of the Marche region', *Economia and Management*, no. 3, Milan.

Stelzer, I. (2004) 'Europe has to reform or keep falling behind America', *Sunday Times*, 25 January, p. 4.

Storey, D. J. and Johnson, S. (1987) *Job Generation and Labour Market Change*, Macmillan, London.

Styles, C. and Ambler, T. (1997) *The First Step to Export Success*, PAN'AGRA Research Programme, London Business School.

Teece, D. J. (1993) 'The dynamics of industrial capitalism: perspectives on Alfred Chandler's *Scale and Scope*', *Journal of Economic Literature*, vol. 31, pp. 199–225.

Wiedersheim-Paul, F., Olson, H. C. and Welch, L. S. (1978) 'Pre-export activity: the first in internationalisation', *Journal of International Business Studies*, vol. 9, no. 1, pp. 47–58.

13 Conclusion

Judith Piggott and Mark Cook

This book has outlined the various challenges, opportunities and threats that European business has faced in recent years, and highlighted a number of areas of concern for the future. It also sets such business in a global context. An overview of the various chapters was given in the introduction so we will not repeat it here. Instead this concluding chapter will set out what we see as the big challenges for Europe in the next decade.

There are a number of major challenges that Europe and European business face in the future:

- Enlargement – where next?
- How far should integration go?
- Internal structure of Europe – which model?
- Challenges from outside Europe – what does the future hold for European business in the global market?
- Demographics – how can Europe cope with an ageing and declining (in numbers) population?
- Innovation and technology – how competitive is Europe in this area?
- Environment – is this the real threat in the future?

Each one of these will be looked at briefly in turn.

Enlargement of the European Union

The last expansion of the European Union in May 2004 increased the member states from 15 to 25, enlarged the surface area of the European Union by 25 per cent and increased its population by 20 per cent up to 450 million (BBC 2004). The European Union is now the biggest single market in terms of population although the North American Free Trade Area (NAFTA) has a higher total gross domestic product (GDP). As seen in Chapter 4, the new entrants are economically diverse. There are also four other candidate countries entering into negotiations soon: Romania and Bulgaria which are looking for entry by 2007, Croatia for 2009, and Turkey. The former Yugoslav Republic of Macedonia has also officially applied to join the European Union and there are possibilities that both Moldova and Ukraine will seek to join. Other possible future applicants are Bosnia-Herzegovina, Albania, Belarus, and Serbia and Montenegro.

Although these countries provide a number of opportunities for European business they also provide a number of problems, as the new applicants are generally quite poor and in some cases relatively poorer than some of those countries in the last expansion of the European Union in 2005. Some richer European states are still not EU members, such as Norway, Switzerland, Liechtenstein and Iceland; however these have chosen to remain separate, but closely linked.

The growth of the European Union may however be restricted for a number of reasons. Some current members of the European Union such as Austria may be unwilling to seek any great expansion after the next wave of entrants. Further expansion of the European Union could take it to the borders of Russia, and this might be politically sensitive. Within the European Union's treaties is the statement that member countries should be 'European'. There is, however, no precise definition of 'European'. Turkey has had its application accepted although the great majority of its territory is in Asia. Georgia might like to join, though it is geographically east of Syria and Jordan. Azerbaijan is geographically European but its chances for acceptance on both political and economic grounds appear remote at present. It also has to be asked, how soon can some of these countries meet the Copenhagen criteria?

These criteria are:

● To be a stable democracy, respecting human rights, the rule of law, and the protection of minorities. Fulfilling these is seen as a prerequisite for starting accession negotiations.
● To have a functioning market economy as well as the capacity to cope with competitive pressure and market forces within the Union.
● To adopt and enforce the common rules, standards and policies that make up the body of EU law.

Whether the further expansion of the European Union to south-east Europe does take place in the short to medium term, the expansion to the east has shown that the decision-making bodies and institutions and the general running of the European Union will need to change to accommodate the new members. Some changes in voting procedures were agreed at the Treaty of Nice in 2001, but bigger changes have been put forward in the way that the European Union makes decisions within the auspices of the EU Constitution (see below and Chapter 4).

Depth of integration

The vision of the founders of the European Union was that of a United States of Europe which would bring an end to a history of conflict within Europe. The initial impetus was political but the emphasis switched to economic for two main reasons, according to El-Agraa (2004): it was too soon after the war for political integration, but economic integration could pave the way to this, and economic integration was needed to survive against the main competition of the United States and Japan.

So where do we stand now? There appear to be two main views of integration at present. First, there are those who envisage the European Union becoming deeper and evolving into a closer union, with the euro playing a central role in this. There are also talks about a possible move towards a common fiscal policy. The main drivers behind this would probably be seen as France, Germany and the European Commission. Such views provided the backdrop for the Convention for the Future of Europe and for the proposed changes in the constitution (see Chapter 4). The other view is to favour a looser, more flexible arrangement with an emphasis on encouraging a wider union (see above for possible candidates), a move which would probably prevent the closer union favoured above. The views of the UK government would probably fit into the second category, together with the Scandinavian countries. So the basic widening versus deepening question still exists.

Internal structure

Not only are there questions of enlargement and further integration, there is also a more fundamental question concerning the future of Europe. What model of the economy should dominate within Europe? On the one hand we have the Anglo-American free market view which believes in low-level intervention in the economy and the power of competition within the market. On the other hand there is the more 'traditional' social market model of the French and German economies, which believes in a much more interventionist approach. This divide within Europe can be seen in the debate over more flexible labour markets (see Chapter 9) and on industrial and competition policy, particularly the reduction of state aids (see Chapter 10). On one side is France supported by Germany, Spain and Belgium objecting to these moves, while on the other is the United Kingdom supported by the Netherlands, the Scandinavian countries and Ireland. The latter group also is strengthened by the support of the new president, Jose Manuel Baroso, and a number of the new entrant countries such as Poland.

A similar divide can be seen in the debate over opening up of services, with the 'ultra-liberals' (as Chirac has called them) in the UK camp, being opposed by the supporters of the social model (*Economist* 2005b).

Changes in the global market

The Lisbon Agreement calls for Europe to become 'the most competitive and dynamic knowledge-driven economy in the world by 2010', but we have seen in Chapter 1 that it lags behind the United States and Japan (and increasingly China) in many areas. It has to be said that in terms of productivity per hour worked, Europe does match the United States, and that Finland is the world's most competitive country (with Denmark, Ireland and Sweden not far behind). Germany and France have some of the world's strongest companies, and Germany is the world's largest exporter (*Economist* 2005a). However growth in Europe is still sluggish and the threat from competition is very real. But what of the competition in the future?

Jacques (2005b) states that the 'EU will continue to play a major global role' but he also points out that, although the European Union has acted as a role model for other trading blocs (especially Mercosur) and proved far more successful than any could have predicted, the United States and 'the other most likely candidates [such] as future global powers – China and India – are all nation states' (Jacques 2005b: 17). These are all giant nation-states, and therefore contain many of the European Union's advantages within their own borders (for example, market size and subsequent scale economies). He rejects the idea of trading blocs such as the European Union becoming one of the future global powers, therefore.

Furthermore the rise of India and China in the global economy will force businesses to engage with very differing societies and economies. Despite the differences there are strong cultural, historical and racial links between Europe and the United States, whereas China and India have very differing roots from the west. India's main link to the west has been colonialism, but this was only marginally true for China. The future for European businesses therefore will 'no longer be overwhelmingly western' (Jacques 2005a: 17).

Demographics

A major problem for all European economies is the ageing population and how a smaller number of workers can support a growing percentage of pensionable population (see Chapter 9). The problem obviously arises from the fall in birth rates in many European countries and also the increasing life expectancy. For example in Italy for every 100 people of working age there are more than 20 over the age of 65, but by 2050 (if nothing changes), for every 100 people of working age there will be 80 over 65, so quadrupling the burden of support on each worker (Environmental Literacy Council, no date).

One way to meet the need for a greater working population is of course more labour mobility and migration, but this has its own tensions and problems. A UN study actually considered what level of migration would be necessary to keep the ratio of working population to retired population as at present. For Italy (used in the above example) to keep a ratio of four workers to one retiree, it would have to accept 2.2 million migrants a year, or alternatively raise the working age to 77 (*Indian Times* 2000). An alternative approach is to encourage women to have more children, and recently (September 2005) the French government offered to increase the benefits received by families for second and third children (*Expatica* 2005). This ageing population obviously will have major implications for European businesses as workers increase in age (and perhaps become less flexible and less productive), but also as a shortage of workers begins to become apparent.[1]

Some of the stress may however be alleviated by technological advances (although in the past technology has not actually replaced the need for workers, just changed the need for certain types – see Chapter 9 for further details).

Technology and innovation

Technological innovation penetrates business at all levels. Innovation in computing, telecommunications and transport is vital to maintain the competitiveness of many European businesses. Furthermore there has been a massive spread of networked information systems to all types of industries in recent years, especially telecommunications and Internet technology, and these have led to the emergence of what has been called the 'new economy' based around electronic networks (Morrison 2002). In fact Ohmae (2000) has suggested that the national borders of the 'old world' are in fact obsolete and that this new world is an invisible continent of cyberspace (also see Chapter 6). The worrying factor is that the new world has the same inequalities that the old world had; over 50 per cent of the US population has access to the Internet but only 0.6 per cent have access in less-developed countries (Morrison 2002). However in order to maintain competitiveness especially compared with the United States, Europe has to keep abreast with new technology.

In terms of innovation, the 2004 European Innovation Scoreboard (EIS) showed that Europe's innovation levels have been maintained, with the Nordic countries, in particular Sweden and Finland, keeping their positions as world leaders. However the European Union as a whole has begun to lose ground against some of its major competitors such as the United States, mainly because of their enhanced innovative capacity and because the new member states have lowered the European Union's average innovative capacity. The EIS scorecard suggested that the weaknesses faced by the European Union were in patenting, the lower qualifications of the EU workforce and lower business R&D expenditure (see Chapter 9). Access to broadband is a different matter, with a greater proportion of broadband connects per household in the United Kingdom than in the United States (*The Times* 2005).

Environment

It could be argued that this is a challenge not just for Europe but for the whole world. Global warming caused by heat-trapping gases, or greenhouse gases, emanating from burning fossil fuels threatens both ecology and human welfare, causing flooding and desertification (Morrison 2002). The Kyoto Protocol set targets for various greenhouse gases for industrialised countries, and came into force on 16 February 2005 after two conditions had been fulfilled:

- the ratification by a minimum of 55 countries
- those who ratified it accounted for at least 55 per cent of the emissions from the main industrialised countries (called Annex 1 countries).

The first target was met in 2002 but the second hit problems when both the United States and Australia refused to ratify the Protocol. However when Russia ratified the agreement on 18 November 2004, the Protocol came into force 90 days later.

Many suggest that the agreement has some fatal flaws. It only aims to reduce emissions from industrialised countries by 5 per cent, yet most scientists suggest something like 60 per cent is needed. Furthermore although China and India have ratified the agreement, as developing countries they do not have to commit to reducing emissions (despite both being major polluters). Finally without the United States and Australia on board, it has been suggested that this protocol is pretty toothless. However, it does present a framework for future negotiations, and is a serious attempt to combat the situation (BBC 2005). Many European countries also are already cutting back emissions by more than 5 per cent and showing the way forward (Morrison 2002) (see Chapter 11 for further details).

But what effect will this have on European business? Already most businesses have seen the 'writing on the wall' and implemented an environmental policy. This can be seen in the move towards far more environmentally friendly vehicles. Eventually all will have to consider the environmental impact of their goods, working practices and processes to ensure their survival business-wise and that of the planet.

The European model and its level of social protection may well have suited Europe and European business over the past 30 years but has increasing come under pressure from the challenges of globalisation and the dominant role of the United States. A future world with a less dominant but still strong United States and with a rise in the economic power of China and India poses a different set of threats to European business. Europe and European business must meet such threats in order to survive during the next decade.

Note

1   That older workers are less productive is a very debatable point; see Chapter 7 and the Hitachi example.

References

BBC (2004) 'Q&Q: EU enlargement', 18 June, *BBC News*, www.bbcnews.co.uk, accessed on 13 April 2005.

BBC (2005) 'Q&A: The Kyoto Protocol', 16 February, *BBC News*, www.bbcnews.co.uk, accessed on 10 April 2005.

Economist (2005a) 'From Lisbon to Brussels', 19 March.

Economist (2005b) 'Outlook: gloomy', 2 April.

El Agraa, A. M. (2004) *The European Union: Economics and policies*, 7th edn, FT/Prentice Hall, Harlow.

Environmental Literacy Council (no date) *Aging of the Global Population*, www.enviroliteracy. org, accessed 30 April 2005.

Expatica (2005) 'Have more babies: France to French women', 22 September, www.Expatica.com, accessed on 23 September 2005.

Indian Times (2000) 'Aging populations in Europe, Japan, Korea, require action', 22 March.

Jacques, M. (2005a) 'No monopoly on modernity: American dominance is bound to wither as Asia's confidence grows', *Guardian*, 5 February, p. 17.

Jacques, M. (2005b) 'Two cheers for Europe', *Financial Times*, 19 March, p. 15.

Morrison, J. (2002) *The International Business Environment*, Palgrave, Basingstoke.

Ohmae, K. (2000) *The Invisible Continent: Four strategic imperatives of the new economy*, HarperCollins, London.

Times (2005) 'Broadband use in the UK surpasses US level', 22 September.

Glossary

Absolute advantage A country is better (more efficient) at producing certain goods than others.

Acquis communautaire The acceptance by all member states (and states wishing to join) of the entire body of community law, and the obligations implicit therein.

Ad valorem A tax or tariff which is a certain percentage on top of the price.

Anti-trust The US term for competition policy.

Arbitrage The mechanism of buying and selling currency in the market, which keeps rates of exchange consistent.

Autarky The position at which an individual nation can maximise its welfare but in the absence of trade.

Barter Exchange of goods with no money involved.

Beggar they neighbour trade policies Trade policy based on the view that one country's gain implies another country's loss. There are no mutual gains from trade in this theory.

Bilateral trading deals Trading arrangements agreed between two countries.

Buyins The ownership of an organisation is transferred to a new set of shareholders who are a management team external to the organisation.

Buyouts The ownership of the organisation is transferred to a new set of shareholders, among whom the incumbent management is a significant element.

Common external tariff The same tariff rate in all the member states against a given commodity from outside the union.

Common market The next stage from a customs union, where not only do commodities move freely between member states but so do factors of production.

Comparative advantage A country has a higher degree of superiority in the production of one good than of others.

Comparative disadvantage A country has a lower degree of superiority in the production of one good than of others.

Competition policy Policy designed to promote competition in business, and often specifically to limit or prohibit the abuse of monopoly (or 'dominant firm') power and to prohibit restrictive trade practices such as price fixing and collusive tendering.

Council for Mutual Economic Assistance (CMEA or Comecon) The pre-1989 trading organisation linking the Eastern European countries and the Soviet Union. Comecon was essentially a system of bilateral trading arrangements.

Counterparty clearing A system whereby individual trades are netted out by the exchange so that traders settle only the remaining balances with the people with whom they are trading (counterparties).

Credit derivatives The entire economic risk attached to an asset is transferred to a counterpart without actually moving the asset itself.

Customs union A free trade area with a common external tariff.

Debt equity swaps A process by which creditors return debt to debtors in exchange for an equity interest in assets owned by the debtors.

Demerger The break-up of a previously merged organisation into separate parts.

Deregulation A process under which government restrictions on markets are reduced.

Devaluation A reduction in the value of a currency against other currencies in a fixed exchange rate system.

Discretionary financial regional support Regional support that is not automatic but at the discretion of the government.

Diseconomies of scale Costs per unit rise as output increases.

Disintermediation The diversion of business away from financial institutions which are subject to controls.

Divestment The sale of non-core parts of the organisation.

Division of labour To divide production into various tasks and labour then specialises in the particular tasks.

Dumping This occurs where a good is sold in an overseas market at a price below the real cost of production.

Dynamic effects A category of factors that influence growth and improve efficiency over time.

Eclectic theory A theory that brings together the different strands of various hypotheses in one comprehensive theorem.

Eco-labelling A scheme introduced in the European Union for products that cause the least environmental damage in all stages of production.

Economic union The next stage from a common market, where there is a high degree of integration of fiscal, monetary and commercial policies.

Economies of scale As production increases, costs per unit fall.

Economies of scope The reductions in costs that can be attained from joint production of two or more products.

Environment Action Programme A series of programmes introduced in the European Union to tackle environmental matters.

Equity markets Markets for equities such as stocks and shares.

Eurocurrency market A market designed to facilitate the transfer of short-term funds (in various currencies) from surplus units to deficit units, in which commercial banks serve as intermediaries.

Europe Agreements A set of agreements between the European Union and a number of central and east European countries. These agreements give the eastern European countries associate status with the European Union. They cover trading arrangements and other broader political questions.

European Central Bank (ECB) The central monetary authority of the European Union which operates the single currency.

Eurosclerosis Term used in the 1970s and 1980s to describe the relatively poor growth performance of the European Union and its job-creating ability.

Exchange rate The price of one currency in terms of another.

Extra-EU FDI Foreign direct investment entering the European Union from outside, notably from Japan and the United States.

Extra-EU trade Trade taking place by EU countries with countries outside the European Union.

Factor endowments The quantity of factors of production a country possess.

Factor intensity reversal This occurs when wage-rent ratios differ across countries and goods.

Factor mobility The degree to which factors of production such as labour are free to move from one country/occupation to another.

Factors of production Factors that are used in the production of goods, such as land, labour and capital.

Foreign direct investment (FDI) The flow of foreign money into the domestic or European economy from countries outside Europe.

Forward rate The rate set for delivery of a currency, commodity or other assets some time in the future.

Free trade area An area in which tariffs are eliminated between member countries but each applies its own tariff policy regarding the outside world.

Futures An agreement to buy a currency at a future date, however this contract is re-saleable up to the time it matures.

G8 The group of eight countries or regions, members of which are the United Kingdom, France, Russia, Germany, the United States, Japan, Italy, Canada and the European Union. They meet regularly to discuss major issues.

Global Triad The three trading regions of North America, Europe, and south-east Asia and Japan.

Gravity model A model which attempts to predict the extent of trade between any two countries or regions on the basis of a small number of factors.

Greenfield investment When investment enters a particular industry for the first time.

Heckscher-Ohlin theorem That countries should specialise in the goods which use intensively the factor of production they have in abundance.

Home country The destination of FDI.

Host country The source of FDI.

Human capital The skills obtained by labour.

Imperfect competition There are a number of firms in an industry each producing a differentiated product.

Import quota A limit on the number of goods imported into a country.

Increasing returns to scale A situation where increase in output is associated with decreases in long-run average total cost.

Industry policy A term with different shades of meaning. Most simply IP can be viewed as government policy (other than fiscal or monetary macro-policies) to try to encourage business success and to increase competitiveness.

Intensity ratio A measure of the extent to which FDI from one country or region is concentrated in another.

Internalisation-specific advantages (ISA) Advantages accruing to a firm when transaction costs of market solutions are too high.

Intra-EU FDI Foreign direct investment flows from one EU member state to another.

Intra-industry trade The trade between two similar sectors in different countries: for example the trade in cars between the European countries.

Joint venture An agreement between two or more firms to cooperate in some way, while typically maintaining the separate identities of each of the partners.

Labour theory of value The value attributed to a good by the amount of labour embodied in it.

Laissez faire To allow the market to work alone, with no government interference.

Law of comparative advantage Each country should specialise in producing the good(s) in which it has a relative (comparative) advantage and trade for other good(s).

Leontief paradox An attempt to prove the Heckscher-Ohlin theorem using US data which actually showed the opposite.

LSA Location-specific advantages, certain advantages that a firm has as a result of its location.

Luddites People opposed to new technology.

Market concentration The share of a market controlled by a given number of firms.

Mercantilism Belief that the aim of trade is to increase wealth in terms of precious metals and so increase exports and reduce imports by various means.

Merger or acquisition (Often called 'concentrations' in EU terminology) A situation where two or more independent businesses come together to form one new legal business entity.

Multinational enterprises Enterprises that own or control production or service facilities in more than one country.

New protectionism Non-tariff barriers to trade which have replaced tariffs as the major obstruction to the free flow of international trade.

Non-discrimination The thesis that a country should treat all its trading partners alike.

Non-tariff barrier In the wider sense, barriers to trade that are not tariffs. They include quotas and health and safety regulations.

Optimum currency area A region where the use of a common currency implies no loss of welfare.

Options A contract giving the right to buy at a set rate or price at a given future date.

OSA Ownership-specific advantage: a certain type of know-how that is specific to a firm.

Over the counter derivatives These include currency swaps and options, forward rate agreements (FRAs), interest rate swaps, options on traded securities, interest rate options, equity forwards, swaps and options.

Partial equilibrium analysis Equilibrium conditions examined in a given market.

PEST Tool of analysis of the environment of a firm: political, economic, social and technological.

Political union A federal state where a central authority controls monetary, fiscal and foreign policy as well as carrying out legislative, judicial and administrative functions.

Portfolio investment Creation or transfer of financial capital.

Price elasticity of demand. Responsiveness of quantity demanded to price changes.

Prisoners' dilemma A special case of game theory based on the idea of two arrested people being interviewed by the police. If neither confesses the police will implicate them both in the crime to some degree; if one confesses he or she will manage to pin the crime on the other and go free; if both confess they will get a higher sentence than if neither confesses.

Production subsidy A subsidy to producers to lower the cost of production.

Public procurement The purchase of goods and services by governments and state-owned organisations, often by contract or by tender.

Purchasing power parity (PPP) The principle that, measured in a common currency, traded goods should cost the same wherever they are bought across the world.

Qualified majority voting A voting system used in the European Union. Each EU member is given a number of votes (according to the size of population) and a set number is required to achieve what is seen as a majority vote.

Quota An upper limit to the level of imports allowed into a country.

Quota licence A licence to import a certain amount into a country.

Random walk A time series where the best estimate of any future value of the relevant variable at any point is that it should remain at its current level.

Reciprocity The thesis that if one country makes a reduction in a trade barrier with another, the second country should also respond with an equivalent reduction in trade barriers.

Repurchase agreement (repo) A form of borrowing with collateral, in which the borrower sells a security to the lender, thus obtaining ready cash, then buys it back again (in other words repurchases it) for a higher price at the end of a specified time period.

Revaluation An increase in the value of a currency against other currencies in a fixed exchange rate system.

Social costs The costs of an activity or output that are borne by society as a whole, rather than the costs borne by the individual or firm carrying out the activity or producing the output.

Specific duty A duty of a set or specific amount.

Specialisation To choose to produce certain goods and not others.

Spot rate The price quoted for the delivery of foreign currency immediately or 'on the spot'.

Spread The difference between the selling and buying price (for example, of a currency).

State aid Financial assistance given by governments to home-based firms or industries.

Strategic alliance An association between two or more organisations, which may be either formal or informal, enabling an organisation to gain access to an external market without having to expand its operations there.

Strategic trade policy A means by which a government can undertake trade policies so as to improve its own welfare and obtain a comparative advantage in the production of a product.

Tariff A tax on imports as they enter the country. These taxes may be a proportion of the value of the product (*ad valorem*) or related to size or weight (specific).

Tariff escalation The process by which tariffs on products increase, the greater the product is developed.

Tariff peaks The highest tariffs in operation.

Terms of trade The price or rate at which goods exchange.

Trading bloc General name for a group of countries that are linked by trade agreements of varying depth.

Trade creation Domestic production is replaced by imports from a customs union partner.

Trade deflection Goods in an FTA enter the area through a country with the lowest external tariff and then circulate through members.

Trade diversion Extra-union imports are replaced by intra-union imports.

Trade expansion The growth of trade created through a reduction in prices (from tariff reductions) on joining a customs union.

Trade Related Property Rights (TRIPs) The ways in which the rights of creators of intellectual property – patents, copyrights, and trademarks – can be enforced outside of the country of origin. A subject of recent agreements by the WTO.

Transparency The replacement of disguised barriers to trade by more overt ones.

Transfer pricing The setting of prices charged by one department of a multinational company to other departments as goods are transferred within the company in the course of the production process.

Voluntary export restraint An agreement by an exporting country to set an upper limit on the amount of goods it will export to other countries.

World Bank International institution set up to promote general economic development in the world's poorer nations.

World Trade Organization (WTO) An international grouping set up to promote and regulate trade. Most major economies, except Russia, are members. The WTO is the successor organisation to the General Agreement on Tariffs and Trade (GATT).

X-efficiency　The efficiency with which resources are actually used in productive activities as a result of the degree of effort and commitment of managers and workers.

Index